Ethnicity
Counts

Ethnicity Counts

William Petersen

TRANSACTION PUBLISHERS
New Brunswick (U.S.A.) and London (U.K.)

Library of Congress Catalog Number: 96-37513
ISBN: 1-56000-296-4
Printed in the United States of America

Library of Congress Cataloging-in-Publication Data

Petersen, William.
    Ethnicity counts / William Petersen.
        p.   cm.
    Includes bibliographical references and index.
    ISBN 1-56000-296-4 (cloth : alk. paper)
    1. Ethnicity. 2. Ethnology—Statistical services. 3. Ethnicity—United States. 4. Ethnology—United States—Statistical services. I. Title.
GN495.6.P49   1997
305.8—dc21   96-37513
                                                        CIP

For Renee,
as always

Contents

Introduction

The accuracy of ethnic data is the principal topic of this book. With details concerning counts in the United States and several other countries, it demonstrates that in a general enumeration a reasonably true classification and accurate count are impossible.

We expect the official statistics of less developed countries to be inadequate, but the quality of data is not generally better in advanced societies, in part because of the very fact that they are advanced. The era when censuses became a routine element of national administration was also when divisions in the population by occupation, education, religion, race, and nationality became more permeable. The son of a peasant was no longer necessarily a peasant, and in his urban setting he retained, often with some ambivalence, only some of his forebears' traits. An open industrial society is inherently fluid, so that neither social class nor ethnic group can be interpreted as identical with the terms as applied in a more nearly static community.

Ethnic groups are real, and often they are of great significance. Their indefinite and variable boundaries, however, make it hard to classify persons into meaningful sectors of a population. And the difficulty is increased by the fact that the collection of ethnic statistics has frequently become a battleground where the professed leaders of the groups being counted contest each element of every enumeration.

There has been a flood of American writings about race and ethnicity in books, scholarly journals, and popular magazines, and it continues with no sign of abatement. Most of these works have pertained to the United States. The dominant theme remains victimology, for the casualties of real or alleged discrimination now include not only blacks and Jews but Hispanics, Indians, and others, as well as females, homosexuals, and the disabled as supposedly parallel cases. Whether excellent or poor by other criteria, most of these books and articles are parochial in the sense that no comparison is made or implied with any other real society. With a concentration on "problem minorities" and a standard set at utopian perfection, the American record seldom deserves, or gets, approbation. The conviction that the melting pot has utterly failed, which has become dogma in many of the works lacking a comparative framework, is not at all evident when the relative acculturation of newcomers to American society is contrasted with the process elsewhere. Over the past two centuries, democrats were right to believe in the promise of the New World.

1

Books that seek a broader understanding in a comparative perspective are much rarer. Two excellent works can be cited—Thomas Sowell's *Race and Culture* and Donald Horowitz's *Ethnic Groups in Conflict*.[1] My book also analyzes ethnicity in several societies, but it differs from both of these in a number of ways. Sowell is an economist, Horowitz a political scientist and lawyer. For these disciplines, demographic data are a given. The emphasis here, on the contrary, is on the procedures by which these source materials come into being.

Many of the general public, no more than semiliterate in matters mathematical, are impressed by any assertion made with numbers and graphs. Even analysts of ethnicity generally show little interest in how ethnic groups are defined and counted. "I am going to write about a particular ethnic/racial group," an author says to himself, "and everyone knows who is a member and who is not. When I want to get some figures to back up my findings, I need only use the census data, for the official statistics are surely a reliable source."

Neither half of this assumption is well based. Who is a black, a Hispanic, a Russian, has not been a firm datum, either in the United States or in other countries, either in the past or at the present time. The lack of consistency and dependability is characteristic of ethnic data per se, not restricted to this or that agency or national bureau. The statisticians and demographers who work in the U.S. Bureau of the Census and its counterparts in other countries are well aware that ethnic data are unreliable. The fundamental reasons are that a complex attribute cannot be accurately measured with a simple indicator, and a more appropriate measure cannot be fitted into a national enumeration. In Central and Eastern Europe, where the right of national self-determination was promulgated in polyglot populations, the art of cooking data was developed into an haute cuisine (see chapter 10). Frequently the state has found it expedient to slant the count one way or the other.

The principal demand of ethnic minorities has generally been for some degree of cultural autonomy, and from the dominant sector's point of view, the main dangers in granting them such rights have been that the nation would be substantially weakened not only culturally but also economically and militarily, and that the demand might escalate into an independence movement. The way to square the circle, it has seemed to many persons of good will, is through a federal structure. Among actual federations, however, secession was the proximate cause of disastrous civil wars in the United States and Nigeria (see chapter 15), of a short but bitter war in Switzerland (see chapter 13), and of a persistent constitutional quandary in Canada. The seemingly promising federation of the two Rhodesias or of the West Indies soon dissolved into their separate parts. A federal system is fragile almost by definition, and the greater prominence of ethnic ambitions the world over has made it more so.

Most figures on ethnic groups in the United States derive from the publications of the U.S. Bureau of the Census, reporting either on the decennial enumerations or on the various types of intercensal surveys (see chapters 4 through 9). To know what the counts by ethnicity signify, we must ask how the Bureau defines the groups it classifies and counts. Have these definitions remained fixed from past enumerations, so that the indicated trends have a firm base in reality? How are individuals assigned who have two or more ethnic lines among their forebears? What pressures by interest groups, Congress, and its own budget affect the Bureau's decisions?

Even the simplest case may involve problems. A census schedule is filled in for everyone living, let us say, in Chapel Hill, and then the total number of persons eventually is printed as "the" population of the town. Before 1950 unmarried students had been enumerated as residents of their parents' homes, often not in that town; beginning with that census, students were defined as residents of the places where they were studying. The population of Chapel Hill, the site of the University of North Carolina, increased from 3,654 in 1940 to 9,177 in 1950, mostly because of the reclassification. Not merely the number of persons but also the reported median age, income, level of education, and so on through every other characteristic were transformed by a shift in how the Bureau defined "residence."

As another instance, the Bureau of the Census decided that in the 1990 count it would designate federal workers serving temporarily overseas as residents of the states to which they would eventually return. As a consequence of this shift in recorded populations, Massachusetts lost a seat in the House of Representatives and Washington State gained one (see also chapter 9).

Census queries on ethnicity have gradually shifted from an "objective" to a "subjective" type. To an objective question there is only one correct response (e.g., in what country was an immigrant born?); the difficulty is that in many cases the answer is not a very useful indicator (in this example, each country of Central and Eastern Europe has included several ethnic groups; see chapter 4). A subjective question permits a range of responses and thus affords a possibly greater relevance (e.g., what is a person's nationality?), but the answer is sometimes ambiguous and therefore not necessarily comparable with earlier figures.

Identities may be particularly susceptible to changing fashion when it is the respondent who is asked to name his ethnicity. In the United States self-enumeration was introduced in 1960 for questions put to a sample of the population, and subsequently it has been used for all census returns. The new procedure saved a good deal of money and it has other advantages, but one can presume that the ethnic identities of many persons changed when self-enumeration was substituted for identification by an enumerator. American blacks were once so classified by the state as a first step in various types of control; a black who passed himself off as white did so to evade those controls (see chapter 5). Persons born abroad have sometimes lacked the opportunities available to the native-born; among immigrants, more males than females have reported themselves as natives, since as workers outside the home men have had both a better basis and a more cogent reason to misrepresent their personal history.

One of the more troublesome characteristics of responses on ethnicity is the "vanity effect"—the tendency of respondents to answer questions in a way that they think may enhance their status. For instance, to vote is considered a civic duty, and when New Yorkers were asked whether they had cast a ballot in a just completed election, 40 percent of the nonvoters in the sample said they had.[2] At any period in American history, the nationalities are arrayed in a loose hierarchical order, with *Mayflower* descendants at the top and the most recent immigrants close to the bottom. How many, when questioned about their forebears, take the opportunity to raise themselves a step or two on the symbolic ladder?

On the other hand, many persons are indifferent to their ethnic background, and their responses are likely to be capricious. When the same question was asked three times in successive surveys over four years, the replies of the whole sample seemingly remained almost constant. On closer examination it was found that four-fifths of the respondents had what might be called nonattitudes. They answered inconsistently and randomly, but the changes back and forth canceled out and gave the impression of overall stability.[3]

Ethnic Group versus Ethnic Category

Until recently the very notion of group rights was incompatible with the American credo (see chapter 3). The founding fathers' ideas derived in part from what might be called the founding grandfathers, the Englishmen who inspired Washington, Madison, Jefferson, and the others. The political theory of John Locke (1632–1704), for instance, emphasized *individual* rights: ultimate sovereignty lies not with some abstraction like Rousseau's "general will" or Lenin's "working class," but with actual persons, each expressing his own choice. The state can act legitimately only by the rule of the majority, which binds everyone; in the later American paraphrase, all three branches of government derive their just powers from the consent of the governed.

Data are collected from individuals, and they are presented as characteristics of groups. Though the distinction between group and category is routinely ignored with respect to ethnic classifications, in many other settings it is recognized as crucial. In a review of a book about the British philosopher Alasdair MacIntyre, as an example from a completely different context, we read:

> Explaining what he means by a practice, MacIntyre takes the example of fishing.... There is a clearly marked difference between a group of fishermen who band together only so long as they make more money than they would by taking up

some other occupation and a group who see themselves as fishermen, bound to one another by ties of friendship and habit, who understand the excellences of their craft, and who would not readily trade in their occupation for a higher paid one. The latter will provide the basis for a community; the former will not.[4]

Or, the latter is a group properly understood; the former is a category or aggregate.

In his interesting study of ethnicity, the sociologist Richard Alba reinterprets the well-documented fact that as individuals white Americans may maintain ties to their ethnic backgrounds:

> [The perception that] if ethnic identities persist, then...assimilation has become bogged down lies at the heart of much of the analysis and scholarship that claims an ethnic resurgence is occurring among American whites.... But the difficulty is that [this diagnosis] offers no conception of how such identities are linked to meaningful social groups....
>
> In contrast to the past, the different European ancestries are not seen as the basis for important social divisions; instead, they create the potential for...a new group called, for lack of a better term, the "European Americans."[5]

His point is that persons of various nationalities engaged in seeking their ethnic roots are not reconstituting the old ethnic groups; rather they are beginning to coalesce the category of European Americans into a brand new ethnic group.

That most analysts of ethnicity ignore the distinction between category and group affects not merely this or that detail but the very core of their analysis. The lack of a convenient noun has induced writers to coin such makeshifts as "ethnic group," which passes over the crucial contrast (see chapter 2). With increasing degrees of self-conscious cohesion, a subnation can constitute successively a *category* or *aggregate,* a *group,* and a *community.* An ethnic group, strictly defined, is a subnation conscious of its distinct attributes but lacking a formal organization; a community is based not only on an awareness of its different religious faith, for instance, but also on the church's organizational structure. Yet the term *ethnic group* is so well established that it could be futile to try to eliminate it.

Analysts of languages differentiate between bilingualism, which is a characteristic of individuals, and diglossia, which is one of populations. Considering simple aggregations, one might assume that where one exists the other must also, but in an interesting essay the linguist Joshua Fishman exemplified the distinctions to be made:

- A monolingual population made up of monolingual individuals, the simplest case, is restricted to very small and isolated speech communities.
- A country with both diglossia and bilingualism is approximated in Paraguay. The rural population there once spoke only Guarani; but a substan-

tial portion, particularly of those who moved to towns, learned Spanish, which in the countryside is also the language of education, the courts, and other government institutions. As a consequence, more than half of the people use both languages.

- In a society with distinct social classes and little movement between them, it sometimes happens that each class has its own language. In some countries of pre-1914 Europe, for instance, the elites spoke French and the common people another language. The small amount of communication required between master and servant was in a pidgin—that is, a curtailed version of either language.

- Bilingualism without diglossia, finally, can be exemplified by the United States during the periods of mass immigration. Newcomers to the country have had a strong motivation to add English to their native language; but their bilingualism has usually been transitory, seldom lasting as a mass phenomenon beyond the immigrant generation or, at most, their offspring.[6]

Whether the discussion is of groups or categories, an unrecognized heterogeneity can distort any comparison between two sets of aggregate data.[7] Since it is hard to discern the paradox in the abstract, a hypothetical case is useful to illustrate it.[8] In the following table, the unemployment rates are 10 percent in Population A and 9 percent in Population B. When the two populations are broken down by color (or by gender, two nationalities, levels of skill, or whatever), it turns out that Population B has a higher rate among both blacks and whites. In other words, a correctly reported comparison can lead to diametrically opposed conclusions depending merely on how much detail is included.

Comparison of Unemployment Rates in Two Hypothetical Populations

	Population A			Population B		
	Labor Force	Unemployed		Labor Force	Unemployed	
		No.	%		No.	%
	1,000,000	100,000	10	1,000,000	90,000	9
Blacks	500,000	75,000	15	300,000	48,000	16
Whites	500,000	25,000	5	700,000	42,000	6

Diglossia and bilingualism can be disjunctive, and the addition of new details can reverse a comparison of two totals. The problem is not, of course, merely with interpretation of statistics on language use or unemployment, for the paradoxes apply also to any index of ethnicity or social status.

In the United States censuses, the principal index of whites' ethnicity is the places of birth of respondents and their parents. If a person and/or one or both of his parents were born in another country, he is classified as part of the foreign stock; if all three were born in the United States, then statistically the respondent disappears into the native population. Take an English-speaking Canadian who immigrates to the United States. He has no equivalent of a Hibernian Society or a Hebrew Immigrant Aid Society; often he is not even aware of the existence of other "Canadian Americans." In one analysis of ethnic data, it was found that the number of Americans born in Canada was more than three times the number reporting Canadian ancestry.[9] But because an individual has reported his foreign birth or that of his parents, he is automatically assigned membership in an ethnic "group" that in fact does not exist.

Next consider an immigrant, say, from Germany. He may be distinguishable by his accent, often by his name, and he is likely to seek a path into his adopted culture by living and associating with other German Americans. Because their backgrounds and problems in acculturation are similar, he and his fellows are likely to coalesce into a genuine group, with some degree of cohesion and a feeling of separate ethnic identity. If the German immigrants join a Lutheran or a Catholic church, particularly if it is one with bilingual services arranged specially for them, then one can say that the ethnic group has become a community.

The development of a subnation's self-awareness is similar to the rise of the same sort of perception in a social class. Marx distinguished between a "class in itself" and a "class for itself." The former consists of all persons who share a particular relation to the means of production—owners of factories, or those who work in them, or small shopkeepers, or any similar aggregate. Because the persons in each such category are likely to come into frequent contact and to discuss their common problems, they may (Marx would say "do") develop a class consciousness and become a class for itself.[10]

The Measurement of Ethnicity

It is important to stress that no census has ever been flawless. There are too many individual steps, taken by too many fallible persons with imperfect tools, ever to achieve perfection.

A book of, say, 500 pages, with text and tables and formulas, may easily contain a total of one and a half or two million signs (including their position). The statistical laws of nature make it virtually impossible that a first printing contain no misprints. Neither can the manuscript from which it is made be free of errors.[11]

But a book of 500 pages would be only a very small portion of the census volumes of a modern nation. The American economist and statistician Oskar Morgenstern illustrated this general point with a sizable error in the 1950 census of Connecticut. The printed table omitted two towns of 20,000 people, seven of 15–20,000, twelve of 10–15,000, and seventeen of 5–10,000, while thirty others were listed inaccurately. The table, once printed, was accepted as dependable and appeared unchanged in several other government publications.[12]

Morgenstern next cited what became perhaps the most famous instance of a census error, "the case of the Indians and teen-age widows," which was solved with all the panache of a good detective story. The 1950 census had a surprising number of fourteen-year-old boys and many widows also aged fourteen, especially among American Indians. The remarkable statistics were the consequence of mistakes in punching the cards as they were processed in the preparation of census publications.[13] That the error was discovered was due largely to the fact that the data were implausible, to put it no stronger. Many errors leading to false but believable statistics are in all likelihood never discovered.

Even if there are no human, technical, or fiscal pressures on a statistical agency, in short, any census will be a product of flawed beings. Moreover, as countries assume more responsibilities for satisfying citizens' needs or desires, more and more interest groups have tried to influence the count, which in many cases determines the distribution of goods and services. As I will note in diverse contexts, enumerations are more and more hampered by demands that the counts be conducted in ways not in accord with good statistical norms.

Some years ago the East-West Population Institute in Honolulu hosted a conference of census officials from various Asian and Pacific countries. Out of that meeting there came the best discussion I know of on two techniques that the Bureau of the Census uses to round out data gathered in the field—"editing" and "imputation." When a form is filled out with an obvious error (a person who lists himself or herself as a male and a wife, for instance), such an inconsistency is corrected either by a census employee or a computer program; this is called editing. And when a space on the census form is left blank, this is filled in with what it assumed to be a plausible response; this is called imputation. Statisticians do not generally object to either procedure when used parsimoniously, but many authorities believe that the Bureau has misused both. If a statistical agency becomes accustomed to adjusting its data in this fashion, it is likely to become a bit sloppier in its controls on field procedures. In particular, "imputing the existence of persons and all their characteristics should be avoided, because everything about such persons is unknown."[14]

The ethnic data in any enumeration depend essentially on three factors: how members of the population regard the distinctive ethnic attribute, the methods used by the statistical agency, and the political or fiscal influences on one or both of these. Of the three elements, the basic one is how the ethnic/racial group is defined and defines itself, what changes have taken place in that self-concept, and how those changes fitted in with their social and political environment. When either the same or a matched person was asked his ethnic origin in Current Population Surveys in successive years, one out of every three gave different responses from one count to the next.[15]

Not only is the size of an ethnic group somewhat indeterminate in any particular enumeration, but it may change in one direction or the other. In his analysis of traditional India, the Indian anthropologist M. N. Srinivas coined a term, *sanskritization,* to indicate the process by which lower castes adopt certain of the customs, associations, and beliefs of a higher caste. By such a closer association over a generation or two, they could sometimes raise their own level in the caste hierarchy[16] (see chapter 16). If we generalize this neologism to mean a group's social mobility by the manipulation of symbols, the statistical reclassification of marginal populations is one type of sanskritization. Upward mobility in terms of such material differences as occupational status or income is likely to be easier after a group has effected a shift in its image.

Media attention to the past several American censuses has focused on the underenumeration of blacks and Hispanics, as well as on the suits to force the Bureau of the Census to make postcensal adjustments. These issues are important, but they merely touch on more basic defects in all ethnic counts, both in this country and generally.

1

Toward the End of Ethnicity?

In the United States the study of ethnicity has long been a key element in analyses of the population's composition, but this was far less true of social disciplines in Western Europe. Such classics of European social analysis as the works of Vilfredo Pareto and Max Weber had little to say on the subject, and Karl Marx's distinctive contribution was to deny the significance of ethnicity altogether. In Britain, John Stuart Mill and Lord Acton wrote on problems associated with nationalism, but with few followers. "It was only after the end of the Second World War, and particularly during the 1960s, that social scientists [in Britain] began to recognize the central place of race relations in the study of society." That is the opening sentence of a book by the English sociologist John Stone.[1]

Two historical experiences stimulated this new interest in Western Europe: the breakup of the various empires and the consequent immigration of sizable numbers of former colonials, who began to create colored minorities in several European countries. Thus it was that England acquired a corps of academics who not only discussed these trends in their teaching, but founded several journals in the field and participated in the new Institute of Race Relations. Building on prior work in the United States and other major areas of immigration, John Rex, another English sociologist, attempted to incorporate race relations into broader social theory.[2]

Today the study of ethnicity and race is a significant component of several social disciplines, not only in the United States and Britain, but throughout the world.[3] To say that this development was not anticipated would be an understatement. For quite a few social scientists, a study of ethnicity represented a provocation to emotional or ideological involvement rather than an invitation to dispassionate analysis. In any case, many used to see problems associated with ethnic differences as transitory, troubles that even with no public intervention would gradually dissipate.

Ever since the early eighteenth century, Western philosophers looked forward to a world in which, among other attractive transformations, everyone would speak the same language and all animosities between nations and races

11

would melt away. Such is the almost comic forecast in William Godwin's *Political Justice* (1793), for instance:

> There will be no war, no crimes, no administration of justice, as it is called, and no government. Beside this, there will be neither diseases, anguish, melancholy, nor resentment. Every man will seek, with ineffable ardor, the good of all.[4]

Such a utopian vista reached an influential climax in writings of the various socialist schools. For Marx and Engels, nationalism was part of the mere superstructure resting on the moribund economy of the merchant-manufacturer class:

> Communists are reproached with desiring to abolish countries and nationalities. The workingmen have no country. We cannot take from them what they have not got.... National differences and antagonisms between peoples are daily more and more vanishing...[and] the supremacy of the proletariat will cause them to vanish still faster.[5]

Under this cosmopolitan rhetoric, it is true, lay Marx's virulent anti-Semitism and a perfervid jingoism.[6] But among Marxists and their supporters, the chauvinist side of the internationalist-nationalist coin has been buried under a mountain of socialist propaganda. The main doctrine on ethnicity that Marxism bequeathed to Europe's social disciplines was the prospect of universal brotherhood.

Matching this internationalism of the Left there was a parallel ideology on the Right. The so-called Sacrum Imperium, made up of the dying Holy Roman Empire and the Papacy, helped inspire a loose federation, the Concert of Europe, through which such reactionaries as Alexander I of Russia sought to establish universal amity. It did set the stage for an unprecedented Hundred Years' Peace, from the final defeat of Napoleon in 1815 to the beginning of World War I in 1914.

Nonethnicity in the United States

When American writings on interethnic relations began to supplement these competing Left and Right ideologies, they influenced the beliefs also of other countries. For more than a century the United States had been the major destination of international migrants, and in the aftermath of that mass movement it became also the birthplace of modern sociology, the discipline most concerned with the ethnic structure of large populations.

In the United States the study of ethnicity/race developed in the context of long and often bitter debates on two policy issues: the Negro's proper place in American society, and, second, whether and how to restrict immigration. The fundamental questions were whether the differences between blacks and whites, and between immigrants and natives, were more or less permanent and therefore significant, or were transitory and thus to be discounted in a longer perspective.

Apart from these two policy issues, those in the American social disciplines were generally as little interested in ethnicity as their counterparts in Western Europe. When Nathan Glazer and Daniel Patrick Moynihan began work on their book *Beyond the Melting Pot,* they reviewed several encyclopedias in search of an appropriate definition of ethnicity. Neither Edward Byron Reuter's *Handbook of Sociology* (1941) nor G. Duncan Mitchell's *A Dictionary of Sociology* (1968) had an entry for either "ethnic group" or "ethnicity." *A Modern Dictionary of Sociology* (1969) by George A. and Achilles Theodorson included "ethnic group," but with a definition that is no longer current.[7] In spite of the enormous body of writings on blacks and immigrants, as well as a library of filiopietistic writings by members of particular groups to celebrate their ancestors, it was only during the past several decades that analysts started to generalize from these beginnings to a theory of ethnicity.

In *An American Dilemma,* a major synthesis of a generation's writings on black-white relations in the United States, the Swedish economist-sociologist Gunnar Myrdal expounded the then-current liberal doctrine on race relations. He held that differences between the two races were of three types:

- those based on false stereotypes (e.g., blacks' "peculiar smell"), which would be eroded by the improved cultural level of enough blacks;
- real differences based on discriminatory institutions (e.g., the lower level of basic skills acquired in poorer schools), which would gradually disappear as blacks were integrated into the general society; and
- real but superficial differences (e.g., skin color), which would become no more important than, say, a contrast between blond and dark hair.

An improvement in blacks' real situation would interact with whites' increasingly positive perception of the other race. By what he called a principle of cumulation (that is, a vicious circle in reverse), as blacks rose economically the cultural divergence between them and whites, as perceived from either side, would diminish and eventually become altogether insignificant. The book ended on a note of high optimism: "The driving force behind social study [is] the faith that institutions can be improved and strengthened and that people are good enough to live a happier life."[8]

Myrdal supervised the composition of a massive scholarly work, rich in detail and discerning in many of its insights, but it was flawed by the social democratic vista of its principal author. It reflected social scientists' general supposition that the movement of a significantly larger proportion of blacks into middle-range incomes and middle-class status would lead to an overall rapprochement between the two races. This is what I wrote myself at the time:

> The American Negro is wholly assimilationist. His many demands can be summed up in a single one—that he become invisible in white society. He wants his ghettos to merge into the rest of the cities they now disfigure; he wants the differentials by occupation, by mortality, by illegitimacy, by any other social statistic, to

become a thing of the past; he even wants (if this were possible) his color to disappear.[9]

Nothing in the assimilationist doctrine prepared Americans for what actually happened. The response to the great improvement in many Negroes' civil and economic condition was a resurgence of black nationalism, often led by those who had moved up farthest and fastest.

Somewhat similarly with respect to immigrants from Europe, Israel Zangwill's play *The Melting Pot* proclaimed the doctrine that in new land all European stocks would blend into a nobler American compound.[10] The play's hero, an immigrant to the United States and, like Zangwill himself, of Russian Jewish origin, married the immigrant daughter of the tsarist official responsible for the pogrom in which the groom's own parents had been killed. "The great Alchemist melts and fuses them with his purging flame—Celt and Latin, Slav and Teuton, Greek and Syrian," and, as represented in the hero and heroine, Jew and gentile. Though it has become routine to deride the metaphor of the *melting pot,* at the time it accurately represented the dominant desire of the insecure immigrant generation to disappear totally, to merge into indistinguishable sameness with "real" Americans.

Zangwill's work is customarily cited for what it said, not for its mediocre literary quality. The same is true of a later play on the same theme by Anne Nichols, *Abie's Irish Rose* (1922), in which a Jewish man and an Irish Catholic woman fall in love and are married by a Methodist minister. Its 2,327 performances marked one of the longest runs in the American theater, and the play also spawned a novel (1927), a radio program (1942), and a movie (1946).

Like the rest of the population at that time, academia was divided on what would constitute a just immigration policy, and some of the most bigoted works were written by one or another professor. But the really influential analysts of ethnicity gave the assimilationist dogma an aura of scientific validity. The most important American sociologist in the early decades of this century was Robert E. Park of the University of Chicago. All interethnic relations, he held, go through an invariable and irreversible four-stage succession of contact, competition, accommodation, and *assimilation.* Progress along this path is inevitable—except when something interferes with it.[11] Once its premises are accepted, the schema is unassailable, for the many subnations that have remained distinct for decades (or for centuries) can be explained away by their special circumstances, and the tenet that full amalgamation will be attained eventually remains intact. As one exponent of the thesis wrote, "Assimilation...goes on wherever contact and communication exist between groups.... It is as inevitable as it is desirable. The process may be hastened or delayed; it cannot be stopped."[12]

Myrdal and Park differed on one important matter. Though Park's theory was labeled "the race-relations cycle," in fact he believed that it applied more to European nationalities than to nonwhite races. Less optimistic than Myrdal concerning black-white interaction, he believed that attitudes, particularly in the South, were too entrenched among all whites to be easily dislodged. In 1939, when Myrdal was starting work on *An American Dilemma,* Park wrote him to express this pessimism concerning Negroes' future in the United States. That distinction apart, the two essentially agreed on the notion that the United States would soon become a country with no significant ethnic divisions; and from the status of the two men one can conclude that this was close to the consensus of the most influential American social scientists of that generation.

The view that group differences are either no more than apparent (or, if genuine, are temporary or unimportant) was reinforced in some influential works on group prejudice. Literally, *prejudice* means prejudgment. The *Oxford English Dictionary,* where it is defined as "a judgment before due examination or consideration; a premature or hasty judgment," gives citations exemplifying this meaning from the fourteenth to the nineteenth centuries. But in the years after World War II, American sociologists and social psychologists redefined the word.

> The term "prejudice" is sometimes used to refer to any kind of prejudgment. This usage would suggest that we are all prejudiced in favor of our friends and our preferred membership groups. To avoid this kind of interpretation we shall use the term in the more limited and usual sense of "prejudice against." A prejudice is thus an unfavorable attitude, and may be thought of as a predisposition to perceive, think, feel, and act in ways that are "against" or "away from" rather than "for" or "toward" other persons, especially as members of groups.[13]

According to a sociology textbook of the same decade, "prejudice refers to those negative attitudes that create a predisposition toward unfavorable responses to a racial or minority group."[14] In the words of four authors of an authoritative *Handbook of Social Psychology,* "by prejudice we mean an ethnic attitude predominantly negative. In other words, for us a prejudice is simply an unfavorable ethnic attitude."[15] Eventually these innovative statements became enshrined as a definition of the concept as simply a negative disposition toward certain ethnic groups, the attitudinal underpinning of discrimination.

With such a perception of prejudice, it becomes very difficult to distinguish negative judgments based on empirical evidence from those of a bigot. According to the Nazi stereotype, Jews controlled both high finance and the Communist movement (both statements were demonstrably false). However, German Jews were indeed very prominent in the cultural fields producing what Nazis called *Kulturbolschewismus*, or cultural Bolshevism.[16] In the United States, similarly, there is a world of difference between an opinion that blacks are frequently poorly educated and an assertion that they are innately unintelligent; to blur the line between such statements because they are both nega-

tive judgments about a minority does not help in combating anyone's irrational and nonempirical biases about other sectors of a population.

The commonly excessive deference to the symbolic-interaction school of
psychology reinforced this redefinition of a key term in social analysis. Indeed,
as those social psychologists held, members of ethnic groups often interact less
on the basis of actual characteristics than on the perceptions they form of both
their own group and other nationalities, religious communities, or whatever.
But it is also true that some perceptions of subnations, even if negative or hostile, are accurate. The test of prejudice, properly understood, is not whether the
appraisal is or is not favorable, but whether it is based on myth or fact.

During the same period anthropologists developed the doctrine of *cultural
relativism*, namely, that one may legitimately judge the worth of any culture
only by the criteria embedded in that culture's own value system. Following
from this postulate, as the American cultural historian Gertrude Himmelfarb
pointed out, the "virtues" celebrated by every Western moralist since Aristotle
have been transmuted into "values," which can be "beliefs, opinions, attitudes, feelings, habits, conventions, preferences, prejudices, even idiosyncra-
sies—whatever any individual, group, or society happens to value, at any
time, for any reason."[17]

In the United States cultural relativism was given a significant impetus by
the eminent anthropologist Franz Boas, and it reached a kind of apogee in the
main work of one of his ablest students, Ruth Benedict's *Patterns of Culture*.[18] Following the precedent set by Boas and his associates, the executive
board of the American Anthropological Association expounded the same view
in a more frankly political context. According to a statement that they jointly
submitted to the newly established U.N. Commission on Human Rights, if
the principle of individual rights were to apply to all of mankind, it would
have to include a respect for the cultures from which the individuals derived
their norms. In order to assist in expanding the concept of human rights in
this way, the team of supposed authorities outlined "some of the findings of
the sciences that deal with the study of human culture," as follows:

1. The individual realizes his personality through his culture, hence respect for
individual differences entails a respect for cultural differences.

2. Respect for differences between cultures is validated by the scientific fact that
no technique of qualitatively evaluating cultures has been discovered.

3. Standards of values are relative to the culture from which they derive so that
any attempt to formulate postulates that grow out of the belief in moral codes of
one culture must to that extent detract from the applicability of any Declaration of
Human Rights to mankind as a whole.[19]

Perhaps the most remarkable element of this statement is its date, 1947,
when the innumerable horrors of Nazi Germany were being brought to light.
Yet three years later, when A. L. Kroeber (with Boas one of the country's two

most prominent anthropologists) wrote a half-century review of his discipline's development, he repeated the same view as its consensus: "Anthropologists now agree that each culture must be examined in terms of its own structure and values, instead of being rated by the standards of some other civilization exalted as absolute—which in practice of course is always our own civilization."[20]

Among British anthropologists, one of the outstanding proponents of cultural relativism was Bronislaw Malinowski. Trobriand Islanders, the subject of several of his early works, were among the most primitive people in the ethnographic record, and he insistently repeated that they should never be judged by the standards of European civilization. A private diary that he kept in the Trobriands, which his widow had published after his death, demonstrated how far this public pose was from his actual thinking. While in his published works he always put the abhorrent word "savage" in quotation marks, in his journal he was jotting down his "general aversion for niggers," his wish that he could beat up his informants "without causing a row," his feeling that he would like to "exterminate the brutes."[21]

In theory the principle of cultural relativism might have meant no more than that, during a period of contact with a band of cannibals or headhunters, a field worker would try to understand their way of life by acting "as if" their customs were merely one variant in the wide spectrum of human differences.[22] In general, however, the thesis has been understood as a faith in the moral equivalence of all cultures—though, as Malinowski's conduct indicates, a product of high civilization who professes to put himself on a level with primitives is likely to indulge in an only partly successful self-deception.

The *International Encyclopedia of the Social Sciences,* published in 1968, has been widely endorsed as authoritative. According to its article on the concept, "Cultural relativism is a controversial doctrine that was quite fashionable in the second quarter of the twentieth century but has since lost much of its support."[23] Cultural relativists, we can say, have overreacted to the ethnocentrism in the theories of progress of the eighteenth and nineteenth centuries. An irrational feeling of guilt for past injustices against blacks or immigrants in the United States, or against the native populations of Europe's colonies, helped establish the axiom that in every significant respect a society's ethnic components are also, one and all, morally equivalent—and, hence, that over time any differences among them would all but disappear.

Almost all the doctrines, whether the melting pot or Marxism, evolved as supports for a political position rather than as an objective analysis of the trend in interethnic relations. Even as ethnic identity was becoming more significant in the United States, many of the society's leaders tried, in conformity with national policy, to disguise the very existence of racial/ethnic differences. In their progress toward "One World," idealists looked with eager anticipation to the predicted obliteration of all ethnic distinctions. Race, of course, would not literally disappear; rather, racial differences would be perceived as less and less significant. Over the past several centuries the decline of religious faith has been repeatedly proclaimed, and the more zealous ecumenicists have come close to asserting that no truly significant doctrinal tenet separates any religion from any other or, indeed, from atheism. For every Marxist denomination, a cultural group is either false or pathological. The demise of one language after another was documented: the last person who used Dalmatian, a Romance language once spoken in the former Yugoslavia, was killed in a mine explosion in 1898; in the late 1930s there were only two speakers of the American Indian language Chitimacha. With the spread of a few dominant civilizations, the people absorbed into them would eventually all speak, if not French or English, then Esperanto.

If all meaningful ethnic differences were disappearing (in fact, in the view of some, they had not disappeared already only because of racists' and capitalists' last-ditch efforts to maintain them), it was incumbent on every person of good will to move ahead of the trend and act as though all such distinctions had already become obsolete. In the 1940s an American professor who commented on "the Jewish vote" or "the Negro vote" would have put himself beyond the pale. The American Civil Liberties Union tried (unsuccessfully) to get the question on race deleted from the 1960 census schedule, and New Jersey did omit race and color from its birth and death certificates for the year 1962 (restoring them, however, one year later). Following the example of the prestigious *New York Times,* for about a decade many newspapers omitted racial identifications of all persons in the news. In new laws or regulations of federal bureaus and local jurisdictions, it was forbidden to require an ethnic identification or photograph on employment applications, applications for admission to college, and similar forms. (In several contexts such regulations overlapped with a later set imposing *de facto* quotas for the admission of students or the hiring or promotion of workers. For a period, thus, American universities and business firms that were not allowed to classify persons by ethnicity/race were required to maintain a stipulated balance among designated groups.)

Attempts to prevent the gathering of particular kinds of social data were based on three main arguments:

• It is morally wrong for a government to require anyone to identify himself by race, for that is an invasion of privacy. (But the color of one's skin is hardly less an element of one's persona than the colors of one's hair and eyes, which appear routinely on such documents as a driver's license or a passport—and excite no one's opposition. Is it reasonable to draw an ethical line at a mere census enumeration, in order to preserve our ignorance of a socially and politically important classification?)

• Race identification on forms is often used to discriminate against the individual identified on the form. (But few jobs are filled without a personal interview.)

- Statistical summaries by race are often used to reinforce stereotypes and prejudices—for example, racial breakdowns of crime, venereal disease, and dependency statistics. (But if a problem is concentrated in a particular sector of the population, to prohibit knowledge of that fact hardly helps in alleviating it and, thus, assisting the persons involved.[24])

The negative stance has included blocking out certain scholarly works. Paradoxically, America's first outstanding analysis of ethnicity, Sumner's *Folkways,* was in some respects the most perceptive. William Graham Sumner (1840–1910) was one of the founders of American sociology. Terms that he introduced—folkways, mores, ethnocentrism, in-group, out-group, and so on—became common usage in subsequent work. For several decades, however, little or no trace remained of his belief that group differences, because they are based on distinctions seen to be more or less immutable, are likely to persevere. One cannot change the mores, he wrote, "by any artifice or device, to a great extent, or suddenly, or in any essential element.... Changes which are opposed to the mores require long and patient effort, if they are possible at all."[25]

From roughly the 1920s, in sum, Americans in the social disciplines gave an aura of verisimilitude to their liberal views, and when their interpretation diffused to Europe and eventually to other parts of the world, it interacted with a parallel tradition based largely on Marx. However different in other respects, these two ideologies were one in picturing nationalism/ethnicity as reactionary and therefore, given the optimistic perspective characteristic of both views of the social world, as the last convulsions of a dying past. In his noteworthy book on ethnic politics, published in 1994, the American sociologist Milton Esman began by reviewing some prior works on ethnicity. The dominant view, he found, was that "in the emergent society, free of ascriptive or communal constraints, people would participate and compete as self-determining individuals valued and rewarded according to their individual contributions and performances.... Ethnicity would survive only as nostalgic vestiges of an earlier and less enlightened stage of historical development."[26] Though challenged by pluralists, this liberal/Marxist view persisted long after any empirical foundation for it had disappeared.

The Origins of Ethnic Groups

The concept of melting pot, once accepted as a plausible interpretation of American society, was later rejected. However, even if we postulate the only half-effective assimilation that critics substituted for Zangwill's metaphor, we must ask how it is that ethnicity has become a more and more important organizing principle of one society after another. The conventional American view of ethnic relations is that subnations come into being mainly through migration, but relative to the world's population, only small proportions have migrated. The dilemma is similar to that faced by pre-Darwinian writers on biology: all species had been brought into being only once, at the time of the world's creation; some had disappeared, as was known from their fossil remains; but the number of species in the world seemed to be growing. Darwin resolved the dilemma by describing how new species arise. It is also necessary, on a smaller scale, to consider the origins of ethnic groups, the process of ethnogenesis.

Lineage

The etymologies of the key terms used to designate cultural or genetic groupings—nation, ethnic, race—reflect their biological origins (see chapter 2). The belief of a group's members that they are descended from a single set of ancestors is a significant bond holding together most nations and subnations.

Residence

In the ninth century, every person in northern France was assigned to a particular parish and forbidden to attend services in any other; and this parochial division, identified as *patriotisme de clocher* (bell-tower patriotism), long persisted as a significant element of French politics. Throughout Western and Central Europe, peasants wove a web of sentiment that attached them to their *pays,* the local area where they were born, lived, and died.[27]

Some areal units of the Roman Empire had an amazing durability. When it fell apart, the principal larger pieces—Hispania, Gallia, Italia—sometimes retained a political identity that transcended their coherence as geographical regions. These fragments of the empire became not ethnic groups, but nations. The local variation of Latin spoken in each area was a unifying force, even though it was only much later that the present languages of Spain, France, and Italy evolved from the main dialects of those countries.

Migration

The conversion of immigrants from a particular country into a specific ethnic group is not a simple process. As noted by the English geographer Paul White, a distinction is made in European languages between "immigrants" and "foreigners": French *immigrés* and *étrangers,* Dutch *immigranten* and *vreemdelingen,* Spanish *imigrantes* and *extranjeros,* German *Gastarbeiter* (a particular type of immigrant) and *Ausländer.* The difference is in the public perception of acceptability, with the first terms used to describe low-status ethnic minorities, with the second usually designating higher-status groups. Research has been concentrated on the first, while the more acceptable foreigners are often passed over. For example, over the past several decades

Britain's Office of Population Censuses and Surveys issued a series of reports on ethnic minorities, but ignored completely the largest, the Irish, as well as all other whites.[28] On 1 April 1996 the country created a new independent bureau, the Office for National Statistics, combining the earlier Central Statistical Office and the Office of Population Censuses and Surveys. It was hoped that this move would cut the criticisms from various private users of government statistics.

Foreign nationals from one country arriving during the same years tend to concentrate in a few localities and occupations, and thus they enter only a narrow span of the receiving country's social structure. Where each flow of immigrants ends up depends on the level of their education and skill and, at the other end, on the opportunities available at that stage of the receiving country's development.

In the United States, where newcomers went was generally decided on the basis of the prior settlement of friends and relatives, supplemented by the aid given through German *Vereine,* Jewish *landsmanshaften,* Chinese *hui kuan,* or the Italian *padrone* system through which contract laborers were distributed. Typically residential concentration led to the formation of ethnic communities, a process stimulated by both natives' frequent hostility and the immigrants' preference for familiar faces.

In the recurrent disputes over how immigrants relate to American culture, some interesting analytical points have been largely ignored. It is not quite true that one can judge the impact of Swedish immigrants, say, by comparing the cultures of Sweden and of the United States, for migrants are never a random sample of the populations they leave and enter. In this instance, since most emigrants were neither urban nor upper- or middle-class, they took with them not the general culture of Sweden but rather a peasant version, expressed in local dialects and made up of regional customs. Free migrants, moreover, are generally already half-assimilated even before leaving home. Before someone left to go to a Swedish-American settlement, he started his acculturation in an American-Swedish milieu made up of New World letters, photographs, mementos, knickknacks—all contributing to what was termed *America fever.*[29]

The Japanese immigrants in the United States were subjected to harsh discrimination, culminating in their internment in concentration camps. Those in Brazil did not suffer from either type of bigotry. Yet, during World War II Japanese Americans were loyal to their new country, while Japanese Brazilians were fanatically pro-Japan. The contrast cannot be explained by examining the way of life of Japanese in the two countries to which they had migrated. "Yet it is readily understandable in terms of the cultural difference which existed between the two groups of Japanese *before they left Japan.*"[30]

Analysts of immigration to the United States often take it for granted that the receiving population is sufficiently large, powerful, and cultured to act as a host to newcomers. In contrast to this pattern, during the decades following the establishment of Israel in 1948, acculturation of Jewish immigrants was not to a host population, but rather to the ideology of Zionism. Migrants formed a dominant sector of the new state's population, but with many ethnic divisions within it (see chapter 14).

Consider also the case of Argentina. Immigration accounted for 58 percent of its population growth over the century from 1841 to 1940, or considerably more than in most countries of immigration; and it was immigrants who became Argentina's modernizing force, the major constituent of the urban proletariat (as in the United States) and also of the urban middle class.[31] Before the mass influx, almost the sole enterprise was cattle ranching; most of the labor force was divided between the owners, renters, and managers of the *estancias,* on the one hand, and the *gauchos,* or cowboys, on the other. Immigrants had no possibility of joining the first social class and no desire to become part of the second. Nine out of ten of them settled in the central provinces, mostly in the Buenos Aires metropolitan area or in other large cities. By 1914 the country was more than half urban, and its earlier two-class structure had broadened. Ethnically the immigrants were Italians, Spaniards, and Polish Jews; but as contrasted with economically and socially conservative rural classes, they were a single modernizing force. The complexities of Argentina's politics, reflecting the rapid and anomalous shifts in the social structure, are related to the only partial integration of an unprecedentedly high proportion of the foreign-born well-to-do.

Conquest

One common form of migration has been invasion and conquest. In *Ethnic Groups in Conflict,* Donald Horowitz notes that this has been a recurrent stimulus to a proliferation of ethnic groups. "The ensuing domination lends itself to the establishment of upper and lower ranks, clientage relations, and an ideology of inferiority for the subordinate groups."[32]

The Europeans who once governed their empires were distinguished from the general population first of all, of course, by their power; and since in most colonies the subject peoples were not Caucasian, the most visible sign of social status was usually race. K. M. Panikkar, one of the most scrupulous of Indian scholars in acknowledging India's debt to British rule, also remarked on the frank racism that "constituted the distinguishing characteristic of British rule in the East in the nineteenth century."[33]

Consolidation

Inhabitants of the Appalachian Mountains provide an example of consolidation-in-process. Their past relations with one another had often been hostile; residents of each hamlet huddled in its hollow perceived those from over the mountain as unwelcome strangers. Even within the small in-group, cooperation used to be the exception. "I know of many mountain communities," the American sociologist Jack Weller wrote in the mid-1960s, "where not a single sustained cooperative activity takes place to this day. Each family makes its own way, even though it is evident that there are needs requiring the strength and assistance of a group working together; the pattern of each depending upon his own talent, strength, and resourcefulness is too deeply ingrained." For decades contacts with the larger society were mostly through revenue men seeking the illicit stills of moonshiners (or blockaders, as they called themselves, to indicate that the defense of an alleged illegality was in fact a local right). Anyone whose identity was not known was suspect, very possibly an agent of the hated federal government.[34]

These isolated pockets of humanity were first defined as a single entity from the outside. In 1895, William G. Frost, president of Berea College in Kentucky, announced the discovery of "Appalachian America, the mountainous backyards of nine states," and in a series of articles over the next decade he tried to generate interest in helping the country's "contemporary ancestors" in this poverty-stricken region.[35] A federal bureau designated the counties making up the Appalachian Region on the basis of their need for various types of assistance. Eventually the common characteristics of the Mountain People, analyzed by such Southern sociologists as Howard Odum, Rupert Vance, Thomas R. Ford, and their successors, penetrated the consciousness of the objects of these studies.[36] Many organizations and institutions are now active in promoting this subculture, and the consequent consolidation may have been assisted by the increased contacts of Mountain People with others and their greater awareness that those who live in the Appalachian region really are distinct. It is at least possible that further acculturation to the general society will be by the circuitous route of uniting into a firmer and more self-conscious subculture.[37]

Promotion or Demotion

Raising a dialect to the status of a language can shift a lower class to parity on an ethnic scale. This has happened in two places discussed later in the book, Norway and Belgium (chapters 10 and 11). In the United States the rise of "Black English" suggests a similar process, though at a far earlier stage (chapter 5).

Sometimes a change in the ruling sector of a country lowers the status of an ethnos. With the persistent tribal dissension in Africa, many peoples have undergone a downward mobility in welfare and security. As the date in 1997 approaches when Hong Kong will be transferred to Communist China, residents become ever more fearful of what will happen to them. The last day that one could apply for a British passport was 31 March 1996, and more than 160,000 desperate people waited in line before the consulate, which stayed open until midnight. Those who succeeded in filing an application would, at best, receive a British National (Overseas) passport, which would give them visa-free access to a number of countries, but not the right to reside in Britain. In other words, wherever they are permitted to stay, they will be a new second-class minority.[38]

Race Crossing

In many works on ethnicity what is termed *amalgamation* is identified as one major route to the formation of new groups. American history challenges the validity of the thesis in at least some instances. African Americans have a high proportion of Caucasian forebears, but apart from the few who have passed into the white population, blacks have been defined in law and general perception as one race, regardless of the degree of admixture. One reads again and again that a new composite race is developing in Hawaii, but even if this were so biologically, it is an unlikely social prognosis (chapter 9). The Cape Colored in South Africa, in contrast to American blacks, do constitute a separate subnation that was brought into being partly by race crossing (chapter 15).

Race crossing is the result of many marriages or matings between persons of different racial identities, but the term *intermarriage,* self-explanatory in the abstract, is very difficult to relate to empirical data. Analyses of intermarriage in the United States pertain to crosses over lines marked by nationality, religion, or race.[39] What is termed an intermarriage, however, may be homogamous along the dimensions that the two persons involved consider most important. Two agnostics, one labeled a Jew and the other a Protestant, may in fact agree on all the moral issues subsumed under religion. Since race is not consistently defined, interracial marriages usually include a proportion that could be otherwise classified. Sometimes the decisive attribute is not considered in an analysis; for instance, a short man usually marries a short woman; someone in the middle class seldom takes one in the lower class as a spouse.

By one or more of these processes—a created lineage, a common residence, migration, conquest, consolidation, promotion, and race crossing—new ethnic groups are continually coming into being. The development is generally through three stages: category, group, and community. Sometimes, however, the progression is blocked or reversed by the contrary process of assimilation. Neither differentiation nor its opposite is ordained, and we know too little even to say which is more likely under specified circumstances. No one, however, can any longer challenge the generalization that ethnicity is here to stay indefinitely. And that is a new fact.

An Ethnic Revival?

Nothing indicates more pointedly the ambiguity of statistics on nationality, race, and religion than the debate about whether there has been a renaissance of ethnic sentiment in the United States. Those who try seriously to trace the changing contours of America's ethnic map have found little to agree on.

The assumption that assimilation is a one-way process proved to be quite mistaken. The hypothesis of "third-generation nationalism" offered by the American historian Marcus Lee Hansen showed an unusually shrewd appreciation of acculturation by picturing it as a cycle, with marked differences between immigrants, their children, and their grandchildren.[40] While immigrants were linked to their native countries by childhood memories and recurrent nostalgia, as well as by immigrant-aid societies, national churches, and other ethnic organizations, their acculturation was not usually impeded by a conscious reluctance to give up most old-country remnants. The aspiration of many immigrants to be more American than a New England Yankee was taken over a little more realistically by the second generation, which often attempted to learn nothing of the language and other culture traits of its European forebears. The third generation, however, often tried to organize a revival of their grandparents' native way of life.

Thus, each of the nationalities that came to the United States was followed two generations later by a succession of amateur historical societies, folklore associations, and other organized efforts to keep alive, revivify, or invent elements of the various overseas cultures. As Hansen put it, it was an "almost universal phenomenon that what the son wishes to forget the grandson wishes to remember." Such a new or revived interest and participation has been called *neo-ethnicity,* "either the revitalization of weak ethnic collectivities (for example, Negro Americans) or the rehabilitation of dwindling ethnic cohesiveness (for example, Irish Catholics, Jews, Italians)."[41]

These aspirations of the third generation were given a certain legitimacy by the American social psychologist Horace Kallen, who developed the concept of *cultural pluralism* in several influential papers.[42] Maintenance of American democracy, he held, did not require that immigrants be totally assimilated; one should distinguish those alien attributes that had to be foregone (in particular, loyalty to a foreign state) from those that could well be retained in a pluralistic society, such as, for example, language and religion. Critics pointed out that precisely the latter characteristics have been proximate causes of conflict the world over. Even insignificant remnants of minority cultures, moreover, would encourage each ethnic population both to maintain a certain coherence and to continue its links to the home country, and the most abrasive charge against "hyphenated" immigrants had generally been that their loyalty to the United States was compromised even by minor cultural traits that persisted in the New World.

In spite of such seeming flaws, cultural pluralism soon supplanted the melting pot as the usual social policy, and the list of acceptable characteristics of the alien stock was repeatedly expanded. It soon included the one attitude that, according to Kallen, had to disappear—a vestigial political rather than cultural adherence to another country. According to the often cited thesis of the American journalist Samuel Lubell, both the interventionists who wanted the United States to support the Allies in World War II and the isolationists who wanted to stay out of Europe's troubles were expressing half-hidden nationalist sentiments. Since it was politically impossible to advocate directly that the United States back Nazi Germany, descendants of Germans in the Midwest voiced this wish indirectly by supporting isolationism. And when Britain's need was dire enough, New England Yankees voted to help her even though they were half a dozen generations removed from immigrant status. In scholarly circles Lubell's work helped establish a link between ethnic blocs and American foreign policy as a customary element of most analyses, and thus to carry out the promise of the title of his book, *The Future of American Politics.*[43]

The argument linking national origin with political attitudes is dubious or, at best, unprovable. Adequate statistics on nationality beyond the second generation or on religion at all did not exist, and associating such data as could be found with secret votes involved all the well-known faults of ecological correlations. Concerning specifically the 1940 election, the one that Lubell used most to substantiate his argument, so distinguished a political scientist as V. O. Key concluded from an intensive study that "foreign policy seemed to have far less bearing on the vote than did questions of domestic policy, [with] a comparatively mild relation between attitudes on foreign policy and vote shifting."[44]

After the melting pot was supplanted by cultural pluralism as the goal of ethnic policy, eventually most writers on ethnicity accepted one type or another of pluralism. The American historian John Higham divided analysts into two schools. What he called the "soft pluralists" followed in the tradition of Kallen, perceiving cultural differences as values to be cherished for their own sake. Others, the "hard pluralists," followed Herbert Gutman, another history professor, in linking ethnicity with social class. In the view of the latter school, only ethnic unity enabled otherwise defenseless workers to resist industrial oppression.[45]

Against a background of constitutionally guaranteed religious freedom, ethnic associations of a dozen types, and the partial persistence or revival of foreign customs and languages, one might ask what rights was Kallen demanding that did not already exist in American society? When the sociologist Milton Gordon complained in his well-known book, *Assimilation in American Life,* that it was more or less equivalent to "Anglo-conformity," he recited a familiar list of past discriminatory practices culminating in "the so-called Americanization movement, which gripped the nation like a fever during World War I." Acculturation, he said, had been "numerically and functionally overwhelming," but "structural assimilation" (his term for entry into clubs and institutions of the host society) "turned out to be the rock on which the ship of Anglo-conformity foundered."[46] In other words, the instruments of cultural pluralism that Kallen hankered after not only existed, but were crucial in maintaining—at least in part—the ethnic diversity that both he and Gordon wanted to preserve. Kallen and Gordon were Jews, and with the rise of Zionism on the one hand and Nazism on the other, more Jews were evincing interest in ethnic analysis.

One main current of Catholic political thought reached a high point in a 1960 book by John Courtney Murray, a distinguished American Jesuit scholar, which linked the "public consensus" of the United States to its Christian past. The "tradition of natural law and natural rights" Murray interpreted as "the central political tradition of the West"—though not of the French revolution and the democracy that evolved out of it. He contrasted the long dominant conservative or reactionary Catholicism in Continental Europe with the same religious faith in the United States, where in his view it had been integrated as an essential part of the democratic ethos. The acculturation that he saw as desirable was facilitated by the fact that both the existent nation and the newcomers he spoke for shared fundamental moral values.[47]

Another prominent exponent of new trends was an American man of letters of Slovak forebears, Michael Novak, who attracted national attention first as a spokesman for Slavs and, thus, indirectly for Catholics. His book on "the rise of unmeltable ethnics" is essentially about politics. Catholics, he wrote, "have special characteristics, needs, and dreams. Their symbolic life, rhetoric, and ways of perceiving are unique." Moreover, and this is the point, "they form a formidable electoral bloc," in which the Irish, only half-welcome, are included mainly because they already possess power that they can share.[48]

According to the American sociologist Herbert Gans, in one of the better expositions of a familiar theme, the ethnic revival has been mainly "a nostalgic allegiance to the culture of the immigrant generation, or that of the old country; a love for and a pride in a tradition that can be felt without having to be incorporated in everyday behavior." This "symbolic ethnicity" has taken on an expressive rather than an instrumental function.[49] As I see it, the difference between expressive and instrumental need not be sharp. "Symbolic" can refer to matters either trivial or of grave import. Chocolate-covered matzohs exchanged as Passover gifts, one of Gans's examples of the frivolous extensions from genuine Judaism, are no more or less symbols than the standard matzohs that observing Jews eat during Passover in place of bread. Indeed, sentiments associated with institutions are generally expressed in symbolic ritual, and this association is instrumental in a sense made familiar in Émile Durkheim's works, namely, by helping maintain a viable establishment.

One reason that ethnicity has become more prominent in the United States is that the number of ingredients in today's melting pot is far larger than when the metaphor was coined. The Southern California Gas Company, which at a recent date served 13 million consumers over 22,000 square miles from the Mexican border to south-central California, has conducted its own surveys to supplement census figures. By its findings, within that territory the population spoke a total of eighty-eight languages and dialects. The company installed a device to transfer any telephone calls not in English to a center where employees answer questions in Spanish, Vietnamese, Korean, Mandarin, Cantonese, and (according to announced plans) Armenian, as well as various Spanish dialects. Manuals on how to hook up a gas stove were made available in Spanish, Vietnamese, Korean—and English.[50]

Commercial firms serving such a polyglot population begin by addressing each sector separately, but soon consumer products reflect interactions among the various nationalities. When an accommodation takes place between several exotic cultures, with a production of commodities new to them as well as to America, should an analyst of native-alien relations rate this process as an indication of more or of less acculturation? In the mid-1990s, Los Angeles lunch counters and small restaurants were owned by such entrepreneurs as Jews, Italians, Chinese, Vietnamese, Thais, Koreans, Mexicans, Cubans, and Greeks. They have developed a style called *fusion cooking*. Novel combinations as compiled by Merrill Shindler, restaurant critic for the Los Angeles *Herald Examiner*, included *chile relleno* with Gujarat-style *alu chole* (spicy chickpeas), served with salsa and Indian bread; kosher-style burritos; a chili-doused and tortilla-wrapped frankfurter identified as an *Oki dog;* as well as a combo of teriyaki chicken and falafel.

Are such inconsequential matters as composite recipes relevant to the question of whether ethnicity is being sustained or revised in a more important sense? A Berkeley professor of Spanish literature, when I knew him in the 1960s, was collecting elements of "Spanish as she is spoke in California." No new housing development, hardly any new avenue, could be completed without doing fresh damage to the language of a neighboring friendly nation. Examples are generally ridiculous, often amusing, sometimes unintentionally vulgar.[51] This mauling of the Spanish language, however, may indicate a potential sympathy with the Latino minority and their aspirations. Consider the analogous intrusion of Yiddish expressions—among others, *meshugge, chutzpah, maven*—into the conversations of gentiles and the columns of general newspapers. The trend has accompanied a marked erosion in anti-Semitism and, at least arguably, facilitates a further decline in anti-Jewish sentiment.

The works of Hansen, Kallen, and Lubell typify a broader discussion that descendants of European immigrants engaged in concerning their nationalities. During the same years, the melting pot, to the degree that it ever applied to blacks, was also rejected by many of them. The Martiniquan poet Aimé

Césaire coined the word *négritude,* the essential quality of black people, and his work was glowingly praised by such Paris intellectuals as Jean-Paul Sartre and André Breton. Césaire tried to resolve "the dilemma of a victim forced to free himself from the shackles of his oppressor by the use of those very shackles."[52] That is, though reason and the technology of white civilization were to be exorcised and replaced by blacks' vitality and "soul," the advance of black people had to come about in part by making use of the very instruments that they were rejecting.

The ferment among black writers over négritude was broadened by the search for roots popularized in the United States by the novelist Alex Haley, who claimed to have traced his black (but not his white) ancestors through 200 years of slavery and oppression. For eight consecutive nights during January, 1977 an estimated 80 million persons watched a television version of Haley's work. According to a check by two professional genealogists, the roots that Haley had claimed to have uncovered were largely fictional. Some of his presumed ancestors did not exist, others were too young or too old to have contributed to the family tree, and still others lived in the wrong place. The cited records "contradict each and every pre-Civil War statement of Afro-American lineage in *Roots.*"[53] This refutation, published in an obscure journal, was generally ignored even by professional historians; certainly it did not disturb the extension of the search for roots from a European to an African context.

Under the fanciful notions of cultural relativism there has often been, at first half-hidden, a will to denigrate Western civilization. The proposition that all cultures are equivalent meant, in fact, that the culture of those offering this view was not superior—indeed, in many respects was inferior. The first chapter of Richard Bernstein's book on multiculturalism is titled *"Dérapage,"* a skid or slide, which historians of the French revolution have used to denote the transformation of the noble aims of the eighteenth-century Enlightenment to the despotism of the Terror. Similarly, the dogma of multiculturalism began with appeals to openness and diversity and soon evolved into a cloak for American *dérapage.* The transformation of American schools' curricula in the name of tolerance has been, in fact, tolerance for every culture except that of the United States or, more broadly, of the Western world.[54]

The unanticipated resurgence of some form and some degree of ethnicity and nationalism made nonsense of the earlier perspective, but nothing has risen to take the place of the melting pot. Both public policy on ethnicity and the social theory that supposedly has guided it (and in fact has often been derived from it) are in disarray. The conventional race doctrine in the United States, for instance, split into two halves, no more compatible than the pair that Myrdal confronted in what he called an American dilemma. On the one hand, some black spokesmen developed an American variant of négritude— the faith that blacks, specifically because of their race, are superior to whites.

On the other hand, the rejection of any biological distinctions whatever has remained the most pervasive expression of the thesis that there are no significant group differences. As another example, though few representatives of ethnic groups are willing to set any limits to their conflicting demands, many believe that all these competing factions will coalesce into a harmonious cultural pluralism.

2

Concepts of Ethnicity

Demography is generally defined as the scientific study of population or, more particularly, of fertility, mortality, and migration. That prior to such study one must define the population to be analyzed is usually left implicit, for generally the authors of demographic works accept what is deemed to be the natural unit—the persons inhabiting a nation-state or a smaller political subdivision. Apart from the possible ambiguity in the definition of residence, the demarcation of populations by nation, province, county, township, and so on is clear-cut, and in some cases such areas can be meaningful units of analysis. But since most boundaries of geographical units are arbitrary, the sectors of the population defined by them are irrelevant to many of the questions asked in the social disciplines.

When analysts try to set precise limits to transnational concepts (Southeast Asia, Northwest Europe, the less-developed countries, and the like), or to divide national populations into appropriate subunits other than geographical divisions, they appreciate how convenient the usual delimitation of their topic is. For each decision whether or not to include marginal groups in a population being studied affects not only its size but also all its demographic rates and, thus, possibly the validity of the whole analysis. The problem is particularly intimidating when dividing a population by ethnic identity.

The English language has been enriched by the incorporation of some more or less synonymous words from two or more sources. The many terms used to analyze ethnicity or nationalism, however, have not contributed to greater clarity. With so complex and contentious a topic, all designations have remained more or less ambiguous, and commentators are often unable to agree on the exact meaning of any of them. As an egregious example, the term *affirmative action* denotes both the earlier attempts to *remove* racial discrimination and the later policy to *impose* it. Everyone who writes on the subject is aware of this, of course, but many are unwilling to clarify the muddle. In any propaganda war it is a major victory to get one's own version of key terms accepted as routine elements of a supposedly neutral presentation.

One might suppose that it would be useful to stipulate the correct meaning of each term. More realistically, the intent here is to trace the meanings as-

31

signed to each, beginning with its etymology and continuing through its connotations in various contexts.

Search for a Terminology

The word *ethnic* derives via Latin from the Greek *ethnikos,* the adjectival from of *ethnos,* a nation or race. As originally used in English, ethnic signified pagan or heathen; not Christian or Jewish. In *The Leviathan* Thomas Hobbes exhorted Christian converts to continue obeying their ethnic (that is, not Christian) rulers. *Nation* comes from Latin via French; its ultimate source is *natus,* past participle of *nasci,* to be born, and the closer one is *natio,* meaning birth.

The biological association suggested by these etymologies was long retained in English, as we can see from some currently obsolete or rare usages. Like dozens of other words, both *ethnic* and *nation* were applied originally to outsiders as a class. With the lessening of what we now term *ethnocentrism,* the range of such words was extended from alien peoples to any people, including that of the speaker. And from their physiological context, the meaning of both terms broadened to include cultural attributes and political entities. But neither of these shifts has been consistent.

With the development of nations, ethnicity also came into being. Just as there were no peasants before the rise of cities (for a peasant is not merely an agriculturist, but one who relates to a rural-urban complex), so the prior adherence to a parochial culture acquired new significance when those united by local patriotisms became identified also as sectors of a larger entity. In the introduction to the *Harvard Encyclopedia of American Ethnic Groups,* the editors noted that the groups discussed in the entries are characterized by one or more of the following attributes:

- common geographic origin;
- migratory status;
- race;
- language or dialect;
- religious faith or faiths;
- ties that transcend kinship, neighborhood, and community boundaries;
- shared traditions, values, and symbols;
- shared literature, folklore, and music;
- food preferences;
- settlement and employment patterns;
- special interests in regard to politics in the homeland and in the United States;

- participation in institutions that specifically maintain the group;
- an internal sense of distinctiveness; and
- an external perception of distinctiveness.[1]

Some of these characteristics are less elements of a definition than behavior patterns that set off particular ethnic groups, but the list as a whole suggests how many threads are woven into the texture of ethnicity.

Ethnic is an adjective; English never fully adopted a noun from the Greek *ethnos*. The lack of a convenient substantive form has induced writers to coin a number of makeshifts, all of which have their drawbacks. Of these, the commonest is *ethnic group*. Unfortunately, those who use this term often forget the crucial distinction between a group, which by definition has some degree of coherence and solidarity, and a category, which denotes no more than a patterned differentiation. Despite the difficulty in determining at what point an aggregate becomes a group—that is, when coherence is established—it is important to maintain the distinction.[2]

As professional jargon, *minority group* is even less suitable, for both its elements are ill-chosen. According to Louis Wirth, whose writings did much to popularize the term, it refers simply to victims of a reprehensible subordination: "the people whom we regard as a minority may actually, from a numerical standpoint, be a majority."[3] But in most of history, as well as in most of the non-Western world today, the dominant social division has been between a small ruling elite and a vast ruled mass; what Tocqueville called "the tyranny of the majority"[4] can arise only in the exceptional democratic society. Wirth's term merely muddles and facilitates a manipulation to fit the political occasion. In the British Isles the Irish are a widely dispersed minority; in all of Ireland the Protestants are a minority; in Northern Ireland the Catholics are a minority. Simply by drawing the appropriate boundary and stressing the self-serving portion of an area's history, partisans can almost always find a way to picture themselves as a victimized minority group.

In the United States, also, the term *minority* has had a capricious meaning. Since, suitably delineated, every ethnic element of the American population can be called a minority, the term has no fixed relation to reality; in the vocabulary of logic, it is a referent without a relatum. In the days of the New Deal it meant in most contexts Negroes, sometimes also Jews or Jews plus Catholics. These quite dissimilar categories had in common two characteristics—that they were victims of discrimination and that, partly for that reason, they were likely recruits for the Democratic party. These two characteristics set the designation also of the indefinitely expansible array of other minorities—Indians, Hispanics, Italians, Slavs—all of whom might be induced to vote for the party that allegedly had done, or promised to do, more for them.

In any coalition, however, ethnic segments are especially likely to compete against one another. The national party that the Roosevelt team assembled began to fall apart already in 1946 (when Democrats lost control of Congress), in 1948 (when the presidential victory was extremely narrow), in 1950 (when Republicans still controlled Congress), and in 1952 (when a Republican president was elected). The main reason was that Democrats could no longer depend on automatic support from the South, primarily because of the party's gamble in wooing the black population. More generally, by its very nature an ethnic coalition affords each sizable unit the possibility of blackmail, with the ransom usually set at action still more affirmative for the most obstreperous group(s). Continually raising the stakes, being rewarded more and more for continued adherence to the party, sets up a counterpart to a class struggle in which all sides have viewed every accommodation as a temporary staging ground for the next battle. With a massive redistribution of money, goods, and services, all on a group basis, those of almost every ethnic background have tried to muster enough collective power to ensure a reallocation favorable to themselves or, as a minimum, to impede the similar efforts of other minorities.

Some analysts have preferred the term *interest group,* which substitutes for the persecution of Wirth's "minority" a competition among many minorities. For most of the ethnic patterns in the United States or Western Europe, this is a far less tainted concept, but it also focuses the analysis only on power relations. There are indeed societies where the denotation *Homo hierarchicus* is appropriate: the book with that title is an analysis of India's caste system.[5] But the tendency to regard all ethnic configurations as hierarchical can be grossly distortive. In most contexts New Englanders and Lutherans are hardly interest groups, yet they illustrate important parts of a comprehensive ethnic classification of the United States. Moreover, the term invites one to pass over the frequent dissension between the self-appointed ideologues who speak in the name of interest groups and the persons they supposedly represent.

In previous works I suggested the term *subnation,* a unit smaller than a nation, but otherwise similar to it. A nation is a people linked by common descent from a putative ancestor and by its common territory, history, language, religion, and/or way of life. Obviously neither all nations nor all subnations conform to every element of this list, and the precise limits of subnations are more difficult to judge because they are less often directly associated with the counterpart of a boundary-protecting state. However, hardly any other analysts have adopted *subnation* in place of the terms I intended it to supplant.

Essentially the word *nation* has two meanings—a cultural entity and a political state. In actual life the two are often intertwined, and some analysts hold that it makes no difference if the two definitions are as confused in commentary as in actuality. From the League of Nations to the United Nations and beyond, common usage rejects the seemingly reasonable point of the American political scientist Walker Connor: so-called international organizations are composed of states, virtually all of which are ethnic composites.[6] The German historian Friedrich Meinecke distinguished between *Staatsnation* and *Kulturnation* or, narrowly defined, state and nation.[7] In contrast to this sharp distinction, Elie Kedourie, until his death in 1992 a professor of politics at the London School of Economics, argued that nationalism is essentially political, a doctrine by which intellectuals use ethnic sentiment in order to weld people into an independent state.[8]

The first meaning of *nationality* was national quality or character, then an ethnic group that is potentially but not actually a nation. The most common current usage in such multiethnic countries as the United States or the former Soviet Union is to designate a nonracial type of ethnic category.

The words *nationalism,* conservative, liberal, socialism, and capitalism all first appeared in English in the middle of the nineteenth century.[9] Nationalism and *nationalist* can pertain to actual nations (in which case they are more or less synonymous with patriotism and patriot), but more often they refer to the sentiments of ethnic groups within a present country. Polish nationalists wanted an independent Poland; Flemish nationalists wanted equal status with Walloons in a continuing Belgian state. It is confusing that we use the same word to designate both black nationalists—virtually none of whom have demanded independence from the United States—and Canada's French nationalists, whose leaders have insisted that Quebec become a separate country.

The term *nationalism* is especially imprecise in describing a shift from one level of group consciousness to another. In multiethnic Austria-Hungary, the creators of a new Slav awareness first demanded no more than greater group rights within the empire; only later did some of the Slav leaders insist on independence for what eventually emerged as Czechoslovakia and Yugoslavia—both of which split again into separate units in the 1990s. In many areas it is less an analytic than a political judgment whether the surviving *tribalism* in black Africa (or, in India, *communalism*) expresses dissent within an essentially unified entity or the strivings of real nations to throw off the dominance of alien rulers.

The word *tribe* (from the Latin *tribus*) originally referred to the three patrician orders of ancient Rome: Latin, Sabine, and Etruscan. It came into English not directly, but in a reference to the twelve tribes of Israel listed in the Bible. In modern usage it has typically signified a primitive people, and when used to allude to a class of persons in a modern society, the intent used to be to suggest derision. More recently, several writers have defined tribe simply as a synonym for ethnic group, with no pejorative connotation.

Interpretation is likely to falter also when words in other languages, even the closely related West European languages, are translated as ethnicity or nationalism. The French word *nation* has the same double meaning as its English derivative, either a community based on common attributes or a political unit. A biological linkage is likely to be expressed by *peuple,* people, and a territorial or sentimental one by *patrie*, fatherland. The word *état*, state, has the convenient derivatives *étatisme* and *étatisation*, which in English are rendered by nationalism (as in economic nationalism) and nationalization— far less appropriately, since it is not the nation, but rather the state that is involved.

Under the Nazi program to delete all foreign words from German, *Nation*, which had usually implied a cultural rather than a political unit, was largely supplanted by *Volk*, very roughly, people, but in fact untranslatable. The adjective *völkisch* denotes the essential, organic character of Germans, usually including more than those living in the Reich. Since 1945, *Volk* and *völkisch* have been used less, for both words were tarnished by Nazism. The French word *ethnie* is similar to *Volk*, denoting those bound by racial, cultural, and sentimental ties regardless of national boundaries; *l'ethnie française* thus comprises not only France, but also the French-speaking sectors of Belgium, Switzerland, Italy, Canada, and so on.[10]

Ethnie is listed in the *Nouveau Petit Larousse* as a neologism, and it may be writers will solve the terminological predicament in English by adopting as a suitable noun either *ethnie*,[11] or the Greek *ethnos*, or the English adjective. In recent popular writing, when *ethnic* has been used as a substantive, it customarily refers only to certain categories: "white ethnics" are Italians and Poles, but usually not Scots and Norwegians. My preference is for *ethnos*, a more suitable term than most alternatives.

Ethnos versus Race

Of the various criteria of ethnicity, race is in many respects the most significant. The characteristics of the body, that most palpable element of one's persona, have been used throughout history to define the commonest type of group identity. Since ethnos with its derivations first pertained to a biological grouping, it was close to what we now call race (probably derived through the French *race* from *ratio*, which in medieval Latin was used to designate a species). In its current usage a biological connotation sometimes adheres to the word ethnic, but not necessarily: some groupings are defined by their genetic heritage, others by their language or religion or another cultural attribute.

Apart from poetry or metaphor, *race* in English has usually referred to a biological unit, but its size has varied from a family line (as in Tennyson's *Sisters*: "We were two daughters of one race") to the entire species (as in Shakespeare's "the whole race of mankind" or the common phrase "the human race"). When Alexander Pope translated a line of *The Iliad* (1715) with "Troy's whole race thou wouldst confound," he was using the word in place of what we would be likely to call a nationality. The nineteenth-century American botanist Asa Gray defined race as "a variety which is perpetuated with considerable certainty by sexual propagation" (1880)—that is, more or less the same meaning as a species. Cognates in other European languages—French *race*, German *Rasse*, and so on—are still used with a seeming indifference to the range of the unit.

As physical anthropologists now use the term, the size of a race depends simply on the purpose of the particular investigator: it means a breeding population that differs significantly from others in the frequency of one or more genes, with "significantly" specified according to the context.

> A race or subspecies is a genetically distinguishable subgrouping of a species distributed within a more or less localized territory that interbreeds with other subgroups of the species in areas of overlap or when brought into contact with them. The frequency of gene exchange between races is highest in the overlap zone and decreases away from it.[12]

Or, more succinctly, a race is "a geographically and culturally determined collection of individuals who share a common gene pool."[13]

In the social disciplines the definition of the concept has never been settled. A symposium on race in *Current Anthropology* (three full issues in 1962–64) indicated how little consensus, how little even of a charitable appreciation of other views, exist among the world's professional analysts of the subject. The symposium was instigated by an attack on *Mankind Quarterly,* another anthropology journal, and on the author of a paper published there.[14] When asked to respond to the statement, "There are biological races within the species *Homo sapiens,*" 52 percent of cultural anthropologist disagreed, 58 percent of physical anthropologists agreed.[15]

There has been a trend in the social disciplines, at least among those who do not believe that the term should be abjured, toward reserving race for mankind's major biological divisions and using another designation for smaller units within them. Thus, many American writers distinguish racial from ethnic minorities, the former being blacks, Asians, and other nonwhites, the latter the descendants of European immigrants or the equivalent subunits of other races. The separation of the two terms has been inhibited, of course, by the confusion in real life between physiological and cultural criteria. Typically a racial group is set off from the rest of a population also by cultural characteristics. Conversely, if the endogamy enjoined or at least encouraged by most religious faiths and other cultural groups continues for enough generations, it is likely to result in a perceptible physical differentiation.

Analysts of Latin America commonly use the term *social race,* for genetic heritage and class structure are more intertwined there than in most other settings. In the censuses of Spanish America, the offspring of persons of different races have often been classified separately. Sometimes attempts were made to delineate with great precision the degrees of miscegenation among whites, Indians, and blacks, with not only *mestizo, mulato,* and *lobo* as the first generation, but also *morisco, costizo, cambujo, sambahigo, calpamulato, jíbaro, coyote, albarazado,* and so on as various degrees and types of crossing.[16]

The disarray in the concept of race is even more pronounced in the Portuguese terms used in Brazil. During the early colonial period, there were very few white women. Many of the Indians, too few in any case to fill the growing demand for slaves, died or disappeared into the category of *mestiço* (or mixed Indian-white). They were replaced by blacks; of the approximately 11.3 million African slaves shipped to the New World up to the year 1870, well over a third were taken to Brazil. White males mated as freely with blacks as they did with Indians, and several new degrees of race crossing began to acquire specific designations. Finally, immigrants from various European countries—plus Chinese and especially Japanese—were added to the mixture. The terminological profusion reflects the thoroughly mixed population; and the meanings assigned to *raça* or its equivalents waver between genetic and cultural components.

In the last decades of the nineteenth century, intellectuals trying to expound an ideology of Brazilian nationalism were impeded by the anthropological theories that then prevailed. Arthur de Gobineau, the French racist, found the Brazilians to be "a population totally mulatto, vitiated in its blood and spirit, and fearfully ugly." Louis Agassiz, the Swiss-American naturalist, discovered there a proof of "the deterioration consequent upon an amalgamation of races, more widespread here than in any other country in the world."[17] Such judgments were circulated in Brazil first as part of the debate about the abolition of slavery in 1888, then again in the 1920s, when Brazilians were discussing its immigration policy. Those in favor of a larger influx also agreed on the absolute necessity of recruiting more agricultural laborers from Europe.[18]

Of the counter statements, the most influential was by the Brazilian sociologist, anthropologist, and social historian Gilberto Freyre. According to his *The Masters and the Slaves,* published originally in 1933, not only had generations of miscegenation not done the irreparable damage charged by critics, but the resultant population was Brazil's immense asset. Brazilians could be proud of their uniquely mixed tropical civilization.[19] Especially the many *mestiços* rising in social status were happy to accept his perspective as a new truth.

Freyre's vision of "racial democracy" was not in accord with Brazilian social reality. According to studies by the Argentine-born sociologist Carlos A. Hasenbalg, whites are much better off than mulattos, who are only slightly better off than blacks. Another sociologist, Nelson do Valle Silva, found that mulattos, presumably because they often compete with whites, suffer more discrimination in the labor market even than blacks. Afro-Brazilians have proposed affirmative-action programs similar to those in the United States, but with little success. One major impediment to race-based organizations or policies is the problem of defining who is black. With the vast array of terms that Brazilians use to identify various skin shadings, they have impeded the effort of militant blacks to institute some form of reverse discrimination.[20]

Brazil's lamentable slums are inhabited for the most part by blacks, and at least some of them deny that they are racially distinct from the upper classes.

> The black Brazilian woman who says that there are no blacks in Brazil is pursuing the national logic. The myth of a Brazilian racial democracy tells her that all Brazilians are treated alike, while her experience tells her that blacks are treated differently. She is led accordingly to conclude that a black cannot be a Brazilian, and since she believes herself to be a Brazilian, she cannot believe that she is black.[21]

The recurrent debate whether race is one type of ethnicity or rather a parallel but separate classificatory criterion pertains not to the real world or even to most ethnic/racial statistics, but to those confusing absolute categories of the last century. At one time the American sociologist Pierre van den Berghe defined a race as "a group that is socially defined but on the basis of physical criteria." Then he decided that it is not useful to retain the distinction: "While I still think that the greater rigidity and invidiousness of racial, as distinct from cultural, distinctions makes for qualitatively different situations, both race and ethnicity share the basic common elements of being defined by descent, real or putative. Therefore, I now tend to see race as a special case of ethnicity, rather than as a categorically discrete phenomenon."[22] My own feeling is that terminology is inconsequential: race and ethnicity are mingled in many situations, but the attempt to foster either understanding or good will with word magic is pointless. "All ethnic groups behave in the same typical manner, regardless of whether the underlying ideologies hinge on religious, political, cultural, racial, or other characteristics and regardless of whether these characteristics are real or fictitious."[23]

In some cases the descent referred to in a racial category has been the contrary—a construction backwards from the present to some mythical past. By a collective quasimemory, each people conceives an image of its past and a lineage from that era to the present. The German word *Stamm* (literally, stem or trunk, hence *stock*) has been used to mark such a route of specious descent—for example, from Germanic tribes of the Roman era to inhabitants of regions where the present dialects of German are spoken. Actually, such tribes as the Visigoths and the Ostrogoths recruited diverse swarms of fugitive slaves; "all war bands were mixed and tended to become more heterogeneous the more successful they were."[24]

In the most remarkable feats of such a reverse lineage, peoples have claimed a divine ancestry. Out of the folk cult of *Shinto,* Japanese militarists fashioned a state religion that bestowed on the emperor not only divine forebears but the personal status of a living god. A belief in *Sharif* descent, which designates Mohammed as a progenitor, proliferated in the Islamic world, with more than 4,000 progeny by the ninth century in Baghdad alone. More recently, several Moroccan dynasties legitimized their rule by officially claiming a sharifian origin.[25]

In the aftermath of the Nazi genocide, a number of anthropologists have argued that we should delete the word *race* from our languages, not only because it is associated with racism, but fundamentally because it is a vague category with imprecise and shifting boundaries. Whether the removal of a word would also eradicate group antipathies is doubtful; one suspects that with another label Jews and Gypsies would have been murdered just as bestially. In any case, deleting the term does not remove the need for some designation. Ashley Montagu, a professor of physical anthropology and anatomy, was among those who argued the case most vociferously; he drafted the UNESCO book on race that propounded the same view.[26]

In the mid-1970s the government agencies of Canada expunged the word *race* from official usage and substituted the phrase "visible minority." Included under this rubric were what the U.S. Bureau of the Census used to term *nonwhites,* whom the Canadian government was to protect against discrimination in employment.[27] The category, however, is as artificial and obscure as its American counterpart. In both cases, in order to get a reasonable picture of social reality, one has to break down the composite into its racial parts. The years of schooling in 1986, taken as an indicator of social-economic status, varied greatly, as can be seen by the percentages of various races that had university degrees:

	Male	*Female*
"Nonvisible minority"	16	12
"Visible minority"	23	16
Blacks	12	7
South Asian	26	18
Chinese	24	15
Filipino	37	42
West Asian and Arab	32	20

The number and boundaries of the world's races have been analyzed many times since the pioneer efforts of Johann Friedrich Blumenbach, who in 1795 divided the human species into five "varieties" based on the shapes of their skulls. As Franz Boas showed in 1911, not only were Americans of European origin about two inches taller than their parents, but the new environment changed appreciably the shape of the skull, which soon thereafter ceased to be used as a major index of racial classification.[28] Rereading some of the main works, the American physical anthropologist Joseph Birdsell found, was "a depressing task," for what he judged to be as sensible a racial schema as anyone has offered since then was compiled in 1775 by Immanuel Kant.

> Kant divided mankind into four major races: Whites, adapted to cold damp climates; Mongoloids, living in cold, dry regions; Negroid, originating in the dry

heat of tropical Africa; and finally the inhabitants of Peninsular India, similar in their dark skins and linear body builds, evolving in a regime of the same climatic characteristics.[29]

Since each person has two parents, four grandparents, and so on, we can calculate the number of a person's forebears by doubling for each generation. The result is thrown off by remarriages and multiple births, but these cause small deviations from a regular exponential succession. If we ignore such aberrations, in the roughly sixty-four generations just since the beginning of the Christian era, the number of ancestors of each person is 2^{64}, or 18,446,744,073,709,551,616. The size of this figure suggests more vividly than any alternative argument how much overlap there has been in sexual relations and, thus, how irresponsible it is to postulate the purity of any genetic grouping.

The notion that analysts should recognize only pure categories is bizarre. It follows from the theory of evolution itself that all biological divisions, from phylum through subspecies, are always in the process of change, so there is never a sharp and permanent boundary setting one off from the next. Blood groups may be the best indicator of genetic inheritance. They are classified according to whether the red blood cells of one person can be mixed with those of another without forming clots. Karl Landsteiner received the Nobel Prize in 1930 for demonstrating the incompatibility of the groups now designated A, B, AB, and O. Subsequent researchers identified almost two dozen other types. The classification discriminates much more precisely than one based on such gross somatic characteristics as skin color. For example, the so-called Lutheran blood groups are concentrated in only one portion of the Caucasoid race, and the antigen Lu[a] can be present in blacks as well as whites, though apparently not in Asians, Eskimos, or Australian aborigines.[30] Now races are sometimes classified with computer-generated calculations of the distribution of traits transmitted by a single gene.

Culturally Defined Groupings

If the demand for pure categories were to be extended to indicators generally used in the social disciplines, acceding to it would bar most discussion, not to say research. For the difference is also partly arbitrary and somewhat mutable between rural and urban, employed and unemployed, literate and illiterate, and so on. As Abraham Kaplan, an American-Israeli professor of philosophy, put it in his classic *The Conduct of Inquiry,* "it is the dogmatisms outside science that proliferate closed systems of meaning; the scientist is in no hurry for closure. Tolerance of ambiguity is as important for creativity in science as it is anywhere else."[31]

The meaning of *language,* probably the second most prevalent indicator of ethnicity, is as ambiguous as that of race. Forms of speech known to be affiliated constitute what is called a *linguistic stock,* made up of related languages and associated dialects. But with the advance of knowledge, the Germanic stock, for example, was recognized as a subunit of the larger Indo-European stock. As Edward Sapir, an American anthropologist of the past generation, put it in his standard work on linguistics, the terms *dialect, language, branch,* and *stock* are all relative, convertible as our perspective widens or contracts.[32]

Often linguistic characteristics matter less in distinguishing between a language and a dialect than the cultural or political status of the subpopulation that uses a particular speech form. Flemish was once one of the dialects of Dutch spoken in Belgium, but now, after the successful effort of Flemish nationalists to establish it as such, Flemish or Southern Dutch is one of the country's two official languages.[33]

Perhaps the strangest case is the acceptance of a second language, Landsmål, in Norway, a country with some four million inhabitants that until then had no significant ethnic differentiation. Because the standard speech used by the educated middle class was close to Danish, agitation for recognition of the new language was based in part on patriotism; and because Landsmål was an amalgam of several dialects of peasants and fishermen, a second appeal could be made based on democracy. After more than a century of agitation, the proponents of a second official Norwegian language achieved their goal, and today the country's schoolchildren must learn both.[34]

What happens when a political leader is in a position to adopt a new language form? When Kemal Atatürk founded modern Turkey, he arranged for Turkish to be written with Latin letters in order to reinforce his country's cultural links to the West. In the early days of the Soviet Union, when the Bolsheviks believed that their initiative would ignite a revolution in Germany and then in the rest of Europe, Lenin enthusiastically linked the Roman alphabet to the new regime in Russia. Still in the early 1930s Cyrillic was dismissed as "the alphabet of autocratic oppression, of missionary propaganda, of Great Russian chauvinism," while the Roman alphabet was linked to "the victory of October over the whole earth."[35] However, once Russian nationalism established the victory of Cyrillic, Soviet linguists developed writing systems in it for Soviet minorities. They were indifferent to whether or not this alphabet was the most appropriate to represent the sounds of those other languages.

One of the more interesting examples relates to Chinese. For about a century linguists worked to fashion a system by which the ideographs could be converted into an alphabet, and apparently most of the technical problems were solved. In some respects such a conversion would be incalculably beneficial, for at present the goal of universal literacy is hampered by the fact that pupils have to learn characters one by one, with few clues to linked meanings and none to pronunciation. Among the six or so main Chinese dialects, differences are slight in syntax, somewhat larger in vocabulary, but very great in pronunciation. A decision was made, apparently in the 1960s, to maintain national unity even at the cost of forgoing an alphabetic system until Mandarin, the official language of the state, becomes the speech of the tens of millions who now speak other dialects.[36]

The meaning of *region,* another ethnic indicator, is also ambiguous. Sometimes it is based on what is termed a *natural area,* that is, a physiographic unit delineated by its topography, soil type, climate, or other physical features. Particularly among primitive peoples, who have relatively little control over their environment, a natural area may overlap with what anthropologists call a *culture area,* which approaches what we ordinarily think of as a region.

In the United States, no one doubts that a complex of distinctive attributes of the South, for instance, sets this area off from the rest of the social world, or even that those attributes can be specified and loosely measured. The various regions have developed a local variation of American culture that is analogous to ethnicity. In spite of the powerful unifying force of a modern nation, maps of dialects in the United States still clearly show such a pattern; and at least according to the myths on which ethnicity thrives, each region has a distinctive type of American living in it.

The bottleneck comes when one attempts to establish exact boundaries and quantify any idiosyncratic qualities. The predecessors of the Bureau of the Census introduced the concept of region in the mid-nineteenth century and designated four large subunits.[37] The South ranges from Maryland and Delaware to Florida, from the Atlantic to Oklahoma and Texas. Around the core of the Confederacy are such states as, for instance, West Virginia, which split off from Virginia when its citizens repudiated Virginia's secession. The northern boundary of the South, the Mason-Dixon line and an extension westward, does not include the southern tier of counties in Indiana and Illinois, where such Southern customs as segregated institutions used to prevail.

In addition to the South, the Bureau of the Census divides the United States into the Northeast, North Central, and West, with each subdivided into *geographic divisions.* All these designations are somewhat arbitrary. Whether there actually are subcultures associated with New England, the Midwest, and so on depends on where one draws the boundaries and which indices one uses to measure the supposed differences. Moreover, if we try to compare the regions' poverty, education, health, and so on, we must always keep in mind that in poor areas statistics are generally poor; the yardstick we use changes as we move from Massachusetts to Mississippi.

In short, not one of the group characteristics, whether cultural or physical, that are used to define ethnicity sharply sets off any subpopulation. A great contrast is likely only when several indices overlap. In Canada the francophone sector resides mostly in the province of Quebec, is Catholic rather than Protestant like most other Canadians, and (to add a nonethnic factor) was until some decades ago concentrated in the lower and lower-middle classes in contrast to the province's anglophone employers and managers. The world-famous amity among Switzerland's language communities and religions, on the other hand, has been partly based on the happy accident that the lines of ethnic division have cut across one another.[38]

The concept of a nation as ethnically homogeneous, which is a common myth especially in Europe, hardly fits the facts. In a paper originally published in the early 1970s, Walker Connor remarked on the lack of coincidence between ethnic and political borders:

> Of a total of 132 contemporary states, only 12 can be described as essentially homogeneous from an ethnic viewpoint.... In 31 states, the largest ethnic element represent only 50 to 74 percent of the population, and in 39 cases the largest group fails to account for even half of the state's population.... In some instances, the number of groups within a state runs into the hundreds, and in 53 states, the population is divided into more than five significant groups.[39]

He argued from these statistics that nation-building out of many diverse elements of former colonies is not likely to be successful, for the very factors that encouraged the establishment of new nations stimulated the demand of ethnic minorities for the same corporate rights and privileges.

A small band of intellectuals may propagandize for decades or for generations before their arguments are accepted by the sector of which they have designated themselves leaders. Very often such pioneers have spoken not for the whole of their supposed constituency but for one part of it, with other parts either represented by other leaders or with no spokesmen at all to express their views. In the United States ethnic pacesetters have acquired their influence through wealth (German Jews in the nineteenth century), professional standing (black clergymen), a place in general American politics (Irish in Eastern cities), and only occasionally through elections in an ethnic organization that is truly representative (the Japanese American Citizens League in its heyday). Self-designated conductors always pretend that the whole of the orchestra is following their beat, even when the cacophony of divergent sections is plainly audible.

In the United States the Bureau of the Census probably helped quicken the consolidation of ethnic groups by granting their self-designated spokesmen more authority than they yet exercised anywhere else. In an effort to improve ethnic coverage, the Bureau established nonprofessional advisory committees, of which many members were militant activists interested in statistical procedure only in order to shape the census count so as to validate their own perception of social reality, or their own hopes concerning the future of their particular movement.

As one example, the especially active Census Advisory Committee on Spanish-Origin Population for the 1980 census produced a large number of recommendations, some pertaining to nomenclature and some to procedures, all in order to raise to the maximum possible the number to be classified as of Spanish origin. It recommended, for instance, that the question on ethnicity appear before that on race: many Mexican Americans might define themselves as either Hispanic or Indian, and many Puerto Ricans as either Hispanic or black, and in both cases the choice might depend on the order of the questions. As another example, the committee recommended that if a person reported himself as part-Spanish, he be classified either in one of the subordinate Spanish-origin categories or in the residual "Other Spanish." The Bureau rejected this recommendation and instead asked a respondent with forebears of several nationalities which of them best described his origin as he saw it. In relation to the 1990 census, as another example, self-appointed representatives of the Taiwanese in this country wanted them distinguished on the schedule from Chinese. Once again, in line with the national policy not to recognize Taiwan as a separate country, the Bureau demurred. Even so, a sizable number of "Taiwanese Americans" used the open choice on the census form to give themselves that designation.

Since the line between category and group is not sharp, no simple indicator can distinguish between them. To ignore the distinction, however, means that the statistics will often be misinterpreted not only by the general public, but also by journalists and social scientists. Similar difficulties have been recognized in various types of survey data, and polling firms have developed methods of coping with them. The American urban economist and demographer Ira Lowry has suggested that after crude measures have identified ethnic groups in a census count, a sample of each category could be surveyed to determine how intensely each respondent feels about his ethnic identification. Possible probes might include questions about family lineage, languages used, and interactions with others of the same ethnicity.[40] Until something of the sort is done, virtually the entire body of ethnic data remains ambiguous.

Official Counts of Ethnic Groups

Age and sex, two characteristics of a population about which almost every census or survey asks, exemplify so-called hard data. The interviewer does not even need a response to specify a person's sex. Age is often misstated, but whether or not the respondent gives it accurately, there is only one true figure. Other attributes frequently included in census or survey schedules, however, are decidedly softer. In classifying persons by marital status, one must decide whether to designate common-law marriages as the equivalent of those that the state has sanctioned, and whether a divorced person who has not remarried is to be counted as single. As another example, the number and diversity of types of work recorded in statistics have often lagged decades behind those in the real world, and in the United States definitions of occupations were so greatly altered in the 1980 census that a commission had to be appointed to align the new data with those of 1970.

Before counting persons with characteristics associated with soft data, one must set certain conventions to define each such attribute, which is thus moved part way from the population to statisticians' concept of it.

Where in the hard-soft continuum should one place ethnicity? According to some analysts, any imprecision or ambiguity is due merely to distortions, and the one most often cited in recent criticisms of ethnic counts, the underenumeration of particular minorities, might be used to support this view. That some blacks or Hispanics are not included, however, need have nothing to do with racial/ethnic identity, and such selective underenumeration is only one of the faults of ethnic counts. Over the history of the American census, enumerations have helped create groups, moved persons from one group to another by a revised definition, and through new procedures changed the size and characteristics of groups. Though some of the resultant anomalies have probably never been discerned, others are so evident that the census volumes themselves point them out. Such deviations from a simple classification may lead one to conclude that essentially race and ethnicity cannot be measured accurately. Or, with a lower standard of precision, one must nevertheless aver that these characteristics differ from age and sex not merely in degree of mensurability but in kind.

However a society's subnations are classified in formal documents, in the self-perception of most persons the truly significant division is the one between themselves and everyone else, between the in-group and the out-group. The name that many primitive peoples have given themselves means Man or Human being: situated at the center of their universe, they place all others at its periphery. Greeks called all non-Greeks *hoi barbaroi,* barbarians, literally the stammerers. In American colleges, members of Greek-letter fraternities also call themselves Greeks, and they used to denigrate students who joined no fraternity as barbarians. Among Jews a gentile is *any* non-Jew and among Mormons, *any* non-Mormon; in India the word means *any* non-Muslim. En route to our word *nation,* the Latin *natio* was used to designated *any* of the barbarian tribes outside the Roman world.

In modern societies there is sometimes a kind of tension between such primitive dichotomies and more detailed classifications. Populations are usually divided between native and foreign-born, and between citizens and aliens. Particularly in tabular data on an ethnic structure, miscellaneous groupings are often lumped together into one heterogeneous bracket. An egregious example is the former practice of the U.S. Bureau of the Census of dividing Americans into whites and nonwhites. The current category of Asian or Pacific Islander might as well have been called "Others."

One notable reason that the analysis of ethnicity is so complicated is that the size and other characteristics of the units keep changing. An ethnos that is large and diverse in a preliminary survey becomes, as one takes a closer view, smaller and relatively more homogeneous. This volatile quality is especially likely when an ethnic group defines itself as an interest group, that is, when sectors of the population are mobilized in order to obtain special privileges, or to prevent others from obtaining them.

The difficulties in defining races, nations, and ethnic groups are so great that one must expect, rather than merely deplore, the typical lack of consistency. A more useful guide to understanding is to suggest why a quest for unequivocal precision flouts reality and is, however paradoxically, unscientific. After World War I, with the dissolution of the German, Austro-Hungarian, Ottoman, and Russian empires, the conventional wisdom was that the new states formed out of the remnants would be more or less homogeneous. In fact, they were not, and Central Europe remained a restive terrain.[41] The breakup of the Soviet Empire resulted in the sudden emergence of twenty new states. The dissolution of other empires was completed, and the maps of Africa and Asia were transformed.

The vagaries of ethnic classification are apparent in the several early United Nations comparisons of the criteria used in the world's censuses. According to the first of these compilations, in 1957, thirty-nine countries divided their populations by a geographic-ethnic criterion, ten by race, eight by culture, twenty-two by a combination of race and culture, eleven by a combination of culture and geography, one or two by origin as indicated by the language of the respondent's father, and several by mode of life.[42] Even when the same term was used, the meaning was sometimes different. Replies to questions on matters reflecting social prestige were probably often false; and the enumerations have not improved since this comparison four decades ago.

In the 1990s a United Nations agency called the Research Institute for Social Development undertook a project to study "ethnic diversity and public policies," based on the new premise that "cultural pluralism is an enduring attribute of contemporary political societies." Modernization does not, as was once believed, erode ethnic associations; in this assessment, it generally reinforces them. Identities are usually multiple, so that ties to a subnation may or may not conflict with so-called nation-building. Only rarely, according to this appraisal, is it possible to avert or mitigate ethnic conflict by following a single policy; the choice is normally no more than to make a series of adjustments.

The conclusions from this worldwide study were appropriately modest. "'Nation-building' homogenization cannot succeed. Nor, over time, can simple ethnic domination serve as a stable formula for rule." "Patience and perseverance can be supreme values." "The search for effective policies will continue on a global scale."[43] A skeptic might respond with several elementary points. It may be that ethnic conflict cannot be eliminated by any state policy and that therefore one need not waste time and money looking for such a policy. If it can, it is unlikely that the same policy or policies will be effective "on a global scale"; perhaps the first step toward a realistic policy is to adopt a dictum that all ethnic relations are local; and if anyone can be helpful, it is unlikely to be a team from the United Nations.

In April, 1992 the U.S. Bureau of the Census and Statistics Canada jointly sponsored a conference in Ottawa to discuss ethnic/racial classification systems. A number of countries with multiethnic populations were represented, including Australia, Malaysia, Russia, and the United Kingdom. It was agreed that ethnicity is an ambiguous and mutable concept, and that one should not expect agreement among countries on whether or how they classify their populations. For the United States the focus of discussion was on Directive 15 of the Office of Management and Budget,[44] developed during the 1970s and now often considered to be a flawed guide for a much changed population.[45]

How much variation is to be found in supposedly invariant characteristics as reported in two or more surveys or censuses? In a review of several comparisons, it was found that reported ages matched in only 83 to 95 percent of the cases, the occupation of the respondent's father in 70 percent, the respondent's education in 62 to 77 percent, and the respondent's income in 50 to 64 percent.[46] Or, to take a different kind of count, consider the obvious fact that for every emigrant from one country there is an immigrant to another one. The U.N. Economic Commission for Europe conducted an analysis of migration between pairs of member countries, that is, nations that in general maintain the best statistical records in the world. For the total movement along 342 paths, the number of immigrants was 57 percent greater than the number of emigrants.[47]

> Economic statistics, immigration statistics, and statistics on innumerable other social variables are subject to huge variations, according to how they are defined, collected, and used. The number of Germans in Australia is ten times greater by some definition of "Germans" than by other definitions. The same has been true of the number of Chinese in various countries in Southeast Asia....
>
> In the United States, Mexican Americans are either (1) rising economically, like other immigrant groups before them, or (2) are stagnating or retrogressing— depending on whether all Mexican Americans are lumped together statistically, or whether those born in the United States are distinguished from those who are still arriving and beginning at the bottom.[48]

The 1980 census of the United States was followed by a monograph titled *The Politics of Numbers*. As the two editors, William Alonso and Paul Starr, wrote in the introduction, a central tenet of the book is that "statistics cannot be constructed on purely technical grounds alone but require choices that ultimately turn on consideration of purpose and policy." The authors of the papers were economists, historians, political scientists, sociologists, demographers, and planners; and their joint effort was to show how and why data collected by United States government agencies are compiled and interpreted to fit the preconceptions of those involved. This is not, as the editors stressed, an indication of corrupt practices but rather an inevitable intrusion of the statisticians' judgments and biases into the data they collect.[49]

A more incisive exposition of the same theme was presented in *The Tyranny of Numbers: Mismeasurement and Misrule,* by the American demographer Nicholas Eberstadt. This collection of his papers shows how "the policies of liberal and affluent states have been miscast or deleteriously directed through an ill-advised use of, or reliance on, statistical data." Some of the chapters pertain to the numbers underpinning the foreign policy of the United States, both during the Cold War and after it ended; other papers discuss, for instance, poverty and the food supply. The novelty of the current problem-solving state, in his words, is "the expectation and belief that an engine fueled by numbers will be capable of drawing the mass of humanity steadily closer to an earthly perfection."[50]

As these two volumes suggest, the inadequacy of data on ethnicity is not unique. Measurement, or the assignment of numbers to specified entities according to a designated rule, is a way of standardizing, and thus, when feasible, it constitutes a truly fruitful process. The weight of all things, no matter how diverse, can be compared using a single unit. A prerequisite to measurement in this simplest sense is that such a constant unit either exists in nature (persons in the count of a population) or can be arbitrarily designated (a pound or kilogram as a unit of weight). But even an elementary count of persons depends in part on how one defines residence as well as how one defines population. There is thus no single answer to such a question as what is the population of the United States or what is the largest city in the world. And the complications are of course magnified when one tries to measure not merely the number of persons but also their characteristics, such as, for example, ethnicity or race.[51]

3

American Politics and the Measurement of Ethnicity

Before the founding of the Republic, policies on immigration and naturalization differed considerably from one colony to another. London imposed some uniformity by setting overall conditions for naturalization. In 1740, for example, Parliament excluded Catholics from the colonies but, in remarkably liberal clauses, exempted Quakers from taking the oath of allegiance required of other Protestants and permitted Jews to pledge with an oath reworded specially for them. Even so, among the complaints against George III listed in the Declaration of Independence was the charge that he had impeded the growth of the colonies' population by overriding their own regulation of naturalization. In fact, two kinds of citizenship existed, one valid only within each colony and the other based on English law.[1]

In several respects, the thirteen colonies that evolved into the United States lacked the characteristics ordinarily associated with a nation. The people were not all descended from one set of supposed ancestors; they spoke different languages; many had migrated in order to practice freely their separate religions. J. Hector de Crèvecoeur (1735–1813), a Frenchman who traveled widely and eventually settled in New York State, wrote a series of essays later assembled as *Letters from an American Farmer*. The work has been routinely cited as an authentic picture of America in the late eighteenth century. The American, he wrote, is "a European or the descendant of a European...whose grandfather was an Englishman, whose wife was Dutch, whose son married a French woman, and whose present four sons have four wives of different nations."[2]

Historians of particular nationalities have traced records of early settlers, sometimes with painstaking care over minute details. Early Dutch migrants, for instance, left traces not only in New York State, but also throughout much of the East and Middle West. Data down to lists of personal names were collected in a massive two-volume work.[3] The immigration of Germans to Pennsylvania began with the founding of Germantown in 1683 and eventually evolved into a "Pennsylvania Dutch" subculture, of which elements survive to this day. Many chronicles of such settlements were exercises in ethnic pride, often marred by an inclination to exaggerate the size of the nationality whose history a descendant was depicting.

> Whether one Tyrker who accompanied Leif Ericson was a German, and whether Captain John Smith's settlement at Jamestown did indeed include some Germans, are matters for the determination of which some antiquarians appear prepared to barter the promise of eternal bliss.... Others seem ready to shed their heart's blood if, by so doing, they could establish as fact the old story that the German language missed becoming the official language of the United States by a margin of one vote in a congressional committee.[4]

Similar myths were circulated from one quasischolarly work to the next about wellnigh every other component of America's population.

Yet these motley elements not only fused into a single nation but, over the following two centuries, absorbed more immigrants than any other country in the world. Many analysts of American ethnicity have contrasted remaining differences in the white population with the total disappearance that the metaphor of the melting pot suggests. If one judges the record not by such an absolute standard but in comparison with other nations, the conclusion must be that assimilation did work in the United States. The historian Marcus Lee Hansen, atypical in this respect, made the point with a telling anecdote. Three ships, he imagined, left Hamburg in the 1840s carrying essentially identical German immigrants to the United States, Australia, and Brazil.

> The descendants of the first group have only a sentimental interest in their origin. If they speak the ancestral tongue it is the result of their school instruction.... The passengers [to Australia] founded a community which retained its German individuality with much more tenacity, in spite of the fact that in Australia they were surrounded by an atmosphere more thoroughly Anglo-Saxon.... The descendants [in Brazil], now [in 1948] in the fourth and fifth generation, speak German, think German, vote German. They constitute a Teutonic state in the Brazilian federation.[5]

Consolidation of the Union

Though English became the language of the new country and other British institutions were incorporated into American civilization, the country was too diverse to become a nation in the conventional sense. Lacking a natural unity based on biology or a common history from an actual or mythical past, Americans—in the words of the historian George Bancroft (1800–1891)—"seized as their particular inheritance the tradition of liberty." Hans Kohn, another historian, emphasized this point by contrasting two historians' views of, respectively, the American Revolution and the one that followed in France. Both uprisings were based on universal dicta, the Declaration of Independence and the Declaration of the Rights of Man, but the struggle to establish *liberté, égalité, fraternité* never catalyzed the consolidation of revolutionary

Europe's heterogeneous population into one people. On the contrary, in postrevolutionary writings French virtues were discovered also in prerevolutionary France, attributes of Frenchmen rather than of democrats. In the works of Jules Michelet (1798–1874), the overseas counterpart of George Bancroft and a model for later French interpretations, the glorious climax to which French civilization rose in 1789 was inevitable, given the excellence of France's people.[6]

A conglomerate population unified by the ideals of civil rights and personal liberty was so novel a concept of a nation, however, that it was difficult to bring the American colonies together and overcome their jealousies. The instrument of this unification was the Constitution. The delegates who assembled in Philadelphia in 1787 to write it were among the new country's most distinguished men. The nation that had been fashioned by the Articles of Confederation was on the point of collapse; Britain and Spain had troops at the borders ready to absorb the pieces if it did fall apart. Whenever differences among the delegates threatened to disrupt the convention, they would remind one another of the urgency of their work.

In the existing Confederation each state had equal power, but the delegates from the more populous states wanted to give equal weight to each person. The compromise was to establish a bicameral Congress: in the Senate, with equal representation from each member of the Union, the less populous states had proportionally more weight; and in the House, with representation based on the population, those with more inhabitants dominated. To maintain this balance, the number in the lower house had to be adjusted periodically to population growth, and the first link between politics and enumeration was thus inscribed in the Constitution itself.

The Constitution also prescribed that no direct tax should be imposed except "in proportion to the census or enumeration." The linkage of representation and taxation had the advantage of reducing the probable error in the count. As James Madison wrote in *Federalist Paper* No. 54, the accuracy of the census would depend on the cooperation of the states, which should therefore not be tempted to increase or reduce the size of their populations. "Were their share of representation alone to be governed by this rule, they would have an interest in exaggerating [the number of] their inhabitants. Were the rule to decide their share of taxation alone, a contrary temptation would prevail. By extending the rule to both objects, the States will have opposite interests which will control and balance each other and produce the requisite impartiality."[7]

It was possible to apportion taxes precisely but not representatives, for with any simple formula a district might be represented by a fraction of a congressman. After a dispute lasting more than a year between states and between regions, the compromise that passed was vetoed by President Washington in the first use he made of that power. In the eventual law, the House of

Representatives was set at 105 members, and the number of constituents per member at 33,000. But the debates over the issue continued, particularly as different rates of population growth began to shift power from the South to the North and from the East to the West.

The North and the South were divided on several issues but most sharply, of course, on slavery. Several Northern delegates at Philadelphia aggressively denounced slavery and especially the slave trade, but to have called for abolition would have brought the convention to an immediate end. Delegates from the Southern states wanted to get representation for all their residents, including slaves. In another major compromise, apportionment was based on all free persons except Indians "not taxed" (that is, not living in the general population) plus three-fifths of "all other persons." For each one hundred slaves in a congressional district, that is to say, it received representation equivalent to that for sixty free persons.[8]

> If none of the slaves had been included, as Northern delegates wanted, the slave states would have had only 41 percent of seats in the House. If all of the slaves had been included, as Southerners wanted, the slave states would have had 50 percent of the seats. By agreeing to include three-fifths, the slave states ended up with 47 percent—not negligible, but still a minority likely to be outvoted on slavery issues.[9]

Up to the Civil War, slaves were probably counted more or less accurately, but with only partial data on even their basic demographic characteristics.

In shaping a diversified population into a single people, the concept of liberty was reinforced by the legal principle that in public life each American is a citizen only, not a member of a particular ethnic group or other sector of the population. In the Bill of Rights and in the traditional interpretation of American law, the political arena comprises only two components: individual citizens and the government that represents them. Indeed, during the first decades of the federal government, states' rights were intermittently an important issue, but after the Civil War this factor in American politics gradually attenuated. The restrictions on group association were not deemed to be oppressive, for subnations could set up and maintain their organizations outside the public arena. With respect to religion, this right was seen as important enough to be confirmed in the opening clause of the Bill of Rights; and no limit was imposed on the organization of nationalities, races, or other types of ethnos—only the convention that these communal societies be private.

If the principles underlying the legal structure were clear, the laws themselves were a muddle. Originally national citizenship was corollary to being a citizen of one of the states, and the definition of naturalization varied as new states were admitted to the Union. The first restrictions set by Congress were in effect canceled by the states' more open policies. Finally, a naturalization law enacted in 1801 set the conditions for the following century. After five years' residence, any white alien of good character could become an American citizen by renouncing foreign allegiance and swearing to support the Constitution, and either state or federal courts could implement the law. The status of free blacks and of those naturalized in the Northwest Territory was ambiguous. Until the Bureau of Immigration was established in 1892, states or cities along the East Coast were responsible for screening immigrants and excluding those that were inadmissible. There was a thriving industry selling false papers to foreign seamen.

The Dred Scott case (1857) showed all too clearly how little precision existed in the law on citizenship. Dr. John Emerson, an army surgeon, moved from St. Louis first to Illinois and then to Wisconsin Territory, taking with him his household servant, a Negro slave named Dred Scott. During some five years Scott lived in places where slavery was prohibited, and on that basis he subsequently sued for his liberty in a Missouri court. A judgment in his favor was overruled by the state supreme court, and when the case reached the U.S. Supreme Court, the nine justices handed down nine opinions.[10] A majority held that Scott was not a citizen of the state or of the United States and, hence, could not sue in a federal court; that his temporary residence in free territory had not made him free after his return to Missouri; and that the Missouri Compromise, by which slavery had been prohibited in Wisconsin Territory, was in any case unconstitutional. The decision aggravated sectional hostility and left the law in a shambles. In 1862 Attorney General Edward Bates, when asked to define a citizen, replied that the topic remained "as open to argument and speculative criticism as it was at the beginning of government."[11]

From the Melting Pot to Ethnic Competition

Once the Republic came into being, it generated a strong tendency toward cultural unity. One reason for the worldwide underestimation of the potency of ethnicity a generation ago was, in Walker Connor's words, "improper analogizing from the experience of the United States," with the consequent spread of "a presumption that the history of acculturation and assimilation within an immigrant society would be apt to be repeated in multinational states."[12]

As early as 1789, as Noah Webster wrote in his *Dissertation on the English Language,* "A new country, new association of people, new combinations of ideas in arts and sciences, and some intercourse with tribes wholly unknown in Europe...will produce...a language in North America as different from the future language of England as modern Dutch, Danish, and Swedish are from the German, or from one another." Such effusions, though for many years routinely repeated on ceremonial occasions and applied not only to speech but to literature and art, social institutions, and national ethos, proved to be false prognoses. Anglo-American remained a single language, with less divergence between the two countries than within either of them. American law was based on English common law. The American public school was a realization of the aspirations of such English innovators as Adam Smith and Thomas Robert Malthus. In short, American institutions were English institutions, shaped by the different physical and social environment and, more profoundly, by the idea of liberty—which, however, was in large part also imported from across the Atlantic.

Initially Protestant church services were in the old-country languages; then they gradually shifted to two services, one in English in order to retain the younger communicants; and finally most non-English services petered out (indeed often to be revived in recent times). Initially many second-generation children were taught in schools associated with the churches. As the public school system evolved, various cities or states responded to voters' demands by fostering bilingual programs, which sometimes lasted for decades (and were also reinstituted during the past several decades). Each wave of immigrants generated a succeeding wave of foreign-language news media. After the exodus from Germany following the failure of the 1848 revolution, the number of German-language newspapers in the United States jumped from one in 1843 to twenty in 1850 and almost eight hundred in the mid-1890s.[13] But generally each generation accommodated more and more to the English norm, retaining old-country institutions mainly as mementos of its ethnic roots.

Apart from the two anomalies, American Indians and Negroes, the population was seen as unitary or, at worst, in the process of becoming homogeneous. The expectation that all whites would assimilate into a single new nation was countered by opposition, usually temporary, to various European nationalities. During the middle decades of the nineteenth century prejudice was strong against Germans and especially Irish, but only for a time. Many of the immigrants' leaders tried to preserve their native languages in the new country, but over the longer term with little success. For, as noted, until recently the dominant impetus from both sides was to foster acculturation, and this was a typical leitmotif of writings on American ethnicity.

While assimilation was taking place, the country was debating whether "New Immigrants" from Southern and Eastern Europe should be allowed to come in such large numbers, for allegedly they were inassimilable into American society. The first major challenge to open immigration had come with the massive influx of Irish Catholics—as many as a million in the decade following the famine of the 1840s, or between a third and a half of all who entered the country up to the Civil War. In the public eye the overall increase of Irish was magnified by their concentration in Eastern cities and the rapid development of an institutional structure of churches, seminaries, parochial schools, colleges, newspapers, and lay societies. These were aliens in the literal sense, targets of an already strong anti-Catholicism. In 1855, the Know-Nothing movement, which expressed its anti-Catholicism in a nativist opposition to any foreigners, controlled six state governments and had some seventy-five members in the House of Representatives.

The Famine Irish, as they were called, arrived as paupers, lived in hovels, and for a generation or two helped perform the country's most menial tasks. When they climbed up, it was only—or so it was believed—to the lower middle class. In fact, however, by the 1960s the average Irish Catholic had risen to levels of education, occupational prestige, and income second only to those of Jews. That this fact was not recognized earlier was due to the lack of official statistics on religion. Irish Catholics, identified only by the Irish half of their dual identity, were confounded with the Scots-Irish, Protestants of whom most had immigrated earlier and had remained low on the social ladder. The critical distinction between the two sectors of Irish was made mainly from a series of polls by the National Opinion Research Center, since this private institution did ask respondents for their religion. The American sociologist/priest Andrew Greeley used its data both to demonstrate the success of the Irish Catholics and to illustrate how this was achieved.[14] Like most other immigrants, the Irish entered the work force at close to the bottom, and interethnic relations were paralleled by class relations. These were given shape, moreover, by opposition between the Republican and Democratic parties (or their predecessors), whose constituents included, respectively, most of the Protestant upper middle class outside the South and eventually virtually all Irish Catholics. Yet this twice reinforced ethnic structure did not freeze into a caste society, mainly because the firm norm at that time was that in national affairs all Americans acted not as members of diverse nationalities, but as individuals.

Studies that opposed immigration were virtually all written by men of English ancestry, with names like Fiske, Burgess, Lodge, Turner, Dillingham, Fairchild, Ball, Commons, Ross, Rossiter, and so on, while the few who answered their arguments were named Hourwich and Stella—and, as an exception to the rule, Willcox. With respect to any one individual such a distinction would be invidious, but the predominant Anglo-Saxon family background certainly influenced the questions that the American scholarly community posed and the answers they usually agreed on.

The Irish Catholic response was not uniform: some spokesmen became defensive, but others tried to accommodate to the established system. Some prelates and laymen answered critics by arguing that Catholics should adjust to American norms, especially by accepting the separation of church and state. As the Boston *Pilot* put it, "The old habits of Ireland will not answer here." Orestes Brownson (1803–1876), a journalist who was raised a Presbyterian and became successively a Universalist, a free-lance minister of his own church, and a Catholic, presented a strong assimilationist program to allay anti-Catholic antipathy, apparently coining the word *Americanization* in the process.[15]

Beginning in the last decades of the nineteenth century, the exclusion of newcomers from Eastern and Southern Europe was first sought indirectly, by banning the immigration of illiterates, and then in a series of new laws. In 1921 European immigration was limited to 3 percent of the number of foreign-born of each nationality residing in the United States at the time of the last available census figures, those of 1910. A second law, passed in 1924, set up another temporary system, more restrictive than its predecessor in two respects: the 3 percent was reduced to 2 percent, and the base population was changed from the 1910 to the 1890 census, when the proportion from Southern and Eastern Europe was smaller. The 1924 act also provided that eventually immigration quotas would be based on the national origins of the total population, rather than merely of the foreign-born; and five years later this was done.[16]

In the transformation to a modern, bureaucratic society, much is given up that later is regarded as valuable. Personal identity is more significant if it is linked to the symbolic meanings given to group identity by differences in body, name, language, history, religion, and nationality. It was hardly surprising, after all, that once the demands of an agrarian society had been met, many tried to escape the impersonality of modern life and retrospectively to establish a fuller emotional environment for themselves. In a book published in 1953, the American sociologist Robert Nisbet accurately foresaw the mood prevalent in the 1990s:

> We are suspended between two worlds of allegiance and association. On the one hand, and partly behind us, is the historic world in which loyalties to family, church, profession, local community, and interest association exert, however ineffectively, persuasion and guidance. On the other is the world of values identical with absolute political community—the community in which all symbolism, allegiance, responsibility, and sense of purpose have become indistinguishable from the operation of centralized political power.[17]

Of course, the cycle was not in every case precisely the three generations that Hansen had forecast,[18] but it was generally true that attempts to acculturate arose from an initial feeling of insecurity and that from a later security there developed a yearning to distinguish one's group from the mass.

In the traditional American view, race, religion, or nationality have no legitimate place in national politics. In voting for national leaders, citizens are supposed to act as ethnically undifferentiated Americans; for an openly double (so-called hyphenated) ethnic identity used to be seen as a sensitive issue in the relations between the United States and other countries. In Continental Europe, on the contrary, a party has typically been narrowly linked to a social class (the Labor, Socialist, or Peasant parties), a religion (the various Calvinist parties of the Netherlands and Switzerland), or both (the Catholic People's parties). They are therefore too small to form a government, which is made up rather of a coalition among several of them. What Americans call a party is by European standards a coalition—a coalition made up of factions roughly equivalent to European parties.

The difference has been crucial. With the tradition of an unofficial and half-hidden link between ethnicity and the loosely bounded factions of political parties, the American ideal of democracy has been until recently a national government of individuals, each acting on the basis of his personal beliefs to make his own political decisions. With the clearly designated boundaries of European parties, in contrast, democratic politics there has been an interplay among sectors of the population. The development of ethnic politics in the United States apparently means that a shift to the European pattern is taking place.

The integration of the black minority into the general population was, of course, more complex. In 1863, acting as Commander-in-Chief at a low point in the Unionist cause, President Lincoln issued the Emancipation Proclamation. He promised that slaveholders who declared loyalty to the Union he would try to get compensation for the loss of their property. This military edict prompted by expediency, as it was labeled by its critics, was attacked in the South, by many in the North, and by news media abroad. Yet manumission changed the civil population fundamentally. A large minority were no longer an anomalous exception to American law, but became in theory the equals of all others. Ethnicity had been expanded to include race.[19]

After the Unionist victory, the Thirteenth, Fourteenth, and Fifteenth Amendments to the Constitution made this civil equality part of the country's basic law. The amendments abolished slavery, guaranteed equal protection under the law, and prohibited a denial of suffrage because of race, color, or previous condition of servitude. Since the purpose of the amendments was to eliminate not only slavery but also the vestigial effects among emancipated blacks, the new directives were in the negative: *neither* slavery *nor* involuntary servitude shall exist; *no* state shall make or enforce any law abridging citizens' rights, which shall *not* be denied on account of race or an equivalent attribute. When their group status as slaves was abolished, rights were afforded not to a category of ex-slaves but, in line with the legal tradition, to individuals. No state shall deprive *any person* of life, liberty, or property without due process of law, nor deny *any person* equal protection of the law.

Of the three amendments, most subsequent litigation pertained to the Fourteenth. According to repeated findings of both state and federal district courts, the guarantee of equal rights did not imply an end to separate public facilities. The issue reached the U.S. Supreme Court in the famous case of *Plessy* v. *Ferguson* (1896). Homer A. Plessy, a man of seven-eighths Caucasian stock, had bought a first-class ticket on a railroad operating within Louisiana; when he refused to accept a seat in a segregated coach, he was arrested and later convicted of violating a law requiring all railroads operating in the state to provide separate coaches for black and white passengers. The Supreme Court held that the protection he sought was of a social right not covered by the Fourteenth Amendment; that the law, not unreasonable on other grounds, therefore did not deny him equal protection, for separate but equal facilities satisfied the constitutional guarantee. The lone dissenting opinion of Justice John Marshall Harlan is better known than the decision itself. "Our Constitution," Harlan wrote, "is color-blind, and neither knows nor tolerates classes among citizens.... The law regards man as man, and takes no regard of his surroundings or of his color when his civil rights as guaranteed by the supreme law of the land are invoked."

For several decades following *Plessy,* the Fourteenth Amendment was cited more often and more successfully to defend corporate "persons" than to uphold the rights of blacks. During the 1920s the Supreme Court was evidently reluctant to accept cases involving what was termed the Negro question, thus in effect giving discriminatory practices the sanction of federal law. In *Corrigan v. Buckley* (1924), for instance, when the court held that it lacked jurisdiction to challenge a restrictive covenant, it in effect upheld residential segregation. Several times the NAACP challenged the rule that in the one-party South, Negroes were barred from voting in Democratic party primaries and thus were eliminated from the only significant election, but for years the protests elicited no effective remedy. In several cases the issue was whether a criminal trial had been conducted under conditions that abrogated due process. In all such instances, those fighting to obtain justice for blacks defined justice as equal *individual* rights, with blacks afforded the same privileges and immunities as all other "persons" protected under a color-blind Constitution. Only reactionaries insisted on classifying blacks as a separate group under the law, a civil category different in kind from the general population.

Even when it was fashionable to deny that race or ethnicity had any legitimate role in national politics, this myth could hardly have been applied with even minimum plausibility to America's multiethnic cities. The main reason for open and unabashed ethnic voting blocs in a metropolitan context was that local governments distributed jobs, contracts, licenses, access to facilities, and so on. In order to get preferential treatment from a ward boss and to impede others from obtaining such favors, a person had to join with others into a smaller, less blunt wedge than the heterogeneous national political parties. One obvious base for mustering such power lay in the quasipolitical, ethnically based social clubs and churches.

After President Roosevelt's New Deal was amplified in President Johnson's War on Poverty, the standard municipal pattern of distributing preferments became the prototype for political patronage by federal agencies, with the consequence that ethnic blocs competed aggressively also in Washington. The search for one's roots would hardly have become so fashionable an element of the country's culture without the material advantages linked with that quest. In combination, ideological and monetary forces were irresistible.

The new emphasis on ethnicity was reflected in basic changes in American law. At one time both immigrants and natives regarded assimilation as the normal culmination of a relatively short process; with the revised expectations, newcomers were met at the border, as it were, by ethnic organizers, happy to welcome recruits to their interest groups. Opponents of immigration have made much of the shift in nationality of more recent immigrants, but the more important change is in the transformation of native institutions. Bilingual ballots were prescribed in place of the earlier requirement that newcomers learn English as part of their naturalization. Affirmative action of diverse kinds favored first blacks, then Hispanics and other ethnic groupings, and then women, the disabled, and in some jurisdictions homosexuals. These transformations coincided with the passage of the Immigration Act of 1965, which facilitated the shift from Europe to Asia and Latin America as the principal countries of origin.

During the same decades the concept of *equality* was revised, with momentous effects on ethnic relations and thus on the significance of how ethnic groups were classified and counted. The moral equality guaranteed in the Declaration of Independence, compromised by the Founders' acceptance of slavery, had been given legal force in amendments to the Constitution following the Civil War. As one can see from the debates on those amendments in Congress, those who framed them wanted to outlaw all legal distinctions based on race, but the Supreme Court ignored this intent. The separate-but-equal doctrine, which it laid down in 1896, was not reversed until 1954, in *Brown* v. *Board of Education.* In that important decision, however, the Court did not set a color-blind polity but, on the contrary, continued with the psychological—rather than constitutional—rationale of the majority from which Justice Harlan had earlier dissented. In *Plessy,* since the Court professed not to believe that racial segregation stigmatized blacks, it did not give the plaintiff the individual right to equal protection under the law. Subsequently, as Justice Brennan argued in defense of the racial quota that barred the white Allan Bakke from the University of California's medical school, the reason was that he was not "in any sense stamped inferior by the Medical School's rejection of him.... [The] use of racial preference will [not] affect him throughout his life in the same way as the segregation of Negro school children in *Brown* would have affected them." As the Court has continued to interpret the law, persons who because of their race are denied access to employment, promotion, a contract, or a place in a university cannot demand such benefits as their constitutional right but must come as supplicants, petitioning for redress from proved deprivations.[20]

Congress also repeatedly insisted that the government remain neutral with respect to race, enacting the Civil Rights Acts of 1957, 1960, and 1964 and the Voting Rights Act of 1968. That these laws were intended to establish a color-blind standard is clear not only from their language but, even more, from the debates in Congress. Opponents of the Civil Rights Act of 1964 worried about the possible effects of Title VII: prohibiting discrimination in employment, they feared, might lead to new racially determined preferences. The bill's sponsors adamantly rejected this interpretation, and finally Hubert Humphrey, who was shepherding the bill through the Senate, became so exasperated with the continued skepticism that he declared, "If...in Title VII...any language [can be found] which provides that an employer will have to hire on the basis of percentage or quota related to color,...I will start eating the pages [of the bill] one after another." Similarly, Title IV of the same act plainly stated that "'desegregation' shall not mean the assignment of students to public schools in order to overcome racial imbalance," and that the act would not "empower any official or court of the United States to issue any order seeking to achieve a racial balance" in public schools.[21] Those who abhor racial distinctions in employment or in access to other benefits happily joined what seemed to be a national consensus in, at long last, establishing a color-blind government in the United States.

However clear the mandate of Congress, it was ignored by federal agencies, federal and other courts, and local jurisdictions, which once again frustrated the will to set standards that did not differentiate by race or ethnic identity. The attempt to equalize education moved from securing equivalent schooling to the peripheral issue of busing children away from their neighborhoods to balance the numbers of white and black pupils. Affirmative action in employment went from equal opportunity as a goal, to testing the efficacy of programs set up to achieve that goal, to equal outcomes and many instances of reverse discrimination. As implemented, the laws were not what their proponents had intended them to be; on the contrary, in many cases nothing mattered so much about a person applying for various types of preferment as race or gender.[22]

In 1979 Robert Earl Lee, an engineer with the Montgomery County (Maryland) Environmental Protection Department, changed his name to Roberto Eduardo Leon and had himself reclassified from white to Hispanic, thus moving a step or two ahead of competitors for promotion. His boss, amused, remarked only that "it's nice to have a Hispanic on our staff," but county officials soon deleted his minority status and ruled that henceforth a committee would review changes in ethnic self-identification. We do not know how many other instances of this new type of passing a diligent search would uncover, but one can be sure that this incident was not the only one.

That such a reidentification was more common than is usually supposed is suggested by the racial restrictions in the San Francisco school system. According to a 1983 consent decree, students in public schools were classified into nine racial groups, with a strict racial cap at each school. No one racial group may make up more than 40 to 45 percent of the student body of any school, and each school must have at least four racial groups represented among its students. At an academically prestigious high school, to which all the best students would like to go, admission tests are evaluated on the basis of race: of 69 possible points for admission, Chinese must score 62, whites and other Asians 58, blacks and Hispanics 53. The school district tacitly allows each student one change in ethnicity during his school career. In 1994 Chinese American parents sued the San Francisco Unified School District to undo the race-based quotas embedded in the desegregation plan; and a year later the case was still in the courts, a "gravy train for lawyers."[23]

"By 1965, counting ethnic minorities had become a serious business, affecting the outcomes of elections, admission to graduate schools, marketing strategies of housing developers, federal contract awards, hiring, firing, and promotion policies of private employers, and the disbursement of federal grants to state and local governments," as well as, a few years later, "the right to hold public offices."[24] The size of ethnic groups thus acquired a new salience: it was no longer the native stock checking on whether immigrants were being assimilated on schedule but rather certain minorities making demands on the public purse in proportion to their numbers.

The most effective argument against affirmative action was made in Thomas Sowell's *Preferential Policies: An International Perspective*. The difference between this work and almost all others on the issue is that Sowell achieves a far better grasp of all questions by examining them in a comparative framework, with detailed discussions of the dozen or so countries that have tried such presumed reforms. The results everywhere are similar. Programs instituted as temporary expedients to benefit the most depressed classes spread to others and remain as fixtures hard to displace. The group for whom the program was initiated does not profit from it nearly so much as others (e.g., in the United States, inner-city blacks versus middle-class women). The incentives to rise in the social scale by work is undercut as the context shifts from economic worth to political activism. Whatever interethnic hostility that exists becomes more impassioned.[25]

According to a 1978 review of public opinion polls, "every major national study shows that a sizable majority of Americans are opposed to remedying the effects of past discrimination by giving any special consideration in hiring or school admissions." When asked whether "ability" or "preferential treatment" should be the decisive criterion, 81 to 84 percent (including 56 percent of black respondents) replied ability; only 10 to 11 percent (or 14 percent of blacks) supported preferential treatment.[26] Subsequent polls did not differ significantly.

The most striking reflection of this majority sentiment is the California Civil Rights Initiative, a measure placed on the November 1996 ballot to amend the state constitution with this proviso: "The state shall not discriminate against, or grant preferential treatment to, any individual or group on the basis of race, sex, color, ethnicity, or national origin in the operation of public employment, public education, or public contracting."[27] It passed by 55 to 45 percent, with a majority of women and many blacks and Hispanics supporting it. The ACLU immediately filed suit to block its enforcement, holding that color-blind justice is unconstitutional. However, those who believe that highly prized goals should not be distributed according to group membership may yet win, for California's precedent has often been followed nationally.

From Race to Ethnicity and Gender

From the beginning of the American experience, race was a fundamental ethnic characteristic in the censuses and eventually in other records. It has been plausibly argued that defenders of slavery exaggerated the significance of race, and reformers trying to remedy the country's social ills also stressed the special disadvantages of being black. The vast expansion of writings on minorities focused, at least initially, on that group. As one index of this emphasis, of the 482 articles on ethnic groups that appeared in the *American Journal of Sociology,* the *American Sociological Review,* and *Social Forces* from 1900 to 1974, 71 percent dealt with blacks, 29 percent with all others.[28]

The extraordinary focus on blacks has been challenged in a number of ways. As I pointed out, a number of anthropologists tried to eliminate the concept of race from the social disciplines. Others alleged that the handicaps of blacks, however specified, are shared by other components of the population. In his work on ethnic differentiation, Thomas Sowell, who is himself black, was obviously struck by the discrimination and humiliations long suffered by Irish immigrants; the many parallels that he pointed out cut across the race line.[29] The broader analysis of America's minorities increasingly transcended earlier filiopietism. Andrew Greeley, who as noted earlier started with Irish Americans in Chicago and then in the whole country, expanded his view to "the rediscovery of diversity" and the importance of ethnic identity in itself, not simply as a function of social class. "We know less about Polish Americans," Greeley wrote, "than about some African tribes," and he joined others in trying to repair that gap.[30]

The shift from race to ethnicity was stimulated, of course, by politics. One of the most influential works in documenting, and thus fostering, this shift was Nathan Glazer and Daniel Patrick Moynihan's *Beyond the Melting Pot.* As a study of ethnic politics in New York City, it started with a milieu in which blocs delimited by race or nationality were traditional, but the interpretation included the whole of American society. The "new ethnicity" of their analysis was not readily accepted. One of the agencies that funded the study withdrew its support; some critics objected especially to the fact that racial groups like blacks and Puerto Ricans were discussed precisely in the same way as ethnic groups like Jews, Italians, and Irish.[31]

There can be no doubt that the nationalities once labeled the New Immigration have suffered, and in many instances still suffer, from discrimination. One early symptom of the resentment building up was manifest at hearings in 1982 before representatives of the Illinois Department of Human Rights on a bill concerning affirmative action and equal employment opportunities. According to Representative Robert Terzich, who had sponsored the bill in the Illinois legislature, its main purpose was to amend the laws prohibiting discrimination in order to give protection also to those defined by national origin. By a threshold set in the bill, any group comprising 2 percent or more of the state's population would be so protected; but according to Representative Terzich, "group" could be interpreted to include "umbrella groups and multiple ethnic communities...similar to grouping of many national origins under the general title of Hispanics." Such "groups" he exemplified as Southeast Asians, Eastern Europeans, and persons from the Baltic states.

Asked to define an ethnic group, Becir Tanovic of the United Yugoslavs noted that neither federal nor state legislation is very specific, but the intent of the bill was "to include primarily East European and South European groups because they have been discriminated [against] and that has been demonstrated well enough over many years." He listed the ones he meant: first of all Poles, well over 15 percent of the state's population, and Ukrainians, Yugoslavs, Czechoslovaks, Hungarians, Greeks, and Italians. How discrimination would be proved was suggested by Roman Pucinski, local president of the Polish American Congress: he cited a recent survey showing that only an infinitesimal fraction of the executives of the five hundred largest Chicago corporations were of Slav origin.[32]

If group-based quotas were to be set for Slavs of various nationalities, Italians, and others not proportionally represented in high-level positions, the Bureau of the Census would be called on to furnish the data on which these new quotas would be based. Presumably the already complex schedule would become yet more so, the already dubious statistics yet less satisfactory.

When spokesmen for various European nationalities complained that their constituents had never been allowed into full participation in American society, their petitions, however understandable, were largely negative and thus destructive. While the *pluribus* of *E pluribus unum* was pampered, they invited us to neglect altogether the *unum*, which was taken for granted.

Advocates of the new ethnicity have not, of course, repudiated the principles of freedom, equality, and democracy,...[but] their approach implicitly denies that there can be a unitary *American* identity based upon common assent to universalist principles, an identity that makes Americans *one people* despite differences of ethnic derivation. And to treat terms like Americanization, assimilation, and melting pot as hateful symbols for reprehensible policies—as the spokesmen for the new ethnicity consistently do—inevitably implies that the nation never represented values and ideals that immigrants could reasonably accept, identify with, and defend.[33]

Ethnic Composition of the United States

The enumeration in 1790 followed the constitutional provisions regarding the census. The population in each district set the number of members in the House of Representatives, and a breakdown of the national total was printed in a pamphlet of fifty-six pages. Since slaves and Indians had a special relation to apportionment, they were distinguished from whites, all of whom were classified together. Before the 1800 census was started, two learned societies sent memorials to Congress recommending that questions be added on, among other topics, the number of native citizens, citizens of foreign birth, and resident aliens; but no move into ethnic statistics was taken at that time. In the fourth census, in 1820, a question was asked to determine the number of unnaturalized aliens. The first six censuses, in sum, were limited mainly to a count of the population classified by age group, sex, and race (subdivided between slave and free); and the attempts to include such other topics as occupations were admitted failures.[34]

From 1790 to 1860 no instructions were given defining racial terms, and each enumerator was free to determine the race of each person in his district. Later, blacks (or sometimes categories within the race) were defined by their supposed quanta of blood, hardly a yardstick that could be readily used in a census operation. At all times the classification of marginal persons undoubtedly reflected local opinion, which for those of mixed blood would depend in large part on the respondent's place of residence and social position. Thus, the association between social class and race was sometimes set not by the generalization that blacks were typically in the lower classes but, on the contrary, that a person in the middle class was ordinarily not black.

In 1840 the first effort to go much beyond the classification in force since 1790 produced a result notably deficient in many of its details. As a consequence of "the manifest and palpable, not to say gross, errors" in the 1840 census, as a Senate bill put it, a central control was established to set uniform practices for the U.S. marshals who supervised the count in each district. In 1850 and 1860, six separate questionnaires were used to make a complete inventory of the nation, with items (in 1860) covering population, wealth, agriculture, manufactures, mining, fisheries, commerce, banking, insurance, transportation, schools, libraries, newspapers, crime, taxes, and religion. So many data, compiled by marshals as one of their lesser duties and tallied by hand, were hardly useful. Much of the information was not published until it was thoroughly out of date, and census officials themselves testified to the many weaknesses in their operation. Yet it is remarkable how few items in that vast mass pertained to ethnicity (apart from race), which up to the mid-century had little or no place in American law and, therefore, in the country's censuses.

The country of birth of respondents has been asked in every United States census since 1850, and the countries of the respondents' two parents from 1870 to 1990 (but not in 1980). These are seemingly straightforward questions that would yield unambiguous and meaningful data, but in fact most of those statistics have what the American economist Oskar Morgenstern termed "specious accuracy": "data are given which even when they have only a very small margin of error are nevertheless useless."[35] Even when it was correctly reported, the country of birth has been a very poor indicator of the ethnicity of immigrants, especially those from the multilingual empires of Central and

Eastern Europe, who made up the majority of newcomers from the 1870s to the 1920s.

Censuses taken during the era of the melting pot reflected concern about newcomers' attributes, real or supposed, and their rate of Americanization. In 1870, questions were added to determine whether either of the respondent's parents had been born abroad. In 1890 foreign-born males aged twenty-one or over were asked how many years they had resided in the United States, whether they were naturalized, and, if not, whether they had taken out naturalization papers. Also in that year all persons were asked whether they were able to speak English and, if not, what language they spoke. After the restrictive laws of the 1920s were passed, interest in ethnic composition waned somewhat; and from the depression decade of the 1930s until a new surge in immigration in the 1980s, questions in the census schedules reflected the greater concern about economic well-being.

Both ethnic leaders and the general community used to pressure aliens to acculturate, and until a short while ago most whites who could be distinguished as different not only aspired to disappear into the broader population but, to a significant degree, actually did so. With the present emphasis on searching for one's roots, on bilingual education and multilingual census schedules, on civil rights defined in racial or ethnic terms, on affirmative action to compensate for the alleged prior discrimination against whole groups, it is easy to forget how recently such official encouragements of differentiation came into being.

In 1980 and 1990 respondents were asked to define themselves as one of the following: "white, black or Negro, Japanese, Chinese, Filipino, Korean, Vietnamese, Indian (Amer.), Asian Indian, Hawaiian, Guamanian, Samoan, Eskimo, Aleut, or other (specify)." The list does not follow elementary rules for constructing a taxonomy—that the classes be mutually exclusive, that all the classes add up to the whole of the population, and that they be of roughly the same order of importance and magnitude.

It should be stressed, however, that this mishmash was not created by the Bureau of the Census. In a directive the Office of Federal Statistical Policy and Standards had designated the races and ethnic groups to be used in all federal reporting and statistics.

> These classifications [the directive warned] should not be interpreted as being scientific or anthropological in nature, nor should they be viewed as determinants of eligibility for participation in any federal program. They have been developed in response to needs expressed by both the executive branch and Congress to provide for the collection and use of compatible, nonduplicated, exchangeable racial and ethnic data by federal agencies.[36]

Ira Lowry suggested the implicit defense the Bureau of the Census might offer for carrying out the procedure that this directive mandated:

Ethnic identity cannot be established by objective criteria, at least in large-scale self-administered surveys. We therefore accept that an individual's ethnicity is whatever he says it is. The Bureau's job is to elicit self-identification and then to group the responses into recognizable categories that (a) are mandated for federal civil rights enforcement [contrary to the directive just cited], (b) satisfy the more vocal ethnic lobbies, and (c) provide enough continuity with past census statistics to satisfy social scientists engaged in longitudinal research.

"However," Lowry concluded, "the Bureau's success in balancing the claims of constituencies was achieved at the expense of its fundamental mission: gathering valid and reliable information about the population of the United States."[37]

Following the "scientific disaster," as Lowry termed the classification by ethnicity in the 1980 census, the Bureau was inundated by some fifty-four lawsuits, based on such charges as that, according to the Bureau's own post-enumeration surveys, the undercount of black males ranged as high as 7.8 percent.[38] Since—to repeat—many federal disbursements to local jurisdictions are based on census figures, errors of this magnitude cost cities and states millions of dollars. The court cases centered on the question whether the Constitution permits or requires the Bureau to adjust figures obtained in an enumeration, an issue that reached the U.S. Supreme Court only in the mid-1990s. The plaintiffs held that the Bureau should use every statistical technique that would result in a more accurate count. The Bureau's response was that it is "prohibited by the literal terms of the Constitution from making any addition to the census figures that is not based on identifiable names or addresses." Vincent Barabba, then director of the Bureau, defended the 1980 count as the best ever,[39] and eventually the courts accepted his defense. Unadjusted counts for states and small areas were released on schedule, then later corrected in successive emendations. But the Bureau's embarrassment over the country's "turbulence," as Barabba called it, resulted in a more comprehensive preparation for the count of ethnic minorities in the 1990 census.

In the mid-1980s the Bureau assembled a working group of representatives of federal agencies that use ethnic data, eventually joined by twenty-eight ethnic specialists from academia or relevant organizations. There were also four ethnic advisory committees, one for each of the protected minorities. No consensus developed even on such relatively minor matters as whether the term *race* should be included in the schedule. The recommendations consisted mainly in proposals that alternative wordings or orders of items be tested in the field before the 1990 count. Six surveys were conducted with different samples throughout the country, and their results helped shape the phrasing and format of the 1990 schedule. In general, this was an improvement over that a decade earlier; but it was still true that spokesmen for various minorities succeeded in shaping the schedule so as to maximize—they hoped—the number of their claimed constituents.[40]

More basically, the 1990 census showed some of the general inadequacies of ethnic counts. For example, those classified as "black" included any who identified themselves as "Jamaican" or "West Indian," not all of whom were necessarily black. On the other hand, blacks who classified themselves as "Hispanic" required a double entry. According to the census report, "specialists with a thorough knowledge of the race subject matter reviewed, edited, coded, and resolved inconsistent or incomplete responses."[41] Most of those who had been classified as in "other races" were transferred through this process to one of the four main racial categories.

America's bicentennial census [in 1990] was conducted by 520,000 workers, or more people than General Motors employs worldwide. The government spent $2.6 billion, or about $1,040 per person counted. Tens of millions of census forms from 3,141 counties, 23,435 places, 49,961 census tracts, and 6,961,150 census blocks were microfilmed, tallied, computerized, shredded, and then placed in warehouse vaults in Jeffersonville, Indiana...where they are to remain until the vast majority of respondents to the 1990 count will have died.[42]

According to the Bureau's estimate, the undercount in 1990 was only between 1 and 2 percent—probably about 1.8 percent—as contrasted with 5.4 percent in 1950. Instead of the actual count of 248,709,873, the estimated population was 253,978,000. The estimated undercounts of minorities, however, remained high.[43] According to post-enumeration surveys, the proportions of various sectors of the population not included in the 1990 count were:

Blacks	4.4 percent
Hispanics	5.0
American Indians	4.5
Non-Hispanic whites	0.7

In other words, the considerable improvement in coverage did not include those at the bottom of the social scale in anything like the same degree. A higher proportion of the so-called protected minorities are hostile to government representatives of all types, and many of them presumably managed to elude the enumeration. This was manifestly the case on some Indian reservations, almost certainly just as important a factor among Hispanic illegal immigrants and the homeless or marginal blacks.

In the mid-1990s the Bureau of Labor Statistics conducted a study on whether to respond to demands for new ethnic/racial categories. Some Arab Americans want to be identified as Middle Eastern rather than white. Some Hawaiians want to be listed as Native American rather than Asian-Pacific. About 7 percent of the population, according to preliminary reports of the Bureau of the Census, say that they would be best identified as Multiracial, which would be a new listing for the approximately two million children of interracial unions. This last figure has more than doubled in each of the past two censuses. In 1997 the Office of Management and Budget is to decide whether any of these labels will be adopted.[44]

In summary, each step toward keeping track of the population's ethnic composition was taken ad hoc, in accordance with new legal requirements or in response to pressures from Congress and sectors of the public. Blacks and Indians, who had an exceptional relation to apportionment, were therefore separately classified in the first censuses; and that precedent set the basic distinction between race and nationality that has been maintained ever since. During the nineteenth century and particularly its later decades, when political debate focused on immigration restriction, the schedules were amended to test how well newcomers were fitting in with their new country's culture. After the restrictionist laws were passed in the 1920s, both the public—and, therefore, the Bureau—saw assimilation as a relatively unimportant matter, and few would then have anticipated how pressing an issue the counting of ethnic blocs would become, or how troublesome it would be for the officials supervising the operation.

As one would expect from something that developed rather haphazardly, ethnic counts have been far from satisfactory. Indeed, there have been very few instances when statistical data were deliberately manipulated to support a political position,[45] but many of the decisions on how a group was to be defined, or how it was to be counted, have had political consequences. Ideally an enumeration should take place with no partisan passions to affect the route to its results. With the development of the welfare state, the financing of many local or private functions was shifted to Washington and, with it, great competition there in seeking preferment. It is a supreme paradox of our time that, not only in the United States but generally, the greater state control over the economy and society has brought about not the growing indifference to nationalism and ethnicity that every socialist since Marx anticipated, but precisely the opposite.

By 1990, the Bureau's operations were more politicized than during prior counts. The groups given preferment under affirmative action are not the only ones who have suffered and still suffer from discrimination, and the nationalities that originated in Asia or Eastern and Southern Europe have shown resentment at what they see as a double discrimination. If group-based preferences were to spread, as some spokesmen for these minorities demand, one can readily suppose that the small tribe of "instant Indians" that federal programs have brought into being[46] would be augmented by considerably larger numbers of "instant Poles" and "instant Italians." The agency in charge of specifying how much federal largesse each of them should receive would make the difficulties of the past censuses seem picayune.

Nor could the Bureau officials easily defend any of their decisions on this matter; for as the Australian demographer Charles Price concluded in a useful review of how ethnic groups are classified, "one has to accept the reality that there is no final certainly in the matter; that estimates, no matter how well based and researched, are only estimates."[47] If, on the other hand, the move in the 1990s to eliminate or greatly curtail affirmative-action preferments succeeds, then the classification by ethnicity will probably become less critical.

What groupings are significant enough to warrant the cost of recording them? Understandably, the census procedure has been to subclassify populations that are well-known in America (thus, English, Scots, Welsh, and Irish, rather than merely British) but to ignore differences of equal or greater importance in less familiar nationalities. On the other hand, the 1990 schedule called on each American Indian to name his tribe. In the Voting Rights Act of 1982 the Bureau of the Census was required to include Eskimos and Aleuts as racial categories on the long form for the entire country, though these two groups are highly concentrated geographically and together number only several tens of thousands. Hispanic civil-rights organizations also argued that the revised law required the Bureau to ask questions concerning them of 100 percent of the population, specifying each Latino in one of the four subcategories. These are striking examples of how money is wasted not to obtain information of even possible utility to the nation as a whole, but to satisfy the demands of particular ethnic organizations.

The most unwieldy category based on race has been, of course, nonwhites, which was introduced in 1960 as an economy measure. A two-category classification by color was defensible for national summaries, in which Negroes constituted the overwhelming majority of nonwhites (92 percent in 1960) or for regions of the country with few Indians, Asians, or other persons neither white nor black—but not in the West. After a good deal of criticism, the Bureau abandoned the term.

Somewhat similarly, the contrived category of "Hispanics" presents an appealingly simple view of the ethnic spectrum: all who speak any version of Spanish, or whose forebears did, coming from no matter which Spanish-speaking country, are lumped together irrespective of cultural, economic, and racial differences that to many persons in the separate minorities are a good deal more important than these criteria. Still more bizarre is the bunching together of all persons with a background in any Asian country or any place in the Pacific islands.

To say that the ethnic classification has not been consistent or logical is to point to the obvious. The issue is rather why this has been so. Four main factors are involved.[48] The first we can label *science*; it designates the effort to classify the population as accurately as possible, using all the techniques available to statisticians and demographers. The second is *law*, the constitutional requirement that the Bureau of the Census count the population in order to allocate seats in the House of Representatives and, following directives in particular laws, to set the distribution of federal funds according to the relative numbers in each category. A legal scholar, Thomas A. Cowan, held that science and law, at best complementary, are often at odds; and in their examination of the 1980 enumeration, Ian Mitroff and his associates made much of this contention.[49]

Laws and regulations have invited in a third factor, *politics,* to participate in each count as a major contender. Some of the dubious decisions of the Bureau may have reflected no more than standard bureaucratic conservatism, but in many instances this was augmented by diverse interest-group pressures. The fourth factor, which can be called *expediency,* is the constant effort to accommodate to fiscal or technical restraints. Imputation, or the computer techniques the Bureau uses to fill in data not gathered in the field, became the basis for many of the legal challenges to the census figures.

There is no way of classifying ethnic groups that satisfies all of these governing principles—*science, law, politics,* and *expediency.* The Bureau has been engaged in a mission impossible not entirely of its own making.

4

Identification of Americans
of European Descent

The discussion in chapter 3 of how ethnic enumerations by American statistical agencies evolved since the founding of the Republic gives only a preliminary impression of the ramifications of this task. One can understand more fully what is involved from a detailed account of how each component of the population changed and how the Bureau of the Census and other federal units responded to their moving targets. This is the topic of this chapter and the ones immediately following.

The classification that matters most to the persons concerned is the one embedded in race-conscious law. If racial attributes are indefinite and mutable, as virtually every authority would now agree, how can a law define the boundaries of groups used to administer remedial preferences? The legal scholar Christopher A. Ford used a Massachusetts case to highlight some of the conundrums.[1] Two brothers, Paul and Philip Malone, tried to qualify for the Boston Fire Department, but failed the examination. Two years later they tried again, this time identifying themselves as black. Under the court-ordered affirmative action program, the city maintained separate minority lists, and even with their poor scores, the two were hired. After ten years of service, when they sought a promotion, their false identities were uncovered. They were fired, appealed, and lost the case. After the state district attorney delved into the matter, eleven other firemen came under investigation on similar grounds.

Ford began his analysis by considering the census questionnaire on race/ethnicity. In 1990 nearly 10 million persons marked the census forms to state that they were of other races than those listed. By the Bureau of the Census computer program known as imputation, respondents with a nonspecified race were assigned to the same race as their nearest family member, housing block coresident, and so on. Thus, according to a communication from a Bureau employee, the number of whites recorded was increased by about 9 million, of blacks by about 500,000, and of Asian/Pacific Islanders by almost 200,000. One racial identity in every twenty-five was modified by such a procedure.

Group-preferential hiring and promotion are mandated by the regulations of the Equal Employment Opportunity Commission (EEOC). The guidelines define a "minority" as persons "having origins in" or as the "original peoples" of various continents. Yet if an employer fails to comply with this indeterminate directive, his contract may be terminated and he may be barred from future contracts. Employers are required to submit reports on the race, ethnicity, and sex of their employees, and this breakdown is compared with that in the local labor market. According to an EEOC manual that Ford quotes, "In the final analysis, availability figures often are more the product of negotiation than they are precise calculation." However, such negotiations depend on comparing the self-reported identities collated in the census with those in personnel files, which are usually based on how outsiders define each employee.

> In attempting to remedy race-related wrongs, our social engineers work with data as conceptually muddy and contextually contingent as our notions of race and ethnicity themselves. Accordingly, it is unwise for courts and administrators simply to assume that the foundations upon which they erect these platforms of public policy and jurisprudence are solid.[2]

Identification of Minorities

Few things facilitate a category's coalescence into a group so readily as its designation by an official body. Most of those leaving the multiethnic pre-1914 empires of Central and Eastern Europe had little or no consciousness of belonging to a nationality. As he saw himself, such an immigrant had four identities. He was the subject of a particular state, for example, Russia; he spoke a particular language, for example, Estonian; he was an adherent of one or another religion; and he regarded a certain province or village as home. Even some of the immigrants from nations that had achieved political unity did not identify themselves as natives of those countries; an "Italian," for instance, was more likely to look on himself as a Sicilian or a Calabrian.

In some cases, thus, it was only after they had left it that migrants learned to identify themselves with "their" country, first by the questions put to them by immigration officials and later in census schedules. The technical requirement that the question on ethnicity be put in a simple form—"What was your country of birth?" or something equivalent—meant not only that superficially valid responses were in a deeper sense false, but that posing them helped solidify new ethnic groups. Having learned that they had been members of a nation, some immigrants submerged their provincialisms into a broader patriotism, possibly even their local dialects into a language. The first Lithuanian newspaper was published in the United States; the Erse revival began in Boston; the Czechoslovak nation was launched at a meeting in Pittsburgh; the very name of Pakistan was coined by students in London.

How loose an indication of ethnicity could be derived from statistics on the country of origin is suggested in a paper by Richard Böckh (1824–1907), the eminent German statistician.[3] During the years 1898 to 1904, when for the first time the United States classified immigrants by stock independently of the country of origin, Böckh calculated that in addition to the 151,118 "Germans" from Germany, there were 289,438 from such other countries as Austria-Hungary, Russia, and Switzerland. Russia was an especially interesting case. Though Slavs (apart from Poles) made up about 70 percent of Russia's population, they constituted only 2 percent of the 625,607 "Russian" immigrants during those seven years. The others were:

"Hebrews"	41.9 percent
Poles	26.5
Finns	11.4
Lithuanians	10.1
Germans	6.8
Scandinavians	1.3

In other words, American immigration and census statistics—or at least, that portion of the data pertaining to pre-1914 Central and Eastern Europe—began to furnish a genuine clue to the newcomers' ethnic identities only shortly before the imposition of national quotas.

Impressionistic accounts of the population when the Republic was founded, as typified by Crèvecoeur's work,[4] depicted a polyglot people amalgamating into a new type of nation. There are no firm data to check this narrative, but in a census monograph W. S. Rossiter (1861–1929), a statistician at the Bureau of the Census, estimated the national origins from the surnames listed in the 1790 enumeration as follows:

English	83.5 percent
Scotch	6.7
German	5.6
Dutch	2.0
Irish	1.6
French	0.5
"Hebrew"	>0.1
All others	0.1

That is to say, by his reckoning the American population in 1790 was overwhelmingly of British stock.[5] Note that most of the "Irish" in Rossiter's list were Scots-Irish, who thus furnished a larger quota to the Irish they customarily denigrated as Papists.

However, many names are common to several nationalities, and in an English-speaking country the tendency would be to assign them to the English component rather than the German, French, or Spanish. According to Rossiter, a larger proportion of the non-English stock was to be found in particular areas, such as New York State with 16.1 percent Dutch or Pennsylvania with 26.1 percent German. One probable reason for this finding is that residents of a German American community retained their Germanic names, while many of those living among persons of English stock changed them to an English-sounding equivalent.

The historian Albert Faust also checked the names registered in the country's first census, but he then compared his results with historical records of German settlements. In counties of Pennsylvania with a population of predominantly German stock, most of the original names had been retained, but not, for instance, in North and South Carolina, where "it was remarkable to see to what extent German names had been anglicized." The total number of German stock so derived was 375,000, which to be conservative he reduced to 360,000.[6] This was 18.9 percent of the 1790 white population, as contrasted with the 5.6 percent that Rossiter had estimated.

There is no reason to suppose that the false estimate was specific to German immigrants, for the same factors applied to all other non-English nationalities. In the 1980s the *William and Mary Quarterly* published several articles on the undercount of other nationalities, including one significantly titled "Why the Accepted Estimates of the Ethnicity of the American Population, 1790, Are Unacceptable."[7]

These calculations would be mainly of antiquarian interest except for the fact that eventually immigration policy was set by an essentially similar reckoning. The Immigration Act of 1924 required the calculation of "the number of inhabitants in the continental United States in 1920 whose origin by birth or ancestry is attributable to [each] geographical area" designated in immigration statistics as a separate country. This task was undertaken by the Bureau of the Census assisted by two experts paid by the American Council of Learned Societies.

One of the committee's "main sources" was Rossiter's estimate, at first accepted as "furnishing the most complete information available" on the national origins of the 1790 population. However, since the committee eventually recognized that there was a "considerable element of uncertainty" in any classification based on family names, the English component was cut by a little more than a tenth, an arbitrary figure that was then prorated among other nationalities according to the (also poorly based) proportions that Rossiter had calculated.

Between 1790 and 1820 no record was kept of immigration, but the allowance made for these newcomers was not thought to be "a factor of very great importance in the final result." Subsequent immigration was recorded, but in statistics of notorious inadequacy. The frequent and untraceable marriages across ethnic lines made it impossible to divide the 1920 population itself into distinct ethnic groups (as the 1924 act required), and the committee undertook instead to measure the proportionate contribution of various national stocks to the total gene pool of white Americans. To the base of the 1790 population were added immigration figures, such as they were, and—for lack of a breakdown by ethnic groups—an overall rate of natural increase. Since the multiethnic empires of pre-1914 Europe had been broken up after the Allied victory, those born in Germany, Austria-Hungary, or Russia were allocated to the new nations not on the basis of their birthplaces, which were not available from the record, but again according to their names.[8]

The immigration restrictions of the 1920s lasted until 1965, when a new law replaced the quotas by country with a single overall figure. In 1986 an Immigration Reform and Control Act conferred legal status on more than 2.5 million residents previously outside the law and, on the other hand, applied sanctions on anyone who employed illegal immigrants. The Immigration Act of 1990 set a supposed worldwide limit of about 700,000 arrivals annually, but with so many exceptions that in 1993 those legally admitted totaled 904,000, the highest number since 1914. In 1994, 8.7 percent of the American population was foreign born, nearly double the proportion in 1970, though far less than the 14.7 percent in 1910. In 1994, more than a third of the foreign-born lived in California. By far the largest national component was Mexican-born, some 6,164,000 persons out of a total of 22,568,000.[9]

In the mid-1990s there has been a widespread clamor for more restrictive legislation. The arguments are eerily similar to those that were circulated from the 1890s until the laws of the 1920s were passed. Earlier those coming from Russia and Italy were pictured as inassimilable; later this has been said of Asians and Hispanics. Immigrants, it is alleged, cost the country inordinate sums by their large numbers on welfare, in prisons, in hospitals, in line for state handouts everywhere. As before, a xenophobic bias is more evident than a solid base in fact.

One myth is the repeated contrast between the golden past, when allegedly immigrants came only to work, and the dismal present, when high proportions are eating up public funds. According to Lawrence H. Fuchs, a student of immigration history and a vice-chairman of the U.S. Commission on Immigration Reform, "The idea that [in the past] immigrants had no charity available, no welfare, is crazy." The statistics are hardly adequate for definitive conclusions, but one can reasonably deduce that the cost of immigration around the turn of the century was much greater than in recent years. The contrary impression derives partly from two anomalous categories—the politically motivated immigrants of the 1930s and the so-called brain drain from less developed countries. These movements were atypical, when a newcomer might be a nurse, a graduate chemist, or even a rocket scientist.[10]

Americans' Religions

People in Western countries have customarily thought of Islam as one religion—until the continual Near Eastern conflicts pointed up the implacable hatreds between various denominations and sects. Many gentiles know that religious Jews are divided into Orthodox, Conservative, and Reform branches; but probably few are aware of how serious the differences have become. Even the conventional division of Christians between Catholics and Protestants should be supplemented by one between modernist progressives and orthodox conservatives.

The national statistical agency published a so-called Census of Religious Bodies every ten years from 1906 to 1936. One was started but never finished in 1946, and the series was canceled altogether in 1956. The data were collected not from individuals, but from questionnaires sent to the headquarters of each denomination. Such statistics depend on the voluntary cooperation of denominational leaders, as well as their avoidance of any temptation to inflate the number of their parishioners. Some sects, in particular Christian Scientists, prohibit the publication of their membership figures; others are hardly equipped to maintain an accurate register. In any case, membership is not defined consistently. Most Protestant churches include only those who have been confirmed and are currently enrolled in a congregation. As defined by the Roman Catholic Church, the Protestant Episcopal Church, and several Lutheran denominations, however, members are all who have been baptized and thus include infants and children up to the age of confirmation as well as adults who have not broken away publicly.

In an analysis of Catholics in Britain and Ireland, the author compared the population sizes derived from five different ways of specifying a "Catholic": self-definition, acceptance by the church, baptismal or marriage statistics, numbers reported by key informants, and registration totals. All these criteria have been used, and the resultant numbers vary greatly.[11]

The many ways of being Jewish have been defined both by the persons themselves and by the societies in which they live (see chapter 14). To designate a person a Jew has meaning, but not a simple one.

Protestant denominations are generally identified by a single appellation— Lutheran, Methodist, or whatever—as though all of the many subdenominations of any Protestant grouping were essentially identical. In fact, Protestants are split within denominations between Fundamentalism and Modernism. The name Fundamentalist derives from *The Fundamentals,* a work in eleven volumes (1910–1915). In a recent restatement, its essence consists of "a very strong emphasis on the inerrancy of the Bible;...a strong hostility to modern theology and to the methods, results, and implications of modern critical study of the Bible; [and] an assurance that those who do not share their religious viewpoints are not really 'true Christians.'"[12] Modernism, as defined by the dean of the Divinity School of the University of Chicago, is "the use of the methods of modern science to find, state, and use the permanent and central values of inherited orthodoxy in meeting the needs of the modern world.... Modernists are Christians who accept the results of scientific research as data with which to think religiously."[13] With respect to theology, social policy, or church structure, the basic differences in American Protestantism are between these two wings. To classify a category of respondents in a poll or survey as "Methodists" (not to say "Protestants") is worse than meaningless; it is grossly misleading.

To some degree the distinction also divides the clergy from the parishioners that they supposedly lead. A Gallup poll of the Episcopal Church showed that in the mid-1980s the clergy differed significantly from the laity on theological and political questions. For example, 60 percent of the clergy believed that the Episcopal Church should be an agent of political change in the United States, but 78 percent of the members held that it should be primarily concerned with worship and spiritual direction. According to the Reverend James Law of the Prayer Book Society, which commissioned the poll, "the Episcopal Church is schizophrenic and there is a gulf, a chasm, and out-of-stepness between the clergy and their people."[14]

Or consider another major Protestant denomination, the Lutherans. From its founding Lutheranism has had a strong schismatic bent, and in the United States more than a dozen subdenominations evolved. In 1960 the most important of these—but not all—reunited into the American Lutheran Church, and according to a 1970 survey of 4,745 Lutherans, including both laymen and clergy, there was a basic adherence to conservative values in all the subdenominations.[15] To the degree that all Lutherans have similar views, however, these need not be exclusively a reflection of their religion. Most Lutherans in the United States are of German or Scandinavian descent, living in the Middle West as prototypes of small-town Americans. Those members of the church who deviated very much from the composite norm, one can reasonably assume, moved away both from that setting and from its religious institutions. In 1986, after four years of negotiations at three conventions, the three main Lutheran churches agreed to unite again into a new Evangelical Lutheran Church in America, which would become the fourth largest Protestant denomination in the country. No doctrinal disputes of any importance had separated the churches, and in the negotiations leading to unity the issues were such organizational matters as where the new church's headquarters would be located.[16] Two of the more conservative organizations, the Lutheran Church-Missouri Synod and the Wisconsin Evangelical Lutheran Church, retained their independence.

If the statistics were accurate, that would still leave in question what they mean concerning the beliefs and behavior of members of the various churches. That a person defines himself, say, as a Roman Catholic provides only a first clue.[17] Catholics in the United States have usually voted Democratic, true; but that is a long way from demonstrating that they vote Democratic because they are Catholic—rather than because they are urban, working-class, or members of trade unions. While Catholic spokesmen have denounced contraception, a vast majority of pious Catholic wives in the United States have long used the means condemned by their church. In a few polls persons who defined themselves as members of the church were asked, for instance, how often they attended mass, whether they performed the Easter duties, how often they went to confession, whether they married in a religious ceremony and are raising their children as members of the church, and so on. But such an attempt to approximate the degree of cohesion in the real world is time-consuming and expensive, and it would be out of the question in a nationwide census.

When no money was allotted for the 1956 Census of Religious Bodies, a question arose whether to include a question on religious affiliation in the 1960 enumeration. This had been proposed earlier, but it was opposed by representatives of Jewish organizations and civil libertarians. A test survey in Milwaukee seemed to support those who wanted a query on religious affiliation: only 0.5 percent of the respondents refused to answer the question, "What is your religion?"—compared with 0.6 percent on the number of respondent's children, 1.3 percent on education, and 7.0 percent on income. In 1957, the Bureau of the Census included the same question in a preliminary survey, which resulted in a partial report.[18] Opposition was voiced by only a very few, but they were so vehement that the innovation was abandoned. A decade later a suggestion to include a question on religious affiliation never got off the ground.

Most of the data collected in the 1957 survey were made public only after demographers resorted to the Freedom of Information Act to force their release.[19] No other statistics had ever been kept secret in this fashion, contradicting the norm that all the Bureau's data not pertaining to identifiable individuals are to be open to public scrutiny in full. According to an official of the Bureau, "Although at one time census reports were treated as state secrets, it is now recognized that a census is not complete until the data are compiled and published."[20]

Data from unofficial sources furnish a general view of religion in the United States. The Princeton Religious Research Center uses reports from the Gallup organization, which has surveyed Americans' religious affiliations since 1947. According to those statistics, the percentage who reported a religious preference rose from 76 in 1976 to 89 in 1991, and the proportion responding that they had "no religious preference" rose over the same period from 2 to 11 percent.[21]

In the nineteenth century dozens of religious or secular communal settlements blossomed in New York, Pennsylvania, and Ohio, but almost all except the Mormons have disappeared. The crucial difference may have been what adherents saw as persecution, for nothing is so likely to nourish a new religion as the martyrdom of its leaders. The long journey to Utah eventually brought about the Mormons' partial isolation, though not an end to hostility. Under two acts of Congress, the polygamy that Mormons practiced was prohibited; the church lost its corporate status, with its property escheated to the nation. What members of the church viewed as a renewed persecution reinforced the devotion of the faithful, and even after polygamy was abandoned in 1890, relations with "gentiles" did not improve greatly. Contrary to the constitutional principle of separation of powers, church and state were joined among Mormons in what outsiders saw as a theocracy. In Utah suffrage meant that church members elected religious leaders, who also became heads of civil government. Even after the controversy about multiple wives was long past, after the isolation of their desert home was breached by improved transportation, the Mormons have remained a distinct group, now set apart less by their religious doctrine than by the social-political organizations associated with the church.

Who is a Citizen?

Statistics on aliens derive ultimately from the prodigiously complex laws on nationality, which differ greatly from one country to another. In the United States a question on whether the respondent is a citizen has been asked in many censuses, but the answers have not necessarily been truthful. In 1940, when for the first time the census data were supplemented with a registration by the Immigration and Naturalization Service, the difference in the figures was great—a census count of about 3.5 million aliens and a registration of about 5 million.

In any case, the concept of American citizenship has undergone fundamental changes.[22] At one time laws on naturalization prohibited a series of specific acts that, in the view of Congress, indicated that the person's primary loyalty was still to another country. According to the Expatriation Act of 1907 and the Nationality Acts of 1940 and 1952, Americans could lose their citizenship if they were naturalized in a foreign state or took an oath of allegiance to it, if they served in the military force or government of a foreign state or voted there in a political election, or if they renounced United States citizenship. In order to inhibit those who desired the benefits of American citizenship while residing in their native country, naturalized citizens were forbidden to live abroad for more than a limited period. In a number of early cases federal courts upheld the right of Congress to set such conditions of expatriation and, thus, the constitutionality of these provisions.

The Supreme Court's stance began to change in *Perez* v. *Brownell* (1958), which upheld—but only by a five-to-four decision—the power of Congress to revoke the citizenship of someone who had voted in a foreign election. According to *Kennedy* v. *Mendoza-Martinez* (1963), a man who had fled to

Mexico to evade the draft and then returned voluntarily did not automatically lose his citizenship. In *Schneider* v. *Rusk* (1964), the Supreme Court held that restricting residence abroad of naturalized persons made them "second-class" citizens and was therefore unconstitutional. Erosion of the law on citizenship up to that point pertained to provisions manifestly from another era (such as revoking the citizenship of a woman who married an alien) or to marginal issues (on military personnel, for instance). In *Afroyim* v. *Rusk* (1967), however, the Supreme Court went considerably farther. After Afroyim, a naturalized citizen, went to Israel and there voted in an Israeli election, the State Department refused to renew his American passport. Writing for a majority of the court, Justice Hugo Black held that, "once acquired, citizenship [was] not to be shifted, canceled, or diluted at the will of the federal government, the states, or any other governmental unit." Seemingly this defined American citizenship as absolute, not subject to control by anyone including, under some circumstances, even the individual himself.

Vance v. *Terrazas* (1980) concerned a man of dual United States-Mexican nationality who, in order to become a citizen of Mexico, signed an application renouncing all other nationalities. It was not his intent, he later claimed, to relinquish United States citizenship, and the Supreme Court unanimously upheld the basic holding of *Afroyim*: whether an American citizen pledged allegiance to a foreign state was no longer a relevant issue unless the act indicated "intent" to forgo his American citizenship. Renunciation of citizenship is effective only if carried out before a diplomatic or consular officer of the United States in a manner prescribed by the Secretary of State. Informal renunciations have no effect.

The most dramatic test of this ruling pertained to Rabbi Meir Kahane, the American-born head of the militant Israeli Kach Party, who had a record of arrests in both the United States and Israel for leading violent street demonstration in support of his extremist views. He moved from the United States to Israel in 1971, and in 1984, when he was elected to the Israeli parliament, he swore "to be faithful to the state of Israel and serve my mission faithfully at the Knesset." According to his letters to American officials, Kahane did not "intend" by this act to renounce his American citizenship; but even so the State Department issued a Certificate of Loss of Nationality, which Kahane challenged in an appeal. At a speech in Washington, he asserted that, though himself a dual citizen, he believed that "a person should not be a dual citizen" and that he would long since have given up that status if he did not fear that the United States government "would place great obstacles in my path in attempting to obtain a visa to enter America for lecture tours," the means that he used to finance his Israeli organization. Kahane's lawyer, Charles S. Sims of the American Civil Liberties Union, charged that the State Department's brief was "an invitation to anti-Semitism," thus assuring his client the most emotional hearing possible. Before the case could be settled by American courts, the Knesset passed a law aimed directly at Kahane, requiring its members to relinquish non-Israeli citizenship.[23]

As it has been shaped by juridical decisions, American law on citizenship can result in strange anomalies. At a time when the United States and Nicaragua were unofficially at war, perhaps as many as a hundred American citizens were employed by the Sandinista government—including, for example, Kay Stubbs, born in Ohio and working as official interpreter for President Daniel Ortega; and June Mulligan, a native-born American in the public-relations office of Nicaragua's armed forces. Peter Rosset of New York, who worked for Nicaragua's Ministry of Agriculture, shifted to teaching at a government-run college of agronomy, for in the latter post his salary was paid by the United States under the Fulbright program.[24]

That Americans gradually acquired the option of virtually unlimited dual loyalty has changed the legal significance of ethnicity also in other respects. Though the European practice of permitting aliens to vote in local or provincial elections[25] has not yet been imitated here, there seem to be steps in that direction. A National Association of Latino Elected Officials issued a report, "The Long Gray Welcome," urging that the process of naturalization (already less cumbersome and faster than in almost any other country) be made easier.[26]

In a more remarkable innovation, lawyers have defended immigrants charged with crimes with the plea that they were only following the norms of their native countries. Thus, Vietnamese Americans who beat their wives claimed to be astounded that they were subject to arrest for exercising their customary marital rights. When a Japanese-born woman, despondent about her husband's extramarital affairs, tried to commit suicide by walking into the sea with her two young children in her arms, the children drowned but she survived. Experts were called to testify that such an act, reportedly common in Japan, would not there be regarded as murder. Several of the 30,000 Hmong from Laos who have settled in the Fresno area in California practiced what an anthropologist termed "marriage by capture" but police called "rape."[27] After a judge half-accepted the so-called cultural defense, a lawyer pleaded in a similar manner for a man who had killed his wife because she took a job with a male employer. When the courts have occasionally permitted a type of defense alien to prior American jurisprudence, they encouraged each minority to relate differently to the United States because of the customs of their native land.

On Paradoxes in Ethnic Counts

During the several decades when the melting pot was the unofficial credo of the United States, it existed in a groove parallel with a contrary ideology. Few believed that nonwhites would ever be melted down with those of European forebears; and the rising number of immigrants from Eastern and Southern Europe generated a flood of articles and books holding that these latest newcomers would also never assimilate. Congress's directive to specify the national origins of the American population from the 1790 census onward was based on the belief that race and ethnicity are fixed characteristics. Quanta of blood could be diluted only by mixed marriages, and the assumption underlying the restrictionist laws was that one could track the resulting partial quanta with statistics on successive generations.

The vogue has now changed, with a revivification rather than a diminution of ethnic sentiment. But the dogma has survived that ethnicity is a fixed quantity and that therefore one can classify the whole American people by nationality, race, or whatever. The very term *ethnic revival* connotes that adherence to a lineage is typical. However, as the European forebears of American whites recede into the distant past, questionnaires about national origins are more likely to evoke only part of the respondents' ethnic antecedents, or to leave them out altogether. Among a sample of third-generation Americans polled in the mid-1980s, up to age twenty a relatively stable proportion reported a single national line of descent, but in the next older age group the percentage was 10 points higher. There was a corresponding downward trend by age in the proportions reporting two or three ancestries. Or, as another type of distortion, when native-born white parents, with the husband and wife each of a single but different national lineage, were asked to report on their children's ancestry, from a third to more than half (depending in part on their nationalities) responded not by citing their own two ancestries, but something else.[28]

Questions about language have been included in the census since 1890, but the data from 1980 and 1990 were hardly congruous with those from prior enumerations. In 1980, following the precedent of the thirteen prior censuses, respondents were asked where they were born, but the question on the place(s) of birth of the respondent's parents was dropped, only to be restored in 1990. Thus, the history of the second generation's background, the key element in studies of acculturation, has had a critical interruption. Whether the innovations in 1980 were justified is a matter of opinion, but the enumeration was barely over when some analysts of ethnicity dissented from the decision of the Bureau of the Census.[29]

Strange to say, ethnic groups have been identified quite differently by various federal agencies. The absurd result is that in the several perspectives of his country's officials, the same person could be classified as a member of various ethnic or racial groups. A 1954 compendium of ethnic data from federal statistical sources listed ninety-two items, with a wide variety in the reasons for collecting the information and, thus, in the premises underlying the process.[30] "'Misclassification' with respect to color might better be termed 'inconsistent classification' of the same person as between one census and another, as between a birth certificate and a census form, or as between the entry made by a Selective Service Board and by a census enumerator."[31]

The two principal sources of statistical information on the population, the census and vital statistics, do not classify ethnicity and race in the same way. An example of a possible consequence was found when a researcher compared white and nonwhite death rates over the period 1925 to 1955. In the first half of each intercensal decade, nonwhite mortality fell faster, and in the second half, white mortality fell faster. A plausible explanation is that during each intercensal period underestimates of blacks rose relative to those of whites. Moreover, with the migration of many blacks to the North and to cities, there was also a probable rise in the number of persons classified as white in the census, but as black on death certificates. Both errors would cut the number of blacks in the denominator and thus raise the black rate relative to the white.[32] Yet the trend in the white-nonwhite mortality ratio is routinely used as one of the more significant indices of whether racial discrimination is being brought under control.

Consider another example: though American Indians generally have high rates of suicide, in Riverside County, California, for the years 1965 to 1969 no suicides were recorded in a substantial Indian population. The reason was that on the basis of their Spanish surnames the suicides were all classified as Mexican Americans.[33]

In a reaction to this shambles, the Office of Federal Statistical Policy and Standards issued a succession of directives designating the races and ethnic groups to be used in all federal reporting and statistics. Merely specifying a list, however, hardly began to deal with the problem. As had been noted, many federal laws pertain to particular ethnic sectors of the population in explicit detail, and the boundaries of the relevant sector were often fixed or at least implied in the legislation. The Bureau of Indian Affairs is mandated to deal with "Indians" as specified in its regulations, and the Bureau of the Census enumerates "Indians" according to another expression of Congress's will. Calling them both by the same name does not make the two populations one.[34]

Tom Smith of the National Opinion Research Center (NORC) and the associated Cultural Pluralism Research Center has used his experience with those two organizations to highlight some of the difficulties in classifying the American population by ethnic identity. How finely should one divide the population; how many ethnic groups should one posit? The NORC uses thirty-nine plus "All other," but of the forty, twenty each comprises 1 percent or less of the population. Classifications specified by forebears, by such a behavioral characteristic as language, and by self-identification do not necessarily jibe. Even when every effort is made to elicit a definite response to a query on ethnicity, some 10 to 15 percent of the respondents can give none. About 35 to 40 percent cite two or more ethnic strains; and of those about a third, or 11 to 12 percent of the total population, are unable to choose between what they regard as equally important elements of their ancestry. Thus, only one American in every two has a single, clearly defined ethnic identity—which, even so, is often stated in such a way as to be ambiguous or false. In sum, national origin is "of all the kinds of basic background variables about a person, the most difficult of all to measure and measure reliably."[35]

Not only the Bureau of the Census but also such other federal agencies as the Social Security Administration have also found that questions on ethnic identity are often not answered or, if they are, elicit confused responses. Before the 1980 count, a panel of the National Research Council made some of the same points at greater length. "The Census Bureau," its report remarked, "has performed some awkward lumping and splitting in an area of great sensitivity in American society."

> It is by no means clear that persons in similar situations and with similar characteristics will answer in the same way. For example, two third-generation persons with Italian ancestors, with similar family, education, economic, and other characteristics, may give two different answers: "Italian" and "American." Each answer is "correct."

The panel speculated that more persons of Irish ancestry would so designate themselves because the date of the count closely follows St. Patrick's Day. Would it have the same effect on Italian Americans if the date was shifted to mid-October, following Columbus Day? Because religious questions are avoided in the census, the category "Jewish" is deleted when a respondent so identifies himself, but "many religious and nonreligious Jews think of themselves as ethnically (as a people, a culture, a language) Jewish, not German, Polish, Ukrainian, etc." Once self-identification was adopted as the criterion of ethnicity, whatever a person chooses to respond is the "truth." Even this dubious version of reality, however, is not reflected in census reports, for very often the schedule is filled in by one member of a household reporting (accurately or otherwise) for himself and all other members.[36] Many of the responses, moreover, are incomplete and are filled in by a computer in the Bureau's office.

Three officials of the Bureau of the Census offered similar comments on ethnic data:

> Historical comparability of ancestry data within and between United States censuses has been complicated by problems not inherent in other types of data.... Collection of ancestry data is more difficult because of the lack of clear-cut definitions, changing terminologies, poor reliability, and lack of knowledge of the degree of affiliation with a group or groups. Although indirect measures such as own birthplace, parental birthplace, and mother tongue help estimate ethnicity because they are less susceptible to change in reporting between censuses, a direct question on ancestry might give more useful information if criteria for inclusion in particular groups could be established with reliability.... Ancestry would reflect identification, but not the degree of attachment or association the person had with the particular ethnic group(s).[37]

In preparation for the 1990 census, the Bureau issued a series of Content Determination Reports noting in detail how it would try to carry out its function. One of these is on Race and Ethnic Origin. It includes several pages listing the laws and regulations that specify how the identities of Americans are to be determined (though the contradictions between these many directives are not pointed out).

As in previous censuses, the one in 1990 was based on two main questionnaires, a short form containing basic population and housing questions, and a long form with additional queries filled in by a sample of only 17 percent of the population. Among the typical pressures from ethnic interest groups, each tried to get questions pertaining to the minorities it supposedly represented included in the schedule with full coverage rather than only in the sample; and, as has been noted, some of them succeeded.

> The Interagency Working Group recommended asking separate questions on ancestry and country of birth of parents on the sample form.... If questionnaire space would not permit this plan, they favored a combined ancestry and Spanish-origin question on the 100-percent form and a parental birthplace question on the sample form. When presented with a choice of including either an ancestry question or a parental birthplace question in the 1990 census, the group chose the parental birthplace question by only a slim margin.

As this excerpt suggests, the panel of agency officials and representatives of other interested organizations was not very helpful in setting clear and definite guidelines. The Bureau tried out alternative procedures in a series of tests during the 1980s, gradually reaching decisions on the wording of the questions, whether to include them in the 100-percent or the sample form, and other matters. No new items were added, but the items on race and Spanish/Hispanic origin were revised considerably, those on ancestry somewhat less. Perhaps the most important revision was that the birthplaces of the respondent's parents, which had been deleted in 1980, were restored.[38]

After data on ethnicity have been compiled and published, anyone using them must not only try to estimate their accuracy, but also decide what they mean. From any set of figures it is impossible to determine whether they pertain to a category or a group, and successive counts can change from one of these two types of ethnic entities to the other. How the units are broken down by other characteristics can affect crucially how one interprets them. If a society is made up of individuals and, in a different perspective, of ethnic groups, there need not be a one-to-one relation between the attributes of persons and those of groups.

5

Differentiation among Blacks

Since the boundaries of ethnic groups are neither precise nor immutable, some have argued that races, or biological differences in general, do not exist.[1] Yet many elements that we discuss and analyze are similarly structured: at the core they have distinctive characteristics; they merge at the periphery into other things or beings; and they change over time.

Take as a totally unrelated example the division of the English language into three temporal classes: Old, Middle, and Modern. Old English, or Anglo-Saxon, is the source of our basic vocabulary, but a present-day reader finds it all but incomprehensible. In the twelfth century, with large infusions of French and Latin, it gradually evolved into the language of Chaucer, which, with a glossary of the words that have become obsolete, is understandable today. Then around 1500 there emerged the language of Shakespeare and the Book of Common Prayer, the Modern English that is almost completely intelligible. No philologist would reject this tripartite division for the reasons that some analysts of race cite for their refusal to use that concept. The language at each stage was quite distinctive, and the fact that the change was gradual, taking place over centuries with occasional detours surviving in dialects, does not affect the validity of the classification.

In his stimulating work on how to conduct research, Abraham Kaplan discusses what he called the "semantic myth," the conceit that the principal trouble with the social disciplines is linguistic. "If only the behavioral scientist were to eliminate vagueness and ambiguity, define his terms, use definitions of the right kind (operational or whatever), all would be well with him." But vagueness is characteristic of most entities in real life. There is first of all the problem of where to draw the boundary between X and non-X, almost never a simple, not to say an automatic, decision. How precisely does one draw the boundary between blacks and whites, or between blacks and Hispanics? Then there is what Kaplan calls internal vagueness. All things are defined by a set of properties, but no property is necessarily characteristic of the whole class. Skin color does not define blacks: Walter White, long head of the NAACP, who in spite of his light complexion and blue eyes defined himself as a Negro, wrote an autobiography titled *A Man Called White*. Finally Kaplan takes note of "dynamic openness": even if a definition is more or less precise at one moment, there is a "permanent possibility of change in meaning."[2] The attributes used to define the category of blacks, whether by statistical agencies or by themselves, have not remained consistent.

If the Bureau of the Census were free to concentrate on delimiting ethnic groups as well as its demographers and statisticians could manage, the result would still be far from ideal. But pressures abound from Congress, interest groups, fiscal considerations, technical problems. The consequence is that often even a reasonable approximation is an unattainable mirage.

Negroes, Blacks, and African Americans

In the past, though with respect to most attributes blacks were much more homogeneous than now, census enumerations identified subgroups within this minority. Until general emancipation slaves were distinguished from freed blacks; and Negroes from the West Indies, like other immigrants, were listed separately. In order to stress how important these two differentiations were, Thomas Sowell titled an essay "Three Black Histories."[3] Most "free persons of color," who constituted 14 percent of the Negro population in the 1830s, lived not on plantations in the black belt, but in cities or small towns. In the District of Columbia, half the blacks were free in 1830, more than three-quarters in 1860. They established their own schools and reduced illiteracy sometimes to nil and always to well below that of even the most favored urban slaves. Those who escaped from slavery before the general emancipation had an enduring advantage, as shown by the fact that they and their descendants were the principal leaders of the black community up to about the time of World War I.

In five censuses between 1840 and 1910 an attempt was made to classify Negroes by skin color, usually between *blacks* and *mulattos,* but in 1890 into four different subcategories. Enumerators were given the task of assessing the proportions of blood, and the instructions given them made it obvious that the administrators thought this was feasible:

> Be particularly careful to distinguish between blacks, mulattos, quadroons, and octoroons. The word "black" should be used to describe those persons who have three-fourths or more black blood; "mulatto," those persons who have three-eighths to five-eighths black blood; "quadroon," those persons who have one-fourth black blood; and "octoroon," those persons who have one-eighth or any trace of black blood.[4]

According to the census report itself, the four-way classification was "of little value" and "misleading."

It is usual to dismiss these attempts to construct a taxonomy by quanta of blood as manifestations of the nineteenth-century obsession with the biology of race. On the other hand, one could take the black-mulatto dichotomy as a rough substitute for the slave-free one, with which there was a significant overlap. In the free Negro population of 1850 there were 581 mulattos per 1,000 blacks, contrasted with only 83 in the slave population. Years of schooling and proportion illiterate also differed considerably between the two subcategories.[5]

Another division in the black population has been between natives and *West Indians,* or immigrants from any of the British islands together with their descendants. Though in some respects slavery was more callous in the islands than on the Mainland, slaves there were assigned land and time to raise their own food, and they could sell any surplus in the market to buy other things for themselves. Thus, when they were freed—a full generation before general emancipation in the United States—they had already developed something of the self-reliance and resilience that their descendants later brought with them to the Mainland. Though West Indians numbered only about 1 percent of the black population, their concentration in the upper levels of the Harlem community made them important. Allegedly they have differed not only in their occupations but in behavior patterns, being more frugal, hard-working, and entrepreneurial. They have had smaller families and lower crime rates than other Americans, black or white.[6]

In the recent period most of the contentions about census counts of blacks have pertained to coverage. Indeed, none of the Bureau's carefully crafted procedures have sufficed to include all, or even an adequate proportion, of lower-class blacks.[7] But in this context it is relevant to consider also the issue of ambiguous identity—at the boundaries both between blacks and whites and between widely separated middle- or working-class blacks and those living in seemingly permanent poverty.

Whatever the past differences between slaves and the free colored, or blacks and mulattos, or natives and West Indians, one might contend that so long as all Negroes were denigrated in law, suffrage, employment, and other major institutional settings, no distinction within the race was of decisive importance. It is still the case that virtually every black, no matter how law-abiding, how respectable, has been subjected to humiliating experiences or worse. It is undeniable that the incidence of street crime, illiteracy, illegitimacy, and some other social inadequacies is notably higher among blacks than in the rest of the population. Is it ever legitimate, in judging a person, to accept color as a first rough approximation? Such a statistical rather than categorical discrimination is the kind of distinction that everyone makes every day. As private individuals, we all weigh the likely effects of our actions on the basis of partial evidence, not probing every situation to determine whether in this particular case the mere probability is a valid guide.

The point can be highlighted by a telling anecdote. Many jewelry stores admit customers only after the proprietor has observed them through a locked glass door, and some owners use the system to exclude young black males, who, on the basis of their experience, are least likely to buy, most likely to rob. Richard Cohen, a columnist for the *Washington Post*—that is, a liberal commentator writing in a liberal newspaper—defended the practice against criticism by some other journalists. "The mere recognition of race as a factor," he wrote, "is not in itself racism." Thereupon the *New Republic,* a liberal weekly, posed a dilemma:

> If you were such a jewelry store owner [the magazine asked several academics and journalists], would you use your buzzer system to exclude young black males? You might take other factors into account—not just age and sex, but style of dress and the time of day—but would you ever take race into consideration as well? Whatever you yourself would do, is taking race into consideration in these circumstances racist? Understandable? Both? Neither?[8]

This example of what some have come to call rational discrimination has become not merely a basis for the behavior of vulnerable persons, but also a topic of heated discussion.[9] A generation earlier the question could not have been raised in a liberal journal, and the dilemma is still difficult for any fair-minded person. In a democratic society the appropriate response, whatever it is for an individual in personal relations, is that in official settings a judgment based on race is never fitting.

Today, now that formal segregation and discrimination are illegal, the earlier statistical subclassifications within the category of blacks have been abandoned. True, there is a substantial immigration of blacks, who are sometimes distinguished as a component of the foreign born (though they may choose to list themselves as Hispanics). Current data on native blacks, however, are often misleading, for along virtually every dimension they are divided into two sharply contrasting subgroups.[10]

In a book whose title proclaims its subject, *The Declining Significance of Race,* William Julius Wilson compared the two sectors of American blacks.[11] On the one hand, as one symptom of the general condition of the black slum, the nonwhite-white ratio of unemployment rates for those aged sixteen to nineteen rose from 1.37 in 1954 to 2.35 in 1974 (in October 1995, 17.1 percent of all male teens were unemployed, but 33.1 percent of that sector of blacks). On the other hand, the number of visits made by recruiters from corporations to predominantly black colleges and universities, which averaged only 4 in 1960, rose to 50 in 1965 and 297 in 1970.

From 1975 to 1990, the number of black seventeen-year-olds who could read at an "adept" level doubled. The number of blacks in college has soared. In 1994, of blacks aged twenty-five years or more, 13 percent had a B.A. or better (compared with 23 percent of comparable whites).[12] Black men in technical jobs earn almost as much as whites, and the chance of a college-educated black rising to a managerial or executive position is about the same as for comparable whites. Among female managers and executives with college degrees, black women make 10 percent more than their white counterparts. Black teenagers have stopped smoking in a higher proportion than white. The use by blacks of pot, coke, crack, inhalants, and hallucinogens dropped between 1991 and 1993, and in the latter year only 0.2 percent of young blacks were smoking crack.[13]

In every respect the contrast is sharp between the black unemployed, many of whom are unemployable at the minimum wage set by law, and the recently risen middle class. When income or any other attribute of blacks is given by a median or average figure, this depicts the bottom of a U-shaped curve, where the smallest number of persons are located. There are many with low or very low incomes and many also with middle-class incomes, but there are fewer between the two extremes.

Whatever one might have anticipated from the improvements in the welfare of many blacks since the 1960s, in fact the division between blacks and nonblacks has widened—"in residence, in school achievement, in economic conditions, in family patterns, in attitudes."[14] The shift in attitudes as indicated by the most prominent black leader has been especially striking, from the integrationist program of Martin Luther King, Jr. to the racist and anti-Semitic ranting of Louis Farrakhan.[15]

Changes in Identity

The past transformation of blacks' social status and life chances brought about fundamental changes in their self-identification. Contrary to what one might expect, when oppression was harshest, the usual reaction was to seek the maximum integration. With the recent considerably reduced discrimination, the greater latitude resulted in a sharp increase in black nationalism, particularly among some of those who had risen farthest. As I have noted in several contexts, this is the opposite of what idealistic opponents of racial segregation anticipated.

As slaves, blacks had no say in any public matter. For many years after emancipation, when it was difficult to advance or in the worst periods even to maintain oneself, the occasional especially talented or lucky individual who succeeded usually modeled himself on the white middle class. Once the barriers had been significantly lowered and large sectors could get ahead, this widespread upward mobility was accompanied by a new emphasis on ethnic values. Elements of past history that once had been deliberately ignored or suppressed were revived to reinforce group solidarity, which it was hoped would result in a further advance of the whole race.[16]

There are now bookshelves full of works on black identity and how and when it had changed. William E. Cross, Jr., an American psychologist who is himself black, has timed one major turnabout, the shift from "the period during which the Negro self-hatred thesis evolved" (1939–1968) to "the period of nigrescence in which Blacks affirmed the evolution of a 'new' Black identity" (1968–1980).[17] The term *nigrescence,* which he apparently coined, he defines as "the process of becoming Black," that is, the transformation of identity from Negro to black.[18] In an appendix he summarized forty-five other analyses of black identity, and in a similar work a dozen more studies are listed.[19] This research has concentrated on the most recent of several major shifts, marked by the move from Negro to black as the preferred identification.

The succession of official or quasi-official designations, as summarized in the *Encyclopedia of Black America,*[20] is one indication of the changes in identity. For some decades after the Civil War the usual polite name was *colored,* which avoided the connotations of both blackness and African origin. Its use declined from the 1950s, and it probably would have disappeared altogether except for its retention in the name of the NAACP, the National Association for the Advancement of Colored People. (The former Colored Methodist Episcopal Church, commonly known as the CME, changed the "Colored" to "Christian.")

The designation *black* became taboo during the first decades of this century, but *negro* (which is Spanish for black) and eventually *Negro* were coming into increasing use over the same period. During the 1960s usages began to diverge among group leaders. Roy Wilkins, long head of the NAACP, wrote in his syndicated column that he would continue to call himself a Negro, but younger or more radical spokesmen insisted on being called blacks (or Blacks), reflecting their "black consciousness" and their desire for "black power." The publishers of the *Negro Digest* changed the name of their magazine to *Black World.* During the same several decades the link to Africa, once regarded as especially offensive, began to be emphasized. Afro-American was popular in the 1960s, and by the 1990s *African American* had become the politically correct designation. However, according to a survey by the Joint Center for Political and Economic Studies, a black think tank in Washington, *black* is the appellation that most in the ethnos still favor.

Each of these changes in designation was insisted on with great emotional fervor. When they were taboo, negro or black connoted, in Low and Clift's summary in the *Encyclopedia of Black America,* "bad, ugly, inferior, bestial, or subhuman." Yet only a short time later many blacks and some whites used comparable epithets to condemn those who did not immediately discard *colored* or *Negro* and substitute *black.* If a person calls himself a Negro and refuses to be identified as a black or African American (or vice versa), what is a statistical agency to do when it is trying to count all in the category irrespective of the current label? The response of the Bureau of the Census in the 1990 schedule was to offer a choice of designations and thus to coalesce the responses into a single aggregate. It would have been interesting if instead the Bureau had accepted the different self-identifications as names of distinct subgroups rather than, as it assumed, alternative names for precisely the same sector of American society. The dogma that all persons in a race are essentially the same has survived the manifest differences between two groups widely separated by virtually every social index.

The group name that most persons in the minority seemingly preferred at various periods, a significant datum in itself, illustrates more general differences that can be exemplified with other indicators. The designations colored, Negro, and black (or African American) roughly delineate three stages in the political orientation of the subnation.

In what we may call the colored period, the ideal girl or woman had a light skin, thin lips, and "good" hair. Some of those light enough to pass as white shifted their racial identity. Obviously any estimate of the number who moved into the white population can be no better than a plausible guess, but apparently the phenomenon was once relatively common, more prevalent in the United States than in countries with a formally recognized intermediate sector of mixed ancestry.[21] In theory, it should be possible to estimate the number who moved from one racial category to another by calculating an intercensal natural increase from birth and death records and then comparing that figure with the growth of population as shown by the two census counts. This has been done to determine the number of blacks who passed[22] and, more recently, the number of light-skinned Negroes previously counted as whites who expressed their black pride by changing their identity in the opposite direction. However, the vital statistics and enumerations of blacks are too imprecise to give much confidence to a calculation that depends on both sets of data.

Several decades ago some small groups with black-Indian-white forebears successfully protested against their classification as Negro in the census and were reclassified as Indian, which in the South of that time was a step up.[23] As noted by a scholar then at the Bureau of the Census, granting a new name for triracial groups was a recurrent problem. In Robeson County, North Carolina, the number of Indians enumerated grew from 174 in 1890 to 16,629 in 1940, a miraculous rise if one interpreted it as the consequence of a natural increase. In 1930 the so-called Issues of Amherst County, Virginia, wanted to be counted as Indians, but state officials insisted they be listed as Negroes.

> The controversy waxed so hot that the census taker refused to enter their race altogether. He turned their schedule in with that column blank and passed the problem on to the district office, where a decision was made to count them as Indian. The mixed bloods of Rockingham County, North Carolina, declared themselves as white to the enumerator. According to the statement of one of their leaders, the enumerator listed them as white in their presence but changed the race entry to Indian after leaving their homes. This they resented very much.[24]

So long as the designation of race was set by an enumerator, his decision was almost a random factor. The Cajuns in Alabama, for instance, were listed by different enumerators as white, Negro, Indian, and Cajun.[25]

The slogan "Black is beautiful," often repeated over the next decades, was intended to transform much more than the perception of beauty. The phrase broadened into a "struggle for the image," sought in both belles lettres and social commentary.[26] Blacks in the United States concurred with those elsewhere in a worldwide celebration of négritude.[27]

The black subculture was once defined as standard American culture truncated by educational deprivation. Summarizing this earlier view with respect to speech, Gunnar Myrdal held that "the so-called 'Negro dialect' is simply a variation of the ordinary Southern accent...in lower-class slang form.... Only a few dozen words and phrases are uniquely Negro, except possibly in some isolated Southern rural areas."[28] Now the fashion is to recognize a way of life with significant transfers from Africa, and accordingly some have now defined the speech of lower-class blacks as a genuine dialect. It is said to have derived along Africa's west coast (as with Swahili along the east coast) for the greater convenience of slave traders.[29]

Black English is said to be superior in some respects to the idiom of middle-class whites. "Because it has a system of tenses which indicate degrees of pastness and degrees of futurity, it can talk about how long ago things didn't happen, or how far ahead they aren't going to happen. English does not do this in its verb system; Black English does."[30] "This language *difference*, not deficiency, must be considered in the educational process of the black ghetto child. In 1953, the UNESCO report regarding the role of language in education stated that: 'It is axiomatic that the best medium for teaching a child is his mother tongue.'"[31] Nor, according to some devoted to the new doctrine, is instruction in Black English merely a bridge to learning English. The author of a work on Negro clergymen, for example, held that they are more successful if they have become "bilingual," preaching to their parishioners in Black English and communicating with the broader community in "'standard' American English."[32] A court in Michigan reinforced the trend and went one step farther. The judge required teachers in public schools to learn enough Black English to communicate effectively with their black pupils.[33]

Models to Emulate

Another index of the several transitions in self-identification is the marked difference in prominent leaders' characteristics. Booker T. Washington (1856–1915), born a slave, was the dominant black spokesman during his lifetime.[34] As president of Tuskegee Institute, he helped teach craft skills to a generation of blacks so that they could become self-dependent. "We shall prosper," he asserted in 1895, "in proportion as we learn to dignify and glorify common labor and put brains and skill into the common occupations of life."[35]

W. E. B. DuBois (1868–1963) was born in Massachusetts, graduated with honors from an integrated local high school, and eventually earned a Harvard

Ph.D.[36] According to an obituary of Booker Washington that DuBois wrote for the NAACP's *Crisis* (December 1915), he was "the most distinguished man, white or black, who has come out of the South since the Civil War." Even so, he bore "a heavy responsibility for the consummation of Negro disfranchisement, the decline of the Negro college and public school, and the firmer establishment of color caste in this land." Both Washington and DuBois wanted an eventual full integration of blacks into American society, but they differed in their timetables and programs, as well as in their perception of the typical black.

DuBois was an elitist, delighted by elegance and aristocracy, an indubitable member of the Talented Tenth that he wrote about, one who was prevented from realizing his full potential by American racism. For some years Herbert Aptheker, a Communist student of American blacks, took every occasion to stroke his ego; and on Soviet-sponsored trips to the USSR, DuBois was greeted everywhere with contrived enthusiasm. Ultimately he joined the Communist party, exiled himself to Ghana, and became a Ghanaian citizen. As a disillusioned fighter for civil rights, he ended as a showpiece for totalitarianism.

To some degree the contrast between Washington and DuBois persists as alternative policies for American blacks. As the American economist Glenn Loury pointed out, when Clarence Thomas replaced Thurgood Marshall as the only black on the Supreme Court, it was as though one ghost had succeeded the other.

> Of course, the DuBois-Marshall view is today's orthodoxy, an orthodoxy defended fiercely by the civil rights establishment from the criticism of radical dissidents (like Thomas).... But there are signs that a new era is dawning, and that...the principles laid down by Booker T. Washington will be rediscovered and play an important role.[37]

A third prominent leader was Marcus Garvey (1887–1940), a Jamaica-born black nationalist.[38] In 1914 (or a year before Booker Washington died), he founded the Universal Negro Improvement Association (UNIA), designed "to promote the spirit of race pride" throughout the world and to foster a movement "back to Africa." Within a few months of its first issue in 1918, *Negro World,* published by the organization, became one of the country's leading Negro weeklies, with a circulation estimated at perhaps as high as 200,000. The following year Garvey was able to purchase a large auditorium in Harlem, which he dubbed Liberty Hall, the headquarters of the UNIA. He also incorporated the Black Star Line, an all-Negro steamship company that would link black peoples the world over; starting with a stated capital of $1,000, it was capitalized at $500,000. Garvey also organized a Negro Factories Organization, whose declared purpose was to build factories in the Americas and Africa and to manufacture "every marketable commodity."[39] However, from a high point at the 1920 convention of the UNIA, Garvey's fortunes quickly sank. In 1922 he and three Black Star associates were charged with mail fraud; Garvey conducted his own defense and was convicted. Two years later he was indicted for perjury and income-tax evasion, imprisoned, and, after President Coolidge commuted his sentence, deported. He died in London at the age of fifty-three, an apostle of race pride and self-help some decades before these became routine slogans of black advancement.[40]

A pioneer of a different type was the white American anthropologist Melville J. Herskovits (1895–1963). He did field work in West Africa, the Caribbean area, and the American South; and in *The Myth of the Negro Past* (1958) he used the data he had gathered on institutions, names, languages, and material artifacts to document his thesis that much of the culture of New World blacks was rooted in Africa.[41] Though transfers of culture traits were both more numerous and more consequential elsewhere in the Americas, Herskovits uncovered them also in the United States. For instance, "African religious practices and magical beliefs are everywhere to be found in some measure as recognizable survivals." Or, "Negroes have evolved a real folk music which, while neither European nor African, is an expression of the African musical genius for adaptation that has come out under contact with foreign musical values." Or, most significantly, "Negro common-law marriages in the United States...are directly in line with African custom...[as is also] the 'self-sufficient' woman who, in the United States, desires children but declines to share them with a husband."[42]

If Herskovits had been a black rather than a Jew, today's "African Americans" would probably acclaim him; but when *The Myth of the Negro Past* appeared, it ran counter to the then prevalent doctrine that slavery had erased all links with Africa and, thus, that the history of the American Negro had started *de novo* in the United States. There was a running debate between Herskovits and E. Franklin Frazier (1894–1962), his generation's leading black sociologist, who resolutely defended the conventional view of the day.[43] The differences between the black family and the general American norm— more consensual unions, a higher incidence of illegitimacy, a more important role of the female—Frazier ascribed exclusively to the destructive influence of slavery and post-emancipation urbanization. He retained this position still in the revised edition of *The Negro Family in the United States,* which was published posthumously in 1966.[44]

A final example is suggested by the reaction to a government report, *The Negro Family: The Case for National Action* (1965). Written by Daniel Patrick Moynihan and issued by the U.S. Department of Labor, this work was intended to lay a basis for remedial action that, it was hoped, would help alleviate the well-documented plight of inner-city blacks. Nothing in the diagnosis was new. Like the title, the general thesis was borrowed from Frazier's *The Negro Family*; the statistics were from government reports and their interpretation from works by competent analysts, both white and black. The flood of scurrilous abuse pitched at Moynihan was remarkable.[45] Most significant was a defense of what came to be called the "one-parent family," rather than any of several terms suggesting that reproduction out of wedlock is morally and socially reprehensible. According to a view evolving at the time, higher rates of illegitimacy among American blacks reflected not a breakdown of middle-class standards, but conformity to a different norm governing not only the family but the whole of black culture. In 1994, 47.9 percent of households of blacks had no spouse present, contrasted with 10.5 percent of those of whites.[46]

Over the decade 1968 to 1977 the U.S. Supreme Court considered fourteen cases challenging a state or federal statute related to illegitimacy, and in ten instances each was judged to be unconstitutional. At the beginning of that decade every state had the right to promote family life by penalizing the parents of children born of extramarital relations. By its end, this deterrent was condemned as "illogical and unjust" to the innocent children.[47]

The change in marital norms, both statistical and moral, was reflected also in the practice of the Bureau of the Census. In earlier enumerations no direct questions had been posed about children born out of wedlock, for it was believed that the responses would not be sufficiently accurate to be useful. In the 1970 census, for the first time, unmarried women filling in the schedule themselves were asked how many children they had borne; those interviewed by an enumerator were asked the question only if children were present. Since 1976 the annual overall Current Population Survey has included questions on the number of children borne and the expected number of additional births, both queries put to women regardless of their marital status.

The Statistical Record

The data compiled on blacks are often of dubious utility, sometimes seriously misleading. The undercount of young black males is so large as to make one question any conclusions relating to the population that includes that sector. A considerable proportion of those recorded as having been counted, moreover, are only imputed. Even if we ignore all the defects in the counts of blacks, there remains the problem of interpreting the figures.

Before the Civil War, slaves were distinguished from freedmen; after emancipation, a similar distinction was made by counting blacks and mulattos separately. But before roughly 1945, or perhaps 1964, the status of being black was overwhelmingly decisive in any person's life, and the subgroups distinguished by these classifications were essentially one with respect to segregated institutions and poor life chances. During the following several decades, the homogeneity imposed by white rule has largely dissipated. Negroes' aspirations differ greatly between the now significant middle class and those in the continuing black slum, and their success in realizing their hopes deviate just as much. Statistical tables about blacks relate to a population with no more than remnants of unifying attributes, and generalizations based on such tables are likely to be at least partly false.

As noted earlier, one of the ten Interagency Working Groups the Bureau of the Census set up to prepare for the 1990 enumeration related to race and ethnicity. This IWG, composed of representatives of federal agencies and other organizations that made use of census data on ethnicity and race, provided a basis for decisions on terminology, what to include, the order of items, and similar matters. Only a few of its recommendations pertained to blacks: that the word *race* be retained; that the category labeled "Other races" be restricted as much as possible, for example, by editing such multiple-race responses as "black-white" into one of the two components. Four tests of alternative procedures were made during the 1980s. The question on race, asked of all persons, "does not denote any clear-cut scientific definition of biological stock. The data represent self-classification by people according to the race with which they identify themselves."[48]

6

Who is an American Indian?

From one enumeration to the next, the Bureau of the Census and its predecessors were inconsistent in setting the portion of the population that it should classify as American Indians, who of all minorities have been counted most erratically. Strangely, most of the vast array of writings on Indians pass over the crucial issue of how this population is to be defined. An encyclopedia on Indians and most of the references it cites, for example, assume that the identity of the minority's members is too obvious to be discussed.[1]

Diversity among tribes was once notable, and to some degree still is. A physical anthropologist might classify Indians as one of the world's major races, and the white men who first encountered them also saw them as one; but the pre-Columbian populations hardly constituted a unit in any other sense. According to the American team of anthropologists, Charles and Florence Voegelin, the Indians of North America spoke a total of 221 mutually unintelligible languages, not including contiguous dialects that permitted a minimal communication.[2] Such other basic cultural elements as means of subsistence, religion, and family organization also differed greatly.

Since American colonies and later the various governmental units of the United States signed treaties with *tribes,* it is especially important to note how much variation existed in political organization. In about half of the California culture area, the extended family was the largest unit; in the other half, two to six extended families combined into tribelets, some of which had definite territories. Even the Navajo, now the largest of the Indian communities, may never have had a centralized political organization. According to Willard H. Hill, a specialist on the subject, "Speaking in a strictly political sense, a Navajo tribe does not exist.... The Navajo have never functioned as a unit in a concerted action...or been brought, even temporarily, under the leadership of a single person or individual group for a common purpose."[3]

In the Midwest and East the commonest organization was a band or village. Shoshone-speaking Comanche, for instance, never got beyond the band stage. Though the Cheyenne had a civil council of forty-four chiefs, none of them could ever exert the force needed to carry out the council's will. The League of the Iroquois (with a total population of 10,000 to 17,000) was the largest and best organized federation—which, however, split during the American Revolution to support both sides.[4]

In other words, not only was the concept of *Indian* (as well as the name) a product of white contact, but many of the tribes with which treaties were signed also had a dubious existence. In what may prove to be a key lawsuit, an attempt in the late 1970s by the Wapanong tribe in Massachusetts to reclaim some 11,000 acres of Cape Cod, valued at more than $30 million, failed in court. The jury found that on several of the crucial past dates the Indians were not a tribe but rather an ethnic community, with no more rights than any other such group.[5]

The wide diversity in cultural and political organization was reinforced by violence, feuds, raids, and wars. According to the American anthropologist Harold Driver's well-documented account, "Probably as many Indians were killed fighting each other after white contact as were killed in wars with whites." On the Plains and in the East, warfare was an established institution, motivated by hope for economic gain, intergroup jealousy, and desire for personal prestige. "No young man ever thought of getting married or of being accepted as an adult citizen until he had slain an enemy and brought back a scalp to prove it." In the East prisoners were commonly "tied to a stake, frame, or platform and tortured with fire, blows, mutilation, stabbing, shooting with arrows, or dismemberment...[for] a few hours to a few days. The remains of the victim were often eaten in a cannibalistic feast."[6] In the area of the first European settlements these methods of combat were used also against whites, some of whom imitated them in reprisal.

Early counts of the pre-Columbian population do not inspire much confidence in their accuracy. Indians in the United States area sometimes used wampum (strings of shell beads) or bundles of little sticks to count people, but unlike the Incas in South America they had neither regular enumerations nor any cumulation of data. Some colonial administrators offered estimates or guesses, most credible when the populations were more or less peaceful. Their figures concerning more distant settlements were generally based on reports or rumors from hunters, traders, or soldiers.[7] According to the seventeenth-century Boston clergyman Cotton Mather, New Englanders of his day felt themselves "assaulted by unknown numbers of devils in flesh on every side,"[8] and it may well be that some of the estimates were influenced by the pervasive fear and were therefore exaggeratedly large.

Among the most knowledgeable of the colonial officials was Cadwallader Colden, scientist and lieutenant governor of New York, who wrote *A History of the Five Indian Nations*—which, however, had no systematic report on their population. Like others at that time, Colden was especially interested in military manpower, whether English, French, or Indian. Colonial governors were under standing orders to supply London with the fullest data possible on the size and state of the militia and its potential expansion in an emergency.

In their reports to the Board of Trade, the governors repeatedly noted how the loss of many young men in conflicts with Indians had adversely affected also the rest of the population. Because of this focus on the defense of the colonies, some estimates of Indian populations comprised only the number of fighting men among hostile tribes.[9]

One of the first official accounts of Indian affairs after the establishment of the United States government was an 1822 report to the Secretary of War by the clergyman and geographer Jedediah Morse. His table of tribal populations totaled only 471,417. As Morse noted in another work, "The hand of Providence is noticeable in these surprising instances of mortality among the Indians to make way for the English. Comparatively few have perished by wars. They waste and moulder away—they, in a manner unaccountable, disappear."[10]

The wide range of guesses about early Indian populations suggested to Woodrow Borah, an American historian who has focused on the pre-Columbian population of Mexico, that more than data went into the construction of estimates. Most who have written on the demography of that period, he remarked, can be identified with either of two schools. The first saw Indians' social structure as simple, their economic surpluses as scanty, and their populations as small until they were affected by social and economic progress. In the typical view of the second school, social structures were complex, surpluses were large, and population trends cyclical.[11] Both points of view are valid, though of different sectors of pre-Columbian populations.

Retrospectively raising the cultural level of Indians north of the Rio Grande reflected the political climate of the 1960s, for the higher estimates of precontact populations implied that the losses from "genocide" were greater and that larger reparations were therefore owed to the victims' descendants. What may seem at first to be an esoteric exercise, the estimation from poor sources by sometimes dubious methods of the numbers of people long dead, became decidedly pertinent to current political issues.

The classic analyses of the population north of Mexico were by James Mooney, an early twentieth-century ethnologist with the Smithsonian Institution. From a tribe-by-tribe compilation he estimated the total of earlier populations to have been 846,000 in the contiguous territory of the United States, 220,000 in British America, and 72,000 in Alaska[12]—figures that a number of subsequent analysts accepted in the main. The highest estimate of the pre-Columbian population of the United States area was almost ten times Mooney's figure, the 8.3 million offered by the American anthropologist Henry Dobyns.[13] Several other authorities have criticized his anomalous figure.[14] Perhaps the best guess, 1.8 million, was made by the American anthropologist team of Russell Thornton and Jean Marsh-Thornton.[15]

Changes in population estimates derived less from improved sources or new methods than from a change in orientation. Generally historians have started from some relatively recent data and worked back through accounts of massacres, epidemics, and other major causes of mortality to a presumed precontact population, which often proved to be higher than in earlier reconstructions. Other components of population loss, however, in particular the disappearance not through death but through race mixture and reclassification, have often been ignored. There has been much "interethnic migration," or a shift in ethnic designation from one enumeration to the next.[16]

South of the Rio Grande race mixture has been more generally noted, but not necessarily accurately recorded. In several countries where mestizos have become dominant culturally and politically, the census defines Indians formally by their mother tongue, in popular usage also by their dress. Concerning Mexico, the American sociologist Wilbert Moore suggested a range of "Indianness" from 100 percent for those who wear Indian clothes and speak only an Indian language to nil for those who wear European clothes and speak only Spanish.[17] As another example, the American sociologist John Early has analyzed a similarly ambiguous classification of the Mayan population in the Guatemalan censuses.[18]

In 1824 the Bureau of Indian Affairs (BIA) was organized informally as an agency in the War Department. Its first duties were to negotiate treaties and regulate trade with the growing number of tribes coming into contact with American settlers. Gradually it took over first custodial duties, then the administration of Indian affairs in general. Formally instituted and transferred to the Department of the Interior, it became mainly an administrative agency, assigned especially to distribute federal funds. The Bureau commissioned the ethnologist Henry R. Schoolcraft to survey the country's Indians, and his six-volume report provided estimates of the tribal populations of the East in 1789, 1825, and 1853, and of the Southwest in 1853 only. When the census volumes for 1850 incorporated some of the results of Schoolcraft's massive compilation, this was the first time any census discussed all Indians as a separate category.[19]

For the nineteenth century generally, the only data on the Indian population were BIA compilations of information it received from the agent or superintendent serving with each tribe. In his outstanding work on the Navajo, D. F. Johnston summarized the data available on that tribe, which can serve, *pars pro toto,* to characterize all the statistics collected on Indians during this period.[20] The "highly fanciful" early figures gradually improved to "inadequate" data. For 1877, as one instance, the agent had added fifty for each sex to the number in 1875, thus recording an increase over two years of precisely 100. This figure became the basis of the following years until 1880, when the agent raised the total by an arbitrary one-third. Other details suggest how difficult it was to get accurate information. Like many other primitives, the Navajo had no sense of precise age. Most reported their children by sex, usually giving first the names of all the girls and then following with a list of all the boys. Since the recording clerks were required to report the age of each person listed, they seemingly adopted the practice of assigning some plausible age to the first child named and then ages at intervals of two or three years to all the succeeding children. Thus, of the seventy families in the 5 percent sample that Johnston studied in detail, only five failed to show all the girls born before all the boys.[21]

Shifting Policies, Instant Indians

Since the beginning of the nineteenth century, federal policy with respect to Indians has gone through six major phases:

- up to about 1850, a continuation of the policy to reduce the threat of attacks and, through education, to prepare Indians for acculturation to American society;
- from 1850 to 1887, the establishment of reservations and the removal of Indians to them;
- from 1887 to the 1930s, the conversion of individual Indians into landowners and farmers by allotting to them a prorated share of tribal property;
- from 1935 to 1950, the reestablishment of tribal authority under the New Deal and continuing beyond World War II;
- from 1950 to 1970, "termination," or a renewed effort to end the special political status of the tribes and to integrate their members as individuals with the general citizenry; and
- since 1970, retribalization or self-determination, a reversal of termination.[22]

With each policy there was a corresponding definition of the Indian, based essentially if only partly on whether the aim was to foster assimilation or to preserve or revive tribal life. Because of the complex relations with various jurisdictions, however, no federal policy determined a single category of Indians. According to a brochure distributed by the Bureau of Indian Affairs, "There is no one Federal or tribal definition that establishes a person's identity as Indian. Government agencies use different criteria for determining who is an Indian. Similarly, tribal groups have varying requirements for determining tribal membership."[23] Each legal definition—enrollment in a tribe, tribal membership, adoption (for example, of a wholly white person)—has its own background of legislation and court decisions, which also varies from tribe to tribe.

Isolation from general American society has recurrently been preserved, or reconstituted, by tribal chiefs and romantic anthropologists. The more Indians have been tied to their relatively unproductive economy, the more they have required outside assistance. The reservations, ostensibly places (somewhat like South Africa's former "homelands") where Indians can develop their distinct cultures in their own settings, are maintained largely at public expense.[24] According to the 1990 census, the four main racial groups in the population broke down into two broad categories, with whites and Asians at the top by most social-economic indicators, and blacks and Indians at the bottom. Indians were better off than blacks by some indices, worse off by others.

Inevitably the legal complexity has increased with the growing number of federal entitlement programs, which established many new relations between individuals and either tribal or general institutions. The BIA has been continually condemned for the inefficiency of its cumbersome bureaucracy. However, whether the Bureau of Indian Affairs is more inefficient than the typical federal agency is moot, and most of its self-contradictory policies were mandated by Congress. That the distribution of public money allocated to Indians should preferentially be administered by other Indians, for instance, may have seemed a strange formula; but long before the term *affirmative action* was coined, it was in effect at the BIA. By a policy first enunciated in 1882 and repeatedly reaffirmed, Indians have received "absolute employment preference." Roughly half of the employees are classified as Indian, as well as probably a larger proportion of the agents in the field.[25]

More than any prior experience, the service of Indians in the armed services during World War II mitigated their isolation.[26] As early as 1911, a small number of well-educated young men had formed the Society of American Indians, which never attracted much support. A generation later such political organizations came into being as, among others, the National Congress of American Indians (founded in 1944) and the National Indian Youth Council (1961). The American Indian Movement, to which the news media have given most attention, may be even more alienated from Indian leaders than from "the white establishment." As one indication, after two AIM members were accused of complicity in the murder of FBI agents, the tribal council of the Navajo voted 48 to 0 against permitting the AIM to hold its convention on their reservation.

In 1948 Congress established an Indian Claims Commission, which was supposed to settle all demands against the United States from the founding of the nation. It was estimated—too optimistically—that its task would take thirty years, with a final cost to the rest of the population of over $1 billion.[27] Claims against one or another government for alleged past wrongs, supplemented by tribal income from such new enterprises as gambling, have induced many Indians to reidentify themselves with the tribes, countering both the pan-Indian movement and the inclination especially of younger persons to find their places in the American culture. According to a report in the *New York Times* (21 March 1976), a presumably authentic Mohawk commented that one consequence of federal programs had been a large-scale production of "instant Indians."

This offhand remark was echoed in a book with the appropriate title *The Invented Indian*. Its editor, James Clifton, is an anthropologist who has studied various tribes over several decades, and he describes "the Indian-rights industry" of his fellow academics with unusual candor. Typical is his account of how the Menomini were retribalized:

> The leaders of the large "restorationist" camp (mainly educated, middle-class off-reservation women), on one side, were the protégées of the liberal wing of Wisconsin's Democratic Party, spurred on also by flotsam on the rising tide of militant paleface feminism. The leaders of the small "pro-termination" party (all elder, mainly male, upper middle-class managers and entrepreneurs) in their turn were aided and abetted by the conservative wing of Wisconsin's Republican Party. And at the third point of this political triangle, the leadership of the late-coming, ferociously belligerent, recently improvised "Warriors Society" (mainly young, urban, lower-class males and the women who adored them) were covertly coached in their deftly played confrontational tactics by a political splinter group— Wisconsin's tiny band of zealous Trotskyites....
>
> On the one hand, the three main Menomini factions were actively milking their external supporters of whatever they could get. In turn, each collaborating with its chosen clique, the outside interest groups were playing out their own special agendas. Whatever the "Menomini people" needed or wanted was nearly irrelevant.[28]

The policy of retribalization, called sovereignty or self-determination by its Indian beneficiaries and their outside allies, Clifton regarded as "political-social segregation and the perpetuation of economic-cultural dependency." As a consequence of these moves of persons into and out of Indian identity, the statistical classification was repeatedly turned on its head.

Some of the regulations have induced tribes, contrary to the general trend, to reduce the number of persons enrolled. In 1954 a bill was offered in Congress to abolish the reservation of the Flathead Indians in Montana, for members of the tribe had become almost fully integrated into the general society. The chieftains, however, were able to forestall this threat to their prerogatives by tightening the rules for membership, so that of the 7,100 who by earlier criteria would have been members in 1970, only 5,500 were listed as actually enrolled. Even so, at the latter date no more than about 3 percent of the tribe's members were full-blooded Indians; one member in two lived off the reservation; and Indians living on it made up only a fifth of the recorded total reservation population.[29]

Thus, if widespread intermarriage and acculturation threatened the present validity of past treaties that Indian tribes had signed, the solution was to bar from membership persons with less than a specified quantum of Indian blood. And as more and more Indians moved into the general society, the preservation of treaty rights has retained special privileges for a smaller and smaller proportion of those once defined as Indians.

Enumerations of Indians

As has been noted, because the Constitution specifically excluded Indians "not taxed" from the population on which the apportionment of the House of Representatives was based, until 1890 they were ostensibly omitted from all enumerations. Because for many years the government had legislated and administered without first deciding over which sectors of the population it had the right to exercise such control, the problem of identifying Indians formally and legally became more urgent in the last decades of the nineteenth century. For example, a case had arisen concerning the allotment of land to which "Indians" were entitled; the Department of the Interior first followed a legal opinion that, as an American citizen, a child of an Indian and a white is not entitled to benefits due to "Indians" and then reversed itself. As early as 1856 the U.S. Attorney General had offered the opinion that the federal government should treat "half-breeds and mixed-bloods" as Indians so long as they retained ties to their tribes; but courts did not follow that lead—or any other. The 1892 report of the Commissioner of Indian Affairs discussed at some length "an interesting question [that] has recently arisen, namely, What is an Indian?"[30]

The routine comment that the 1890 census was the first to essay a count of all Indians is not really valid. Both in that year and in the immediately following censuses, tribal Indians were counted by agents attached to the reservations and nontribal ones by census enumerators, with many possibilities that those at the margin were counted either twice or not at all. In other words, the two sets of data continued as before, and that both were printed in the same volume was also not entirely unprecedented.

The volume of the 1890 census having to do with Indians is a mammoth ethnographic compendium to which data on population were almost incidental.[31] No reason was given why, with no change in the constitutional provision, it was decided to institute a complete count in that year, but one can suppose that it was because a new and more complex relation between Indians and whites had started with the end of the prior direct conflict. The number of Indians had fallen drastically during the nineteenth century, mainly because of the ravages of infectious diseases spreading through a fresh population, but also because of wars, relocation, social disorganization, and reclassification. According to Russell Thornton, the nadir was reached in 1890, when the 600,000 estimated for 1800 were down by almost two-thirds[32] (other approximations of the depletion have been higher). The year 1890 was also the time of the nativist movement associated with the Ghost Dance, which would revive the dead and unite them with the living in a regenerated land cleansed of white intruders. Membership in the new sect spread rapidly among Plains Indians and, as Thornton showed, especially in those tribes that had undergone the greatest losses in population.

The 1890 enumeration lists were destroyed by fire, and those from 1900 are therefore the earliest ones now available from a census after it was decided to include all Indians. When the 1900 enumerators' schedules were used to contrast returns from Navajo and Hopi, it was apparent that, though for different reasons, between a fifth and one-half of the two tribes had evaded the count.[33] Because most Navajo were seminomadic, they were so difficult to count that an agent asked for permission to exclude them from the 1900 census. His request was denied, but the published volume made no claim to accuracy. Both tribes opposed assimilation and, what they generally saw as a step toward it, the education of their children in government schools. In both cases such omissions affected not only the total count but also the age structure, which is a crucial datum for any demographic analysis.

The indicated number of Indians, 248,253 in 1890, fell to 237,196 in 1900 and then rose again to 265,683 in 1910. The decline and subsequent rise can be plausibly explained by the greater effort to include all who might be classified as Indians in 1890 and again in 1910, the years when special volumes were issued. As early as 1910 only 56.5 percent of those counted were portrayed as full-bloods, and the race mixture was interpreted as a symptom that tribal life was coming to an end. The "vanishing Indian" has been a recurrent theme of anthropological and popular writings.[34] The 1910 census was seen as a last chance to make a full count.

> In 1910 a special effort was made to secure a complete enumeration of persons with any perceptible amount of Indian ancestry. This probably resulted in the enumeration as Indian of a considerable number of persons who would have been reported as white in earlier censuses. There were no special efforts in 1920, and the returns showed a much smaller number of Indians than in 1910. Again in 1930 emphasis was placed on securing a complete count of Indians, with the result that the returns probably overstated the decennial increase in the number of Indians.[35]

With these changes in procedure and definition, the population fluctuated as though suffering from recurrent disasters. In 1940, when the count was again more restricted, the number enumerated remained almost static, presumably because the fall in the proportion of those included was canceled by the increase in actual population.

Several recent censuses have been subjected to a review by knowledgeable scholars, with disconcerting results. In 1950 the approximately 345,000 Indians counted did not include about 75,000 persons who would normally report themselves as Indians on such documents as birth and death certificates (30,000 mixed-bloods, plus almost 45,000 enrolled in federally recognized tribes). In addition, at least 25,000 persons not classified as Indians were entitled to legal benefits as members of tribes.[36]

From 1960 to 1970 the growth in the number of enumerated Indians was 67,000 more than the increase as measured by births and deaths. The excess was too large to be explained by errors in registration, an undercount in the 1960 census, or net immigration from Canada or Mexico. Seemingly a major part of the large difference was due to a shift in self-identification; persons who were listed as whites in 1960 chose in 1970 to be classified as Indians.[37]

In sum, there has been an intermittent but persistent growth in the indicated population, but what this means is difficult to say. There are several possible components: a real growth in numbers, perhaps a major fraction in the most recent period; a more nearly complete enumeration, based on the sometimes readier access to remote parts of reservations and the usually easier communication with Indians; a shift in self-identification, including the creation of "instant Indians" by various federal agencies.

There are approximately 300 Indian reservations and 500 tribes (including about 200 Alaska Native village groups). Many reservations have non-Indian landowners and residents, and fewer than half of the roughly 1.9 million persons classified as Indians live on or adjacent to reservations. The 282 federally recognized tribes merge into a single composite only in relation to the relatively few laws and administrative procedures regarding all Indians. Antipathies often persist from wars of the past, and some suits to validate one tribe's claims have been against not only the federal or another government, but also other tribes' competing claims. If even so one attempts to aggregate all those who are in some sense affiliated with any of the tribes, one should not expect consistent response to the query, Are you an Indian? Shifts in government policy, it is reasonable to conclude, have left the modal Indian with a thoroughly confused identity.

As an Indian, a person has been able to share the wealth of the tribe and acquire special access to education, employment, and medical care; and as a white he has evaded discrimination against Indians. Most writings on marginality stress the negative consequences of living in two cultures, but an individual can sometimes gain by alternately playing each of two roles. Indeed, Park's depiction of an incompletely assimilated immigrant as a marginal man was attacked particularly by Jews, who pointed out that life at the edge of two cultures could be not destructive but enriching, resulting in a greater creativity.[38]

One might suppose that the identity listed on a census schedule would be neutral, no matter how the respondent answered the same question in other contexts. However, the Bureau of the Census itself has insistently stressed the material advantages from a full count of racial minorities. In Chicago as in other cities with a sizable Indian population, local officials of the Bureau called a meeting to solicit help in improving the 1980 count.[39] In past censuses, group leaders were told, the significant underenumeration of minority groups (including Indians) had cost cities and their poorer inhabitants federal funds allocated according to recorded numbers. The discussion that followed, however, showed that many Indians were reluctant to be counted in the city because they were already reckoned as part of a reservation's population. When other factors are equal, tribes want to increase the number of those officially enrolled, for this figure also sets the amounts dispensed under various federal programs. Even the slightest sentimental attachment to the tribe would induce a potential member to enroll, if only because he would then become eligible for his share. Indians away from the reservation who avoid being counted because they are drawing benefits elsewhere might thus be recorded by the Bureau of Indian Affairs but not in a census.

In preparation for the 1990 count, the Bureau of the Census established an Interagency Working Group to set procedures with respect to American Indians or Eskimos and Aleuts. Overall guides to the selection of questions in the census was headed by a basic criterion:

> First, only essential data were considered—those with a broad demonstrated societal need and those needed to meet Federal, State, and local statutory data requirements and to administer governmental programs. These data would have to be needed for relatively small areas (local governments and small statistical areas) or numerically small population groups.[40]

The Interagency Working Group held two rounds of regional meetings with representatives of urban Indian organizations and officials of tribal or Alaska Native village governments. Advice was solicited on the content of questionnaires, enumeration procedures, census tracts, and outreach. Tests of various alternative formats were made as part of surveys during the 1980s. In spite of the general guide restricting the range of data to be collected, the Bureau decided to ask for the tribal affiliation of everyone who identified himself as an American Indian. Tribes are indeed "numerically small population groups," but one wonders about the supposed "broad demonstrated societal need."[41]

The report on the 1990 census warned the reader to use the counts of two Indian nations "with caution," for the Onondaga and Tuscarora officials did not permit enumerators to complete their count.[42] The census counted 1,878,285 American Indians, or 37.7 percent more than a decade earlier, but one should not take this figure as gospel. "In 1990, 8 percent of the 1.8 million people who identified themselves as American Indians then said they belonged to these tribes: Haitian, Polish, African American, Hispanic, or Arab."[43]

Conclusions

The United States government has never solved the question of how to deal with American Indians. It is hardly surprising that the vacillating general policy should have been reflected in inconsistent counts by the Bureau of the Census. The public has the worst of all possible consequences from this capricious lack of policy. More money is spent per person enumerated, one can assume, than with any other group in the population, for the listing of the tribal affiliation of every person who identified himself as an Indian meant a considerable increment in every step of counting, collating, and printing the data. Yet the statistics are so ill based that they are virtually worthless.

7

The Creation of Hispanics

The debate about immigration policy that ended in the restrictive laws of the 1920s has been repeated in the 1980s and 1990s. The principal difference is that in the second round the focus of attention has been on those entering the United States from Mexico. The issue cannot be precisely drawn, for we do not know the migrants' characteristics or even their number. Mexican Americans vary racially and culturally. The tradition that supposedly shapes their behavior is often crassly stereotyped and in any case differs greatly depending on where in Mexico they or their forebears grew up and when they came to the United States. There was a certain unity so long as most Mexican Americans were field workers in the Southwest, but a diversification has followed from the spread to other regions and to industrial jobs or professions in metropolitan centers.

The ambivalence of Mexican American identity derives in part from the ambivalence of Mexican identity. In the mid-1980s publishers in Mexico issued several books on the national culture—in particular, Guillermo Bonfil's *México profundo: Una civilización negada* (Deep Mexico: A Disowned Civilization), Enrique Alduncin Abitia's *Los valores de los mexicanos,* 3 vols. (Values of Mexicans), and Roger Bartra's *La jaula de la melancolía* (The Cage of Melancholy).[1] These authors' thoughts on the complexities of Mexican identity can be exemplified by the lines from the country's national anthem that Bartra quotes to introduce his work: "Its ruins exist, saying, This was the fatherland of a thousand heroes."

Who Are Mexican Americans?

"Attempts to form national alliances of Mexican American organizations have failed over the question, 'What do we call ourselves?'" and selecting the proper ethnic label has postponed or interrupted important social programs.[2] In the opening paper of volume 1 of *Aztlán,* a journal devoted to *Mexican American* interests, the literary scholar Fernando Peñalosa offered a tentative three-way classification:

- "Americans of Mexican ancestry," who regard their forebears as of little importance one way or the other;

113

- "Mexican Americans," who are constantly conscious of their ancestry, usually with an uneasy blend of positive and negative feelings about it; and
- "Chicanos," who are committed to the defense of Mexican American subcultural values as they view them.[3]

Omitted from this classification is the most distinctive subgroup among Mexican Americans—the *Hispanos,* descendants of those already residing in the Southwest when that territory was annexed by the United States. Most of them used to live in isolated villages somewhat reminiscent of Appalachian hamlets, where they were cut off not only from the outside world, but also from other Hispanos. There they maintained a way of life little changed from a century earlier. According to an appraisal written in 1945, their status was "a vicious downward spiral of ignorance, apathy, poverty, squalor, antiquated agricultural methods, badly balanced diets, shrinking and impoverished fields, resentment against discrimination, lack of confidence rooted in a feeling of inferiority, and exploitation by their own political leaders."[4] Over the following decades a shift to cities was followed by a significant rise in education, increased rates of out-marriage, and a greater use of English.

Another attempt to define Mexican Americans was made in a detailed comparison of Mexican politics in two American cities. In San Antonio, an economically depressed city where the average member of the minority has a slight chance of advancement, the political leaders have followed the traditional politics of assimilation. In Los Angeles, with far less racial discrimination and much better opportunities for moving up, Mexican American leaders have used the device of defining the group as victimized. The paradox arises, in the author's analysis, from the fact that the current political clichés, largely generated by universities and the media, have a greater impact in southern California than in the barrios of San Antonio.[5]

No Mexican American leaders of the past personify contrasting ideologies as precisely as Booker T. Washington and W. E. B. DuBois did for blacks, but the sociologist Ralph Guzmán has described three prototypes.[6] The first of these, José Vasconcelos (1881–1959), popularized the designation *La Raza.* A pious Catholic, he abstained totally from sexual relations and opposed the article in the Mexican constitution that in his opinion favored Protestant missionaries. Rather than an immigrant, he was an intermittent political émigré, waiting across the border for a chance to take his place in Mexican politics. He saw all Mexican Americans as *el México de afuera*—Mexico Abroad.[7] While in temporary exile, he sought the support of American officials and businessmen—for example, by defending "Yankee imperialism" in Latin America as the importer of capital, science, and technology, and by attacking American trade unions for excluding unnaturalized aliens from membership. In his view the mixed races of the world, including in particular Mexican mestizos, were genetically destined to become a *raza cósmica,* a superrace, that one day would inherit the earth. This racist doctrine, in Guzmán's view, was "the earliest and clearest case of a Mexican American ideology."

The second of Guzmán's prototypes, Arthur L. Campa (1905–1978), was a Mexican-born American, a Protestant and a Republican, a professor of modern languages at the University of Denver and director of its Center for Latin American Studies. His principal professional interest was in Hispanic folklore and culture, and in his view there are both racial and cultural cleavages between Latinos and Anglos. Though for centuries Iberians preferred lighter skin tones, in his opinion they did not reject darker shades or even dislike them. The American emphasis on punctuality, thoroughness, and practicality are alien to the Mexican folk culture, and Mexican Americans tend to react to their subordinate position not by acculturation, but by defense mechanisms that prove to be inimical to both sides.

George Sanchez (1906–1972), born in New Mexico and reared there and in Arizona, became the statistical director of the New Mexico Department of Education, later a professor of Latin American Studies at the University of Texas in Austin. He is best remembered for *The Forgotten People: A Study of New Mexicans* (1940)—"forgotten" because the Anglos who write history books ignore or obfuscate the part that Mexicans played in it. For Sanchez, Americans of Mexican descent are true patriots, a sentiment prominent among his middle-class contemporaries but hardly among the ideologues of the later protest movements.

Chicano, the currently fashionable designation of a Mexican American, used to mean a lower-class Mexican recently arrived in the United States, typically an unskilled field worker in this country temporarily. As used by Mexican Americans, it originally had decidedly pejorative overtones, but it began to acquire a kind of glamorous aura in the popular culture of the 1920s. A *corrido,* "El Chicano," begins with the line *"Ya me voy a trabajar al norte pa' ganarme yo much' dinero"* (I'm going to work in the north to earn a lot of money). From this sentimental usage, the word spread in the 1960s as an ideological label of young activists, who used it to designate all those of Mexican descent irrespective of class (though often, as in the case of "black," against the preference of the professional and middle classes).

In one explication, the word derived from *mexicano,* Mexican, with the first syllable truncated. Many children learning to speak Spanish change the velar consonant represented by x to the sound *ch*; presumably it was from this babyish form that chicano derived. An alternative conjecture is that the word came from *chico,* boy, once used in commands by Anglos to Mexicans: for the "Come here, boy" of the South in past times, the Southwest substituted "Come here, chico." With the suffix *-ano,* as in *mexicano* or *americano,* this became chicano, which softened the depreciating condescension of "boy" and eventually took on a positive value.[8]

As with black in place of Negro, Chicano was almost immediately adopted by official agencies as an alternative designation for those of Mexican heritage. Various lower courts in the Southwest used the term to identify an ethnic group guaranteed the rights listed in the Fourteenth Amendment and various federal statutes. When the Bureau of the Census offered the choice of Chicano or Mexican American in the 1980 and 1990 schedules, it was following the precedent set by other official bodies. The cooptation of a symbol of revolt was rapid and eventually almost total.

Like the Africanism of American blacks, Chicanismo has included a rejection of American society, marked by the search for symbols of social militancy in such heroes of the 1912 Mexican revolution as Pancho Villa and Emiliano Zapata. This Left orientation was the main political difference between generations, for the older Mexican American leaders had progressed far enough to see a brighter future for themselves and their kin in the United States. "To the middle class, social acceptance by the Anglo world was both desirable and possible. To the lower classes [and the radicals who wanted to attract their support], social acceptance was clearly impossible and thereby rationalized as undesirable. The first turned to the United States and the second to Mexico."[9]

But however much Chicanos have identified with Mexico, whenever the Mexican government tried to establish contacts with persons or groups powerful in the United States, it typically passed over persons with Mexican forebears. None of the various types of Mexican American leaders has been able to attract support south of the border. Businessmen seeking special consideration in getting contracts with the Mexican government have reportedly had little success. Intellectuals, though they have been more critical of the United States than of Mexico, would not be welcomed to conduct an independent analysis of the other government's record. Political appointees, who must be circumspect, are hardly able to foster relations with a foreign government. If leaders of Chicano organizations deal with Mexican officials, they risk undercutting their efforts to win concessions for the American minority they ostensibly represent. Members of Congress and other elected officials generally have constituencies of several ethnic backgrounds, and even the few whose districts are solidly Mexican American would not find unanimous support for establishing special ties with Mexico. One of the few officials who broke through the border was Ángel Gutiérrez, a judge of Zavala County, Texas, and founder of La Raza Unida party; thanks to his efforts, Mexico allocated $9 million to fund Chicanos' medical training in that country.[10]

Counts of Mexican Americans

Until 1920 immigrants from Mexico were treated in census statistics like Europeans, classified as part of the foreign stock for two generations and then not distinguished as a separate grouping. But the procedure did not seem to fit: the Spanish-speaking minority in the Southwest, it appeared, was not acculturating to American society but rather remaining more or less distinct.[11]

In 1930, the Bureau established the classification "Mexican" and placed those in it under the rubric "other races" (or nonwhites). This new designation was seemingly in accord with the sentiment developing in Mexico itself that its destiny depended on the exceptional quality of its mestizo population, but both the Mexican government and the U.S. Department of State objected to the new label as racist. In any case, there was a misclassification of the native-born of Mexican descent, particularly among those of lighter complexion or in the middle class. Hispanos do not see themselves as "Mexicans" or "Mexican Americans"; in 1930 they refused to accept those labels, as they still do.[12] New Mexico had an estimated 200,000 Spanish-speaking people, or about half the state's population. The census count was only 61,960 "Mexicans."

The fact that the racial criterion failed particularly in New Mexico, then the only bilingual jurisdiction, may have suggested to census officials the index that was substituted for it. In 1940, when a sample of the entire population of the United States was asked for its mother tongue, the response refuted the common assumption that the use of foreign languages generally disappears by the third generation. Nearly 22 million whites, or 18.6 percent of the white population, reported a mother tongue other than English. Of this rather large number, moreover, some 13.5 million were native-born, and almost 3 million of those had native-born parents. Among the languages listed, the most important were, in order of the numbers of persons using them: German, Italian, Polish, Spanish, Yiddish, and French.[13] Since the size of these ethnic minorities was not the same, the percentages retaining another language differed from this ranking, but Mexican Americans were clearly not the anomalous group they had been thought to be. According to a study in Los Angeles, Chicanos' shift to English was faster than had been anticipated, and the seeming loyalty to Spanish was due to the continuing large immigration.[14]

The Voting Rights Act of 1965, which was intended to protect blacks from procedures that limited their effective suffrage, was amended in 1975 in response to protests from Mexican Americans in Texas and elsewhere. The principal innovation in the amendment was that bilingual elections, which a few courts had already sanctioned, were made mandatory if more than 5 percent of the citizens in the jurisdiction were members of a single minority, if fewer than half of voting-age citizens voted in the 1972 presidential election, and if the materials pertaining to that election were only in English.[15] In reaction to such laws, a movement developed to establish English as the official language of the United States.

Since demarcation by race or language had proved to be unsatisfactory, in 1950 and 1960 the same population was counted on the basis of Spanish surnames. To the almost 7,000 Spanish names collected earlier by the Immigration and Naturalization Service were added some 1,000 others provided by specialists in Romance languages. Then one analyst supplemented the 7,718 names used by the Bureau with 11,262 others (including some from such subcultural regions as Galicia, Catalonia, and the Basque country), thus raising the number of American respondents classified as of Iberian origin by 21 percent.[16]

Since the name of the head of the household, at that time almost always the male, was used as the indicator, Hispanic women who married out of the group disappeared statistically, and non-Hispanic women who married in were added. A study of Spanish-surnamed Californians found that between a third and two-fifths married out, with little difference by age or sex.[17] According to one standard source, Martin is the tenth commonest name in Spain, but the Bureau omitted it from its list because it occurs frequently also among those of English, French, or German origin. Some persons with a Spanish surname had changed it to an Anglo-Saxon one. Among natives of such countries as Chile and Argentina, as also among the small proportion of immigrants from those countries, non-Spanish names are common. On the other hand, many Filipinos, who are classified as Asians, have Spanish surnames.

For all these reasons, using a Spanish surname as the index of ethnic origin resulted in a very large error.[18] Of those so identified, the proportion falsely classified as Hispanic with various coding techniques ranged up to 63.3 percent. Of those who identified themselves as of Spanish heritage, the range of those classified by name as non-Spanish went as high as 69.1 percent. In the five states of the Southwest, 81 percent of those with a Spanish surname identified themselves as of Hispanic origin, and 74 percent of those who identified themselves as of Hispanic origin had a Spanish surname. Outside the five states those percentages fell, respectively, to 46 and 61. By a rather relaxed standard, the Spanish surname "appear[ed] to provide a fair approximation of Spanish origin" in the Southwest but not outside that area.[19]

In 1970 the short form, distributed to 80 percent of the nation's households, had no question related to Hispanic identity. A long form distributed to 15 percent asked questions on birthplace, surname, and language, and another long form distributed to the remaining 5 percent asked about Spanish origin. With four ways of counting Hispanics, the Bureau of the Census produced four different estimates of this population, ranging from 5.2 million to 9.6 million. Inevitably criticisms of these efforts followed the publication of the results.[20] According to a letter to the Bureau director from a Chicano organization, the 1970 count of persons of Spanish origin was "a waste of taxpayers' money...wholly without scientific basis." Allegedly Spanish Americans were underestimated by half, with a resultant loss to the community over the following decade of "at least" $10 billion in revenue from federal programs based on the enumeration.[21]

Even if the data on the number of Mexican Americans were considerably better than they are, they would be rendered almost meaningless by the large component of illegal immigrants. By definition, their number is unknown, and guesses vary with the politics of the person offering the figure and other spurious factors. The number of illegal Mexicans apprehended and/or deported is often taken as an indicator of the size of the immigration, but a more important factor is how firmly the border is controlled at that particular time.[22] About 4 million people live close to either side of the 1,966-mile border between Mexico and the United States. Each day tens of thousands of Mexicans cross the border to work, and before the disastrous fall in the value of the peso, an almost equal number went to shop.

The flow back and forth, which has received recurrent official attention, is not new. Though formally the Western Hemisphere was not included in the immigration acts of the 1920s, consuls in Mexico were then instructed to enforce more rigorously existent laws limiting visas to literate persons who would not engage in contract labor or become public charges, thus cutting the movement by about three-quarters in one year.[23] Over the long run it has been the demand for agricultural and other low-skill labor that set the number of Mexican immigrants, many of them illegal under laws that are routinely ignored. It is thought that undocumented migrants now fill large proportions of the jobs in hotels and restaurants, the meat industry, furniture manufacture, and rubber and chemical plants. Whatever the size of the illegal population, it is likely to grow in the 1990s, for with the sharp contraction of their country's economy, the number of Mexicans who will want to seek work in the United States is bound to grow.

The Bureau of the Census intended to include illegal immigrants in the 1980 count, but whether an accurate count was possible no one knows. Because political representation and federal grants are allocated on the basis of the population counted in each district or state, it was possibly illegal to add such persons as part of the base. An organization called the Federation for American Immigration Reform (FAIR) brought suit to prevent the Bureau from including illegal aliens in the recorded population. After a lower court ruled against FAIR, the Supreme Court declined to review the case. For census officials the primary objection was technical: how could those in the country illegally be distinguished by normal enumeration procedures?

The relation between immigration regulation and the conduct of the count can be illustrated by one incident. After about 1,500 Phoenix citizens complained that they were being denied jobs because of unfair competition from illegal aliens, some 800 Mexicans lacking appropriate documentation were deported from that city. The reaction from the local Chicano organization was to denounce this as "a racist directive. Maybe they don't want Chicanos counted in the census." The local affiliate of an international Spanish-language radio network stopped its broadcasts of materials endorsing the coming enumeration. These protests were supported, moreover, by the local director of the census, who declared that the ten days of raids had undermined years of preparation, making it impossible to conduct an accurate count in the area.

Finally the Immigration and Naturalization Service announced that it would conduct no more sweeps until after the enumeration had been completed.[24]

The large influx of newcomers has seemingly aggravated whatever hostilities existed among Mexican Americans. Working-class Chicanos sometimes resent what they see as unfair competition that results in lower wages and higher unemployment, as well as a loss of status in the wider community. According to a *Los Angeles Times* poll in the mid-1980s, 40 percent of Latino respondents held that there were "too many" Mexican immigrants in California. From the other side, many of the recent immigrants see well established Chicanos as *Mexicanos falsos* or *pochos* (literally, overripe beings), people who have become so anglicized that they have forgotten their origins. Several officials of Mexican American organizations have voiced fears that relations between the two subgroups, already bad, would get worse.[25]

Inventing Hispanics

To recapitulate: reacting to the widespread belief that Mexican Americans retained much of their distinctive subculture beyond the second generation, the Bureau of the Census tried to find a measure that would supplement the standard data on the birthplaces of the respondent and his parents. In line with the general preference at that time, the first indicators were objective—race, mother tongue, and Spanish surname. The subjective criterion used for the first time in 1970 and then exclusively in 1980 and 1990 was in line with the present procedure of asking all persons to identify their ethnic origins.[26]

One fortuitous consequence of the experimentation with the several indicators of Mexican American identity was that a new grouping, *Hispanics* or Latinos, came into being; for not only Mexican Americans, but also many others spoke Spanish in their childhood and/or had a Spanish surname. Hispanic homogenization was not, of course, merely a process carried out by the Bureau of the Census. As the various countries of South and Central America attained independence from Spain, their political and intellectual leaders argued about how much their own national identities derived from a common Spanish heritage. In the United States the term *Hispanic* arose, according to some accounts, as a means of countering Chicano and Puerto Rican nationalism. During the 1960s two quite separate movements developed on the basis of both class and nationality, César Chavez's farm workers union and the Young Lords among radical Puerto Ricans in New York. In 1969 President Nixon proclaimed a Hispanic Heritage Week in tribute to the Spanish-speaking Americans and to promote ties with Latin American neighbors. "The question of why the very different historical and cultural legacies and experiences of the Mexican Americans and the Puerto Ricans were now to be homogenized precisely when their movements were emphasizing their indigenous Latin American roots, rather than Spanish European legacies, was never addressed."[27] According to an interpretation several decades later, Nixon's proclamation was "a conscious effort...to build a historically European Spanish-based and Spanish-dominated group rather than a regional 'Latin' group or a regional 'American' group."[28] Accordingly, Left intellectuals have rejected the designation *Hispanic* and substituted *Latino,* thus replicating the dispute over terminology of blacks, Chicanos, and most other militant groups.

As often as Hispanic/Latino spokesmen have demonstrated the diversity among the nationalities subsumed under that designation, most of them have also welcomed the greater political power derived from a larger sector of the American electorate. Not only in Washington but in many localities, such issues as bilingual education, the curricula in schools and colleges, alleged discrimination against Latinos, and so on have helped bring together at least some portions of the diverse aggregates.

The supposed unity of Hispanics is based on the fact that they all, to one degree or another, by one index or another, derive from Spanish culture. However, even if one ignores the different degrees of acculturation to the English language and American society, the varieties of Spanish differ significantly among the several subgroups, as is clear from studies of the distinctive dialect or language of Chicanos. A passage quoted from a 1953 manual, Pauline Baker's *Español para los Hispanos,* noted the "lamentable decadence of Spanish in the United States.... Every day one feels more the necessity of correcting the errors of poor Spanish that one must avoid and to develop the good Spanish that one ought to use." However, the deviations from Castilian or from standard Mexican are consistent among Chicanos and therefore, it could be argued, are acceptable as the beginning of a genuine new language.[29]

For the first time the 1970 census schedule asked respondents to identify themselves as of Mexican, Puerto Rican, Cuban, South or Central American, or other Spanish origin. The official census count of Hispanics originating in those countries was 1,508,886, contrasted with fewer than 600,000 in both the 1969 and the 1971 Current Population Surveys. As the Bureau noted in its report on persons of Spanish origin, "Some respondents apparently...interpreted the category 'Central or South America' to mean central or southern United States."

In the questionnaire for the 1980 census, the phrase "Central or South America" was deleted as confusing, and persons from that area were expected to identify themselves as Other Spanish. Indeed, over three million persons, or about one out of every five persons identified as Hispanic, did so. In ten states, the category Other Spanish constituted half or more of the total population of Spanish origin.

Perhaps no demographic estimates vary so wildly as those for the Hispanic population, ranging from 16.5 million to 30 million in 1985. Some researchers claim that Hispanics already outnumber blacks (they don't); others that the Hispanic population is growing by 6 or 7 percent a year (it isn't).[30]

In the counts from 1970 through 1990, the various ethnic groups of Hispanic origin varied greatly in median age, family type, fertility, education, level of occupation, proportion below the poverty line, median income—thus, on virtually every social indicator on which there are data.[31] Even commercial firms seeking customers among Hispanics often take care to differentiate among the several groups, following several notable gaffes. For instance, when an insecticide company launched one of its products on Spanish-speaking television, the commercial boasted that it was infallible in killing *bichos,* which in Mexico means insects, but in San Juan refers to penises.[32] When the Anheuser-Busch company translated its advertising slogan, "This Bud's for you," it found it expedient to produce four versions of the jingle: a hot salsa beat for Puerto Ricans in New York, a chiranga style for the Cubans in Florida, and two different mariachi arrangements, one for the Mexican population of Texas (who come mostly from the border region) and the other for those in the rest of the Southwest (whose subculture derived more from the area around Mexico City).

Puerto Ricans

Migration of Puerto Ricans to the Mainland has been greatly affected by the island's special relation to the United States. Ceded by Spain in 1898, the island first became an "unincorporated territory"; then, in 1917, Puerto Ricans were granted American citizenship. There was some talk of independence, but with a poverty-stricken population and an economy dominated by sugar plantations, Puerto Rico would have been devastated by the termination of its special federal benefits. Luis Muñoz Marín, a prominent *independista,* reversed his position and organized the Partido Popular Democrático, which for several decades governed the island under his leadership. Since in his opinion neither independence nor statehood was feasible, Muñoz argued for an intermediate "commonwealth," which was established in 1952. Under the so-called Operation Bootstrap that Muñoz helped establish, firms that located on the island not only gained by the lower wages there, but also paid lower local taxes and no federal taxes or tariffs on exports to the Mainland. (The special advantages have lasted a long while; it was not until the mid-1990s that Congress, anxious to balance the budget, talked of ending them.) By 1980 Puerto Rico had the highest level of living south of the Rio Grande.

As American citizens, Puerto Ricans have no legal barriers to their movement back and forth; and like other internal migrants, many go to the Mainland for a period and then return. According to a series of surveys in the 1960s, one of every three persons born in Puerto Rico had lived on the Mainland, typically staying there for about ten years during his or her adolescence or early adulthood and then returning to bring up a family or to retire.[33] The Spring 1968 issue of *International Migration Review,* which was devoted in its entirety to an analysis of Puerto Ricans on the Mainland, portrayed them as upwardly mobile and successfully assimilating to the general culture. Still in the 1970 addendum to *Beyond the Melting Pot,* Nathan Glazer and Daniel Patrick Moynihan saw "ground for optimism in a substantial shift into white-collar work," particularly by children of migrants from the island.[34]

However, judgments based on the immediate post-1945 decades proved to be oversanguine. It is true that those who live outside New York's Spanish Harlem are better off by almost every index, whether economic, familial, or social.[35] But about 60 percent of Mainland Puerto Ricans live in New York City, and they are close to blacks in education, level of occupation, income, fertility, and social pathologies. According to some sociologists, the "circular migration" of Puerto Ricans impeded their social and economic advance on the Mainland, for they never put down roots in the United States.[36] Such other analysts as Linda Chavez have pointed to the invitation in Spanish Harlem to become dependent on welfare.

[Puerto Ricans] have been smothered by entitlements, which should serve as a warning to other Hispanics. Paradoxically, the Mexican immigrant, even the illegal alien, who comes to East Los Angeles to work in a low-skilled job has a better chance of improving his economic condition and ensuring a better legacy for his children than the Puerto Rican born in New York City who ends up on welfare.[37]

The "Ricans," "Neo-Ricans," or "Nuyoricans," as the second generation in New York call themselves, speak a mixture they call "Spanglish." Their self-perception as depicted by some Left intellectuals has been dominated by a concern about language. One typical expression is a 1978 manifesto by a "Language Policy Task Force," which proclaimed that a "struggle over language in Puerto Rico" had resulted from the attempt to impose English on a hostile population, a policy supposedly being carried out through bilingual schooling. The statement originated at the Centro de Estudios Puertorriqueños of the City University of New York. After circulating in draft form, it was rewritten to accommodate comments from a dozen or so critics. This final version, thus, apparently represented the opinion of at least one substantial circle. The authors contrasted this "neocolonial" policy of bilingual schools with that in the Soviet Union, where, after some faltering under Stalin, minorities were "privileged" and their cultures were "protected." When it posed the question, "Can a Puerto Rican be Puerto Rican if he speaks only English?" the Task Force answered with a ringing "No."[38] A review of Puerto Rican culture in New York, as another example, followed the same political line. For instance, the dominant musical form, the salsa, was found to act as "an instrument of cohesion for oppressed people" and also to contain "all the corrosive features of a bourgeois cultural commodity."[39]

The concern over language became a principal issue in programs in bilingual education. Established initially as a means of teaching Hispanic children both English and other elements of the school curriculum, bilingual education was quickly transformed into an instrument for maintaining the children's native culture. Teachers who tried to maintain it as a bridge to quicker and easier acculturation were ostracized.[40]

Other Hispanic Sectors

In the heterogeneous category of Hispanics, the immigrants from Cuba are at the other extreme from Puerto Ricans. Fidel Castro came to power in 1959, and most of the immediate emigration was politically rather than economically motivated. Initially more than half of the exodus was classified as professionals, managers, and skilled workers, but over the following years the emigration became more diverse.[41] Since most Cubans migrated as adults, their population pyramid has been like an irregular rectangle, contrasted with the broad-based triangles of Puerto Ricans or Mexican Americans. Though many came as émigrés, intending to return as soon as Castro was overthrown, or as refugees, needing assistance to get settled, eventually most accommodated very well to a permanent stay in their new country. Both in Miami and in their smaller settlements in New York City and New Jersey, *Cubans* have established prosperous communities, with low rates of public welfare and other social pathologies.[42]

Cubans seemingly dislike being classed with other groups among the Hispanic population. In the opinion of Manuel A. Bustelo of the National Puerto Rican Forum in New York City, similarly, "The use of 'Hispanic' rather than specific groups has distorted realities. In many instances this has served to convey a more positive picture of overall advancement, while concealing the fact that Puerto Rican communities on the mainland are worse off than in previous years."[43]

Perhaps the best evidence of how different the various groups within the Hispanic category are is in a work titled *Latino Voices*. The authors write that "we share the view that recognizes the several Latino national-origin populations as distinctive and consider it culturally demeaning and conceptually indefensible to aggregate a priori all these groups under a single label."[44] They conducted a survey of 1,546 Mexicans, 589 Puerto Ricans, and 682 Cubans, defining each respondent as a member of that group if he or she, one parent, or two grandparents were solely of that ancestry. In 1990 these three subgroups made up almost 80 percent of those that the Bureau of the Census designated as Hispanics.

Overwhelmingly the respondents identified themselves by their national origin. When asked for their ethnic identity, more labeled themselves "American" than "Latino." Even so, they mostly agreed on what could be called the core elements of a liberal domestic agenda. But those who rated themselves from slightly to very liberal included only 28.5 percent of Mexicans and Puerto

Ricans and 22.9 percent of Cubans. More than 90 percent of all three ethnic groups supported the proposition, usually identified as a conservative position, that citizens and residents of the United States should learn English. Of those who voted in the 1970 presidential election, 62 percent of Mexicans voted for Michael Dukakis, 86 percent of Cubans voted for George Bush, with the Puerto Ricans almost evenly split.[45] Such political positions can be taken as a summary statement of the three typical cultural stances.

According to a Bureau of the Census survey, in May, 1994 the several components of the Hispanic population varied considerably in size and in several key attributes.[46] Two-thirds of the category were Mexicans, less than 5 percent Cubans. The median income ranged from just over $20,000 to more than one and a half times that. The percentage of the population rated as under the poverty level ran from a seventh to a third of the designated nationalities. Other characteristics varied by similar proportions, as suggested in table 7.1.

TABLE 7.1

	Percent of Hispanic Population	Median Family Income	Percent of Families below Poverty Level
Mexican	64.3	$23,714	26.4
Puerto Rican	10.6	20,301	32.5
Cuban	4.7	31,015	15.4
Central and South American	13.4	23,649	27.0
Other	7.0	28,562	21.7

Not only is the whole Hispanic population a miscellany, but none of the five units within it is really homogeneous. Why, then, did the Bureau of the Census establish the category "Of Hispanic origin"? Undoubtedly one main reason was convenience in summary tables, but this has proved to be a false hope. The Interagency Working Group on Race and Ethnicity, set up to prepare the procedures for the 1990 count, had more than the usual difficulty with Hispanics. It formed three subcommittees: Race and Spanish Origin; Ancestry, Place of Birth, Citizenship, and Year of Entry; and Language, each of which pertained to questions on how to delineate Hispanics.[47]

Within the Hispanic category, whatever differences there are between whites, blacks, and American Indians are masked, since those who classify themselves Hispanic may be of any race. Indeed, the most prominent procedural fault of the 1990 census was the overlap between nationality and race in the persons of Hispanic origin, who even in summary tables are listed in a separate column marked "of any race." Then there are two sets of racial categories, the first of totals and the second of persons "not of Hispanic origin."

The Bureau of the Census might point out, of course, that anyone interested in data pertaining to the particular nationalities included under the umbrella "Hispanics" can find such statistics if he goes beyond the most available sources. Indeed, but the public will get most of its impressions from the composite data. A compendium brought out by a private publishing firm offers data on Latinos in a presumably more convenient form. An occasional table breaks down the aggregate, but the bulk of the work presents the data pertaining to three populations: Hispanics, Whites, and Total. One table on persons below the poverty level gives five different definitions of that measure, but uses the dubious composite Hispanics, the even more dubious one Whites, and Total to inform the reader.[48]

8

Americans of Asian Stocks

To identify the ethnic background of European immigrants the Bureau of the Census asked them in what country they were born. This seemed to be a reasonable procedure, but most of those who came from Russia, as an egregious example, were not Russians. Then the Bureau took not one country but many quite different ones and combined them and their progeny into the heterogeneous category of Hispanics. With respect to Asians, the Bureau selected not a country but the largest continent, orchestrating into a single unit people with a background in any part of it, and then it added those with forebears from any of the quite diverse Pacific Islands.

It is true that anyone with enough interest can go beyond the summary tables and find data on each of the main Asian peoples. But it is also the case that most of those who use census data will depend on the aggregate source, which will thus be the basis of the interpretation given the general public. Moreover, several countries of Asia are no more homogeneous ethnically than Russia, so that even those who seek single-country statistics will not necessarily find numbers that can be meaningfully interpreted.

Compared with the number of Americans of almost any European lineage, there are relatively few whose forebears came from Asia. They nevertheless warrant a special discussion, for the influx from Asia has increased substantially, and unless immigration law is made more restrictive, this trend will continue.

Chinese

Settlements of ethnic Chinese in Malaysia (including Singapore), Indonesia, and Thailand were started in the seventeenth century. By the mid-1960s the total population of the so-called Overseas Chinese in Southeast Asia was around 12 million. An up-to-date estimate would not be more adequate, for the boundaries of ethnic Chinese are fluid, with shifts of identity in both directions. After the colonies in the area achieved independence following World War II, the already existent hostilities often grew sharper. In Indonesia tens of thousands of Chinese were slaughtered, allegedly because of their affinity with Communism. Singapore detached itself from Malaysia in large part because these two countries are dominated, respectively, by ethnic Chinese and Malays. In the 1960s the government of the Solomon Islands debated whether to deport all Chinese.

Of the large body of writings on Overseas Chinese,[1] one of the most interesting is by the British anthropologist Maurice Freedman, who challenged many of the routine stereotypes.[2] Some Chinese did not assimilate; others intermarried, adopted the native language, and lost most of the ties to their ancestral homes.

Manchu China forbade emigration, and both those who attempted to leave and officials who connived with them were subject to beheading. Like most of the country's other laws, this one was enforced mainly in the sense of enveloping emigration in crime and corruption. Many contract laborers, perhaps most, were kidnapped and shipped against their will. One of the most thorough of many investigations of how contract laborers were recruited and treated was undertaken in 1876, when Chinese, British, and French members of a commission gathered testimony in Cuba. Of a total of 40,431 Chinese shipped to that island, 80 percent had been decoyed, 10 percent had died in passage, and the survivors were taken to "man-markets" where they were "stripped and their bodies examined in the manner practiced when oxen or horses are being bought." Sold to the highest bidder, most went to sugar plantations.[3]

An annotated bibliography of works on Chinese in California goes back to 1850.[4] In the century and a half since then, the number of Chinese Americans has grown to only about 1.6 million. As immigrants to a population predominantly of European origin, they were set apart by their religion, culture, and social organization—as well as their race, under which other attributes were often subsumed.

However, American opposition to Chinese immigration in the nineteenth century, generally perceived in retrospect as simple racism, was actually more complex. Antipathy was often similar to classical anti-Semitism, a hostility toward a successful group that for a period retained a primary loyalty to its own members. The most principled opponents of Negro slavery were prominent in the effort to prevent what they saw as another system of slave trade.[5] In an outlandish alliance they joined forces with racists opposed to admitting any Asians. At first their efforts had little success. The Burlingame Treaty of 1868, which affirmed the right of Chinese to immigrate, led to riots in San Francisco and elsewhere along the West Coast. Two years later Chinese were barred from becoming American citizens, and China agreed that the United States had the right to "regulate, limit, or suspend" but not "absolutely prohibit" the immigration of Chinese laborers.[6] In line with those provisions, the Chinese Exclusion Act of 1882 suspended immigration of Chinese laborers for ten years, so that to remain in effect the bar had to be renewed each decade. The provision meant that anti-Asian agitation was given a recurrent focus, an issue around which those striving for a full and permanent ban could rally.

Statistics were especially deficient on Chinese immigration. They were prototypical sojourners, working abroad for a period with the intention of returning home. A large but indefinite number entered the country illegally, and Congress raised the issue time and again, taking testimony on the many means used to evade the exclusion law. Chinese going home would change places with seamen who deserted their ships. When anyone who had established a legal residence died, the document certifying his legitimate status was sold. According to one analyst, "the Exclusion Act actually helped thousands of Chinese, Americans, and Europeans to make millions of dollars by taking up smuggling as a regular and profitable business."[7]

On the basis of incomplete returns in a California state census, the number of Chinese in 1852 was 25,000; another local authority thought that 17,000 was more probable; and S. E. Woodworth, the legal representative of the Chinese community, gave its population as 11,787.[8] As in this example, estimates were often much influenced by attitudes on political issues related to immigration. For a considerable period more Chinese left than arrived, and many of those who remained lived in physical and economic isolation in Chinatowns, where the usual business was either to serve the Chinese community itself or to offer exotic foods and other commodities to tourists.

Other Chinese built the transcontinental railroad, then worked in mining camps and as field laborers. Many were relegated to tasks that white men regarded as women's work, and as late as 1920 more than half of employed Chinese worked in either laundries or restaurants. Legal impediments in imaginative variety were contrived to block their advance to middle occupational ranks. San Francisco, in a memorable instance, imposed a special tax on laundrymen who delivered their loads with a pole rather than by horse and wagon. Under a law that California enacted in 1913, persons ineligible for citizenship were not permitted to own agricultural land or to lease it for more than three years. After the U.S. Supreme Court found it to be constitutional, California's initiative was followed by ten other Western states.[9]

Whatever their number, most immigrants from Asia were young men. For example, according to the censuses of 1880 and 1890, the more than 100,000 Chinese males on the Mainland contrasted with only about 4,000 Chinese females. Until the laws were declared unconstitutional, Western states generally prohibited interracial marriages, so that for several generations a normal family life was all but impossible for most Mainland Asians. In Hawaii, however, Chinese often mated with women of other races, especially native Hawaiians.[10]

Most of the earliest Chinese immigrants originated in a small area of Canton province, and in their Chinatowns they painstakingly preserved family and community institutions. After more permissive regulations took effect in 1952, a sizable new influx started from Hong Kong, including many who had fled there from northern China when the Communists took power. Generally these newcomers could speak neither Cantonese nor English, and they usually had to live at the lowest level of the Chinese American economy. Many of their sons and daughters refused to accept that as their lot. Paradoxically some became vociferous supporters of Maoism. The number of hoodlums or criminals snowballed in the Chinatowns of New York and San Francisco until drastic actions by the municipal police forces reestablished control.

Japanese

Laws and regulations that discriminated against the Chinese, who were the first to arrive, were adapted to other peoples from Asia. For instance, restrictions against contract laborers, applied on a racial basis to Chinese, were extended also to the Japanese who followed them some years later. Sex ratios almost as skewed as those of the Chinese were characteristic also of the Japanese during the first decades of their immigration. The outflow from Japan, however, differed crucially from the shipment of Chinese coolies. After the institution of a new regime in 1868, the government of Emperor Meiji sought the maximum interaction with the West by bringing in foreign experts to restructure the country's economy and state agencies, and by giving aid to students and other Japanese traveling abroad. The government also encouraged emigration, much of which took place under official auspices and thus with continuing protection from Japan's consular officials.

In 1906, when the political machine ruling San Francisco decided to segregate all Oriental children into a single inadequate school, this local scandal developed into an international incident. President Theodore Roosevelt received an official complaint from Tokyo, and he dared not ignore it: Japan had defeated China and Russia in rapid succession, demonstrating itself to be a power that other nations had to respect. After almost two years of negotiations, Roosevelt signed the famous Gentlemen's Agreement under which the Japanese government undertook to restrict emigration to the United States to nonlaborers and relatives of United States residents. These relatives, it later turned out, were to include "picture brides"—that is, women in Japan married in absentia to men already in the United States. In substance the difference from the 1882 exclusion of Chinese was slight, especially after courts decided that Japanese were also ineligible for American citizenship. But temporarily face was saved on both sides.

From 1898, when Hawaii was annexed as an American territory, to 1959, when it was admitted as a state, confusion concerning its status in national statistics was a constant source of error, and this muddle affected especially the counts of Asians. For example, when the 1920 census reported that there were only 81,338 foreign-born Japanese in the United States, many questioned the accuracy of the datum: ten years earlier the census count had been

67,655, and during the decade the net immigration amounted to 67,108. If one allowed for the probability that in a population with many old people mortality would have been slightly greater than fertility, the 1920 figure represented an underenumeration of some 45,000, or about 55 percent. The racist press made much of the supposed error, but the discrepancy was only in how two federal agencies defined "the United States." By the usage of the Bureau of the Census, the territory of Hawaii was excluded, but the Commissioner of Immigration included territories—in both cases with no special warning to those using the tables. When the figures were assigned to the proper populations with estimates of the probable changes during the decade, the count in 1920 proved to be not lower but slightly higher than an extrapolation from 1910.[11]

Asian residents of the United States reacted to the series of discriminatory measures in sharply contrasting fashions: the Chinese retreated, the Japanese persevered. The typical Japanese grew or sold agricultural produce and was thus in constant and growing competition with white farmers, whose organizations amassed great political power during the interwar years. Most Japanese lived in one of the small rural communities scattered widely throughout the West. In several respects, thus, the Japanese were more vulnerable to legal and other harassment.

Even the modest number of Asians was pictured as a potential catastrophe. So prominent an academic as the sociologist R. D. McKenzie wrote a paper entitled "The Oriental Invasion" (*Journal of Applied Sociology*, 1925), and a book by the less distinguished Jesse F. Steiner, *The Japanese Invasion* (1917), had an introduction by Robert Park himself. By the 1920s, first through state laws or the decisions of state courts, eventually through actions of their federal counterparts, the restrictionists' program against Asians was achieved in a series of steps. The laws already enacted that targeted the Chinese were extended to all resident aliens who could not become citizens. Up to World War II, thus, however much the Chinese and Japanese differed, in the United States their similarities were greater, because of both the common elements of the two cultures and the parallel discrimination under American law. But during the war Chinese Americans benefited somewhat from the good will toward America's ally (in particular, the exclusion act was repealed), while Japanese Americans were stereotyped as enemies.

Across a large part of the West all Japanese Americans—a total of more than 110,000 citizens and aliens, men and women, grandmothers and babes in arms, gardeners and professionals—were transferred en masse to "relocation camps," where they were kept behind barbed wire and guarded by armed soldiers.[12] No charge of disloyalty was brought against any person; the basis for the evacuation of one whole ethnos (not German Americans or Italian Americans anywhere, or even Japanese Americans in Hawaii) was a loosely specified "military necessity." Indeed, in time of war extraordinary precautions are appropriate, but before the mass internment was conceived, the FBI and naval intelligence officers had already rounded up suspects, screened them on the basis of evidence concerning particular individuals, and imprisoned any who might have constituted a danger.

By the forced sale of their property or its destruction during their absence, the interned Japanese Americans incurred losses estimated by the Federal Reserve Bank at a total of $400 million. Under a postwar compensation program, payments totaling about $38 million were made to approximately 26,500 claimants, the last of them in 1965. Grudging justice was so long delayed that many plaintiffs had died before their heirs received amounts barely sufficient to pay the legal costs.[13] In 1988 the federal government tendered each of the approximately 60,000 surviving camp inmates $20,000 plus a formal apology.

During the post-1945 decades both Japanese and Chinese advanced at an extraordinary pace. According to most indices of economic and social well-being, by 1970 these two Asian minorities ranked higher than any other ethnic group identifiable from census statistics. The key figure may be the median number of school years completed—12.5 for Japanese and 12.4 for Chinese, contrasted with less than 10 for blacks, American Indians, and Hispanics. In part because of their better education, by 1970 Chinese and Japanese had markedly lower rates of unemployment, a higher proportion in upper-level occupations, larger incomes, and, as indicated by their housing, a better style of life.[14]

Beginning in the 1960s some Asians in the United States became politically active, joining a wide variety of organizations that sometimes cooperated in what was called "the Movement." The main base was the almost 110,000 Asian American college students, the main issue opposition to the war in Vietnam. A subordinate goal, more significant in this context, was to develop an identity and culture of their own as a basis for political power. In 1969 there was a conference about "Yellow Identity" on the Berkeley campus of the University of California. According to a sympathetic account by a former activist, "An estimated nine hundred Asian Americans, mainly Chinese and Japanese Americans from the West Coast...learned about 'Asian American history and destiny, and the need to express Asian American solidarity in a predominantly white society.'"[15] The political aftermath was slight. "Many of the early activists who had come to the program 'with energy, idealism and love' [left] feeling 'scorned, defeated, and burned out.'"[16]

Ironically, the accomplishments of Chinese and Japanese Americans were so great that new moves were made to block their advance. As an egregious example, in the mid-1980s the University of California reacted to the large number of highly qualified Chinese and Japanese applicants by setting quotas restricting the number of Asians that could be admitted. In 1995, after a law suit brought by Chinese Americans, the university's Board of Regents voted to rescind race-based quotas and permit Asian students to take the places they had earned.

Filipinos

When the American judiciary extended the exclusion of Chinese to other Asian nationalities, the U.S. Supreme Court found it impossible to set precise racial boundaries. Chinese and Japanese were unambiguously inadmissible, and in various decisions the same exclusion was applied to Koreans, Burmese, and Malays. "White" persons were found to include such marginal groups as Parsees, Armenians, Syrians (though in two instances only on appeal), and Mexicans (that is, not an Asian minority). What the Court did concerning persons of mixed antecedents was more confused, and confusing.[17] Finally this kind of restriction, modified in a series of immigration acts, was repealed altogether in 1965, thus redefining the community of potential Americans to include newcomers from anywhere in the world.

While exclusion was in force, Filipinos were in an ambiguous status, reflecting the quasicolonial relation of the archipelago to the United States. Spain's political rule had ended with the Filipinos' successful war of independence. In the Treaty of Paris (1898) concluding the Spanish-American War, however, dominion over the islands was transferred to the United States. The Filipinos fought a second war of independence and lost it, but the status of the country continued to be debated both there and by the American Congress and public. A 1916 law extended home rule and promised eventual independence, which after many vicissitudes finally was granted in 1935.

Six years later Japanese forces attacked without warning, and a joint Philippine-American army had to withdraw to Australia. After the war, the reestablished independent Philippines coped with a land devastated by fighting, a destroyed economy, and a population grown accustomed to political violence. In spite of some occasional hopeful signs, there was little to suggest that poverty and political corruption would soon end.

Several elements of Philippine history have been reflected in the characteristics of emigrants to the United States. When the islands became a territory in 1899, Filipinos were classified as American "nationals" rather than citizens. As such, they had the right to enter the United States freely but, once here, were subject to the same restrictions as other Asians. No one was happy with this compromise. Increasingly immigrants favored independence for their homeland, and nativist Americans wanted to block the loophole through which one nationality had evaded the bar supposedly erected against all Asians. Congress tried in several ways to adjust Filipinos' status. Under a repatriation act the government paid the passage of any in the United States who wanted to return home, but only one in twenty accepted the offer.

In recent decades more than two-thirds of Filipino immigrants have qualified as "professional, technical, and kindred workers," whose skills were needed in the United States. As a striking example, when many foreigners were being granted licenses as nurses, two-thirds of them were Filipinas, who were fluent in English and trained with a curriculum based on American standards.[18]

Apart from small minorities of Negritos (negroid pygmies) and Dumagats (related to the Papuans of New Guinea), Filipinos are Malays, conventionally divided by language and other cultural attributes into eight groupings. Some seventy languages, including nine important ones, are spoken by the islands' inhabitants. Tagalog, the speech of the provinces adjoining Manila, was the basis of Pilipino, which in 1946 was declared the national language.

Filipinos in the United States are divided into three somewhat antagonistic language communities. The mother tongue of most is not Tagalog or Pilipino, but rather Ilocano or Cebuano (a dialect of Visayan), and each group has established social and business relations in separate neighborhoods among its own kind.[19] Neither within itself nor from the outside does the category of "Filipino American" have firm boundaries. Even when they are correctly classified and counted, the statistics pass over the most meaningful cultural boundaries, namely those setting off each language community from the others. In the complaint of a would-be ethnic leader in San Francisco, "we are always lumped as Asians, Spanish-speaking, or whatever seems politically expedient."

Koreans[20]

Migration of Koreans to the United States started in the last decades of the nineteenth century as a movement of agricultural workers to Hawaii. Until contacts were established through America's post-1945 occupation of Japan and Korea and the subsequent Korean War, only a scattering of Koreans lived on the Mainland. In the following decade approximately 21,000 refugees and wives or children of American servicemen immigrated. Since restrictions on Asians were rescinded, Koreans have been one of the Asian nationalities settling in the United States in significant numbers.[21]

Most of the recent immigrants went to Los Angeles, where in one decade the number of Koreans grew from 5,000 to 150,000. About half of them have had a college education, and their move to the United States often entailed a fall from professional or administrative position to an initial low-status occupation. In the 1970s there were reportedly over 200 Korean Christian ministers in the Los Angeles area, most of them unemployed. The most frequent route to a better livelihood has been to establish a small business.[22]

Some Koreans have organized themselves into dozens of churches, schools, and ethnic organizations, of which the most important is the Korean Association of Southern California. Many, however, have taken no part in the ethnic community and have lived in relative isolation among strangers. Lines of tension developed between war brides (often of lower-class background), political émigrés (who seemingly expected the deference they had once enjoyed), and the later arrivals (who sometimes resented the established position of those who had preceded them). Too few have been in the United States long enough for the community to become interested in American political debates, but involvement with political struggles in Korea has also generated dissension. During their initial period in their new country, Koreans have had high rates of divorce, mental illness, suicide, and juvenile delinquency.[23] There has been a larger remigration than among other Asian Americans.

Indians and Pakistanis

Natives of India, who in other countries are called simply "Indians," in the United States had to be distinguished from American Indians. They have been labeled with several inappropriate designations, in particular "East Indians" (which used to refer to parts or the whole of Southeast Asia) and "Hindus" (alluding to only one of the religious components of India's population). The usual present term, *Asian Indians*, is preferable.

Whatever the designation, American courts long found it difficult to decide how to classify immigrants from India. Whether they could become citizens depended on how one interpreted a 1790 statute, which limited the privilege to "free white persons" (plus, according to an 1870 amendment, "aliens of African nativity or persons of African descent"). As "Caucasians," it was decided, Indians fitted under the rubric "white" and were therefore eligible. Between 1908 and 1923, as many as sixty-seven Indian nationals acquired citizenship through judicial procedures in no less than seventeen states. Bhagat Singh Thind, who was naturalized in an Oregon court, had his citizenship upheld on two appeals. On a subsequent appeal to the U.S. Supreme Court, however, the prior decisions were reversed. Justice George Sutherland, who had just written the majority opinion denying citizenship to Takao Ozawa, a Japanese, on the basis of race, followed with one denying it to Thind on the basis of color. In Western states authorities tried, only sometimes successfully, to rescind the citizenship of naturalized Indians and to prevent them from keeping the agricultural land they owned. Then, by another reversal of policy, in 1946 Congress passed a new immigration act under which "persons of races indigenous to India" could be admitted and naturalized.[24]

According to various indices, Asian Indians generally have no strong attachment to either the United States or India, but are tied rather to one of the many ethnic subdivisions of India's heterogeneous population.[25] Of the more than 100,000 who immigrated during the years 1965 through 1976, only 8,500 acquired citizenship—a seeming inconsistency with the earlier judicial disputes.[26] A number of natives of India testified before Congressional committees in opposition to the "authoritarian" regime of Indira Gandhi and the "demise of democracy" that she had wrought.

Several dozen social-cultural associations that are based on the Muslims' religion or, in the case of Hindus, on language and region of origin, were brought into a loose unity in two umbrella organizations, the Association of

Indian Americans (AIA) in New York and the India League of America (ILA) in Chicago. These associations have differed on such matters as, for instance, how Indians should be classified in the census. In a resolution of earlier disputes, Asian Indians have been classified as "whites," and some were pleased with this symbolic acceptance into American society. A different identity, on the other hand, would furnish a more accurate picture of the ethnic group, as well as laying a legal basis for eliminating discrimination in employment and housing. The AIA wanted to have Indians designated as "Asian Americans," the ILA wanted "Indics." Though with some internal dissent, both organizations thus preferred a new designation that would make the entire ethnic group one element of the nonwhites favored in affirmative action. One Indian resident of the United States wrote to oppose the shift from "Caucasian": "In its drive to seek minority status for Asian Indians, the [AIA] is ready to deny the racial heritage of the people it is supposed to represent, and to my mind, it is the height of political opportunism."[27]

Virtually all the Pakistanis in the United States immigrated after restrictions were lifted in 1965. Most are Sunni Muslims, with small proportions of Shiites, Ahmadis, Hindus, Christians, Buddhists, or Parsees. About half speak Punjabi as their mother tongue and a third Urdu; the native languages of the others are Gujerati, Sindhi, Baluchi, and Pashto. While middle-class urbanites are likely to ignore language barriers, immigrants from the countryside tend to associate only with their own kind. About 200 Pakistani civic and social organizations have been established in the United States, but only the Pakistani League of America and two student associations (most of whose members will presumably return home) have as many as a thousand members.[28]

Indochinese

There were so few Vietnamese coming to the United States before American involvement in the war between the two countries that until 1966 the Immigration and Naturalization Service included them in the miscellaneous category of Other Asian, and until 1975 the agency lumped Laotians with Cambodians. The first significant movement from Indochina to the United States was of wives and children of American servicemen, and then the very much larger outflow of refugees started.

Cambodia had been conquered by the Communist Khmer Rouge, which slaughtered a sizable proportion of the population.[29] Political opponents and virtually the whole ethnic Chinese minority tried to flee Indochina, and many succeeded. Most of the Vietnamese, leaving with almost nothing, escaped by sea in sometimes leaky boats that frequently failed to reach the shores of neighboring countries. In the mid-1970s refugees were entering the few havens that still accepted them at the rate of 50,000 a month.[30] Some countries, notably Japan, denied them asylum altogether, and those that found the increasing numbers burdensome became reluctant to accept more. In 1988 Hong Kong announced over international radio and on the envelope of every letter mailed to Vietnam that henceforth it would treat all new boat people—the journalists' sobriquet for Vietname refugees—as illegal immigrants. Almost all of those who nevertheless came were put in prison rather than refugee camps—a total of 10,500 over the next six or seven months. United Nations representatives arranged a so-called voluntary repatriation program, but no more than 250 of those in prison, giving up hope for any other resolution, signed up. In the same week two more boats arrived with 127 Vietnamese.[31]

The United States had a special obligation to accept the refugees, for when American forces withdrew from Vietnam they left behind most of their former allies. In the one week of 21–29 April 1975, the American embassy in Saigon precipitously arranged for the evacuation of 60,000 Vietnamese in especial danger of Communist reprisals, and 70,000 more arranged their own departure. A new refugee act was passed in 1980, and an Office of Refugee Resettlement established in the Department of Health and Human Services began to coordinate the relief and acculturation programs of private and state agencies.[32] Much of the cost of resettlement, initially borne by local entities, was shifted to the federal government.

For more than a decade following the American exodus in 1975, immigrants from Indochina made up about half of the refugees admitted to the United States. The illegitimate children of black American soldiers who had served in Vietnam were subject to discrimination there, and fifty-five resettlement communities were set up in the United States to facilitate their acculturation. With the traumatic experience of the war, evacuation, life in a camp, and adjustment to the sometimes ambivalent or hostile reception in American communities, Indochinese have taken longer than other Asians to make their way. According to press reports, many Vietnamese returned from the United States to their homeland, where they were welcomed for the dollars they brought with them. On the other hand, by the early 1980s enough Vietnamese were establishing successful restaurants and other small businesses to generate hope that the despair and destitution of the others would soon end. There were recurrent accounts of the extraordinary record set by some of the young refugees.[33]

Who Are Asian Americans?

As in earlier censuses, the 1990 enumeration combined all Asians with Pacific Islanders, referring to the bizarre amalgam as API. Detailed information was collected and tabulated on certain of the groups included in this API aggregate. When a census advisory committee suggested various adjustments in the enumeration procedure, the Bureau responded by pointing out that the thirty-two languages into which the long and short forms of the census schedule were translated included Chinese, Korean, Vietnamese, Cambodian, Laotian, three Philippine languages, and Samoan. The very list suggests how artificial the grouping is in actuality. It is as though the pre-1914 immigrants were lumped together as "European Americans." Those coming from Asia are less familiar and, for the time being, have immigrated in smaller numbers, but they are not more homogeneous.

Data were collected in 1990 from 100 percent of the API population, rather than from only a sample, as a decade earlier (see Table 8.1). According to the 1980 and 1990 censuses, those who reported themselves of Asian ancestry included the following:

TABLE 8.1

| | Population (-000) | | Increase, 1980–90 | |
	1980	1990	Number (-000)	Percent
Chinese	894	1,649	755	84
Japanese	716	866	150	21
Filipino	782	1,420	638	81
Korean	357	797	440	123
Vietnamese	245	593	348	142
Cambodian	16	149	133	831
Laotian	48	147	99	206
Hmong	5	94	89	1,780
Thai	45	91	46	102
Asian Indian	387	787	400	103
Pakistani	16	82	66	625
Indonesian	10	30	20	200

Source: U.S. Bureau of the Census, *1990 Census of Population. Asians and Pacific Islanders in the United States*. 1990 CP-3-5 (Washington, D.C., 1993).

No one can be reasonably identified merely as an Asian American, but the category has a factitious reality. In the simplistic, not necessarily prejudiced view of white Americans, finer distinctions are passed over for easier perception. However, Asians in the United States differ in many of their attributes and frequently disagree on public policies that affect them.[34] How wide the differences are among the Asian nationalities (ignoring the altogether dissimilar Pacific Islanders) is suggested by Table 8.2, which gives some of their social and economic attributes in 1990. Children ever born per 1,000 women, a standard measure of fertility, ranged from 6,215 for the Hmong to 1,651 for the Japanese; similarly, per capita income from $2,692 for the Hmong to $24,877 for the Chinese. Such contrasts indicate the wide differences in both the native cultures and the degrees of assimilation to American society.

TABLE 8.2

	Children Ever Born per 1,000 Women	Median Family Income	Per Capita Income	Below Poverty Level
Chinese	1,897	$41,316	$24,877	35.9%
Japanese	1,651	51,550	19,373	7.0
Filipino	2,089	46,698	13,616	23.9
Korean	1,824	33,909	11,178	42.3
Vietnamese	2,686	30,550	9,033	25.7
Cambodian	3,550	18,126	5,121	46.6
Laotian	3,563	23,101	5,597	34.7
Hmong	6,215	14,327	2,692	64.9
Thai	1,797	37,257	11,970	12.5
Asian Indian	2,085	49,309	17,777	33.1
Pakistani	2,507	37,557	13,921	34.2
Indonesian	1,989	34,339	12,559	25.2

Source: U.S. Bureau of the Census, *1990 Census of Population. Asians and Pacific Islanders in the United States.* 1990 CP-3-5 (Washington, D.C., 1993).

In several metropolitan areas (Los Angeles, Long Beach, San Francisco-Oakland, and San Diego) surveys were made in order to pretest alternative formats concerning questions on the API category. The principal problem in collecting these ethnic data pertained to the offspring of intermarriages. The Bureau's consultants recommended that the number classified in the miscellaneous category of Other Races be held to a minimum, and that persons be asked with which of two or more races of their forebears they identified most.[35]

According to the 1990 census, there were 2.7 million Asians in California, or 9.3 percent of that state's population. A plausible projection puts the figures at 15.6 percent, or about 6 million persons, by the end of the century.

The trends can be seen in microcosm in Monterey Park, a suburb of Los Angeles. Since it was incorporated in 1916 with a small WASPish population, there have been successive waves of in-migrants: Japanese, Koreans, Hispanics, and especially Chinese. Along any main avenue of the business district, the only buildings without Chinese script are likely to house a chain like McDonald's or the post office. The town has also been a training ground for liberal Democrats, several of whom moved successfully into state politics. In 1983 Lily Chen was elected mayor and Monterey Park was celebrated as one of eight All-American Cities. By 1989 she had been succeeded by Barry Hatch, a white who came to symbolize old timers' resentment of their town's transformation. There is group hostility, but no official act worse than a reasonable proposal that in an American community the city council take steps to favor the English language.[36]

Statistics on particular Asian nationalities are like the earlier data on "Russians"—that is, peoples of sometimes widely divergent cultures who happened to come from the composite population of one or another country.[37] Immigrants from Taiwan, as I noted above, asked that the Bureau of the Census distinguish them from those from Communist China, but their request was denied, presumably because the United States does not recognize Taiwan as a separate country. However, according to the 1990 census report, of the 1.6 million Chinese in the United States, some 74,000 are listed as Taiwanese. These people used the option of specifying a nonlisted ethnic unit, but they represent only a portion of the population derived from Taiwanese forebears. Cantonese Chinese and those from Hong Kong or northern China do not understand one another's speech, and their relations have sometimes been violently hostile.

Naichi (or Japanese originating on the main archipelago) look down on Okinawans (a substantial minority among Japanese Americans in Hawaii), who are not distinguished in the official records. Filipinos in the United States not only speak several of the quite different languages of their home country, but have organized themselves into competing language communities. Asian Indians and Pakistanis reflect some of the enormous variety of cultures in their native subcontinent, as well as the hostility left over from several wars between their native countries. Indochinese, who were so unfamiliar to American officialdom that they were initially categorized as one, are now classified by nationalities that make better sense; but the culture farthest from American norms, that of the Hmong, was originally labeled Laotian.

These less than impressive results of the census operation must be discounted also for the considerable proportion of the data that was imported into the record by imputation. As one example out of many, "Persons who reported that they spoke a language other than English at home but whose ability to speak English was not reported were assigned the English-language ability of a randomly selected person of the same age, nativity, year of entry, and language group."[38] At one time, before the use of the computer facilitated such manipulations, printed tables used to have a row at the bottom labeled "Unknown" or "Not reported." That would be a better, because more honest, procedure also today.

9

Hawaii

For its size, Hawaii undoubtedly has the most heterogeneous population on earth. Since many of the sectors defined by race or ethnicity have moved either up or down in social status, they also illustrate the relation between social class and ethnicity. Over the past century the government of the Islands shifted from kingdom to republic, then to American territory, and finally to one of the United States. The corresponding changes in the agency responsible for gathering population statistics meant that the definitions of the Hawaiian subnations were under continual review. Romanzo Adams, a sociologist of the past generation, and Robert Schmitt, for many years the state statistician, have delved into this mass of data and analyzed them in a series of significant works. Hawaii may therefore be the best place to observe how a society undergoing several types of change reflects these transformations in its ethnic data.

Europe of the eighteenth century, taught by Rousseau and his followers to value primitives' way of life, saw each newly discovered South Sea island as a partial realization of utopia. Full sexual freedom, in civilized societies merely advocated in earnest tracts, was expressed in these little paradises with the abandon of an adolescent's daydreams. During his several voyages to the Hawaiian Islands, Captain James Cook was not able to prevent intercourse between the native women and even those of his crew he knew to have a venereal disease. He could prohibit his men from going ashore, but he could not keep the Hawaiians from coming aboard. "No women I have ever met were less reserved," he wrote in his journal in 1779; "indeed, it appeared to me that they visited us with no other view than to make a surrender of their persons."

The widely publicized delights offered the crews of visiting ships induced a number of American and European men to settle in the South Seas and adopt a quasi-Polynesian life-style. In Hawaii the heyday of these beachcombers lasted from 1787, when their presence was first recorded, to 1820, the year the pioneer missionaries arrived. Still in 1873, when an English lady visited the Islands and wrote a series of letters home about her experiences, a few beachcombers "lived infamous lives, and added their own to the indigenous vices of the Islands, turning the district [of Waimea] into a perfect sink of iniquity."[1] The earlier pattern of casual interethnic contacts certainly continued; and the present-day counterparts of beachcombers live in small transient colonies. Citizens' meetings have protested the presence of these feckless whites, who allegedly have sought sexual pleasure with both the daughters and the wives of today's solidly Christian Hawaiians.

From an approximation of their number, one can calculate that there were about 1,500 beachcomber years of exposure, with probably as high a fertility as this figure would connote in any other social context. For all of the South Seas, the progeny of the beachcombers some five or six generations later has been estimated at some 200,000, or half of the total Polynesian population (not including Maoris) of 400,000.[2] The degree of admixture in Hawaii, one can assume, was not less than this average.

For more than a century after Europeans discovered the Islands, the Hawaiian royalty and chieftains retained effective control. Their white advisors, whether missionaries or businessmen, depended on the good will of the native upper class, and the interracial bond was often reinforced by marriages between white men and Hawaiian women of noble or even royal blood. Some of the proudest white families—the Bishops, the Wilcoxes, the Shipmans, the Campbells, out of a total of perhaps thirty well-established, upper-class lineages—have Hawaiians among their legitimate antecedents. In many cases their present power and wealth derive from the land acquired through such relationships. The white elite thus found it inexpedient to raise legal or even social barriers to the miscegenation of others. Unlike almost any other plantation society or, for that matter, the rest of the United States, marriage across race lines has been both common and accepted.[3]

So long as Hawaii's chief contact with the outside world was through whaling, about six hundred ships (ten American to one European) docked at the Islands' ports each year. While the ships were restocked and repaired, the lusty young men that sailed them visited with native women. Their contacts were concentrated in the port towns and thus among only some of Hawaii's women, but during the ensuing generations the sizable deposit of alien genes spread through the population. During the 1860s, with a smaller number of whales, Confederate attacks on ships during the American Civil War, and the discovery of petroleum in Pennsylvania, the market for whale oil could no longer absorb the rising costs of gathering it.

The base of the Islands' economy shifted to sugar, which started an all but insatiable demand for plantation workers. They were recruited from other islands of the Pacific, from China and Japan, the West Indies, various European countries, and the United States. The great diversity was due to the endeavor, in the words of the U.S. Commissioner of Labor, to find "a population that would at the same time supply a civic and an industrial need"—that is, people who would work efficiently in the fields but would also be acceptable politically and socially. "But nowhere was a people found combining the civic capacity to build up a state with the humility of ambition necessary for a contract laborer."[4] The white managers viewed each of the successive immigrant waves first with approbation, then with doubt, and finally with apprehension. The Chinese, initially praised for their obsequious diligence, were seen after their numbers increased as the Islands' main economic and civic threat. The Japanese, who were brought in specifically to counter the Chinese, became the largest component among plantation laborers and thus, in the eyes of the upper class, an even more serious menace. They were succeeded by colonial Portuguese and then Filipinos.

Since most of the immigrants were males, they could establish families, or even have sex relations, only with females of another race. Many of the associations that elsewhere would have remained extramarital were legally ratified and thus, one can presume, resulted in a larger number of offspring.

The racial mixture resulting from this history was delineated in a 1967 study by three geneticists at the University of Hawaii.[5] The racial identifications of parents listed on the birth certificates of 179,327 babies born from 1948 to 1958 were found to be substantially reliable when checked against samples from the Hawaii Blood Clinic. Fathers and mothers were placed in one of the following groups: Caucasian, Hawaiian, Chinese, Filipino, Japanese, Puerto Rican, and Korean, plus combinations of each of these primary categories with each of the other six. With 28 possible racial identifications for each parent, there were 804 possible crossings, of which 524 were found in the record. According to the serological evidence, several decades ago the group identified in the censuses as Hawaiians had an 8.5 percent Caucasian and a 13.7 Chinese admixture. Most of the other supposedly pure racial groups also included a usually significant component from other sectors of the population.

In a 1970 sample survey of Hawaii's population conducted by the State Department of Health, each respondent was asked for the race of each of his parents. With this survey as one pole and the 1950 count (the only one when an attempt was made to measure mixed stocks other than part-Hawaiians) as the other, Schmitt extrapolated the ethnic structures to 1960 and compared the two. The differences were not trifling. Puerto Ricans, counted as Caucasians in the census, were distinguished in the sample survey. Part-Hawaiians were misclassified either as pure Hawaiians or as non-Hawaiians. Differences between the two counts ranged as high as 24 percent for some of the groups.[6] The exercise was a warning to any user of the statistics who assumed that official data more or less represent objective reality.

Fluid as the society was genetically, it was no less so in its social structure. Compulsory education had been started under the influence of missionaries, and the sons and daughters of field workers were thus prepared for new opportunities as they became available. That only some 5 percent of the population was in control of politics and the economy was hardly in accord with the universalist aspirations fostered by both Congregational evangelism and, later, the American credo. The contrast encouraged leaders to add other democratizing institutions to universal education. Though foreign-born Asians, a majority at the time of annexation, were excluded from the political process, their native-born offspring could take advantage of blanket suffrage.

The plantation system itself, paradoxically, helped undermine the static ethnic stratification that is ordinarily associated with it. By 1867, when whaling was almost over, production of sugar was already nearly 10,000 tons, rising to more than 4 million tons at the turn of the century, more than double that in the 1930s, and about 10 to 11 million tons in the mid-1960s. The succession of immigration waves, with a new source tapped every two or three decades, each time facilitated the upward mobility of those who had come earlier. Since there were hardly ever enough field laborers to match the increasing production, sugar companies were under constant pressure to mechanize. Eventually the cane was gathered with mechanical shovels, transported in trucks, and refined in mills operated by a handful of skilled technicians. By 1990 sugar production was the most efficient anywhere; the yield in that year was 204 tons per hectare, compared with a worldwide average of 61. With the virtual disappearance of the lowest stratum, the gap between the top and the bottom of the social structure shrank.[7]

The statistical agencies that interpreted these changes in ethnic and social structure also underwent repeated changes. During a little more than a half-century, the Hawaiian government conducted no less than twelve censuses.[8] The first of these, in 1847, was rudimentary; the last, in 1896, was in Schmitt's judgment "sophisticated, accurate, and comprehensive to a remarkable degree." After annexation, the territory (and later the state) of Hawaii was included in enumerations of the United States.

Principles of Ethnic Classification

Because of the fluidity of racial classification in Hawaii and the mass of data available on the process, one can hypothesize about why certain changes were made. This example suggests some principles of ethnic classification. Though the analysis is restricted to Hawaiian data, the reasoning applies more generally.

• *The subnations of any society are classified only partly according to their objective characteristics, partly also according to other criteria.*

It is useful to begin by rejecting the notion that all knowledge can be expressed in statements about immediate experience. Even though the definitions of races and ethnic groups typically imply that the classificatory system derives solely from their attributes, it requires no more than a cursory digging to show that statisticians play a crucial part in orchestrating their statistics.

• *The nonobjective criteria by which any population is classified into subnations are chosen according to the view that the politically dominant group has of the society.*

If one accept the first proposition as valid, this one follows automatically, for the agency responsible for collecting and interpreting data will share the view of the politically dominant sector of the population. A striking example is the changing designation of offspring of unions between Hawaiians and non-Hawaiians. In the first censuses of independent Hawaii, they were designated *hapa-haoles,* half-foreigners. Later, when the Hawaiians' place in the social structure became more ambiguous, the same group was termed halfcastes. Still later, in the censuses under American administration, they were first termed Caucasian Hawaiians or Asian Hawaiians, depending on the race of the second parent. And finally, in 1940, these two subcategories were discontinued and both together were designated Part-Hawaiians. No significant change took place from hapa-haole to Part-Hawaiian, but the designator shifted from Hawaiian to Caucasian.

• *The dominant ethnos, whether in numbers or in power, is given the most statistical attention.*

According to a pleasant myth in Hawaii, until these sentiments were imported from the Mainland, the Islands' people were almost unaware of race and certainly felt no racial antipathies. That whites were divided into subgroups when other races were not may indicate various attitudes, but hardly a relative lack of race consciousness. All the Japanese in Hawaii were classed together, even though those from the main islands are set apart from those from Okinawa by mutual antipathy, subgroup endogamy, dialect, and some of the other distinguishing characteristics of white nationalities.[9] The same is true of the Tagalogs, the Visayans, and the Ilocanos among the Filipinos; the Punti and Hakka among the Chinese; and the various distinct nationalities or races classified together as South Sea Islanders.[10]

• *In any classification of subnations, one of the main criteria is to distinguish insiders, variously defined, from outsiders.*

The most general application of this proposition, the universal distinction between natives and aliens, was complicated in Hawaii by the movement of Caucasians from one status to the other. The word *haole,* which means stranger or foreigner, was at first applied to all non-Hawaiians. As the white administrators working for the royal house acquired more prestige and power, the meaning of the term was gradually restricted to the most influential aliens, often with a connotation of upper-class status. But how to classify the haoles from Asia? According to the *Honolulu Advertiser,* expressing an opinion apparently common at the time, "In many respects the Japanese are in advance of Western nations, and at all events they cannot be classed as 'Asiatics.'"[11] In the 1860 census Chinese were classified as Hawaiians if they were resident in Honolulu, but as foreigners if elsewhere in the kingdom. By the next count, in 1866, they were sufficiently numerous to warrant their own category; the breakdown was into Native, Halfcaste, Chinese, and Other foreigners.

• *When the relative power of a subnation declines, it may nevertheless retain its earlier place in a statistical classification.*

By most indicators, Hawaiians and part-Hawaiians are now close to the bottom of the social scale, but the old relation between Hawaiian royalty and their American advisors sometimes persists in a symbolic alliance of the two races as contrasted with all others. "In some cases, haole families did take the place of feudal chiefs. The Baldwins and the Shipmans, like the feudal chiefs of old, took care of 'their Hawaiians.'"[12]

To be designated a Hawaiian today affords one a special access to schooling, homesteads, and certain occupations. Pride in the Polynesian past is fostered by all the devices of the large tourist industry. According to official definitions, a person with a known trace of Hawaiian ancestry is classified as either Hawaiian or part-Hawaiian. Schmitt estimated that less than a tenth of the "full Hawaiians" reported in the 1960 census could accurately claim an unmixed ancestry,[13] and the record has not improved since then.

• *The designations of an ethnos are often changed from one synonymous term to another because of shifts in their emotional or political connotation.*

A subnation with a designation it deems to be derogatory may demand not merely a new term, but a reclassification. The Negroes so designated in the 1900 census, mostly of Mainland birth, made up only a few hundred out of the several thousand who would have been so classified elsewhere in the United States. While whaling was Hawaii's main industry, ships recruited crews in the Cape Verde Islands and other Portuguese colonies in Africa; and these men, partly or purely Negro, bred with the Islands' women. In the early counts under American administration, their descendants were classified as part-Hawaiian, in later censuses often as Portuguese. Similarly, the sizable number that immigrated from Puerto Rico had some American Indian and some Spanish but mainly Negro antecedents, but few if any were classified as Negroes.[14]

The 1900 census had no provision to specify subnations not represented in the Mainland population, and in the general tables Hawaiians, Part-Hawaiians, and South Sea Islanders were included with whites "in a form suitable for comparison with the statistics for states and territories of the United States proper."[15] The term *Caucasian,* introduced in 1910, was used to classify whites together with many who on the Mainland would have been designated as mulatto, and apparently this statistical medley did not occasion "any local protest from real Caucasians, i.e., the white people. Probably this was because the term had no traditional use and that it was in effect ignored."[16]

Either intentionally or inadvertently, the 1910 breakdown was revised in 1930, when the designations Portuguese, Puerto Rican, and Spanish were restricted to those of presumed pure white descent, while the 7,000 or 8,000 of interracial descent were transferred to the residual category of Other Caucasian. A decade later, in 1940, most of the Portuguese and Spanish retained their distinctive neighborhoods, pattern of life, and level of occupation and income; but they induced local census officials to maintain the classification of a decade earlier as Caucasians. This symbolic ascent virtually started their mobility into the middle class.[17]

• *A decision not to classify a population by subnations, although it is often justified by a statement that ethnic differentiation is unimportant, is generally based on a reluctance to publicize significant ethnic-class or ethnic-political correlations.*

The full assimilation of Hawaii's minorities, some "two or three hundred years" off in the opinion of Romanzo Adams, will result in a "stable race mixture" of a "culturally homogeneous" people.[18] Other analysts have implicitly predicted a much shorter period. At the time that Adams was writing, there was only one substantial work that pictured assimilation in Hawaii as a process with definite limits, setting a future with a plural society in which each subnation will both participate in universal institutions and take good care to protect its own particular domain. This exception to the rule was written by an outsider and published abroad.[19]

• *An important influence on any classificatory system, particularly as this is applied to a small and atypical population, is the convenience of the administrative agency that sets the criteria.*

Understandably, officials of the Bureau of the Census in Washington take a broad view of their task. Weighing monetary or other costs against national pertinence, they sometimes block proposals that, in a local perspective, strike one as obviously excellent. Within bounds, this is what is expected of an agency that deals with the matter as a whole. But when Hawaiians and Part-Hawaiians were classified as white (as in 1900) or as nonwhite (as in 1960), those who needed to use the statistics contended that the balance had swung too far toward presumed overall efficiency, neglecting the local interest altogether.

The 1960 census had a table headed "Race by Sex for the State, by Size of Place, 1960." In it the entire population of Hawaii was first divided between 202,230 whites and 430,542 nonwhites. Then the nonwhites were divided between 4,943 Negroes and 425,599 Other Races. Finally these Other Races were listed as follows:

Indian	472
Japanese	203,455
Chinese	38,197
Filipino	69,070
All other	114,405

Included among the "All other" were Hawaiians and Part-Hawaiians, a distinctive and significant group who by any reasonable criterion should have been classified separately.[20] The irrelevance of the classification to the local population was even greater when the data were broken down in subsequent tables. Among females residing in places of 1,000 to 2,500 population, for instance, there were eight Negroes, four Indians, and 2,492 in the "All other" miscellany. The state had to pay for a new summation of the 1960 data, giving census tract totals by the earlier racial classification.[21]

When the Bureau of the Census shifted from a de jure to a de facto definition of residence, this had a marked influence on Hawaii's reported racial composition. The armed forces and their dependents, who reside for a while in Hawaii but in most respects are not part of its society, in 1960 constituted 16.4 percent of the state's total population but 43.2 percent of the white sector and only 3.8 percent of the nonwhite sector. Not only the racial distribution but also the reported age structure, mortality, fertility, income level, and so on through the whole range of demographic and social indicators were greatly altered by a new definition of "residence."[22]

At a time when most people thought there had been a net migration from the Mainland to Hawaii, the state officials were chagrined when Washington reported that, on the contrary, there had been a net movement out of the state. The principal reason was that very many of the young wives of servicemen had a child or two during their stay in Hawaii and then took these dependents with them when their husbands were transferred to another post.[23]

Conclusions

The racial classification of Hawaii's heterogeneous population has been inconsistent, for the identification of subnations depends in part on such factors as their relative prestige, power, and size; the sensitivity of particular races or ethnic groups to a particular label, or sometimes to any at all; the cost and utility of the classification as these are perceived both by the Bureau of the Census and by local groups that may affect its decisions.

Very many classificatory systems can be applied to a population like that in Hawaii. In general, the local statisticians did better than those in Washington. In the 1896 count, the last before annexation by the United States, data were collected on twelve races or ethnic groups. "Beginning in 1900 less information was obtained regarding ethnic stock, housing, and religion. In many cases it was impossible to make direct comparisons between results of the United States censuses and those taken by the Hawaiian government. Comparability with census findings for the Mainland was of course greatly increased."[24] Adams twice reworked the 1900 distribution correcting the misclassification particularly of Hawaiians.[25]

The problem is to distinguish, as Adams put it, "a statistical aggregation" from "a real social group—one with memories common to its members and with common traditions."[26] In most cases those with mixed genes are part of only one subculture. In American society generally, the public used to try to validate the melting-pot proposition by underplaying any ethnic sentiment as temporary, insignificant, or reactionary. To some degree Hawaii continued this posture after it waned on the Mainland. In the common parlance of the Islands, those who are diverse in cultural as well as biological heredities are grouped together as Cosmopolitans, and some officials have suggested that this category be included in the next censuses. In fact, the various ethnic groups, however mixed genetically, very often maintain cultural and social boundaries.

When I lived in Honolulu for a few months, my landlord was a Chinese-Hawaiian. At his invitation I attended his daughter's graduation ceremony at a Chinese-language school, where each pupil recited a short piece in Chinese. As another example, an instructor in Japanese at the Kauai Community College surveyed the local population to test whether more courses in the language were desired. The response was generally positive: businessmen hoped that after such instruction they could talk more easily with Japanese tourists, and Japanese Americans wanted to improve their knowledge prior to a planned trip to Japan.[27] There is a Research Committee on the Study of Japanese Americans in Honolulu, which has started issuing a series of monographs: "Toward the Development of Statistical Analysis for the Study of Comparative Cultures: An Attitudinal Study of Honolulu Residents" (1979); and "Honolulu's Japanese Americans in Comparative Perspective" (1984). In short, the physiological amalgamation of Hawaii's peoples into a cosmopolitan unity does not mean that all cultural differences will also disappear.

10

Some European Nations and Subnations

Tracing the successive counts of the races and nationalities of the United States leaves one with a shambles. As I have noted in previous chapters, the enumeration of some groups has been so inconsistent that we can hardly guess what the trend in numbers has been. The counts of other peoples have been better, but none as precise as other demographic data. So long as immigrants were expected to melt into the native pot and they themselves wanted to do so, there was pressure to exaggerate the pace of acculturation. Some decades later, when the nostalgic search for roots was reinforced by group preferments in education and employment or, among other races and nationalities, by group resentment at reverse discrimination, a contrary tendency set in to overstate the persistence of ethnic identities. That is, some of the failures to record accurately the ethnic structure of the United States were specific to this country's recent history.

Were such fiascoes therefore not to be found in nations with a different history? In fact, the problems occur in all attempts to classify peoples by subnations. English social scientists, for instance, have reviewed the frustrations of the U.S. Bureau of the Census, in effect warning their government off the treacherous terrain of ethnic and racial enumeration.[1]

In Europe, *nation* is usually understood literally, as a community based on common descent, in contrast to the American concept of an obviously heterogeneous population that derives its unity from a shared political faith. But even the smaller European nations are not genetically homogeneous. One common mode of resolving the contradiction between image and reality is to depict ideal types: "the" Swede is tall and fair, "the" Frenchman is short and dark. Apparently such a quasi-empirical classification can persist even with little factual underpinning.

When circumstances induce Europeans to discard the traditional assumption that a nation is based on its biological heritage, they are likely to shift to their cultural heritage. The most frequent symbol of that supposed common descent is a collective *language*. At a time when Latin was the language of learning, a number of eighteenth-century scholars in France and Germany became advocates of the vernacular. Perhaps the most influential was Johann

Gottfried von Herder. In this context his major work was *Über den Ursprung der Sprache* (On the origin of language), which was followed by some of the earliest studies in comparative philology. In his view, language and poetry are spontaneous expressions of human nature, to be couched in the language of the people. This was a message that pleased Goethe, Herder's good friend, and all the other Romantics both in Germany and elsewhere. More recently a number of analysts and historians of ethnicity/nationalism have also followed Herder's lead and emphasized the central importance of culture, and especially language, as the essence of ethnic identity.

Europe does contain a few isolated ethnic pockets like the Basques, who deviate markedly from their neighbors in both blood groups and language. More generally, however, the rough association between the two kinds of heritage is far less than most assume, and scholars have long tried to break the connection in the popular mind between race and language. As the eminent nineteenth-century German philologist Max Müller once remarked, "An ethnologist who speaks of Aryan race, Aryan blood, Aryan eyes and hair, is as great a sinner as a linguist who speaks of a dolichocephalic dictionary or a brachycephalic grammar." Certainly the best comment on Nazi stereotypes was a construction of the pure Aryan type out of Nazi Germany's leaders: "as blond as Hitler, as dolichocephalic as Rosenberg, as tall as Goebbels, as slender as Göring, and as manly as Streicher."[2]

Max Weber remarked on the generally slight political salience of a shared language in nineteenth-century Europe.[3] The ethnic Germans in Eastern Europe then had no interest, in his view, in joining a greater Reich. "Until a short time ago most Poles in Upper Silesia…were loyal if passive 'Prussians,' but they were not 'Germans.'" In Western Europe, on the other hand, "the term nationality does not seem to be quite fitting" for such multilingual states as Belgium and Switzerland. Tocqueville also saw Switzerland as a non-nation, which, "properly speaking, has never had a federal government." In his opinion, such diverse cantons as Uri and Vaud made up a union that exists only on the map, as would become evident "if an attempt were made by a central authority to prescribe the same laws to the whole country."[4]

However many authorities like Max Müller have tried to separate genetic from linguistic classifications, in a practical sense those who persist in confusing the two are often partly right. How a belief in either type of heritage affects behavior is likely to be very similar. Indeed, whatever characteristic marks the separate ethnic groups, it has usually made little difference in the intensity of feeling, the typical demands of adherents, or even the symbols of communal belonging. "In nationalist doctrine, language, race, culture, and sometimes even religion constitute different aspects of the same primordial entity, the nation. The theory admits here of no great precision, and it is misplaced ingenuity to try and classify nationalisms according to the particular aspect which they choose to emphasize."[5] Disputes in Europe have been based on differences in both race (England and France) and language (Belgium and Norway), but also in religion (Netherlands and Northern Ireland), nationality (Switzerland), and region (Germany).

Though there are many definitions of nationalism (as many perhaps as there are writers on the subject), only one differentiation strikes me as important. Anthony Smith, an English sociologist, distinguishes between *national sentiment,* comprising "sentiments, consciousness, attitudes, aspirations, loyalties, more or less clearly articulated," and, on the other hand, *nationalism,* which refers to "doctrines, ideologies, programs, activities of organizations, movements."[6]

Nationalism, one of the strongest ideological forces of modern times, was a European invention. As it spread through the rest of the world, social and political analysts repeatedly prophesied its imminent demise on the continent of its birth; and, in fact, there has been a cyclical rise and fall in nationalist cohesion. The Romantic movement of the early nineteenth century—the historical novels of Walter Scott and his imitators, the accumulation of ballads and folk tales, the quest in language or folklore for the cultural roots of one's ancestors, the gradual accretion, in a word, of national sentiment—can be interpreted as a reaction against the rationalist, somewhat arid cosmopolitanism of the Enlightenment. In spite of the subsequent vigorous and sometimes bellicose competition among European powers, they constructed an elaborate and successful international system based on such key institutions as the balance of power and the gold standard.

Nationalism in Europe reached a new peak in a later generation. Its most frenetic expressions, paradoxically, reflected less a folk ebullience than a relatively weak cohesion in states that had achieved formal unity only late in the nineteenth century. Fascist movements, the most extreme purveyors of nationalism, were generally unsuccessful. Even in Spain the Falangists had to share power with the army, the church, and the upper bourgeoisie. But in Italy and Germany, where divisive regional loyalties persist to this day, the fascists were able to take full power.

After the carnage of two world wars and the loathsome excesses particularly of German nationalism, the Continent again sought routes to cooperation, and Europe may be "an emergent nation," as in the title of the American political scientist Carl Friedrich's survey of internationalist sentiment and institutions.[7] His book was written almost a generation ago, and since then powerful integrative trends have continued, but there is hardly a European consensus. "In contemporary Europe there now seems to be an in-built interplay between supranationalist or Pan-European pressures, nation-statism, and minority nationalism."[8] Indeed, sometimes the two themes are united into one. "Europe does not exist; it is neither a continent nor a culture, nor a people, nor a history; it is defined neither by a single frontier, nor by a collective fate, nor by a common aspiration." However, just because the author

finds it appropriate to label the continent with the ambivalent term "Europe(s),"
he finds it critical that Europeans make every endeavor to overcome their
many differences.[9]

In the recurrent shifts between a greater and a lesser unity among European nations, those trying to establish a new arrangement commonly jumped
over the immediately prior generation to earlier models. There is no necessary political implication in this temporal ordering; the Humanists are not
dubbed reactionary because they sought new inspiration from the ancient
Greeks and Romans. Nor is it generally appropriate to classify nationalist
movements per se as either reactionary or progressive.

In the usual stereotype, Scottish and Welsh nationalisms, for instance, are
a quaint hodgepodge of amateurish antiquarianism and ultraconservative
politics, which hostile commentators have exemplified with highly selective
tidbits. "It is the myth of a Celtic Scottish past that serves as the popular
historical perspective of many Scots.... Scottish history is seen as a single
broad path leading straight to the present...part of a common, unique and
shared heritage.... The inaccuracy of historical perception is irrelevant."[10]

In fact, Scottish nationalists have not only competed with socialists, but
have done so on the basis of similar appeals: demands for a better economic
return to relatively impoverished areas and for a more satisfactory communal
life. In the 1920s the British Labor party refused to support Scottish home rule
because it hoped that Scotland would become a Labor stronghold and give the
party the next election.[11] In the following decade, "the Scottish National Party
flourished most in the middle-class suburbia, and notably in the New Towns,"
because the new middle classes were "ready to adopt new ideas and new values,"[12] but also, one would suppose, because these agglomerations of freshly
constructed houses needed a social bond. The restlessness, the anomie, that
frequently seem to be fostered by the complexities of modern society can be
countered by a renewed relation to a simpler past, even a mythical one.

The quest for community, in short, has no necessary political coloration
and indeed defies a classification based on Right and Left pointers from another century. In the Swiss Jura, a present-day leader of the nationalist movement was completely comfortable with his mélange of seventeenth-century
local heroes and Lenin, as well as with his program of achieving a simple
pastoral life through ultramodern terrorist means.

Parallel with the developing European federalism that Friedrich analyzed,
some of the separate nations have begun to disintegrate. Many countries of
Europe are both too small and too large—too small to afford the maximum
efficiency in economic production and distribution, but too large to give their
heterogeneous populations a full and natural sense of identity. The Continent's
elements are being attacked at both ends, by a partial transfer of nations'
prerogatives to both international and subnational units. "Ethnicism is becoming one of the incontestable expressions of federalism," for "only a fed-

eral society provides the conditions in which a complete freedom can blossom for all ethnic groups, large or small, compact or dispersed."[13]

The Rise of the Minuscule?

Whether by genetic stock, language/dialect, or any other attribute that subnations use to mark themselves off from all others, the potential number of self-conscious ethnic units in Europe is staggering.[14] Moreover, since nationalist aspirations are bounded by no inherent limit, yielding to the first demand is as likely to excite the appetite as to satisfy it. The farcical trend in the United Nations, now overrun by delegates from postcolonial states too small to exert a force in any other arena, suggests the possibilities, happily not yet realized, in Europe. However, the successes of two lilliputian groups, the Romansh and the Frisians, may be indicative.

Romansh (also called Rhaeto-Romance or Ladin) is spoken by tiny populations, most in the Swiss province of Grisons, but also in portions of South Tyrol and of Friuli, the neighboring area of Italy. In Grisons it is divided into four official and six school dialects, and the total number speaking all of these constitutes less than one-hundredth of the Swiss population.[15] Even so, in 1938 the Confederation recognized it as its fourth national language—according to one interpretation, as an expression of the Swiss nationalism resurgent after World War I.[16] This gesture did not halt the decline of Romansh, for migrants continued to leave the isolated valleys and they (or, at the latest, their children) forgot the language and spoke German, French, or Italian. The main consequence of the policy for the Romansh minority has been to aggravate its cultural isolation and to make it more difficult for peasants' sons and daughters to advance. Nationalist spokesmen are inclined to view upward mobility as disastrous: for them, the survival of the group is a cause to which the welfare of individuals in it must be sacrificed.

Another example is the Dutch policy toward Frisian, an ancient Germanic language surviving mainly among some inhabitants of the Dutch province of Friesland and the German islands off Schleswig-Holstein. According to one survey, most Dutch Frisians could speak the language, but more than 30 percent could not read it, and 69 percent could not write it. The differences by age and rural-urban residence, moreover, suggested a continuing decline.[17] Even so, The Hague encouraged nationalists who wanted to reverse the trend and establish Frisian as the first language of "their" province. Previously school administrators had been permitted to begin children's education in Frisian and shift to Dutch in the fourth year; henceforth they were required to do so as a means of teaching pupils "their" language. Any periodical in the Frisian language that managed to get at least 250 subscribers could thereafter shift some of its costs to the central government, which beginning in the 1970s subsidized at least four such publications. The province got its own tax-supported regional museum and archival society. These concessions to what had been seen as one regional dialect reverberated to other portions of the Netherlands. Groningen, a province adjacent to Friesland, has been building a regional literature, and in eastern Overijssel and Gelderland small groups have been propounding a regional ideology.

In these two cases the central governments of Switzerland and the Netherlands, following the spirit of their democratic institutions, seem to have been steered by what one might call the preposterous demands of self-appointed spokesmen for minuscule groups. It has been argued that only such a group is likely to develop a nationalist movement:

> Unless the number of individuals in a group is quite small, or unless there is coercion or some other special device to make individuals act in their common interest, *rational self-interested individuals will not act to achieve their common or group interests.*[18]

This assertion seems to beg the question, for "coercion" is very often a condition that exists, or becomes intolerable, only as a nationalist movement develops its forces. Indeed, only pitifully tiny cliques have followed many of the self-appointed leaders,[19] but it adds little to assert that a movement begins small and then sometimes grows, but not always.

One might postulate an optimum size of an ethnos, small enough to foster a genuine social identity and yet large enough to furnish its members with more than a parochial culture. It is true that this notion, like the analogous concepts of the optimum populations of a country or a city, cannot be defined precisely. Either end of a size continuum, however, would be beyond an optimum range.

The Romansh and the Frisians, it is also true, represented no conceivable threat to the nations that gave them special rights. They are not only small, but also without meaningful links to foreign powers. Many of the ethnic minorities in Europe, on the contrary, speak the language of a neighboring state and, irrespective of their other characteristics, are often regarded as potential fifth columnists. Sizable numbers of so-called *Volksdeutsche,* or ethnic Germans, became a widespread problem during the Nazi period. Similarly, small enclaves of ethnic Slavs in Western Europe were the object of an analogous attention during Stalin's *Drang nach Westen.* Until diplomats and journalists had their curiosity piqued by the many Soviet references to "the Wends," few of them had ever heard of these several tens of thousands living along the upper reaches of the Spree River, who speak a variety of Slavic dialects collectively known as Sorbian.

The myth of a core national type has been reinforced by the fact that the most obvious deviations are located at the peripheries. Alsace, Brittany, Trieste, Schleswig, Memel, and so on are at the edge of the countries of which they are parts. Many European nations have no natural frontiers, and those that exist are often inhabited by the same peoples on both sides. Among the mountain ranges, for instance, the Pyrenees divide Basques from Basques, and even so high a barrier as the Brenner has German Tyrolians to the south as well as to the north.[20]

Self-Determination for Whom?

From the American and French revolutionary regimes, the idea spread to other peoples that they too might establish their own state, in which they also could realize both political and cultural independence. The political tenets of the Jeffersons and the Voltaires were embedded in the formal philosophy of the Enlightenment, but this eighteenth-century Classicism gradually yielded to the more emotional nineteenth-century view of the arts and life, which included as an important component the acclaim of popular language and folklore. Nationalist movements derived strength both from the Enlightenment, which gave them the rational impetus to seek a wider range of independence, and from the contrasting Romantic sentiments, from which this hope acquired the flesh and blood of popular enthusiasm.

France helped establish militarism as another typical concomitant of nationalism, particularly after Napoleon's "wars of liberation" stimulated his adversaries to modernize their defenses. Following France's example, Prussia also abandoned the hiring of mercenaries and drafted a national army with recruits motivated in part by an appeal to their patriotism. From the twin doctrines of democracy and militarism, there evolved the thesis that every ethnos may establish, by force if necessary, its own national independence. "The revolutionary theory that a people had the right to form its own constitution and choose its own government for itself easily passed into the claim that it had a right to decide whether to attach itself to one state or another, or constitute an independent state by itself."[21] This new right of self-determination, espoused by political leaders as different as Lenin and Woodrow Wilson, became a dominant principle in the reorganization of Central Europe following World War I, with the disintegration of the German, Austro-Hungarian, Russian, and Ottoman empires.

All four of these empires had been multiethnic composites, and of the four Austria-Hungary was the most complex. Around its German-Magyar core were Czechs and Slovaks; Serbs, Croats, and Slovenes; Ruthenians and Poles; Italians, Romanians, and Jews. This diversity in languages and incipient nationalities, moreover, was enhanced by other types of ethnic division. After the post-Napoleonic settlement in 1815, the German elite in Vienna divided again into *grossdeutsche* and *kleindeutsche* factions, promoting, respectively, the incorporation of Austria into a pan-German empire and the maintenance of Austrian independence. This dispute remained a basic issue of Habsburg statesmanship for a century.[22]

Hungary was divided by religion, and a communal memory of the brutal wars of the seventeenth century still survived. Protestant pastors had then been given a choice between recantation and serving as galley slaves; estate owners suspected of nonconformity had had their land confiscated; urban burghers had lost both their property and their lives.[23] Over the years Slovak linguists and intellectuals had gradually constructed a firmer base for distinguishing their language from Czech. Ruthenians, in language closely identified with Ukrainians, had been converted to the Uniate Church, which divided them from the Orthodox faithful to the east.[24] The effects on interethnic relations of all such differences were aggravated by the Habsburg court's maneuvers to balance potential allies against current adversaries.

These convolutions climaxed in 1848 and 1849, when the revolution in Paris reverberated throughout the Habsburg dominions. Major uprisings in Vienna, Budapest, Prague, and Milan were accompanied by clashes and riots elsewhere. Prince Metternich resigned as state chancellor, marking the end of the post-Napoleonic settlement; Emperor Ferdinand abdicated, to be succeeded by the eighteen-year-old Francis Joseph I. In the Habsburg setting, democratic aspirations were often couched in ethnic terms, but of the half-dozen constitutions that were drafted and the high hopes they symbolized, little remained after the fighting ended. The immediate consequence of the revolutions of 1848 was the imposition of stricter controls.

Aware that eventually the empire broke up largely because of ethnic pressures on it, we can very easily overstate the earlier importance of these conflicts. The dissolution was put off as long as it was precisely because temporarily other factors were more compelling. The empire was prosperous. New industry was concentrated in Bohemia and to some degree Hungary, rather than Austria; new rail lines and the abolition of internal tariffs facilitated the spread of material well-being if not equally, at least more widely. The major split in the Austro-Hungarian society was between the upper classes of whatever ethnicity on the one side and the peasantry and the new urban proletariat on the other. In the aftermath of 1848, "no one among the rising classes wanted the demise of an empire that guaranteed order against the dangers of rioting and revolution and seemed capable of diverting foreign war from the internal territory of the monarchy."[25] Hungary's Independence party, for instance, long demanded that Magyar be substituted for German in its army, but when a bill to establish universal suffrage was brought before the Hungarian parliament, all agitation about language was promptly dropped.

It would be an egregious error to divide the empire's population into "majority" and "subordinate" ethnic sectors. The hatreds that had developed over centuries were partly diffused by the very complexity of the ethnic pattern. In cosmopolitan Vienna especially, members of the multiethnic empire shared in its rich life. Around 1880 about a third of the city's population was Czech, mostly humble folk with schools in their own language. Among the many

Jews who migrated to the city from Polish Galicia, a large number advanced rapidly to the higher levels of business and the arts and sciences. On the other hand, the empire's Italians, who wanted to be united with their fellows on the peninsula, could not be bought off with economic advantages. Croats, Slovaks, and Romanians, who all derived great benefits from the material progress, were restless and opposed especially to the Hungarians, whose leading classes were also divided about the distinctive arrangement with Austria. Part of the Bohemian aristocracy and middle class, similarly, was *Kaisertreu,* loyal to the Emperor, while another part hoped to gain more from increased corporate rights in a federal structure. In Galicia, Polish was the administrative language, and the province's governor was always a Pole. Of the three empires that had jointly absorbed Poland, Austria-Hungary was much preferred to Russia or Germany.

After World War I, one of the main tasks of the several conferences setting policy was to find substitutes for the prior governments. President Woodrow Wilson was mainly responsible for setting self-determination as the chief guide both on how new borders should be set and on who would live within them. When the criterion of language did not suffice to set fresh boundaries, the plan was to use plebiscites, but fewer were conducted than diplomats had anticipated. Allied representatives disagreed on where they would be appropriate, with the British generally in favor and especially the Italians opposed. A recurrent problem was how to define the population permitted to vote. For example, after Germans had annexed Alsace-Lorraine in 1871, perhaps as many as 300,000 French left. Now that this territory was returned to France, should not the sentiment of those who earlier had voted with their feet also be taken into account?

Europe was "on the move." Refugees as a mass phenomenon began with those fleeing battlefields and grew from the oppressive measures targeted at particular ethnic sectors of postwar populations.[26] The breakup of Austria-Hungary generated a large emigration. In the Balkans a series of population transfers was effected under state control, officially to bring about more homogeneous populations within the newly established borders, unofficially to serve the political interests of the victorious Allies. The largest transfer was set by the Treaty of Lausanne in 1922: Greece was compelled to accept a million ethnic Greeks forcibly expelled from Turkey, and Turkey had to welcome 400,000 ethnic Turks from Greece. Over 50,000 ethnic Greeks also had to leave centuries-old settlements in southern Russia to be "repatriated."[27] Those ousted from homes where their families had lived for generations, having left with a fraction of what they had owned, arrived in "their" nation carrying mainly a well-founded hatred of their prior home country, a sentiment that they disseminated among their new conationals.

Even if all ethnic enclaves had been eliminated in this fashion, most of the resultant nation-states would have been of marginal size. In fact, enough of the newly defined aliens were forced out to exacerbate hostilities, but not enough to remove continual disturbances resulting from substantial ethnic minorities. Poland's population included more than 30 percent of non-Poles, Romania's 25 percent of non-Romanians. In the reallocation of East European boundaries ostensibly following the principle of self-determination, those denied that right had to live in states in the full flush of exclusionary nationalism.

The Making and Unmaking of Czechoslovakia

Early in the nineteenth century sectors of the Austro-Slav middle classes and aristocracy used the remnants of earlier patriotic associations as bases for popular ethnic organizations or, when necessary, founded new ones. Typically it was the *matica* (so called in Serbian, and by similar names in other Slav languages) that disseminated enlightenment. If the editors of a literary journal, for example, needed help from a sufficiently numerous body of ethnically conscious well-to-do, a *matica* was set up to bring money and talent together in order to propagate ethnic awareness.[28]

In Bohemia there were attempts to stimulate writing and publishing in Czech and to establish a museum focused on Czech themes. These mostly abortive efforts fed into an organization founded by the eminent Bohemian historian Francis Palecký (1798–1876) and his associates. It published books and pamphlets in Czech, maintained a folk museum, offered prizes for the best works in Czech, exchanged books with other Slav institutions and then with learned societies around the world, and fostered the use of Czech in the germanized universities.[29]

Following 1848, when the Czech renaissance started anew, no significant sentiment existed for a break with the Austro-Hungarian Empire. As even Palecký, "the father of the Czech nation," put it, "If Austria did not exist, she would have to be invented." Until the very eve of the war of 1914–1918, no Czech leader suggested independence. Even Tomáš Masaryk, later the country's first president, wrote: "We cannot be independent outside of Austria, next to a powerful Germany, having Germans on our territory."[30] In 1903 Louis Eisenman, a French expert on Central Europe, suggested what he called a "monarchic Switzerland," and "if this were to prove impossible, it would be a pity for Austria-Hungary and perhaps also for Europe." Similarly, in 1906 a Transylvanian intellectual, Aurel C. Popovici, wrote a book titled *Die Vereinigte Staaten von Gross Österreich*—the United States of Greater Austria. The details of his scheme pertained to the complexities of the area, but the central idea was federalism, following the successful model of the United States. Such Austrian Socialists as Karl Renner and Otto Bauer proposed more complex patterns based on the same federal principle.[31] The common element of such works was to reject *both* domination by Austrians and Hungarians *and* the suggested cure of self-determination for nationalities too small to survive on their own. The economic unity of the empire would have been maintained, but within it each ethnos would have acquired specified cultural rights.

Since the subsequent demand for independence was in no sense a culmination of earlier political efforts, some of the patchwork in the making of the new state was due to sudden reversals of policy. Several fortuitous circumstances helped bring about the independence of Czechoslovakia: the potential or actual revolutions throughout the region, the helplessness of the Bohemian Germans after Germany's defeat, the desire particularly of France to build up anti-German allies along Germany's other borders, and, tying all these together, Masaryk's adept maneuvers to take advantage of his unanticipated opportunities. In 1916 he announced the formation of a government in exile, with himself as president. Amazingly, this demand by an obscure professor living abroad, the leader of a small party, was taken seriously: the Allies proclaimed that their war aims included the "liberation of Italians, of Slavs, of Romanians, and of Czechoslovakia from foreign domination."[32] The very use of the designation "Czechoslovakia," which distinguished these two peoples from other Slavs with a brand new joint identity, was a signal victory for Masaryk's group.

Masaryk argued for self-determination as the most universal of principles. But as first president of the state in the process of formation, he opposed its application to other peoples. "Does it apply only to a whole people," he asked, "or is it valid for sections of a people? A minority, even a big minority, is not a nation. Nor does 'self-determination' carry with it an unconditional right to political independence."[33] That in the abstract the "right of self-determination" is a corollary of a basic moral maxim, while in any particular situation its range is ambiguous, makes this slogan a rather indeterminate guide to policy as well as a frequent stimulus to violent conflict.

The territories assembled to make up Czechoslovakia—Bohemia, Moravia, part of Austrian Silesia, Slovakia, and Carpatho-Ruthenia—had never before been united as an administrative unit, not to say an independent state. Two alien or semi-alien peoples, Slovaks and Bohemian Germans, were brought into the new state in numbers and by methods that made their eventual consolidation unlikely; each acquisition of territory sacrificed not only others' rights but also their good will. Slovak territory could be brought under Czech rule only through military action. According to a Slovak spokesman, Masaryk and Eduard Beneš, who succeeded Masaryk as president, "deliberately altered the original conception of the Czecho-Slovak state.... They practiced a policy of denationalization toward the Slovak identical with the one of which the Magyars had been guilty. Instead of a federative state they organized a centralized one."[34] The issues included not only language but also religion, for though both were Roman Catholic, generally Slovaks were much more pious than Czechs. The programmatic differences were symbolized by the names the proponents gave the new state: Czechoslovakia versus the Czecho-Slovak state.

According to the census of 1921, on the basis of mother tongue Czechs and Slovaks together constituted almost exactly two-thirds of the country's population, with almost all the remainder being Germans. Masaryk's argument for including them was mainly that it was necessary to incorporate Sudetenland, the border area they inhabited, in order to establish a natural geographical boundary. Two groups among the Bohemian (or Sudeten) Germans issued declarations of independence. Others pleaded for plebiscites that would permit these roughly three million people to exercise their right to self-determination. The issue was settled by Czech troops, who invaded the territory and against slight opposition incorporated it into the new state.[35]

In Sudetenland some symbols of Czech dominance were the more irritating in that they represented mere pettiness—for example, the ruling that every commune had to have a Czech or Slovak name. Unable to pass the Czech language test "made expressly too difficult for them," many Germans civil servants were dismissed or, when they retired, were replaced by non-Germans. In the empire German speakers had made up 40 percent of the postal service; almost half of those in the state, provincial, and rail services; and 70 percent of the army.[36]

A third area, the Duchy of Teschen, was important not for its population or territory but for its large coal deposits, heavy industry, and a rail line connecting Bohemia with Slovakia. The population was mixed and not easily specified.

The Hungarian statesman, Count Teleki, tells a story concerning the district of Teschen over which Czechoslovakia and Poland disputed. He once asked a Czech politician how many Poles there were in this district, and was informed that the numbers varied between 40,000 and 100,000. Upon Teleki expressing surprise at such a remarkable reply, the Czech added: "Well, the figures change. The people of certain villages are changing their nationality every week, according to their economic interests and sometimes the economic interests of the mayor of the village."[37]

A projected plebiscite would almost certainly have allocated Teschen to Poland. The vote never took place. A majority of an Inter-Allied Commission recommended that it become an independent state, with roughly 80,000 to 100,000 inhabitants, but after a protracted and acerbic dispute Teschen was incorporated into Czechoslovakia.[38]

In retrospect, it is easy to see that the principle of self-determination should not have been applied to Central Europe, and especially not with the fanaticism that would have made independent ministates of places like Teschen. The populations were thoroughly jumbled. Since the breakup of the empire entailed a considerable economic and cultural loss for virtually all concerned, the very process of establishing the new states resulted in an enduring bitterness.

As long as the prosperity of the 1920s continued, it was possible to ignore the portents of serious disunity and hope for the best. Social Democrats, the largest and most powerful of the Sudeten German parties, were also the most accommodating to Prague. In 1921, however, the Left wing had split off and formed the Communist party, a schism from which the Social Democrats never fully recovered. The Nationalist Socialist Party, like its counterpart in Germany, seemed to be fixed at the size of a noisy but not truly dangerous nuisance. It was on the point of dissolution when Hitler came to power across the border. In Czechoslovakia the combination of a severe economic depression and victorious Nazism changed everything. Given the manner of their incorporation into the state as well as their status in it, it was hardly surprising that many of the German-speaking minority sought support from a resurgent Germany, which would soon renew Prussia's expansion under Nazi auspices.

As Masaryk saw the future, any threat would be from Germany and Hungary, and it would be met by a pan-Slav union consisting of the Soviet Union with three other Slav states—Poland, Yugoslavia, and Czechoslovakia. But Poles were outraged by the theft, as they saw it, of Teschen. Many Slovaks were less than delighted with their subordinate status in the joint state. According to George Kennan, then an American diplomat stationed in Prague:

> For twenty years Czech officials worked industriously in Slovak communities, accomplishing a good deal for Slovakia in comparison with some of the former masters of that country, but constantly antagonizing the more easy-going and imaginative Slovaks with their aloofness, their suspiciousness, and their schoolmasterish attitude. Above all, they failed (and it is idle now to attempt to apportion responsibility for this failure) to do what they were originally expected to do: to train and make way for a new and indigenous Slovak intelligentsia.[39]

The Slovak movement that arose was hostile enough to seek support from the Germans against their Slav "brothers."

The makeshift structure of Czechoslovakia began to fall apart with the Munich Pact of 1938, by which Germany acquired about 10,000 square miles of the country's territory inhabited by about 2.8 million ethnic Germans and 700,000 Czechs. Within a week Poland sent troops into Teschen and incorporated it. Hungary annexed some 5,000 square miles with a mixed population of about a million. The rump of the country was renamed "Czecho-Slovakia" to mark its new federal structure. None of these statelets had enough power to stand on its own; in effect, all were German satellites. Less than six months after the Munich Pact had effected—in the famous words of the British Prime Minister, Neville Chamberlain—"peace in our time," Nazi Germany showed itself ready to extend its claims beyond German-speaking populations to whatever areas were weak enough to be readily absorbed.

The defeat of Germany in World War II was followed by an extension of the Soviet Empire to include satellite states throughout Central Europe. However, the reconstituted Czechoslovakia was no more unitary than the first version. Following the collapse of the Soviet Union, after almost two years of increasing dissension, the country broke up into Slovakia and the Czech Republic on 1 January 1993. The Sudeten Germans are still trapped inside a country they never wanted to be part of.

As Poles knew but Czechs had to learn, the threat to the small states of Central Europe after World War I would be from the west and from the east, from Germans and from Russians. The failure to guard against both aggressors was an invitation to disaster.

Minorities in European States

When the Allies founded the League of Nations in 1918, one of its functions was to safeguard the rights of minorities. Provisions incorporated in the peace treaties committed both vanquished nations (Austria, Hungary, Bulgaria, and Turkey) and new or enlarged states (Poland, Czechoslovakia, Yugoslavia, Romania, and Greece) to follow specified guidelines. And when other countries applied for membership in the League, they were pressured into making formal declarations with similar guarantees. Italy and Germany, the two principal defeated nations, remained outside the system, but in all the other countries the League professed to protect ethnic groups defined by a difference in nationality, race, religion, or language. In President Wilson's draft of the League Covenant, the guarantees to minorities were so broad that they virtually negated the principle of national sovereignty that he had also championed.

As they were eventually defined, the rights regulated in detail the acquisition of citizenship, and anyone dissatisfied with conditions in his new state had the right to migrate and become a citizen in another (thus, it was hoped, removing irreconcilable nationalists and reducing ethnic conflict). Individuals were guaranteed freedom from discrimination, and groups were to receive "positive equality"—that is, the right to maintain their own language and schools and thus to "preserve and develop their national culture and consciousness."[40] Though protection by the League was no more effective than any of its other functions, because of its efforts member states tried to identify those in specific minorities more precisely than in the past.

At the 1928 meeting of the International Statistical Institute, Alajos Kovács, a statistician with Hungary's Central Statistical Office, presented a long critique of nationality data, which he judged to be quite misleading when used to classify the thoroughly mixed populations of Central and Eastern Europe.

As he pointed out, partly on historical pretexts, partly for economic or military reasons, the borders of the new states had been drawn with little or no regard to where ethnic groups lived. According to his estimate, postwar changes in boundaries had created 40 million members of new minorities, defined as inhabitants of states with languages different from their own. A census that posed a question on nationality invited diverse responses related to forebears or family name or whatever, and the resultant data could be obscure or false, rendering nugatory the right of a minority to use its own language.

Since 1880, his own country of Hungary had supplemented nationality statistics with data on "mother tongue"—defined as the language that at the time of the census the respondent freely declared to be his own, or purportedly the same as the usual meaning of the term, the language spoken in the respondent's home during his childhood. With many cross-classifications based on Hungarian statistics, he showed how with data on language use it was possible to apportion a population more meaningfully than by nationality alone. The tone of his presentation can be deduced from its peroration: to collect better ethnic statistics "would do more than serve the interests of science; it would also help ensure a durable peace by silencing the accusations and counter-accusations based on the imperfections of nationality statistics and the impossibility of checking on them."[41]

At the same conference Wilhelm Winkler, the distinguished Austrian statistician, read a paper on ethnic data. He proposed that, because of the importance of the topic, the International Statistical Institute should organize its next meeting around enumeration by language and nationality. The suggestion was killed, according to the Institute's report, by Corrado Gini, the best-known Italian demographer of that period. As an Italian nationalist, Gini was unlikely to encourage a discussion that certainly would have included South Tyrol, annexed by Italy and populated by German speakers who in a 1921 plebiscite had voted for union with Germany.

Some fifty years later the faculty of political science of an institute in Trieste published a book by Mario Strassoldo, *Language and nationality in the compilation of demographic data.*[42] What for Kovács had been mainly a technical problem Strassoldo interpreted as an instrument with which each country could collect and compile data so as to present the image it wanted the world to see.

The index that Kovács had recommended, mother tongue, is one of three queries on language that have been used to gather demographic statistics. The other two are the language spoken, or most often spoken, in the respondent's present home and, third, his ability to speak one or more out of a list of designated languages. How each of these alternative questions is worded can affect interpretations of the data collected: for example, a question on the ability to speak one or more languages yields dubious results unless "knowledge" is precisely defined. Such a question had been included especially in such bilingual populations as in Belgium, Canada, and the whites of South Africa. As Strassoldo illustrated from Austrian censuses, "the usual language" was specified differently from one enumeration to the next. In fact, this rather vague concept acquires an unambiguous meaning only if it is specified according to the frequency of use, the motive for using the language and the occasion or environment in which it is used (work, study, social relations, etc.), the type of communication (speaking, reading, writing), the degree of competence in the language, and whether under equivalent circumstances the respondent would prefer to use this language.[43]

In some instances, a country's statistical bureau may have selected a particular index with no regard to its effect on the resultant breakdown, but some choices were certainly part of a purposeful manipulation. Political ends can be served by grouping languages into units one wants to aggrandize, or by dividing others into smaller units. In the old Austrian censuses Yiddish speakers were classified as part of the German majority, which thus became larger. In Germany's censuses the two dialects of Kaschub and Masurian were counted as separate from Polish, but no less distinctive German dialects were incorporated as identical with High German. Another way to minimize the size of an ethnos is to ask about minority languages only in areas where it is thought that a considerable number use them. According to Strassoldo, only one Italian census, in 1861, asked all families on language use. In 1961 and 1971, for instance, the survey was limited to Bolzano and Trieste, though other provinces (Valle d'Aosta and Friuli) had appreciable numbers of persons who used such non-Italian languages as Romansh, Provençal, and French.[44]

A contrast between the 1910 census of Austria-Hungary and the 1921 census of Czechoslovakia indicates the cumulative effect of such biases. Between the two enumerations the number speaking German (including Yiddish) fell from 3,750,325 to 3,304,423, or by 13.7 percent. The number of Hungarian speakers in Slovakia fell from 1,070,850 to 745,431, or by 43.6 percent. Indeed, there were losses from wartime mortality and emigration, but a good part of these massive changes was a consequence of classifications by the two states in a manner that favored the nationality dominant at the time of each census.[45] Alternative indices of ethnicity, such as nationality or ethnic origin, were subject to the same type of imprecision and fraud.

However little success population transfers had in the 1920s, they became an almost routine expedient after 1945. As one might have expected, those first affected were the defeated countries. The ethnic Germans in Central and Eastern Europe were moved en masse "back" to a country that many of them had never seen. An important reason for the tens of millions of refugees that have become a permanent element of our era is that, in seeking to become genuine nations, many new states pushed out those they defined as aliens. According to a report by Worldwatch Institute, the officially recognized refugee population worldwide reached an all-time high of 23 million in 1995, having risen by almost 4 million in the prior year.

An alternative policy can be exemplified by Bulgaria's draconian measures to assimilate the country's Turkish minority, estimated as a tenth of its population. According to the Bulgarian press, anthropologists at the Sofia Institute of Morphology had been conducting surveys over three decades in areas with sizable numbers of Turkish, Macedonian, or Greek minorities. The Bulgarian, these experts reported, is unchanged since the Middle Ages, racially uncontaminated in spite of repeated foreign invasions over the past millennium. Members of the Turkish minority are genetically Bulgarians who, it so happens, speak Turkish.[46] Schools in Bulgaria stopped all lessons in Turkish, and the state bussed children of Turkish parents to schools where they would be taught to be good Bulgarians.[47]

According to a report by Amnesty International, beginning in late 1984 Bulgarian authorities had stepped up their *gleichschaltung,* as the Nazis termed the amalgamation of aliens into the German *Volk.* Domestic Turkish-language publications and broadcasts were banned, and radio and television broadcasts from Turkey were jammed. Mosques were closed. It was forbidden to wear traditional Turkish-style trousers. Men and boys were inspected to see whether the law prohibiting circumcision had been violated, and offenders were sentenced to seven years in prison. After villages had been circled by tanks, militiamen went from house to house with legal documents to change every Turkish name—Ismail to Ivan, Mehmet to Mihail, and so on—and with all surnames to be chosen from an approved list. Those who resisted this Balkan-style acculturation were shot, and according to reports from affected areas, deaths totaled several hundred. At a debate on the issue, Patricia Byrne, an American ambassador to the United Nations, remarked that earlier Bulgarian censuses had shown three-quarters of a million ethnic Turks, but that the most recent enumeration listed none. "What happened to these people?" she asked. Bulgaria's response was that good Bulgarians, forced to assume a Turkish guise by officials of the Ottoman Empire, had reverted to their true nationality.[48]

In May, 1989, ethnic Turks organized a series of demonstrations to protest the assimilation campaign. Their signs read: "We want our real names"; "We want to speak our language"; "We want to practice our religion freely." Several thousand of the most active protesters were expelled to Turkey.

> In most cases the police went to their homes or workplaces, informed them that they had several hours or at most several days to leave the country, and required them to report to the police station to pick up their passports. Those who resisted were forcibly escorted out of the country. Some did not even have time to see spouses or children.[49]

With the breakup of the Soviet empire, fourteen countries became independent, and three of them—the Soviet Union, Yugoslavia, and Czechoslovakia—fragmented into twenty-two nations, of which fourteen are in Europe.

The demise of the former Soviet Union can be viewed variously as the disbanding of the last colonial empire;... as the strength of centrifugal forces in the secession of peripheral areas from a dominant and resented center; as the liberation of its larger nationalities; as political democratization; as a Communist command economy shifting haltingly toward a market economy; as the failure of the Communist Party and Communism; or as a combination of some or all of these.[50]

These new states are based on specific nationalities, but they are not nation-states: every one of them has its ethnic minorities. The basis of differentiation varies. The populations of Serbia, Croatia, and Bosnia share a common language, called Serbo-Croatian, but they differ in religion. Some of the new Slav countries have related languages, but the differences are reinforced by the use of two alphabets, Cyrillic in Russia, Ukraine, Belarus, and Macedonia; the Latin one in Slovakia, the Czech Republic, Croatia, and Slovenia. Both alphabets are used in Bosnia and Hercegovina, and Moldava is changing from Cyrillic to Latin. Six countries are predominantly Eastern Orthodox, five predominantly Roman Catholic, two Lutheran, and one Islamic.

Based on nationality, the most homogeneous of the new states are the Czech Republic, with 94.5 percent Czech, and Slovenia, with 87.6 percent Slovene. In Bosnia and Hercegovina, as constituted before the civil war, the most numerous sector, the Muslims, were only 43.7 percent of the population. The new Russia still includes about thirty different European nationalities, each with more than 100,000 people. On the other hand, each of the former components of the Soviet Union has large Russian minorities, especially in the capital cities. The economic and political challenges, already extraordinary, are greatly aggravated by divisive sectors of all the populations.[51]

Immigrants: Legal, Quasilegal, and Illegal

Most countries of Northwestern Europe have experienced a marked increase in the number of alien or quasi-alien residents. Those willing to accept low-level jobs have generally differed markedly from the typical natives of industrial countries. Guestworkers, as their name suggests, were supposed to be temporary by definition: the policies of receiving countries defined them as a means of furnishing a work force during a labor shortage without adding a permanent sector of foreigners. By the 1970s, the labor shortages that had followed World War II had eased. Many migrants became guests who stayed beyond their welcome. Though juridically the foreigners were temporary, socially they became a part of the society in which they lived, and demographically often a rapidly increasing one. According to the regulations that the European Union itself set, free movement was supposed to be permitted within the whole region. In every country they went to, guestworkers acquired the legal right to have their wives and children join them. Added to their number were an estimated one to five million labor migrants who circumvented the controls and entered the receiving countries more or less illegally. The roughly

15 million alien residents of Western Europe were often called the tenth member of the Common Market, larger in total population than several of the member countries.

Labor migration is generally analyzed in an economic framework, but sentiment regarding aliens is largely based on ethnic differences. From ethnic jokes to physical violence, German antipathy to Turks has been largely cultural rather than merely an expression of competition for jobs.[52] Violence against blacks and Asians in England became notorious. In France the sizable minority has become a permanent and insoluble problem. About a fourth of France's population are either immigrants or the children or grandchildren of immigrants. Legal influx continues at about 100,000 a year, plus an estimated 30,000 to 100,000 who slip in illegally. The principal change has been not in numbers but in the sending countries; nearly half of recent newcomers are Arabs or blacks from Africa. Unemployment, almost 12 percent in the mid-1990s, is widely attributed to competition from immigrants—whose jobless rate is three times that of the native French.[53]

The background of the large movement from less developed to industrial countries can be illustrated with details about one receiving country. As recently as a generation ago, Sweden had been almost entirely homogeneous, with 99 percent of the population speaking the same language, sharing the same national culture, and at least nominally belonging to the same Lutheran Church. When a sizable migration started from Finland, another member of the Nordic Union, these newcomers were guaranteed the same working conditions and access to housing as natives.[54] Sweden's fertility was well below the replacement level, and unless such acculturated aliens as the Finns replenished the stock, it was feared that Sweden would disappear.

The flood of later immigrants, brought in to supplement the depleted work force, was larger and from quite different cultures. By the mid-1980s, 1.2 million persons out of Sweden's total of 8.3 million were immigrants or their children. Adult aliens, who are entitled to 240 hours of free Swedish-language classes during paid working hours, often cost the employer more than would native workers, had they been available. Sweden's schools have provided 120,000 immigrant children several hours' instruction a week in about fifty languages, including—in order of the numbers enrolled—Finnish, Spanish, Serbo-Croatian, Greek, Polish, Turkish, and Arabic.[55] As a symbolic gesture, the term *utlänning* (alien), which was regarded as pejorative, was changed in all official documents to *invandrare* (immigrant).[56] Even so, ethnic hostility in Sweden was expressed in an incident as ugly as any in Western Europe: native hoodlums in forty cars converged on thirty Middle Eastern migrants and beat them up. According to an activist in the *Vitt Ariskt Motstånd* (White Aryan Resistance, or VAM):

> The issue is...the fact that two million in this country have to be exterminated because they are racially inferior or traitors. It might sound hard, but you have to be realistic. That's the way it is.[57]

About a third of the immigrants have left, in spite of the government's efforts to make them welcome.

From Flawed Enumerations to No Census

Ideally a census count should be conducted in a political vacuum. If it did not matter to anyone what the result of an enumeration was, then everyone could respond honestly and fully; but in that case, the government bureau would not bother to ask the question. The fact that ethnic identity is important makes it incumbent on the statistical agency to include questions about it in a census schedule, and also often renders the result unreliable. The world over, disputes over census results in ethnically divided societies are common.[58]

In Europe, censuses have been postponed or revised in response to pressures from one or another sector of the population. In 1976 the Slovenes in Carinthia, Austria's southernmost province, tried to sabotage a census called to determine how many citizens of that country spoke languages other than German. Great Britain omitted the unsettling question on race from the 1981 schedule. More general protests against a census took place also in Switzerland. In West Germany, where the enumeration became an issue in the 1982 election, about a thousand suits were filed charging that the questions invaded respondents' privacy; the count scheduled for April, 1983 was postponed until the courts could decide the issue.

The most drastic action took place in the Netherlands. Dutch law requires an enumeration every ten years, and in 1970 it was amended to increase meaningfully the existent safeguards against any invasion of privacy. Even so, a significant number refused to respond to the questions in the 1971 census, and many more were "not at home." Pilot surveys to prepare for the 1980–1981 census had so high a nonresponse rate that the responsible minister decided to postpone the count until 1983, and it was also not held then. Indeed, according to a Dutch demographer,

> census taking may not now be a viable form of data collection in the Netherlands. Whether the census law will be repealed is unclear; it is quite possible that for the next half century or so, a solemn decision not to conduct a census will be made at regular ten-year intervals.... The country is left with the problems of providing many varied societal services, while being unable to gather the kind of data that would help the distribution of such services.[59]

Up to the mid-1990s, there has been no Dutch census. Estimates are compiled from the population register, in which every person is supposed to record a move from one residence to another, the birth or death of family members, and other demographic or social data. The several times I was a resident of the country, since I stayed longer than the exempt period specified in the law, I should have noted my presence at a police station, but I never got around to it. It is hard to imagine that a people that rebels against a census will voluntarily register the year-to-year mutations of the size and structure of the population. In fact, the Netherlands, an advanced country in the middle of Western Europe, has no reliable population statistics.

This revolt against enumeration by the state represents more than opposition to questions on ethnicity, though in many cases that has been a significant factor. In a broader sense even the distinction between natives and aliens has been blurred. Throughout Northwestern Europe foreigners have acquired access to benefits once reserved for natives. The temporary/permanent status of guestworkers changed fundamentally when several countries granted them the right to vote in local and provincial elections. This innovation began in Sweden[60] and from there spread to Norway, Denmark, Finland, Iceland, the Netherlands, some Swiss cantons, and for Commonwealth immigrants the United Kingdom.[61] Even France, at one time among the most xenophobic of nations, adopted the system in 1985; in Mons-en-Baroeil, a small town in the North, an election was decided by the votes of Algerian, Senegalese, and Vietnamese noncitizens, and the losing candidates protested the vote on national television.

The motive for the changes in electoral laws derived not from ethical norms, but rather from competition among political parties. For any who want it, naturalization in Sweden requires a residence of only two to five years, but most aliens there preferred to retain their own nationalities. That nevertheless the Social Democratic government gave them the right to vote presumably was motivated by its hope of gaining more supporters. The voting turnout of foreigners started at a lower level than that of citizens and then fell, apparently because aliens' votes did not affect the only issue in Swedish politics that interested them, their own situation.[62] The Labor party in the Netherlands also hoped to gain adherents by shortening the usual route to suffrage, namely, by acquiring Dutch citizenship. Such a fundamental shift in the meaning of citizenship and nationality has affected the significance of ethnic statistics, no matter what their quality, by blurring the main contrast, that between native and alien.

11

A Comparison of American Blacks
and Belgian Flemings

An American sociologist who undertakes a study of the relations between the two language communities of Belgium can hardly avoid a continual feeling of *déjà vu*. Time and again situations familiar to him from his knowledge of black-white relations in the United States seem to recur with only minor variations. Of course, the differences between the two countries—and even more between the two subnations—are important. Negroes were brought to the United States as slaves, and during most of the postemancipation period their sufferings were far more onerous than the relatively milder discriminations imposed on Dutch-speaking Belgians, or Flemings.

Nor is it intended to depict the Flemings as the Negroes of Belgium.[1] The Flemish-speaking people of Flanders have always been part of the relatively homogeneous West European culture, so that any contrast between them and the French-speaking Walloons is likely to be less sharp than one between blacks and whites in the New World. Blacks in the United States are a relatively small minority; Flemings have always made up a majority of the Belgian population. Just because of these basic dissimilarities, the parallels are all the more striking.

These parallels are anomalous also in relation to ethnic theories, which generally stress the unique significance of race *or* language—*or,* for that matter, religion, region, or any other marker of ethnicity. Relations between ethnic groups depend far less than has often been supposed on which of their attributes happens to designate them.

Most who read this chapter, I assume, will know a good deal about race relations in the United States. Indeed, many of the points made are discussed more fully in chapter 5. Each of the sections, thus, begins with (A), a short statement about American blacks, intended merely to recall familiar facts or interpretations, and then continues with (B), a more detailed exposition of the Flemish parallel.

Research for this chapter was completed in the mid-1970s, and only a few additions were made to bring some details up to date.

Intergroup Relations One or Two Generations Ago

(A) Between the two world wars, American blacks were congregated in the lowest occupations, from which they were typically the first to sink into unemployment. Discrimination, seemingly justified by their "low standards of efficiency, reliability, ambition, and morals" were "caused, directly or indirectly, by poverty...and by discriminations in legal protection, public health, housing, education, and in every other sphere of life."[2] The main route out of low-level jobs was into the Negro middle class, whose members served as professionals in segregated schools, hospitals, and other institutions.

> The entire Negro middle and upper class becomes caught in an ideological dilemma. On the one hand, they find that the caste wall blocks their economic and social opportunities. On the other hand, they have, at the same time, a vested interest in racial segregation since it gives them what opportunity they have.[3]

Most who succeeded in rising in social status, one by one, imitated the life style of middle-class whites, moving both physically and spiritually as far from the black slum as possible. Having achieved a middle-range income, the "black bourgeoisie," as Franklin Frazier labeled them, generally tried to consolidate their new status by living between black and white subcultures.[4]

(B) As the author of a survey of Belgium remarks in the very first sentence of his book, it is "the most contrived country in Western Europe."[5] Like many new nations of Asia and Africa, it got its boundaries and its very existence not from a unified history or cultural coherence, but from manipulation by more powerful neighbors. Its borders are all artificial, with no natural feature to mark the political demarcation. The most important cultural division, the boundary between Romance languages to the south and Germanic languages to the north, runs through the middle of the country.

From 1795 to 1815, when the area was part of France, an effort was made to convert it into a francophone province. Then the architects of the post-Napoleonic settlement, afraid that revolutionary France might rise again from its grave at Waterloo, fashioned it into a buffer state on the French border. Today's Netherlands and Belgium were united under King Willem I of the House of Orange, who established Dutch as the official language. After an almost bloodless revolution, independent Belgium was founded in 1830.

In the new state, French was again the only official language, used in all governmental contexts and also by both the mercantile and industrial bourgeoisie and the prelates of the Catholic Church. The mostly illiterate peasants spoke one of the several local dialects of either French or Dutch. Elementary schools were established in both languages, but all middle and higher education was in French.

Dutch-speaking Flemings constituted about two-thirds of the population. Upper-class Flemings spoke Dutch to the servants and French among themselves, and with the democratization of Belgian society, this link between language and social class gradually spread. Since it was the dominant medium of administrative, cultural, and commercial communication, the acquisition of a fluent and accentless French was a prerequisite for a Fleming who wanted to rise above his father's level. Acculturation to the French culture of Wallonia was both a means of upward mobility and a symbol of its achievement. In other words, the most successful Flemings were in the same ambiguous status as the black bourgeoisie in the United States, at the top of their community but subordinate to the francophones, whom they imitated by adopting French as their main public language.

This ambivalent rank became more uncomfortable with the rise of a movement to raise Dutch to a par with French in Belgian public life. At first this movement consisted of grouplets under the leadership of such diverse types as a professor of literature at the Catholic University of Louvain, a minor government official who had opposed the establishment of an independent Belgium, and a novelist who led a group of literary intellectuals in Antwerp. In spite of the weakness of their efforts, in the 1870s three language laws permitted the use of Dutch in criminal cases, public administration, and education above the primary level—modest victories, especially since in practice the statutes were often ignored. In 1898, in a symbolic success, the French and Dutch texts of laws and royal decrees were declared to be of equal validity, and in the following decades there were some similarly small advances.

Relations between the Two Subnations

(A) The significant improvement in many blacks' economic status, which began before World War II, continued during the postwar years. Progress in the status of blacks was faster than at any time since Reconstruction. There were, however, two quite diverse subgroups: those who took advantage of the expanded opportunities and those who, because of age, region, or family structure, found it difficult or impossible to do so. If we control for those three factors, as early as 1970 the contrast in income by race disappeared: "[T]here was no apparent difference in 1970 between the incomes of white and Negro husband-wife families outside the South where the head was under 35 years."[6]

Social scientists generally supposed that, in accordance with Myrdal's principle of cumulation,[7] the movement of a larger proportion of blacks into middle-range incomes and middle-class status would bring about a rapprochement between the races. Instead, the very improvement in blacks' status helped aggravate intergroup hostility. So long as upward mobility was difficult and exceptional, the energy of most Negroes was focused on achieving it. When discrimination was effectively prohibited and then in some cases reversed into affirmative action, their attention often shifted to a search for group identity.

(B) Though the base had been laid earlier, the rapid development of the Flemish economy really got under way after World War II. While Amsterdam and especially Rotterdam were suffering the Nazis' final depredations, Antwerp had been successfully protected by the Belgian resistance movement, which in that area was almost entirely Flemish. In subsequent years the port became the nucleus of a greatly expanded industrial region, which contrasted with a declining Walloon economy based largely on almost depleted mines and obsolescent factories.

In the post-1945 years the struggle for Flemish self-realization finally attained a mass base and significant successes. Under a revision of the constitution, Dutch was confirmed as the official language of Flanders and French of Wallonia, while in the bilingual Brussels area the matter, though formally settled, remained a contentious issue. The few francophones still living in Flanders were vestiges of the upper class or personnel of the Catholic University of Louvain. (Later the university split into two, and the French half moved south to another site, in Wallonia. Similarly, in the United States the desegregation of universities led within a few years to the self-segregation by race of all student-controlled facilities.)

After having recovered from its wartime decline with an almost miraculous speed, the Belgian economy suffered a long slump during the 1950s. One of the government's measures to accelerate the recovery was a thoroughgoing decentralization. It drew up a national plan by region—Flanders, Wallonia, and Brabant (the province containing the bilingual capital of Brussels)—and for each an economic council and public/private corporations were set up to foster investment and further development. In spite of the continuing concentration of financial administration in Brussels, the potential advantage that Flanders had gained could now be realized through the relative independence of the Flemish economy.[8]

The Flemish movement changed radically.[9] Despite the minor dispute in Brussels and its environs, the effort to establish Dutch as an official language of Belgium, on a full par with French, was completed. But an ideologically based movement does not necessarily wither away when its purpose has been achieved. On the contrary, among some adherents the very success heightens partisan fervor.

Many Flemings were bilingual, but they still acquired prestige by reporting themselves as francophones. According to a 1970 survey by two sociologists, only 17 percent of the population of the Brussels area, or far fewer than most persons had estimated, reported their principal current language to be Dutch.[10] Spokesmen for the Flemish cause attacked the survey in the press and in Parliament. The two authors, who eventually shifted to market research, refused even to discuss their earlier work with me.

In fact, the dimensions of the two language communities in Brussels and the surrounding suburbs have been very hard to determine. Depending on whether one asks what language the respondent spoke as a child or what language he currently used more, the statistics have varied considerably. As the two languages became the criterion for more and more political decisions, data on their use became ever harder to assemble and analyze.[11] In the 1970s census data on languages were thoroughly out of date, and alternative sources of information—particularly for the nineteen bilingual townships of Brussels, the area of the most acerbic disputes—might have been compilations, respectively, of French or Dutch identity cards, civil marriage ceremonies, or army service. But none of these necessarily represented what it seemed: though in these situations each person could ostensibly select either language freely, actually the choice was often distorted.

Most officials in the Brussels area were francophones and, unless a person made a point of demanding a Dutch identity card, allegedly he was often given one in French. Even Max Lamberty, one of the best known of the senior Flemish leaders, had a *carte d'identité* rather than an *identiteitskaart*. Similarly, civil marriage ceremonies could be performed in either language at the couple's option, but in many cases neither the Brussels *burgemeesters* nor the couple themselves (whose bilingual status sometimes meant a knowledge of standard French and a Flemish dialect) were genuinely competent in Dutch. Thus, the bride and groom chose the less inconvenient as well as the more chic vehicle for an occasion they wanted to go smoothly. The Belgian army, finally, was divided into two components: officers were required to be minimally competent in both languages, and soldiers could choose a unit using one or the other. However, many Flemish draftees deliberately chose to serve in a Walloon unit in order to perfect their school French. In short, none of the apparent substitutes for census data furnished adequate statistics on language use, and whenever these sources were cited, the polemical heat would be raised by a vigorous challenge to their suitability.

Official Encouragement of Separatist Tendencies

(A) The surge of black nationalism caught not only American sociologists unawares, but also the public and the federal government. According to the eighteenth-century theory of democracy as expounded in any of the classical works, the political unit is the single voter, and the norm that the country was struggling to realize was that eloquently voiced in Justice Harlan's opinion in *Plessy* v. *Ferguson*: "all citizens are equal before the law," for "our Constitution is color-blind." The first benefits that Negroes received through federal intervention, thus, derived either from the removal of special impediments or from social welfare, of which beneficiaries were specified not by race but by need.

In the very years that this tradition was moving toward its fullest official expression, the Civil Rights Act of 1964, a countertrend was developing: the Constitution is *not* color-blind; justice consists *not* in removing ethnic impediments, but in reversing them. The two federal programs to implement this new canon both evolved out of bureaucratic interpretations of antidiscrimination norms.[12] The Act of 1964 established an Equal Employment Opportunity Commission, which more and more intervened to set employment quotas by designated minority groups and gender.

The second program developed from an executive order of 1941 prohibiting defense contractors to discriminate among potential employees by race. Eventually every firm doing any business directly or indirectly with the federal government (at that time a total of a quarter of a million companies, employing about a third of the American labor force) was required to submit in writing a schedule spelling out its proposed "affirmative action." A business firm (or an academic institution) that wanted to improve the quality of its work force had to take as its baseline the performance of the poorest worker (or professor) ever hired during a tight labor market and retained perhaps only out of inertia or even charity. "It is increasingly evident," one commentator remarked, "that government programs have undermined some old-fashioned notions about hiring on the basis of merit."[13]

During the same period the official stance toward minority cultures was also reversed. Under the prior arrangement each ethnos had used fraternal orders, historical societies, and the like to inculcate its norms into its members. Public institutions and particularly public schools, however, emphasized rather the common foundations of the multiethnic society. As early as 1972, according to a study of the American Council on Education, almost half of the 2,578 colleges and universities in the country (virtually all of which, whether nominallly public or private, depended on tax-based funding to a crucial degree) were offering at least one course in black studies. In the following decades the trend spread in several ways—to virtually the whole of American higher education; to such imitations as Chicano Studies, Native American Studies, and Women's Studies; and from a single course to programs in which students could get degrees. Some of the courses were academic in the conventional sense, others were such caricatures as "black mathematics." In his *Race and Class* (1987), Professor George Ghevarughese Joseph, for instance, advocated the inclusion in the teaching of mathematics "traditional African designs, Indian *rangoli* patterns, and Islamic art," as well as "the languages of counting systems found across the world."[14] Scholarship was routinely compromised in missionary efforts to generate a racial, ethnic, or gender consciousness.

(B) In Belgium the parallel developments did not start from the same base. No one had ever held that the differences between the Flemish and the Walloons were merely the factitious product of discrimination. Many of the country's institutions, including political parties, were organized by language community. The trend was rather to reinforce the separation, to minimize the opposed theme of Belgian unity. The counterpart to such phenomena as Black

Studies can be illustrated with the activities of the Cultural Council for Flanders, which since its founding in 1959 has been busy using public funds to enhance the self-consciousness of Flemings. As early as 1961, it established commissions to consider national problems; juridical questions; fine arts; pedagogy in primary and secondary education; movies, radio, and television; literature and libraries; and the theater and music.[15]

In Antwerp's twelve or thirteen museums, the glories of the past are thoroughly recorded, including also the quite recent past. When I visited it in the mid-1970s, the whole first floor of the Royal Museum of Fine Arts, for example, was devoted to modern Flemings. The theme of folk pride dominated especially the exhibits in the Archive and Museum of Flemish Culture—meaning the efforts of Flemish writers, musicians, and artists to establish the base of an independent regional culture. The heroes of the Flemish movement were all here. A yellowing newspaper clipping, included to illustrate attitudes of a past age, quoted one-time Prime Minister Charles Rogier: "The best thing that Flemish girls can do is to learn French as quickly as possible, so that they can become houseworkers in Wallonia, where because of their industry and cleanliness they are much in demand." Even music, often a politically neutral art, was presented so as to show the contrast between a score handwritten in Dutch and a printed composition in French. Many of these artists, bohemians most of them, must have been revered rather little in their own lifetime. René Vermandere, a minor writer, was shown with an identity card on which his occupation was listed as *"Zonder"*—None; literally, "Without." A scant generation or two after their death, their defiance of the parochial norms of Catholic Flanders was celebrated in a nationalist museum.[16]

All museums exist, of course, to give elements of the past a present significance. The special characteristic of museums in Flanders is that this significance is so often defined in a Flemish rather than a Belgian framework.

What Do They Call Themselves?

(A) For a nationalist movement in the process of building a tradition, details that established peoples take for granted can acquire great importance, and none is more critical than the name by which each person wants to be known. Negroes came to the Americas bearing African names, a considerable number of which survived in an altered form,[17] even though for decades such a link to their African origin was deemphasized. After emancipation many former slaves took the surnames of their past masters, and presumably many of today's names derived from that source. With the high incidence of family disorganization and illegitimacy that developed among lower-class blacks, it has been common for half-siblings to have either their mother's name or the several names of their fathers. Given names have often been diminutives that seemingly connoted a subordinate status or, possibly as a reaction to that tradition, an uncommon or even unique substitute. In other words, for many American blacks that most intimate of the links between a person and his world, the name by which he is known, is likely to carry one or another vestige of a past often seen as humiliating.

In all the writings on blacks' identity crisis, little attention has been given either to nomenclature or to means of coping with it. Some few—for instance, Malcolm X and his followers—have used their pseudonyms to emphasize their lack of any place in American society. A few others—such as LeRoi Jones, who chose to be known as Imamu Amiri Baraka—have adopted African or pseudo-African names. With conversions to Islam, some have adopted Arabic names. But the vast majority carry on with the names they were given, and as more Negroes of the past are recognized as of historic significance, or as more move up into the middle class, these family names are gradually acquiring an honorable tradition that may overwhelm their earlier connotation.

(B) The personal names of Belgians often reflect the country's situation on a major language boundary. Among Flemings, thus, there are seeming parallels with American Negroes, though the psychological import is undoubtedly quite different. Many persons with solidly Germanic surnames have French given names. Among those listed under the letter A in the *Encyclopedia of the Flemish Movement,* one finds Achille van Acker, Hilarie Allaeys, and (with a combination of English and French) Edward Camille Anseele. There are three possible reasons for such combinations. One is a mixture of the two nationalities, whether genealogically or otherwise. The father of the Flemish novelist Hendrik Conscience was a Frenchman who had served as an official during Napoleon's time, and the first name of his son suggests his acculturation to Antwerp. Perhaps more common was the touch of gentility that parents a generation or two ago bestowed on their children with a name suggesting a link to the upper classes; and some, it would seem, themselves brought about such a change later in life. Sometimes, however, the francophone official would himself translate the given name on a birth certificate, thus effecting a symbolic acculturation.

De Autotourist, the monthly publication of the Flemish Tourist Club and the Flemish Automobile Club, has had a regular feature, "What Does My Family Name Mean?," which has been proceeding slowly through the alphabet. After more than five hundred installments, in the mid-1970s it was halfway through the letter D. Variants are listed by towns in which they occur, and all who learn that they share a family name (for instance, De Saeger, De Saegher, Desaegre, De Sager, De Sagers, De Sagher, Desagher, Desagre, De Saar, and De Saer) are presumed to acquire a sense of community from the knowledge that all these surnames derive from *houtzager,* one who saws trees into planks.

De Autotourist is a good example of how Flemish sentiment permeates day-to-day life. The magazine of a nonprofit organization that parallels the activities of commercial competitors, it tries to stimulate the national consciousness of its members. Another regular feature, titled "For a Better, Prettier, and More Flemish Flanders," consists of an exchange between the editors and club members on matters usually unrelated to automobiles, travel, or distant places. "Sun and Shadow over Flanders" consists of snippets of news culled in order to gratify or anger any good Fleming.

What is Their Designation?

(A) Since before the founding of the Republic, the designation of Negroes has been in dispute, and the use of one term rather than another has been a kind of political declaration. At the time of the slave trade, the usual term was black or negro (the same word in Spanish), and both words acquired an association with the servile status. The institutions of free Negroes sometimes used African (for example, the African Baptist Church, founded in 1779), but this association with the continent of their origin was also typically avoided. As early as 1830 the most acceptable term had become *colored,* followed by *negro* with a lower-case n. On 15 March 1930, with its fulsome, rounded pomposity, the *New York Times* announced that henceforth it would capitalize Negro, thus marking what was seen by many as an important victory.[18]

(B) In Belgium, a fascinating essay had the title "The Difficulties in Giving Our Language a Name."[19] In the ancient Teutonic tongue the word *theudo* meant people or folk, and when it appeared as an adjective in the old High German phrase *diu diutisca zunga* (in which the *th* had been transformed into a *d*), this referred simply to the language of the people, as opposed to Latin, the language of scholars. In one form or another, this adjective *"diutisca"* appears in all Germanic languages, but with many different meanings. During the Middle Ages two variations evolved in the Low Countries: *dietsch* in Flanders and *duitsch* in Brabant and Holland, both used originally to signify what today we would call Germanic, the generic word for Teutonic languages. During the sixteenth and seventeenth centuries, a new terminology developed to distinguish the precursor of modern German, which had undergone a considerable evolution (*Hooglandsch Duitsch,* Upland Germanic, or eventually *Hoogduitsch*), from dialects or languages that had not done so (*Nederlandsch Duitsch,* Lowland Germanic, collapsed into *Nederduitsch* or *Nederlandsch*).

In modern Dutch with the current spelling, these designations have acquired narrower meanings: *Duits,* German, the language of *Duitsland,* Germany; *Nederduits,* Low German, the composite term for languages and dialects that are differentiated from *Hoogduits,* High German; and *Nederlands,* Dutch, the language of *Nederland,* the Netherlands. *Nederlands,* however, is in fact the language of a people that transgresses the boundaries of *Nederland,* and the double meaning of the word, one geographic and one linguistic, can result in confusion. Thus, *Nederlands* can mean either a number of similar dialects (*Gronings* and *Drents*, among others, in the Netherlands and *Vlaams* and *Brabants*, among others, in northern Belgium) or, on the other hand, the single dialect, *Hollands*, that because of the commercial and cultural dominance of this province in the seventeenth century came to be the official language of the whole area. Thus, *Holland* is sometimes used as a loose synonym of *Nederland*.

Faced with this confusing choice, what words should proponents of the Flemish movement have used to designate themselves and their evolving language? Nothing quite fits all occasions, and (as with Negro/black/African American) the selection of one or another alternative is seldom neutral. In its narrow meaning *Vlaams*, Flemish, is one of the several Germanic dialects spoken in northern Belgium. All of these dialects were given a composite name, originally by the country's alien rulers: *flamenco* (in Spanish) and *flameng* (in French). Thus, "when the inhabitants of Brabant or Belgian Limburg call their language 'Flemish,' they are unconsciously maintaining an originally French (and Spanish) usage."[20] The proper term, some insist, is not *Vlaams* but *Nederlands*, and on this point most supporters of the Flemish movement agree. However, in the name of what everyone called *de Vlaamse beweging*, the Flemish movement, no one objects to the use of *Vlaanderen*, Flanders, to denote the whole of Dutch-speaking Belgium, rather than only the historic Flanders, where the Flemish dialect is spoken. Foreigners (including Walloon Belgians) who want to indicate a sympathetic understanding of the region's developing consciousness are likely to fall into one of the traps that have been set. When I asked in a bookstore for works on particular topics in "Vlaams," the young clerk sternly informed me that there is no such language.

In fact, "Flemish" had a quite illustrious history associated especially with the world-famous painters of Flanders. In the sixteenth century, when various pseudoscholars were offering their own languages as a substitute for Hebrew as the language in which God spoke to Adam, one Goropius Becanus argued that this must have been Dutch, or particularly the dialect of Antwerp. The ancestors of that city's burghers, not present at the Tower of Babel, had preserved Adam's language in all its perfection. This so-called Flemish thesis survived even into the nineteenth century, when another proponent asserted that Flemish "alone is a language, while all the rest, dead or living, are but mere dialects or debased forms more or less disguised."[21]

The complexities of the Dutch terminology were compounded when the various designations were translated into other languages. In a list giving the number of American tourists that had visited various European countries, the U.S. State Department, no less, once cited Holland and the Netherlands as different countries. One must suppose that some Frenchmen understand *hollandais* and *néerlandais*, similarly, to be two languages. In Dutch *Nederland* (singular) is the country and *de Nederlanden* (plural) is the binational region.

In English the first term is ignored and the latter becomes, in transliteration, the Netherlands and, in translation, the Low Countries. In French the translation *les Pays-Bas* (plural) ordinarily means, on the contrary, the single country, but before Benelux was coined it was occasionally used also to designate the region.

In English and American slang, the word Dutch has a number of opprobrious connotations dating from the Anglo-Dutch wars of the seventeenth century. The word reminds Europeans of its cognates *deutsch* and *duits,* German, and indeed sometimes still means that (as in the Pennsylvania Dutch, who came not from the Netherlands but from southern Germany). Some "Dutchmen," having become aware of this range of suggested meanings, tried after World War II to introduce "Netherlandish" as the English name of their language, but with little success.

The Subnations' Foreign Relations

The world's subnations, generally the end products of one or another assortative process, sometimes retain a vestigial association with their homeland, even when (as with Zionists, for instance) there has been no contact for centuries. How members of a minority define their place in the society in which they live depends in part on how they relate to the land of their ancestors.

(A) A generation or two ago, American Negroes felt little or no sentimental tie to Africa. There had been the temporary aberration of the Garvey movement, and in the 1920s a few black intellectuals were discovering African art and music. But more generally Negroes saw themselves as "quintessential Americans," in the words of Horace Mann Bond. "In practically all its divergencies, American Negro culture is not something independent of general American culture. It is a distorted development, or a pathological condition, of the general American culture."[22] This was the view of America's most distinguished black social scientist, Franklin Frazier, who defended it repeatedly in his long debate with Melville Herskovits over whether African vestiges were to be found in the American Negro culture.[23]

The search for roots in Africa, with few guides from a stored common memory, has depended on myth even more than most other efforts to develop nationalist sentiment. The *dashiki* and the Afro hairdo, two of the adaptations that have been symbols of Afro-Americanism, are hardly to be found in Africa. Swahili, now taught in Harlem's public schools at the insistence of black nationalists, is a *lingua franca* of East Africa, more than a thousand miles from the area where American Negroes' forebears originated. A combination of Arab and Bantu vocabulary built on a Bantu grammar, it was developed originally for the convenience of Arab slave traders. When British administrators introduced it as a language of instruction in the East African colonies, the black nationalists there demanded that the authorities substitute

English, for no degree of competence in Swahili could lead students to higher education or other advancement.[24]

The few American blacks who have paid a visit to their "homeland" have often found it a frustrating experience. Paradoxically, they are set apart not only culturally but also physically: American blacks are typically lighter in skin color than Africans. The inhabitants of former British colonies believed that their English-based institutions were superior to the American counterparts, and in contacts between Africans and American Negroes there has been a tendency on both sides to condescend to the other.[25] In the words of a Cambridge-educated Nigerian judge, "That young American assumed that he and I had some special common bond. But all we really have in common is that we both have black skin, and that's evidently more important to him that it is to me."[26]

(B) In some respects the association of Netherlanders and Flemish in *Groot-Nederland* is analogous to the association of American Negroes with Africa. The best presentation of Greater Netherlands is in the works of Pieter Geyl, one of the outstanding Dutch historians of the past several generations.[27] The decisive historical divide has been along the language border, which—as I have noted—except for the Brussels area has remained virtually unchanged for 1,500 years. As Geyl pointed out, a series of accidents cut off the southern sectors of Dutch speakers from their cousins to the north; the army of Philip II of Spain (like that of General Patton three centuries later) was stopped at the Rhine and the Meuse, and in 1830 the great powers recognized a composite Belgium as a buffer on the border of a possibly resurgent France.

Geyl took as his main target the life work of his no less eminent Belgian predecessor, Henri Pirenne.[28] Tracing the history of a fictive nation back through the centuries, Pirenne made an almost plausible case for the existence of Belgian patriotism antedating the establishment of his country. But Geyl's thesis has a *prima facie* reasonableness. The natural rapport that flows from language and tradition is in the case of Belgium more divisive than cohesive, for it unites not Belgians so much as Flemings on the one hand and Walloons on the other.

The affinity between Flanders and the Netherlands does not mean that they will unite to form a single nation. Very few on either side of the border have expressed such a wish. Holland's political and social institutions were long divided along religious lines, with the Catholics constituting a plurality of the population. If a generation or two ago the Flemish Catholics had been absorbed into the Netherlands, this plurality would have become a majority and disrupted the balance of Dutch politics and culture. Yet in earlier years the principal advocates of a cultural association were usually Catholic partisans, whether individuals or such institutions as *Streven* (Striving), a Dutch-language periodical with a binational editorial board.

In the long struggle of Flemish nationalists to raise their region to cultural and political parity with Wallonia, they tried to substitute for the various dialects spoken in Flanders what is called A.B.N. (*Algemeen Beschaafd Nederlands,* General Cultured Dutch). In the series of commissions that reformed Dutch spelling in both countries, more and more Flemish scholars were brought in to consult with their Dutch colleagues. But the principal standard that both used was the long-established language of the Netherlands rather than an evolving *Zuid-Nederlands* (Southern Dutch), the speech of cultured Flemings—which differs from that of Holland about as much as standard American English does from the cultured English of England. The words and expressions to be avoided in Flanders are especially those that derive directly or indirectly from French; for example, the standard word for newspaper in the Netherlands is *krant,* which derives from the French *courant,* but the Flemish sometimes use the solidly Germanic *dagblad.* In the Netherlands, on the contrary, an occasional French phrase suggests a cosmopolitan chic.

A subservience of the Flemish to Dutch standards (like that of Walloons to Parisian standards) could not but be a source of strain in a nationalist movement that seeks roots in the speech and customs of the common people, using folklore as a step to folk history, trying to redefine a dialect as another language. Now that Dutch has been fully recognized as one of Belgium's two established languages, some proponents of Southern Dutch show a greater independence. As one Fleming wrote,

> We are aware that for various reasons Flemings feel it necessary to cultivate their Dutch. But to our alarm we discover that in practice that cultivation amounts to a great impoverishment of the language. Is not the present effort of Flemings in large part an *imitation* of Hollanders?...The result can be nothing but *artificial,* a language in which a writer cannot bare his innermost being.... In fact, I believe, the reason that the Fleming has so much difficulty in learning to speak and write a pure A.B.N. is that A.B.N. is the expression of another psyche.[29]

Achievements of the Two Movements

(A) It would not be possible to sum up in a few lines so complex and polemical a subject as the achievements and limitations of the African American movement. My judgment of the Black Studies departments in various universities is negative; the programs have helped lower the standards of higher education, and in my opinion the students enrolled in such programs are being indoctrinated rather than educated. There has been a prodigious rise in the number of black writers, but on the quality of their writing I do not presume to judge. Beyond any doubt one benefit from the early years of the civil rights movement was that, for a certain period, race was removed as a criterion for jobs, promotions, entrance to college, and other important opportunities. Has the one-time obsequiousness of some Negroes really been supplanted by a new self-confidence or by the obverse of obsequiousness, a sometimes exaggerated truculence? If the latter, is this only a transition to eventual better relations between the races? I think no one knows the answers to such questions.

(B) In one or two generations the Flemish have risen from an economically and culturally subordinate status to parity with francophone Belgians. The local dialects of peasants have been forged into a unified language, the discourse of several universities. In this context the cultural renaissance is more interesting than the economic prosperity of the Antwerp area.

In the years 1972 to 1973 the association of Flemish publishers surveyed a total of 3,092 families, chosen as representative of the Flemish population. On the average each spent 1,800 francs during the year to purchase eleven books, as well as borrowing twenty-one others from public libraries. Most of the books were used by more than one member of the family. Of those that had been bought, 92 percent were in Dutch; almost all those in French, English, or German were technical works with too small a market to have been translated.

In the dispute between the language communities, the point was often made that while French is a world language, Dutch manifestly is not, but one should not conclude from this fact that the Flemish are culturally deprived. A 300-page advertising brochure issued by the same publishers association (*Het Boek in Vlaanderen, 1973–1974*) describes the works to be available during the coming year from either Flemish firms or publishers in the Netherlands that marketed their books also in Belgium. Browsing through this gives one an impression of extraordinary variety and wealth. Many of the publications offered for sale reflect in one way or another this people's search for roots, for group identity. The outpouring of travel, history, and art books, since they are mostly in Dutch, is not mainly for the tourist trade. There are works on the Flemish provinces, on towns and cities, and not only the most prominent. One series has thirty booklets on what the conscientious Flemish visitor should see in thirty Flemish towns.[30]

From such a recital of Flemish successes, one is likely to draw the conclusion that there have been no costs, monetary or other, in maintaining a bilingual country. Complete parity between the languages demands not only that both be used, but that the order between them be neutral. Streets in Brussels have two names, sometimes entirely different. Particularly when one seeks contact with nationalist spokesmen on either side, it is hardly a matter of indifference whether a letter requesting an interview is addressed to the *rue* or the *straat*.

According to one of the language laws of the 1930s, signs in town halls, police stations, and other public buildings of Wallonia and Flanders (thus, not the Brussels area) were supposed to be only in the language of the region. In Wallonia, where generally the signs were already in French, the law had no effect, and in Flanders it was often ignored. In 1937, a former teacher named Flor Grammens started a one-man campaign to paint out the illegal public announcements, name plates, and signs throughout Flanders. Time and again he was arrested and imprisoned, but his example was widely followed. For example, one trolley line out of Brussels goes to a small place called Tervuren, where when I happened to pass there the exit was marked with *Uitgang* and also *Sortie,* with the latter visible through an attempt to obliterate it—or, better, to show that it had been there and was symbolically removed.

Most sizable towns and even some villages have two names, one French and the other Dutch.[31] On highway signs, which for good practical reasons should be short and easily read, the rules are rather complex. In monolingual areas the names of the towns are given in the language of the area; but in the environs of Brussels both names are given, with the Flemish name first for towns in Flanders and the French name first for those in Wallonia. Thus, on the road from Brussels to Liège (which happens to meander back and forth across the language border), one starts out with two kinds of bilingual sign (Liège-Luik but Leuven-Louvain) and along the way the sign is only to Liège for some miles, then only to Luik, then again only to Liège. The difficulties that foreign motorists have in reconciling a map showing the way to Namur, for instance, with a road sign pointing to Namen, or Malines with Mechelen, or Waremme with Borgworm, are not viewed sympathetically by *De Autotourist* (11 October 1973). Those who visit a bilingual country, in the view of its editor, should acquire a minimum knowledge of both languages.

Newspapers reported that mail addressed to smaller Flemish towns identified by their French names was often returned to the sender with a request for a better address. According to one francophone professor at the University of Louvain, for instance, ordinary letters sent to Louvain arrived with no trouble, but special delivery mail (which was handled by the telegraph office, in this city more Flemish-minded than the post office), went astray unless it was addressed to Leuven. "Mistakes" of this type are part of the ammunition of nationalist debates.

Over the decades the most fundamental victory of the Flemish movement was that Dutch was gradually substituted for French in the secondary schools and universities in Flanders, so that children learned French relatively late as a foreign language or, in some cases, at the option of their parents, learned some English as well as some French. Walloon schools followed the converse pattern. In this bilingual country there seem to be rather few young people who know both languages well.

If one were to extrapolate the apparent trend in Flanders, it might seem that English would increasingly supplant French, but this is improbable. Whatever the formal arrangements of the country's regional system, firms doing business in Belgium will generally continue to require personnel who are fluent in its two languages. But if the educational system established in Flanders reduces the typical student's competence in French, then it will diminish an important advantage that bright ambitious Flemings used to have, a full mastery of Belgium's other language.

Conclusions

So careful a scholar of sociolinguistics as Einar Haugen wrote that "any pair of languages functioning within the same cultural framework inevitably approach one another."[32] If this generalization had been valid of Belgium, a mixture of French and Dutch might have developed as the new national language, but one very seldom sees examples of such a merging. The formal Dutch spoken and written in Belgium differs from that used in the Netherlands partly, as noted above, because of the Flemings' aversion to French intrusions, and guardians of Belgian French also abjure borrowings from the country's other language. Haugen's postulate is no more correct than the more general assimilationist dogmas of Myrdal and Park. With language as with other ethnic markers, there are two possibilities. One might rephrase the postulate: Any pair of languages functioning within the same cultural framework tend to approach one another unless they become the indicators of competitive subcultures, in which case the differences are more likely to remain constant or to increase.

Is the appetite of nationalist movements ever satisfied, or does it continue to grow from being fed successes? Will the trend toward increasing federalism in Belgium stop short of the ultimate dissolution of the country that some on both sides have suggested? Two Flemish parties, the extremist *Vlaams Blok* and the more moderate *Volksunie,* have both declared that in a constitutional reform anticipated within the next few years, they want outright Flemish independence. The mainstream Christian People's party found it expedient to accommodate partway to this demand. Its proposal would shift virtually all central functions except defense and foreign policy to the two sectors, which would administer jointly a downgraded Brussels. Such a devolution was made more likely by the move to establish, for instance, a single European commerce and currency, for such innovations would in any case reduce national responsibilities considerably.

On a world scale the Flemish and Walloon factions must be characterized as moderate. Compared even with other nationalist groups in Europe (in the Swiss Jura, the Basque country, Northern Ireland, not to say the Balkans), which have used terrorism and explosives at least occasionally, the Belgian adversaries strike one as essentially reasonable, operating within the framework of a democratic system that neither side has tried to overthrow. The point is worth emphasizing, for in Belgium labels like "extremist" have been used rather frequently. Apparently the successive language laws were in conscious imitation of the Swiss rule that each canton shall determine the language in its public schools and thus, in the long run, that of the descendants of any in-migrants. Responsible spokesmen on both sides often cited Switzerland as a prototype of how to combine national harmony with wide diversity.

More generally, a comparison of the language community of Flanders with the racial group of American Negroes suggests several hypotheses. As upward mobility becomes easier for members of a subordinate ethnic group, a number of changes occur:

• The narrow focus on economic demands, once a prerequisite to any important advance, expands to include also political, cultural, and other goals. Once a higher place, since it was anomalous, was therefore also precarious; but when many move up, all of the newly risen are reassured.

• The reference group of the upwardly mobile, formerly their parents or their less successful prior associates, shifts to the members of the dominant ethnos. By this new yardstick, even moving up farther brings less satisfaction.

• Mobile individuals who rose one by one and then tried to acculturate to the dominant ethnos are supplanted by the upward movement of a substantial portion of the entire subnation acting as a pressure group. By this change, the special opportunities of the exceptionally gifted are sometimes sacrificed to the welfare of the whole subnation.

• Under the new circumstances, those who have moved up farthest are more likely to support the nationalist ideology, for group pressure both bolsters them in their new positions and helps them effect a further rise.

• With their relatively comfortable way of life, the successfully mobile seek their group roots. Thus, the signs of identity that previously were avoided become symbols of ethnic or racial pride. In particular, the history of past oppression is continually reviewed, sometimes building up resentment during a period of improved welfare.

• In view of all these similarities between a linguistic and a racial subnation, one concludes that the attribute used as a marker in ethnic relations makes less difference than was once supposed.

12

Ethnic Relations in the Netherlands

In any survey of countries with noteworthy ethnic institutions, the Netherlands holds a special place. For several generations this small nation was almost entirely compartmentalized; except that it was not hierarchical, its social structure was similar to India's caste system. In English-language works the Dutch word *verzuiling* has been termed vertical pluralism, segmented pluralism, consociational democracy, confessionalization, or, in a direct translation, *pillarization* or columnization. The image to be evoked is a row of *zuilen,* or pillars, representing the various religious denominations or, after an extension to humanists and socialists, the various groups with distinct philosophies of life. Each rises from its ideological foundation and stands independent of all the others, yet in combination they jointly support the pediment, the Dutch nation. Like another such metaphor, the melting pot, *verzuiling* is both descriptive and prescriptive, a representation of Dutch society both as in many respects it was and as some thought it should be in totality.

Pillarization, for many decades the traditional pattern of Dutch society, began to erode under the Nazi occupation during World War II, but it was not until the mid-1960s that its decomposition was clearly evident. I happened to be spending a year in the Netherlands just as this disintegration was getting under way. By now, with a virtually complete *ontzuiling,* or *depillarization,* it is possible to analyze the system's effects not only while it prevailed, but also after its climax and atrophy.

The Background to Pillarization

The pillarized structure of Dutch society was brought into being by an improbable collaboration between Calvinists and Catholics—improbable not only because of the inherent differences between these two faiths but also because disputes over several centuries had aggravated those contrasts and left a residue of resentment and antipathy. Holland attained its sovereignty in an Eighty-Year War against the Spanish Habsburgs (1568–1648), and this war of independence has generally been celebrated as the victory of Protestant Holland over Catholic Spain. Some Protestant commentators have gone farther: because Calvinism was the unifying force in the war, it became the essential element of the Dutch national character.[1]

The seventeenth century has been dubbed Holland's Golden Age, and with good reason. For Dutch Catholics, however, Holland's victory brought no triumph. Limburg and North Brabant, the two provinces in the South where the Catholic population was concentrated, were governed like colonies. Catholic rites were proscribed, and a part of the heavy taxes was used to support the established Calvinist church.[2]

The Dutch society and economy then declined, touching bottom at the end of the eighteenth century with a humiliating French occupation. From a francophile Batavian Republic it was converted into a quasi-independent semimonarchy under a Grand Pensionary, who was soon replaced as King of Holland by Louis Napoleon, the Emperor's brother. Finally the country disappeared altogether and was merged into France as one of its provinces. For Dutch Calvinists, the French administration epitomized the evils of secular statecraft. Dutch Catholics remembered mainly that it was under the French that they were given parity with the Calvinists. In a book written to commemorate the centennial of "our national independence," the Catholic author recalled that "1795 brought the French Revolution's ideas of freedom also to our country."[3]

After Napoleon's final defeat, the victorious Allies combined what we know as the Netherlands and Belgium into a single country, designed as a buffer to insulate France's northern border.[4] The dissension between the Protestant king and the Catholic Church was one important reason that the artificially created state lasted only fifteen years, from 1815 to 1830. The Liberal constitution of 1848 brought, in the words of a Catholic historian, "the fight for full religious freedom to a glorious end."[5] But the Catholic Church still lacked its usual ecclesiastical structure; and when a Liberal-Catholic coalition agreed that the hierarchy should be restored in the South, opposition to this move was so strong that the government fell. Liberals split into smaller groupings, principally over the issue of how far and how fast to extend the suffrage. The resultant political vacuum was then filled by a coalition of Catholics and Orthodox Calvinists, both lower-class minorities aspiring to a greater share of national power.

Catholic Holland flourished. In an extraordinary literary revival, newspapers and journals were started by the dozen, manifestoes were written and distributed to the Catholic population. In the 1880s, after several false starts, a Catholic State party was founded by Herman Schaepman, a priest who had become a professor of church history and the editor of *De Tijd,* which developed into one of the most influential of Catholic newspapers.[6]

The other half of the future Christian coalition was the Anti-Revolutionary party, which grew out of a conservative reaction against the French Revolution and several schisms in the Netherlands Reformed Church. The history of these schisms, complex in itself, is often garbled in English-language works. Before the French occupation the official state church had been called the *Gereformeerde Kerk,* Reformed Church; and in 1816, after the French were expelled, it was reestablished as the *Hervormde Kerk,* Re-formed Church. Since the schismatics wanted to reinstate the earlier doctrine and discipline, they generally included the earlier *gereformeerd* in the names of their sects. To follow a common convention and translate both *gereformeerd* and *hervormd* as "reformed" coalesces the two opposed tendencies into one. I have translated *hervormd* as reformed and designated all of the various *gereformeerde* sectarians together either with the Dutch word or as Orthodox Calvinists.

The first of these dissident groups, the Separatists, broke off in 1834.[7] Thirty years later Abraham Kuyper, a renowned Calvinist preacher, organized a new schism and fashioned a coalition between the 1834 Separatists and the 1886 Dissenters. The new church was known as the *Gereformeerde Kerken* (Reformed Church*es*), for the two wings maintained different attitudes toward the Netherlands Reformed Church: Separatists regarded it as false and Dissenters as degenerate, so that the latter saw themselves as members of the mother church in separate congregations. After bringing them together, Kuyper became the revered leader of some 600,000 Orthodox Calvinists, who gave his political ambitions a solid base.

Although both their places in the country's class structure and their social programs encouraged a rapprochement between Catholics and Anti-Revolutionaries, there were serious impediments to its culmination. Orthodox Calvinists looked back nostalgically to the Reformation as the time when the Protestant base of their present-day liberties had been laid, and for the Catholics that was a past whose history needed rewriting. For both Schaepman and Kuyper political expediency overrode ideological differences, but they had difficulty in winning over their followers to what some of them called a monstrous coalition. In 1878, when a routine bill was introduced to raise the salaries of teachers in the public schools, members of the two religious parties collected almost half a million signatures against it, or about five times the total number then permitted to vote. That the bill gave no subsidies to religious schools was no novelty; new was that the two religious parties were ready to act. The bill passed, but it proved to be a pyrrhic victory for its Liberal sponsors. A few years later, in the largest increase in the electorate up to that time, suffrage was extended beyond the barely 100,000 men then eligible to vote. The following year, with all the new Catholic and Orthodox Calvinist voters, the first Christian cabinet was installed.

One of the first acts of the new government was to pass a law requiring all schools to charge their students a fee (in order to eliminate the unfair advantage of the free public schools), with the state subsidizing all elementary schools, secular or religious, out of tax funds. Thus, free public education (in the sense of without a direct charge to the pupils' parents) ended in the Netherlands,[8] and what in Dutch is called "free education" (meaning that parents may choose among three tax-supported systems) came into being.

In 1901, after a Liberal interlude, the Christian coalition won again, and Kuyper was installed as prime minister. Though the four years of his administration accomplished little, it "initiated a completely new period, preparing the ground for future cabinets that could continue the constructive work on a Christian basis."[9] When a law came into effect making primary education compulsory, the coalition used the occasion to enact subsidies for building new Catholic and Calvinist schools. A bill extending state support to religious universities, after provoking the bitterest opposition in the whole long conflict, was passed. Building subsidies were extended. Teachers in religious schools were given the same salaries, pensions, and other perquisites as those in secular schools. Other tax-based aid was granted. After a grand pacification arranged in 1918, secularists no longer had the forces or the spirit for more than minor skirmishes.

The importance of the conflict over school funding in shaping Dutch culture cannot be overstated. As the system eventually evolved, if in any village or neighborhood the parents of forty pupils or more (that is, perhaps no more than ten families) requested a state-funded Catholic school or a Calvinist "School with the Bible," the government was obliged to comply. Division by religion began in childhood and usually continued throughout life. Typically a Dutch child played only with children of his own faith, and he learned early that the *andersdenkenden*—those with other points of view—were alien species.

In the development of the Christian coalition, in sum, the two major issues were complementary. After the first large extension of the vote, the triple school system was established, and as the suffrage was enlarged again and again, many of the new voters supported the measures they had learned to revere in those schools. Primary education built group boundaries strong and high.

The association of political parties with churches has been common in modern European history. There have been democratic multiclass Catholic parties in Germany, Belgium, France, Switzerland, Austria, and Italy; but in crucial respects the Dutch party was atypical. In the decades following World War II, some 85 to 90 percent of Catholic voters in the Netherlands supported their party, while over approximately the same period the percentages were considerably lower for the corresponding parties in the other European countries. "The Catholic party in the Netherlands was unique."[10] Among Protestants, militant Lutherans invigorated the Conservative party in Germany, and in Switzerland Calvinists took over the Liberal party. But "with the exception of the Calvinist party in the Netherlands, Protestants founded no distinctively confessional party."[11] "In no other Western country has an important sector of orthodox Protestants been so active and so militant."[12]

The fact that the religious parties were culturally conservative but socially progressive made the Christian coalition, once it was formed, relatively impervious to threats from the Left. The single labor law enacted before the first Catholic-Calvinist government prohibited the hiring, except for household and agricultural work, of children under twelve years. From this modest beginning, a full and elaborate labor code was gradually enacted, setting the conditions of work for women, for those in dangerous trades, eventually for all workers; establishing insurance against accidents, disability, old age, and sickness; setting up bureaus of various kinds to enforce such regulations.[13] A mere listing of the social legislation passed during the 1930s would take several pages. In short, measures enacted elsewhere by Left liberals or socialists were pushed through in the Netherlands—often, it is true, with important differences in detail—by the Christian parties.

One significant consequence was that the Netherlands had the lowest age-specific mortality in Europe. In his work on Europe's population, the American demographer Dudley Kirk contrasted each country's deaths with the number there would have been if Holland's age-specific rates in 1939 had obtained. For Europe as a whole, the excess deaths, so defined, amounted to 35 percent of the total number, and for Northwestern and Central Europe they were 23 percent.[14] This was a dramatic way of stressing the effectiveness of the Dutch health system, but much of it was so closely related to the specific culture that it could not readily have been transferred to other nations.

Competition between social classes was generally less important than elsewhere. Though the Right wing of the Anti-Revolutionary party split off and founded the Christian Historical Union, and the Right wing of the Catholic party continually threatened to break away (and eventually did over the issue of Indonesian independence), for several generations the main axis in Dutch politics was what Kuyper called the antithesis—that is, the opposition between Christians and pagans. This relegated modernist Protestants to the pagan sector, where they dwelt not too comfortably with humanists and socialists. The religious parties were the center of Dutch political life.

Verzuiling in Full Bloom

The evolution of the Netherlands into a fully democratic society differed fundamentally from that of other Western nations. When official churches were disestablished in the United States, for example, it was by separating church from state. According to the equity inaugurated in the Netherlands, the governmental perquisites originally reserved to the Netherlands Reformed Church were not abolished, but rather prorated among other churches and eventually also humanist and socialist organizations.

After the French were expelled in 1815, three Protestant denominations in addition to the Netherlands Reformed Church were designated as legally entitled to state funding, and thereafter petitions to establish new livings were granted seriatim. By the late 1950s the government recognized a total of eighty-five Protestant, Catholic, and Jewish denominations. In addition to their annual salaries, clergymen generally received a home and household expenses, a special family allowance for each child up to age twenty-one, various miscellaneous emoluments, and a pension after forty years of service. Provinces and townships supplemented these benefits in various ways.[15]

Radiating out from the churches, each pillar was built on a three-part base of school, political party, and newspaper, and each of these foundations expanded virtually without limit. Pillarized education not only ranged from kindergarten through university but also encompassed trade schools, libraries, reading rooms, cultural and neighborhood clubs, resorts for vacationers or for soldiers, as well as societies devoted to sports, gymnastics, movies, music, dancing, crafts, or travel. To the several daily newspapers of each pillar were joined weeklies, women's magazines, radio, and television.

As part of each pillar, organizations based on social classes were set up among workers, farmers, the middle class, intellectuals, and employers. There were also cooperatives, general and farm credit societies, and health-insurance plans. Many associations were specifically for men or for women, others for the elderly. Rehabilitation of prisoners, family assistance, child protection, and other types of social work, as well as health care, hospitals, and the several counterparts of the Red Cross were all subsidized according to the number of clients of each religion or ideology. Even utopians promoting worldwide amity through the dissemination of Esperanto did so through antagonistic associations based on the pillars.

Social research, the means by which the average person was given, directly or more often indirectly, a perception of what was going on in his country, was thoroughly pillarized. There were three main research organizations: the Institute for Social Research on the Dutch People (ISONEVO), with a social democratic orientation; the Catholic Social Research Institute (KASKI); and the Sociological Institute of the Netherlands Reformed Church. In the mid-1950s, three other research agencies were founded: a Calvinist Sociological Institute, an Institute of the Convention of Christian Social Organizations, and a Humanist Institute.

In fact [the Dutch sociologist J. P. Kruijt wrote in 1959], one can more expeditiously cite areas not (yet) pillarized: relations with neighbors, friends, acquaintances; with business colleagues, suppliers, and clients; in the army. And even in areas ostensibly not yet hemmed in, there are exceptions—for example, building societies and residential organizations based on ideological inclination, attempts to discourage Roman Catholics from joining general organizations of employees, instances—which certainly exist, however difficult they are to quantify—of selecting suppliers or employees within one's own pillar.[16]

When my wife and I lived in Amsterdam in the mid-1950s, our landlady, a Catholic, took us aside one day to tell us that she had seen us coming out of a

Protestant-owned department store. She understood that, as Americans, we could not be expected to know the identities of the city's businessmen, but she assumed as a matter of course that, once informed, we would not repeat the gaffe. She did not know that we were not Catholic, probably assuming that only persons of her pillar would have chosen to live in her boarding house.

Professor Kruijt's short book on pillarization was later revised as a long paper, on which Kruijt, a Protestant, cooperated with Walter Goddijn, O.F.M. They began by defining *verzuiling* precisely:

> An organization (a trade union, recreational club, broadcasting society, school, newspaper, political party, and so on) is structurally pillarized in our terms if it is explicitly and collectively founded on a principled weltanschauung. It is not essential that every member (subscriber, pupil, voter) support this philosophy of life, for exceptions change nothing basically.[17]

Excluded from the pillars as they defined them were church choruses, Bible clubs and similar study groups, and other organizations that formed an integral part of a church or ideological equivalent. The definition did not fix the number of pillars. Any short list would pass over what the authors termed "dwarf pillarettes," which were all jealous of their lilliputian distinctions. To concentrate on four pillars only—Catholic, Orthodox Calvinist, modernist Protestant, and general or secular (sometimes, but mistakenly, called neutral)—mapped out the main topography but passed over many details. That the Catholic pillar was dominant is suggested by the fact that its adherents generally showed the highest allegiance to each type of Catholic organization. One cannot understand how pillarization operated or particularly how the system fell apart without some background specifically on Dutch Catholicism.

The Place of Catholics in Dutch Society

During the decades that Schaepman and Kuyper struggled to build the Christian coalition, the Orthodox Calvinists' uncompromising firmness was mainly a source of strength, but later it became a liability and the Anti-Revolutionary party declined. Allied as the junior member of a coalition first with the Liberals and then with the Anti-Revolutionaries, the Catholic party left each partnership with its power enhanced. The isolation of Catholics persisted—first of all, geographically, for the nucleus of Catholic life remained in the two southern provinces, which were peripheral to a nation centered in Amsterdam and The Hague. The South was cut off also by the fact that it became the industrial region of a nation that lived mainly from trade and agriculture.

Unlike the Anti-Revolutionaries, Catholics were able to adjust to new circumstances and maintain a balance between popular democracy and traditional social values. In 1946, after the Roman Catholic State party changed its name to the Catholic People's party (*Katholieke Volkspartij,* KVP), it continued to grow in members and influence. As the largest pillar and also the fastest growing one, the group long maintained the pose of a persecuted minority, recalling long-past abrogations of their civil rights and demanding "emancipation." So important a man as C. P. M. Romme, then parliamentary leader of the KVP and editor of the largest Catholic daily, wrote that "full Catholic emancipation" could be achieved only when "our people will have become Catholic in the vast majority."[18]

The hope of some Catholic writers that their sector would become a majority of the Dutch population fitted in with the extremely pronatalist norms enforced by the church. In Dutch Catholic writings of several decades ago, it was "certainly false to posit from overpopulation an obligation to practice birth control." Any policy instituted for the purpose of limiting births would be an impermissible interference in marriage and family life. The state's task, on the contrary, was to develop the economic prerequisites for its citizens' full life, including marriage and the family. The typical goal of a proper family policy was the maximum number of children, whether or not the parents themselves could afford them.[19] Within a short time such injunctions had moved from the anomalous programs of small organizations like the Netherlands Union for Large Families to the goals of the most powerful political party, and thus from a local to the national arena. According to a 1957 document of the Catholic People's party, "Family policy extends widely over government activities and covers practically the entire range of Catholic policy."[20]

The fertility of Dutch Catholics was higher not only than that of other sectors of the Dutch population, but also than that in the contiguous Catholic areas of Belgium and Germany. The reason was not the church's moral principles per se, but rather those principles applied in the context of the Catholic pillar, with virtually every institution strongly reinforcing the church's pronatalist doctrine.[21] The effectiveness of the combined religious-political-social-cultural stimulus was demonstrated with a laboratorylike precision in one small area. In 1949, as part of a rectification of the Dutch-German border, the bailiwick of Tudderen was transferred to Netherlands sovereignty. Of the 6,300 inhabitants, only 1,100 were Dutch. Almost the whole of the population was Catholic, and ecclesiastically they remained under the German administration of the Bishop of Aachen. After the transfer, however, the people of Tudderen were attended by Dutch Catholic *social* organizations—among others, a trade union and its women's auxiliary, the Limburg Green Cross (the Catholic counterpart of the Red Cross), and social workers of various types who concerned themselves with medical-ethical instructions on parenthood and childrearing. The birth rate of the transferred territory rose from 19.5 in 1949 to 25.0 in 1959, while in the adjoining German territory it fell over the same period from 16.3 to 12.9.[22] It is seldom in the analysis of social factors that one can so certainly say, Q.E.D.

Compliance with the church's precepts concerning procreation was part of Dutch Catholics' extravagant adherence to religious obligations of all kinds.

Until the mid-1950s Dutch Catholicism was, by most indices, the most traditional on the Continent. It had the highest rates for weekly mass attendance, the lowest rates of defection into the ranks of the unchurched. It was also the heaviest per capita exporter of priests, nuns, and religious workers—for though it represented only about 1 percent of world Catholicism, it produced 10 percent of all missionary personnel in the international church. Both Pius XI and Pius XII singled out Dutch Catholicism as a model church for others to follow.[23]

From Disenchantment to Depillarization

During the Nazi occupation of the Netherlands, oppression pushed all its victims closer together. In the postwar years sizable numbers of people from diverse backgrounds migrated to the Netherlands. These newcomers, of whom most were thoroughly alien to Dutch culture, made distinctions between elements of the Dutch stock seem less significant, differences that with the spread of pillarization had become more and more obtrusive.

In retrospect, it is clear that one important reason for the beginning depillarization was that the system had become too successful, too nearly all-encompassing. Several writers poked fun at it, and their contributions may have been a clearer symptom of its imminent demise than any solemn statement:

> The Dutch people is a people that, in contrast to all other peoples, consists entirely of minorities that imagine themselves to be both irreplaceable and threatened. One knows the names of these minorities, such as the lower middle class, the young Catholic horticulturists, the old Gereformeerde railroad workers, the Frisians, the bachelors, or the unmarried mothers. They are all the same. They designate themselves not a minority but a "forgotten group," and they feel themselves threatened in turn by the upper middle class, the old Catholic horticulturists, the young Gereformeerde railroad workers, the Saxons, the married, or the married mothers; and they want a larger family subsidy and lower taxes. Usually they have a newspaper or at least a newsletter with which they harp on their irreplaceability and bewail the menacing of their certitudes, and twice a year they convene in an assembly where everything they say is written down by apprentice reporters, whose copy an older and embittered editor throws into the wastepaper basket the next morning....
>
> In the Administrative Board of the Society of Young Catholic Horticulturists, there is talk of a certain minority grouping, which fears that its rights are threatened by the majority. The majority itself, consisting of the chairman, the secretary, and three members, are in their hearts silently engaged in a bitter fight between two of the members on one side and, on the other, the chairman, secretary, and the third member. Besides, the secretary feels himself to be a minority as against the chairman, and the third member agrees with nothing the board has done and would like to align himself with the other two members were it not that on principled grounds (the issue of whether to do planting on Sundays!) he cannot share their views and is in fact convinced that only the introduction of his own ideas about young Catholic horticulturists could save the Society....
>
> One day the secretary of the Administrative Board of the Society of Young Catholic Horticulturists, after having discussed it at length with his wife, can no

longer accept responsibility for his fellow members' manipulations, and resigns. With some like-minded members, of whose dissatisfaction with the present maladministration he was long aware, he founds a New and Separate Society of freshly Young, though still Catholic, Horticulturists, and becomes chairman.[24]

Sketches like this were not the only indication that sectors of all the major pillars, surfeited with the absurdities of *verzuiling,* were disposed to seek new alliances across formerly impermeable boundaries. Many modernist Protestants, liberals in the American sense, were quite prepared to cooperate with secularists in a moderate Left partnership. A schism in the Gereformeerde Churches had split off the more extreme tenth of the membership, which founded the "Gereformeerde Churches Maintaining Article 31 of the Dordrecht Synod." That synod, which took place in 1619, had presumed to settle issues that were still a matter of impassioned controversy three centuries later.[25] Among the nine-tenths remaining in the mother sect, an outsider could perceive a move from the "neo-Calvinism" of Kuyper to "classical Reformed" doctrine and even toward "general Christianity," and this shift implied a desire for a more open contact with other churches.

A greater restlessness was evident in the Catholic pillar. Under its new name proclaiming its broader appeal, the leaders of the Catholic People's party themselves helped stimulate an exploratory mood. With the sizable number of intellectuals, an efflorescence that had been seen as a triumphant product of *verzuiling,* it was no longer feasible to maintain the strict discipline of the earlier rigid isolation. Typical of the mood of young Catholics anxious to explore beyond the narrow boundaries permitted them was a lay Catholic magazine, *Te Elfder Ure* (At the Eleventh Hour). Founded in 1954, it announced in the opening issue that it would be guided by a principled openness to those from other blocs.

The most remarkable expression of the new mood was the founding of the Labor party. Leaders of the prewar Socialist Democratic Workers party, whose sectarian Marxism had repelled many potential supporters, tried to assemble a large constituency from the entire moderate Left through a so-called *doorbraak,* or breakthrough: religious divisions in political, social, and cultural institutions would be supplanted by a competition between progressives and conservatives. Initially the effort went well. Several small groups with similar programs coalesced to establish the Labor party; and the first postwar government, a Labor-Catholic coalition, was soon joined by the Christian Historical Union, the Liberals, and the Anti-Revolutionaries.

For several years the *doorbraak* became *the* topic on which every political commentator had to have a say. The most important response to the Labor party's initiative, an official Pastoral Letter from the Catholic bishops of the Netherlands, "The Catholic in the Public Life of Today" (30 May 1954), defended *verzuiling* uncompromisingly and characterized the *doorbraak* as an attack on the church and its institutions.

A "breakthrough" to the Labor Party is at the same time a breakdown of our own Catholic party. The consequence of such a "breakthrough" cannot be ignored, particularly with regard to realizing a Catholic social program on which so much depends.... The Labor Party, lacking any foundation in true Christian politics, can offer no guarantee for a program [based on such norms]....

We hold, therefore, that it is not permissible for a Catholic to be a member of socialist associations, such as the NVV [Netherlands Federation of Trade Union Leagues] and the unions affiliated with it, nor to attend regularly socialist meetings, to be a regular reader of the socialist press, nor to listen regularly to the VARA [the socialist broadcasting program]. We maintain that the Holy Sacraments must be refused—and, in case of death without conversion, the last rites as well—to any Catholic who is known to be a member of a socialist association or who, without being a member, still regularly attends socialist meetings or is a regular reader of socialist periodicals or papers.[26]

In retrospect, it became evident that the strength of the Catholic institutions was only on the surface, as the bishops undoubtedly feared from their more detailed knowledge of the inner workings of the church and its extensions. As a Catholic journalist wrote:

Anyone who knows what is going on, what the young people are thinking, knows that in a few decades the breakthrough will be a fact. Now it is still possible for us to guide it; later it will be impossible.[27]

In fact, only his timing was off. The breakthrough came much sooner than he predicted, and it was not what he and the Labor party had anticipated.

From 1966 to 1970 the number of Dutch priests who left their vocation annually rose from 74 to 243, and the number ordained fell from 277 to 48. Of all Roman Catholics over age seven, the percentage attending Sunday mass fell over the same period from 64.4 to 47.2. Of all weddings in Catholic churches, the percentage of mixed marriages rose from 8.7 in 1966 to 12.4 in 1969.[28] By the mid-1970s it was clear that the Catholic People's party had lost most of its support. As a faint echo of the once-powerful Christian alliance, the Catholic party and two Protestant parties united into the Christian Democratic Appeal.[29] In a sense this was a culmination of the long awaited *doorbraak*, with Dutch politics tending toward a polarized opposition between Liberals (in the American sense, conservatives) and Labor moderated by a much weakened Christian center. More fundamentally, it was less a consequence of Catholics' rejection of *verzuiling* than of their renunciation, partial or complete, of their faith.

One can hardly find the words to characterize so rapid and so complete a disintegration of what had been the country's most powerful pillar. Commentators used metaphors like a "steam kettle" that blew up or "long-brewing pressures that finally exploded" to sum up the widespread disaffection. Elsewhere such estrangements had not disrupted the church because in other Catholic countries the sharpest critics had long since left it. Even more startling was the changed relation with the Vatican, a transformation of the Dutch church within a few years from Rome's most dutiful daughter to an *enfant terrible,* creating what an anonymous Italian called "the worst crisis since the Reformation." French travel agents advertised tours to the Netherlands to see not the tulips but Dutch Catholicism.[30] Not only were malcontents' demands far more pointed than earlier, but in the interim the dissidents had been joined by the bishops. In the disarray that the Second Vatican Council (1962–1964) both reflected and stimulated, members of the Dutch hierarchy were the most insistent in their support of fundamental change.

Between 1966 and 1970 the entire membership of the Dutch Catholic Church was invited to participate in a National Pastoral Council, which organized conferences throughout the country. In each diocese a commission prepared résumés of the dialogue, which were widely distributed. Elected representatives, with laymen in the majority, voted on virtually any issue of pastoral policy. Though discussions of contraception, priestly celibacy, and lay participation got more attention in the press, a more serious challenge came in *The New Catechism for Adults,* which Rome interpreted as an affront to the magisterium, the church's teaching authority. Approved by the Dutch bishops as a safe guide to help laymen follow the colloquy at the Vatican Council, the book became an instant best-seller. In the dispute with several Vatican commissions, the Dutch church won on some points and ignored those on which it lost. I happened to be in Italy during this period and noticed that the Italian translation was featured in the window of a Communist bookstore in Rome—a weapon with which to attack the Vatican, the Italian church, and the Italian Catholic party.

On the Depillarized Society

In the Netherlands, a racially and culturally homogeneous society, ethnicity was defined essentially as religion, more broadly as *Weltanschauung. Verzuiling* came to define almost completely each individual's place in society. The norm was that no one in any pillar would have any meaningful contact with the *andersdenkenden,* those in other pillars. Once started, the process became cumulative.

Pillarization was an amazing success. It ended, however, as an ailing monarch, unable either to rule or to yield to any potential successor. The country's entire institutional structure remained frozen in a mold that had been set by ideologies once revered but now, at first covertly and then more and more openly and insistently, were rejected as obsolete by a majority of the electorate. As it dissipated, the structuring by ethnicity might have been supplanted by the usual opposition between social classes. Behind its grand phrases, that was what the Labor party intended with its breakthrough. However, the mitigation of all degrees of class conflict had long been one of the genuine benefits from *verzuiling,* for each person's main allegiance was to everyone in his pillar, irrespective of whether he was his boss, his fellow worker, or his employee. As depillarization got under way there was nothing in Dutch society to replace it beyond remnants empty of current content. It is true, of course, that during the 1960s mindless rebellion was epidemic all over the Western world, and such manifestations in the Netherlands were partly a local variant of the international craze. But the aberrations were often more serious and more persistent in that country, and it is not fanciful to assert that in great part they were specific to a culture from which values had been systematically drained by institutions that were protracted long beyond their useful life.

In the 1960s much of political interaction in the Netherlands disintegrated into smaller and smaller "action groups," which used picket lines and street demonstrations to try to force the government to protect the environment, to grant larger subsidies for housing, to reject nuclear war. At the time this was a political style in all Western societies, but in the Netherlands it was less an appendage to conventional political institutions than a partial substitute for them. In the mid-1970s there were an estimated 3,000 of these "piranhas of Dutch politics," as a resident American diplomat termed them,[31] and an extraordinarily high proportion developed into small political parties. In some national elections as many as a hundred "parties" were listed on the ballot. Shaky multiparty coalitions alternated with governments under caretakers. (Even so, in 1973 several Dutch researchers undertook a conventional survey of Dutch elites, culminating in a book that barely mentioned the country's turmoil.[32])

The government was able to function only because Parliament distanced itself from the fragmented electorate. A democratic system linked to too volatile a mass half-converted itself into a more or less permanent civil service, responsible less to the voters than to the members' concept of the national interest. In 1972 there was a 163-day interregnum with no government; in 1977 an even longer interval when no coalition of parties could agree. In 1981 a coalition that was formed lasted for a short time only. In 1992 the government legalized brothels and sex clubs; the following year it banned discrimination on the basis of sexual orientation. In 1994 the popular Catholic prime minister Ruud Lubbers withdrew from politics; the Catholic and Labor parties lost heavily, with sizable increases in support to the far Right and the far Left. A three-party coalition was formed of the Liberals, Labor, and D66 (another Left party).

There was a parallel transformation of Dutch universities.[33] Most students, not generally interested in the *corpora* (the equivalent of American fraternities), were organized into Left groups that soon were able to seize some control of academic affairs. Efforts to cope with disorganization were largely ineffective, and one important reason was the structure of Dutch cultural institutions. No association of university professors existed, as in the United States or West Germany, for instance—it would have cut across the boundaries of the pillars. In spite of the diversity of the seven universities and five specialized institutions of higher learning, all were subsidized by the state and presumably subject to its central control. A 1970 University Governance Reorganization Act was designed to cope with higher education as a whole, but its implementation, in the view of a visiting American academic, differed "incredibly" among the various universities and even among faculties and subfaculties at each of them. Neither the Ministry of Education in The Hague nor the administrators of each institution had the will and power to combat student rowdyism effectively.[34] Those attending universities were candidates for the thoroughly radicalized "action groups" or "Provos," whose targets ranged well beyond the usual limits of politics and social welfare.

As another example, within a few years the Netherlands was competing with Denmark to be Europe's center of obscenity. In no other country was the birth-control movement so intimately tied to the promotion of pornography. The Neo-Malthusian League, forcibly disbanded under the Nazi occupation, had been reestablished after World War II as the Netherlands Society for Sexual Reform (*Nederlandse Vereniging voor Sexuale Hervorming,* or NVSH), whose program included the advocacy of nudity, homosexuality, and sexual freedom broadly defined. Only by attacking Calvinist-Catholic puritanism as a whole, the NVSH held, would it be possible to propagate contraceptive practices effectively. The organization had no paid staff, and volunteers who supported various causes of their own got control of parts of the organization. A faction of orthodox Freudians was mainly responsible for the excesses that they labeled "sexual reform." A Communist faction centered in The Hague objected to any linkage of birth control to population pressure, since the only proper way to control an excess growth of numbers was to establish a socialist society. Since the usual themes associated with neo-Malthusianism were lacking, the pornography and near-pornography were more prominent.

Official connivance at widespread illegality was applied to drugs. In the 1960s each morning men would come to hose down the Damrak (the large square in front of Amsterdam's cathedral), waiting patiently while the drugged crowd that had slept on the pavement overnight moved from one side of the square to the other. Then the municipality provided free accommodations, ostensibly because sleeping outdoors during a Dutch winter was unhealthful, really because it was politic to get the all too visible young people off the streets. Many of them were not Dutch, for as the city was becoming famous on the international drug circuit, more and more foreign addicts came to Amsterdam.

Two large clubs, called Paradiso and Fantasio, were opened in downtown Amsterdam, with the municipal and national governments contributing about a third of the operating costs. In each of these psychedelically lit premises, as many as a thousand people were to be found on any night, strewn about on benches and on the floor, while pushers moved from group to group offering free samples as an inducement to sales. The city's police chief said that he was happy that there was less trouble in the streets. The principal complaint came from a radical social worker who remarked that the clubs reduced political pressure. According to a survey conducted for a University of Amsterdam dissertation, virtually all of the 958 in the sample used hashish, and most also used amphetamines, LSD, or opium and its derivatives.[35]

In 1978 the government declared marijuana to be "relatively innocuous" and unofficially dropped all criminal penalties for using it. A twenty-six-year-old American started a formally illegal marijuana seed bank in an Amsterdam loft and produced hashish in his refrigerator. Dealers sell tons of "hash" and "weed" in hundreds of storefront "coffee shops," and the authorities' indifference to their law-breaking certainly helped to deflate overall respect for the law.[36]

Those addicted to heroin could be treated with methadone in a publicly financed clinic; its head estimated that the number of addicts increased from fewer than 100 in 1970 to between 8,000 and 10,000 only five years later. From 1978 to 1983, the number of burglaries, thefts with violence, and murders all doubled, and Amsterdam police blamed heroin addicts for much of the increase. According to the chief narcotics officer at the Ministry of Justice in The Hague, "I don't think Marseille is the central point of drug traffic in Europe any longer. Amsterdam is, for sure."[37]

France refused to sanction a proposed open-border pact with seven states of the European Union until the Netherlands instituted a genuine control of its drug-infested society. "Like mad cows and a single currency, it became a pithole on the road to European unity."[38]

Such lawlessness has been embedded in a generous extension of the social welfare that was started under the Christian coalition. The *Algemeen Ouderen Verbond,* formed by the union of three prior organizations into a General Union of the Elderly, won six seats in the Second Chamber; and every politician was fearful of gray power. According to the 1986 profile of the Netherlands by the Organization for Economic Cooperation and Development, labor-market flexibility and mobility were probably affected there by very high marginal taxes and generous income-related transfers. More bluntly put, individual initiative and diligence have been discouraged by the combination of high taxes and tax-funded subsidies for both necessities and a wide variety of semiluxuries.[39]

The changed relation between social attitudes and participation in the economy is suggested by a way of life based on the dole. Anyone who loses his job receives 70 percent of his wages or salary for a full year; anyone who is declared disabled receives the same proportion of his annual earnings for life. According to official 1986 statistics, unemployed and disabled combined made up more than a quarter of the labor force. In 1994 the cost of the country's social welfare programs amounted to 80 percent of the Gross Domestic Product.

No demand has been too extreme to be met by the government. When squatters occupied empty houses in Amsterdam, the state bought and restored them—down to antique fireplaces—and leased the whole houses to the squatters at a nominal rent. When artists complained that no one wanted their paintings, the state bought them and stored them in warehouses. Dutch soldiers, a component of the NATO forces, have a powerful union to stand up against military discipline; the long-haired ones wear hairnets to avoid jamming their weapons.[40]

What can one say about the validity of Dutch ethnicity data? As I have noted earlier, the rebellion against legal authority eventually made it impossible to take censuses in the Netherlands.[41] The route to this crisis, moreover, was along a road marked by ever increasing hostility to what was widely viewed as a pointless invasion of privacy. Even before enumerations ceased, one can presume that the statistics gathered were far from accurate.

Considering its long duration and firm placement, the breakdown of *verzuiling* came suddenly and, for many observers, unexpectedly. One reason for the inaccurate forecasts was that analysts assumed that the entities favored in the pillarized programs were cohesive groups. Especially the Catholic bloc, but also the modernist Protestant and even the Orthodox Calvinist, were all undergoing tremendous internal transformations, while to the outsider all seemed to be continuing more or less as in the past.

The most salient data in a pillarized country were obviously the statistics on religion. Every pillar, whether of Catholics, of either Orthodox Calvinists or modernist Protestants, or of socialists, was being split apart, with factions taking sides concerning the step-by-step depillarization. Take the number of Roman Catholics as the prime example. When Schaepman started working toward a popular Catholic party, he appealed to the general body of church members over the heads of the small Catholic contingent in the Liberal party and most of the higher church prelates. That all concerned on both sides were labeled "Catholic" was all but irrelevant. This was even more the case later, when the Catholic Peoples party began to disintegrate. The defensive mandement of the bishops divided everyone in the church between traditionalists and rebels. And when the Dutch bishops switched and themselves became rebels against the Vatican, they were still opposed by a considerable number of church members. In short, during two generations when Catholics were at the head of momentous changes in Dutch society and politics, the statistical marker "Roman Catholic" was of no help in defining the boundaries of the competing camps.

13

Two Case Studies: Japan and Switzerland

The countries discussed so far typify particular patterns of ethnic relations. At its founding the United States was a trailblazing nation, based on the concept of individual liberty rather than on a common biological or cultural heritage. Belgium illustrates a bilingual state. In the Netherlands the segmentation by religion or secular weltanschauung became a highly divisive social structure. In each case the analysis could pertain with some emendations also to other countries with similar ethnic arrangements, but there are also other patterns.

Among the world's major powers, Japan is ethnically the most unified. Switzerland is famous for the cooperation among its competing components. While these additional prototypes still do not exhaust the entire range of the world's ethnic structures, they extend the reach of the prior chapters.

The Homogeneous Japanese

According to a consensus among archaeologists and historians, Japan's original inhabitants were the *Ainu.* This self-designation means men; in Japanese the usual term is *Ebisu,* meaning barbarians. Most Ainu today live on the northernmost island of Hokkaido, with small settlements in two areas now under Russian rule, Sakhalin and the Kuril Islands.

During the last decades of the nineteenth century, the Japanese government undertook to assimilate the Ainu completely. They were to adopt Japanese names, to register as Japanese subjects, and to learn to speak and write Japanese. Inevitably, a small people, lacking a written language of its own and dependent on the Japanese for many commodities and services, acculturated to the national norm. Traditional dances and clothing survived less as remnants of the past than as tourist attractions. Even genetically, the Ainu are thoroughly mingled with the dominant people, with only an estimated 300 full-bloods remaining a generation ago.[1]

The history of the Japanese themselves starts about 300 B.C. Why the many fissiparous influences over the two millennia since then failed to create significant ethnic divisions is something of a puzzle. Chinese chronicles of the Han dynasty (206 B.C.–A.D. 220) speak of Japan's "thirty countries."[2] But in the seventh century every local functionary was required to set up an image of the Buddha and make Buddhist scriptures available, and this laid one base for a unified nation.[3] Over more than a thousand years the country was administered through its sixty-six provinces, many of which were separated by water or mountains or distinguished by their traditional land use, settlement pattern, and political organization.[4] In a volume of his authoritative history, George Sansom apologizes for discussing the interclan battles "in what may seem tiresome detail," but in the years 1334–1615 "warfare was almost incessant."[5]

At the beginning of the seventeenth century, the head of a minor clan defeated his adversaries and had the Emperor declare him *Shogun,* or military commander. He launched the Tokugawa era, which from 1603 to 1867 kept the country at peace. Japan cut itself off from the rest of the world, with minor contacts restricted to a segregated area in the single port of Nagasaki. The first edition of the *Encyclopaedia Britannica* (1768) summed up the knowledge available in the West with a single short sentence giving the country's latitude and longitude. In 1854, when Commodore Matthew C. Perry of the U.S. Navy sailed up Suruga Bay and refused to leave until Japan ended its self-seclusion, his action was a last dramatic blow to a disintegrating regime. Japan did not become a colony of a Western power, but in the view of its leaders over the following decades, this was a fate that always threatened.

Since for two and a half centuries Japan had been almost completely cut off from alien influences, modernization during the Meiji era (1868–1912) started from close to zero. The new regime brought about not a revolution but a "restoration." It did not overthrow the country's established institutions, but used them as a foundation for a remarkably rapid and successful transformation. Within a few decades Japanese industry was competing well with England's. In two wars Japan defeated China and Russia, thus acquiring the first of a series of colonies.

From its beginnings Japanese culture borrowed so copiously from all available sources that some East Asian historians have regarded Japan, like Korea, as a variant of the Chinese prototype. In the early period, however, "the introduction of foreign ideas and methods served to strengthen rather than to weaken native tradition, since the use of the Chinese script permitted the Japanese to record their own history and give literary expression to their inherited ideas about life and society."[6] When Japan adapted China's familistic culture to its straitened economy, the dominant goal remained the same—to ensure an unbroken male lineage. This was to be realized not by a numerous progeny, as in China, but by sacrificing numbers to quality without weakening the family's hierarchal structure.

Filial piety went to extremes that a Westerner can hardly credit. The family was fundamental in reinforcing the country's dominant culture, not only in itself, but in a number of extensions. Many unrelated persons were brought into it through adoption, which had a much wider function than in the West.[7] The relation between *oya* (parent) and *ko* (child) spread to such nonkin pairs as boss and worker, employer and employee, leader and follower, so that some familial attributes permeated the whole society.[8] In the usual designation used by Japanese firms, workers and employees are called "members," as of a club or a family.

Japanese Identity

No element of the Meiji Restoration in 1868 was more dramatic than the abandonment of the Tokugawa policy of isolation. By 1872 at least two hundred foreign technical experts were in Japan as officials, reorganizing the army and government, introducing a banking system and commercial enterprises. Industrialization was more efficient than anywhere else up to that time, partly because when it began the Japanese people had existed for a thousand years with hardly any ethnic, linguistic, religious, or cultural divisions.

As individuals Japanese had (and to a considerable degree, still have) little identity independent of their family and community. Each person has his prescribed place, with a welcome security but sometimes onerous restrictions. Since for outsiders there is no such niche, the social structure is almost impermeable. "All foreigners living in Japan become resigned to the fact that they will always be *gaijin* (literally, outside people), welcome as temporary visitors but never admitted to the village community."[9]

A telling early example is Lafcadio Hearn, a nineteenth-century writer of fantastic tales whose search for the exotic led him to Japan.[10] Rejecting his own cultural background (a naturalized American of Greek and Anglo-Irish parentage), he interpreted Japan to the West in a series of well-received books, eventually being rewarded as a distinguished foreigner with a professorship at the Tokyo Imperial University. Then he made the mistake of becoming naturalized, marrying a Japanese woman, and adopting the name Koizumi Yakumo. No longer formally a foreigner but still one in Japanese eyes, he had his salary cut and after a few years, notwithstanding his naturalization, was fired as an unsuitable alien.

Of cultural divisions within the Japanese population itself, perhaps the most important used to be the diversity in *language*. Linguists distinguished twelve main dialects, and several generations ago farmers from different districts had difficulty communicating. But standard Japanese has been taught in all schools, with primary education universal since the 1880s, and more recently the country's radio and television have helped standardize its language. By 1940 the "almost total uniformity of education experienced in the first six school years of the life of every Japanese child [produced] a homogeneity of popular intellectual culture which has probably never been equaled" in a society with that many people.[11]

As regional dialects gradually eroded, the language of the urban elites, studded with foreign (especially English) words, became distinguished from the common speech. I have become well aware of this trend from terms in demography as rendered in Japanese: squatter, *sukuwōtā*; cohort in its demographic sense, *kōhōto*; data, *dēta*; denomination, *dēnomineshon*; minority, *mainoriti*; follow-up, *forō appu*; morning-after pill, *mōninga āfutā piru*.[12] But these differences between cosmopolitan professionals or intellectuals and the rest of the country hardly disturb the medium common to both.

To suppose that Japan's great diversity in *religion* might have created wide cultural gaps would also be simplistic. Japan has remained almost impervious to Christian proselytizing: in spite of the nearly 5,200 foreign missionaries in the mid-1980s, fewer than 1 percent of the population identified themselves with Christianity. None of the country's three main religions—Buddhism, Shinto, and Confucianism—is quite what a Westerner might expect of any faith. In the mid-1960s there were 142 Shinto sects, 169 Buddhist, 38 Christian, and 30 other. In a population of less than 90 million, there were 145 million members of these various sects; in other words, more than half the total adhered to more than one religion.[13] "A popular religious leader of the early nineteenth century urged his followers, 'Revere Shinto, Buddhism, and Confucianism, and cherish sincerity in all.' A literal observation of this command obliged a man to believe simultaneously in the Shinto gods, Buddha, and the nonexistence of both; yet this contradiction did not disturb the Japanese."[14]

Neither doctrine nor liturgy is central to any of the country's main religions. In reinforcing the national norms of behavior and such central institutions as the community and the extended family, Japan's religions transgress what an outsider might perceive as fundamental differences and help unite the people into a homogeneous nation.

Koreans

Though strongly influenced over several centuries by China and Japan, Koreans form a distinct people both racially and culturally. The language is thought to be related to the Altaic stock (which includes Turkic, Mongolian, and Manchu). It was written with Chinese ideographs until the mid-fifteenth century, when a royal commission devised a script better suited to the quite different speech.[15] Eventually Korea tried to protect itself from Chinese and Japanese incursions by closing its borders, so that in the West it acquired the sobriquet the Hermit Kingdom. In the mid-nineteenth century, Germans, French, and Americans tried to open the country to foreign trade, and in 1876 a Japanese naval force succeeded in imposing a treaty that granted commercial and other concessions. In part to offset Japan's influence, Korea signed similar treaties with other countries. During its victorious wars against China (1894–1895) and Russia (1904–1905), Japan installed troops in Korea. The country was annexed in 1910 and retained as a Japanese colony until after World War II.[16]

As in other parts of their growing empire, the Japanese in Korea were efficient, initiating vast social and economic changes, and thoroughly ruthless. As part of a program of Japanization, the military government forbade the teaching of the Korean language or history, and it imprisoned or executed Korean patriots. Koreans of all classes migrated in substantial numbers to Japan. Young men of the middle class, encouraged to go to college in Japan, often used their learning (like colonial students in London and Paris) to oppose the alien rule over their homeland. Their relatively small migration was supplemented by much larger numbers of tenant farmers and unskilled workers. By 1930 more than 400,000 Koreans, and by 1940 1.2 million, were competing with unemployed Japanese for low-level jobs.

Given the combination of a mass base and nationalist students, Koreans in Japan organized a Communist party called the North Wind Society. So long as Japan's military expansion was succeeding, such dissidents had a limited impact. After 1945 Koreans hoped to become a counterforce to the Japanese, but American occupation authorities defined Korean residents not as a liberated people, but as Japanese nationals. Newly established Korean schools in Japan, welfare for the unemployed, the attempt to register Korean residents— every program involved disputes, which persisted until they were overshadowed by the war in Korea (1950–1953). Then all Communists in Japan, both Korean and Japanese, did their best to organize riots against the American occupation. After the war Japan tried to stimulate a repatriation to either North or South Korea, but of the more than 600,000 Koreans then in the country, only some 50,000 to 100,000 returned, almost all to North Korea.[17]

Koreans have children and grandchildren born in Japan, none of whom acquired citizenship by that fact. Like other aliens, they can become naturalized; but few do, for they know that neither prospective employers nor potential spouses will ever accept them as genuine Japanese. According to a survey in the mid-1980s, Koreans in Japan numbered about 700,000, of whom three-quarters had been born and raised in Japan, with Japanese as their first or only language. As in Korea, they were divided politically between pro-Communists and anti-Communists. The Communist organization, the General Federation of Koreans in Japan, was highly bureaucratized; it ran its own schools, with instruction in Korean and an emphasis on nationalist themes. In contrast, the Korean Residents Association in Japan, a loose anti-Communist federation, was less effective in protecting the welfare of its members. "The term 'Korean' is still a derogatory one, even in the school playground, and most Japanese still hold stereotyped views of Koreans."[18]

The Pariah Caste

Japan's "very strongly ingrained racism," a deep folk belief, is strongly reflected also in academic writings. The fundamental tenet is that "Japanese 'uniqueness' is biologically based."[19] The confusion between biological and cultural characteristics, which is often encountered and condemned in Western writings, is built into the Japanese language. The Japanese word *minzoku* means both nation and race; the word for racism is also used to denote nationalism.[20] Moreover, in contrast to the West, where racism has served mainly to denigrate others, the Japanese have concentrated on why their race is unique and how this uniqueness makes them superior.

Among Japanese, physical homogeneity is a highly prized attribute. In English works members of a pariah caste are usually termed the *Eta,* which during the Tokugawa era was the official designation but is now generally avoided as offensive: the Chinese characters used to write the word mean full of filth. Now the commonest designation is *burakumin,* or resident of a *buraku,* or hamlet. (The euphemism is similar to that in some Latin American countries, where a slum area is called a *barrio,* or quarter of the city, and a resident a *barriano.*)

As the vegetarian regimen stipulated by Buddhism spread through Japan, the *burakumin* acquired a monopoly of such crafts as butchering and leather work, which were taboo for others. Under the Ashigawa shoguns (1338–1573), they had a stable community life and a moderate prosperity, with their land exempt from taxation. The Meiji regime revoked their special privileges without compensation, and they became targets of aggression.[21] Today most Japanese eat meat; and butchers, tanners, and shoemakers are usually not outcastes. Many of the *burakumin,* on the other hand, have moved into agriculture. No longer confined to segregated villages, they still generally live in isolated communities. Indeed, the only way to identify an outcaste in contemporary Japan is to know his place of residence. Like light-skinned Negroes in the United States, some try to pass; but every Japanese national is required to be registered in a record that lists both the current and all previous residences. In spite of important changes in the culture, many other Japanese still regard *burakumin* with disgust, fear, and an ostentatious curiosity. Parents try to control their children's choice of a spouse by recounting the disastrous consequences of marrying someone whose antecedents had not been thoroughly investigated by a marriage broker.

During recent decades *burakumin* have organized into militant parties. Matsumoto Jiichiro (1887–1966) ran on the Socialist party ticket and was elected to the postwar Diet in 1947, followed by almost a dozen other outcastes. In 1970 the government established *dowa* (integration) projects, which were intended to facilitate desegregation in occupations, housing, education, and health care. The programs have had some marked local successes but with little change over all. One reason is that outcaste leaders have rejected integration as a goal and stressed the importance of accepting the group identity as not shameful.[22] That the Japanese distinguish, however artificially, a minority estimated at only about 2 percent of the population highlights the homogeneity of the rest.

In sum, Japan is the only major state that is naturally also a nation in the classic sense. Differences in race, language, religion, or other characteristics that define ethnicity pertain only to minuscule groups, are generally insignificant, and in some instances are disappearing. Statistics on subnations hardly exist, for there are few elements of the population that would be included in such a category. Ainu are half-assimilated and live off by themselves in small communities. The pariah caste is small and not clearly distinguishable from the general population. Koreans, like all other foreigners, are never permitted to acculturate. This leaves the homogeneous Japanese as a single ethnic unit.

In the most recent period Japan has been changing radically, and some of these breaks with tradition suggest that a transition in national character may be in process. Market crashes, banking crises, political impotence, regulatory intransigence—this piling up of troubles has been compared with Britain's loss of self-confidence when its empire disappeared, or with the American malaise following the defeat in Vietnam.

> Because Japan, historically and culturally, has deemphasized the individual in favor of a collective identity, it gives people little...motivation when they lose faith in the national "team" effort.[23]

A startling symptom of this deterioration of self-confidence is the remarkable choice in 1996 of an American, Henry D. G. Wallace, to be president of Mazda, the country's mammoth car manufacturer. Ten years earlier no *gaijin* could have aspired to such a position.

The Swiss Confederation

The nucleus of Switzerland was a union in 1291 of three tiny states, called the forest cantons, formed to defend themselves against the Habsburgs. Over the following centuries these three were joined by surrounding areas, all of which were careful to retain their local authority as new cantons. For a brief moment a fully centralized government was imposed in Napoleon's Helvetic Republic, which did not last even as long as the emperor himself. After the defeat of Napoleon, every one of the cantons sent a separate delegate to the Congress of Vienna in 1814–1815, and representatives of actual nations had to untangle their competing claims.

The post-Napoleonic settlement that was finally reached (though still opposed by four of the then nineteen cantons) established less a nation than an arena for ideological dispute. When several urban cantons sought to give the central government the rights to tax church property, establish secular schools, and guarantee freedom of worship, seven Catholic cantons responded by setting up a so-called *Sonderbund* (Separate Union), a half-secession that in their view renewed their medieval federation to protect what they regarded as their ancient liberties. This confrontation between Catholics and Liberals, between the country's rural nucleus and urban radicals, climaxed in a three-week civil war in which the Catholic forces were decisively defeated.

In 1848, Liberals fashioned a new Constitution, which with amendments remains the country's basic law.[24] It has been said that the model used in accommodating national unity to disparate local rights and traditions was the U.S. Constitution,[25] but in fact it approximated rather the earlier and much looser Articles of Confederation. The Swiss Constitution established a single citizenship in a nation with one foreign policy, a single national economy with one customs union, and the right of any Swiss to settle in any canton. Apart from provisions prohibiting new monasteries and banning the Jesuit order, the Constitution relegated to the cantons the governance of church-state relations. It recognized three languages—German, French, and Italian—as official throughout the country and the three language groups as equal; but schools, the instruments of cultural continuity, stayed under the cantons' jurisdiction. The general allocation of power is suggested in Article I: "The peoples of the twenty-two sovereign cantons of Switzerland form together the Swiss Confederation." Many of the prerogatives of statehood, in short, were reserved to the cantons. "If it is the function of a national state to guarantee the political means by which a people united through its common characteristics and environment can further its particular needs and interests, this can be carried out nowhere better than in the Swiss cantons."[26] Or, as the same appraisal might be phrased less positively: "Diverse European cultures have not so much come together in Switzerland as they have coexisted by turning their backs on each other."[27]

The Swiss Confederation has been remarkably successful. As noted above, scholars as perceptive as Tocqueville and Max Weber doubted that so heterogeneous a population could ever constitute a viable nation.[28] Without coal, iron, oil, or colonies, it developed a truly extraordinary prosperity, and from its heterogeneity there arose a national culture of the highest quality. From 1901 to 1960 the number of Nobel laureates per million inhabitants was 2.62 for Switzerland, first in the world and almost twice as high as Denmark, which ranked second.[29] Achievements of this order foster an overall national pride that restrains internal divisions. Yet Switzerland constitutes an anomaly of intergroup harmony, which depends on a complex and sometimes precarious institutional balance of still hostile forces. The wisdom of the nineteenth-century statesmen was reinforced by a number of fortuitous circumstances, which in sum have made the survival of Swiss nationhood possible.

Swiss Identities

The three main language communities, each speaking a tongue in common with a contiguous foreign country, have inevitably shared these alien cultures in some respects, yet the fissiparous effect has been less than one might have anticipated. In the mid-1990s almost two-thirds of the native population is German-speaking, not quite a fifth French-speaking, less than a tenth Italian-speaking, and 0.8 percent Romansh-speaking. According to Hans Kohn, in the middle of the nineteenth century "many German-speaking Swiss felt a dual loyalty: the Swiss canton was their political fatherland, the still ill defined Germany their cultural homeland." After the defeat of the 1848 revolt, this adherence to the larger entity was reinforced by German radicals who found refuge in Switzerland, having lost their battle against German autocracy. Several decades later a professor at Bern University, Ferdinand Vetter, marked the opening of a Germanic museum in Nuremberg with the assertion, "We are happy to celebrate this German institution among Germans, because we German Swiss are spiritually Germans and hope to remain so."[30]

This view, however representative it may have been, was countered by the cantons' fierce independence, which not only impeded their assimilation to Swiss unity, but also blocked even a quasipolitical adherence to Germany. The poet and novelist Gottfried Keller, a greater national hero than any professor, offered an image of Switzerland identical to the American idea of nationality: "a community not determined primarily by biological factors but representing the idea of personal liberty."[31] With the rise of Prussia and particularly after the Nazis took power, the cultural bond with Germany was overridden by growing political alienation. There was even a movement in the 1930s to drop the German language and substitute the Teutonic dialect called Allemanic. It came to nothing principally because the various dialects of Swiss German are both too different and too precious to their users to be easily consolidated.

How and why do the francophone Swiss differentiate themselves from the French, the philosopher and critic Denis de Rougemont asked, and his reply is an apt statement of a similarly ambivalent relation.

> Culture in our cantons is not linked with the state and has never been used as a means of power by the state. Culture in our country exists within small natural or historical compartments, which have never been unified or standardized by a central power.... We are not only neighbors of the Germanic world, but we are in an osmotic relationship with it.[32]

An article on regional identity in French Switzerland gives a different view: "One should not speak of [the francophone sector known as] Romandie," for the differences are too great between Geneva and Vaud, between Valais and Neuchâtel, between Fribourg and the Jura, even within Vaud between particular portions of the canton. The article was written in German, but the statement had a footnote to a book by Alain Pichard in French, *La Romandie n'existe pas.*[33]

From the other side, there has been a mood in France to bolster its hegemony with cultural dependencies, which would take the place of lost colonies and waning political influence. President de Gaulle himself ended a speech in Montreal with the slogan, *"Vive le Québec libre!,"* and there have been movements to "liberate" francophone minorities from non-French "oppressors" in such countries as Canada, Belgium, Italy, and Switzerland. In the mid-1980s President François Mitterand established a worldwide "Francophonia," which with massive padding had fifty-three member nations a decade later. France spends more than $1 billion annually to support the agency's efforts to enhance the use of French. As the first language of perhaps 100 million and an occasional language of another 30 to 40 million, French ranks ninth in the world, while still retaining its place as one of the two official means of communication in international bodies. The intention of this propaganda, obviously, has been to place France at the head of all francophones. Instead it may have relegated France to a place as one of several French-speaking nations. *The Oxford Companion to French Literature,* published in 1959, has been succeeded by *The New Oxford Companion to Literature in French,* published in 1995, with more than 200 entries on Canadian, African, and Caribbean authors. Efforts to promote French in other countries are supplemented by regulations at home intended to guard the purity of the language from Anglo-American intrusions. The most recent measure was the *Loi Toubon* of 1994, which tried to ban the use of any foreign expression for which there was an "officially approved' equivalent.

> So, please, let us repair to a *restovite*—not *un fast-food*—To have *un remue-méninges* together, not—*mon dieu!*—*un brainstorming* to discuss our latest plan for *marketing*—sorry, *mercatique*.[34]

A French-speaking population is more likely to accept cultural or even political guidance from Paris if it lacks self-confidence. One index of the relation of language to provincial cultures is the work of professional linguists, who it so happens differ fundamentally between French Switzerland and Walloon Belgium. In both areas, as one would expect, the study of local dialects has been a dominant concern, but the significance of this topic has not been the same. Ferdinand de Saussure, a native of Geneva and professor at its university, founded a school in linguistics important enough to transcend national boundaries. In Belgium, on the contrary, one of the main interests has been in "preserving *'le bon usage'*; as peripheral users of French they are highly conscious of regional differences in their language, and locked as they are in an ethnolinguistic struggle with their Flemish co-citizens, they fear to lose grip on linguistic standards."[35]

The contrast is not limited to philologists. Rougemont takes a typical stance when he writes of the French and the Swiss francophones simply that "we speak more or less the same language." In Belgium a book titled *Chasse aux Belgicismes,* published by an Office du Bon Langage, became something of a best-seller.[36] The belgicisms to be "hunted down" include especially the regional accent and also distinctive elements of vocabulary and idiom, particularly if they derived from Dutch.

The generalizations about French-speaking Swiss do not pertain, however, to the inhabitants of the Jura in Bern canton, whose demand for a canton of their own has been the country's most explosive ethnic issue. The rationale for the demand, at least in the publications of the militants, goes back to the Thirty Years' War of 1618–1648. In 1815, the main separatist organization sent a memorandum to each of the signatory states at the Congress of Vienna, which had granted jurisdiction of the area to Bern canton rather than to its earlier ruler, an autocratic Prince Bishop of the Principality of Basel. The issue was less simple than a one-to-one confrontation:

> In the Bernese constitution the Jura is viewed as a single entity under the designation "the Jurasian people," but in fact the Jura is divided into three parts: North Jura, which according to the 1959 vote is inclined to be separatist; South Jura, inclined to be antiseparatist; and the district of Laufon, where the people speak German. One must take this division into account if one wants to try to propose a durable solution to the Jura's problem.[37]

When subnations differ not by one but by several overlapping characteristics, the combined divisive force is of course greater than from any one of them. Most of the population of Bern canton were German-speaking Protestants, and Jurasians who either spoke German or adhered to Protestantism were content with the status quo. It has been among the Catholic francophones that the separatist movement developed.[38] Its principal organization, the Rassemblement Jurassien, derived its name from de Gaulle's Rassemblement du Peuple Français, and its journal, *Le Jura Libre,* got its ideology from the same source. On the other side there were several antiseparatist organizations that together represented a substantial opposition to the proposed new canton and especially to the arson and bombings used to bring it about.

When the separatist movement was revived in the 1940s, Bern made a number of concessions. In 1950 a very large majority of the canton's electorate revised its constitution to specify French as the sole official language of the six francophone districts and to guarantee the Jura two seats on the canton's executive council. It was even decreed that a new Jurasian flag be flown next to the Bernese one. However, in the view of the Rassemblement Jurassien, all German-speaking inhabitants of the Jura should have been denied a vote, and all French-speaking "Jurasians," including those who had emigrated permanently, should have been given it. The vote (by more than six to one) in favor of a compromise that the federal government and Bern canton had jointly proposed, was rejected by the separatists because these *jurassiens de l'extérieur* had not been polled. In the summer of 1974 another vote was taken, overwhelmingly in favor of the formation of a twenty-third canton in the francophone Catholic area.

Neither these concessions nor subsequent ones satisfied the rebels, and an independent "République et Canton du Jura" came into existence in 1979. According to the vote, eighty-two communes became part of the new Jura Canton, and sixty-two communes voted to remain part of Bern canton. The Rassemblement Jurassien announced that it was not satisfied with this compromise: it would not rest until South Jura is reunited with North Jura in a single canton.[39]

The opposing sides in the Jura conflict illustrate a structural feature that applies to Swiss history on a broader scale. In the nineteenth century the cantons were predominantly either Protestant or Catholic, and the compromise of 1848 resulted in an initially sharp division between the two sectors, Catholic-rural-traditional versus Protestant-urban-modernizing, with what Swiss history books speak of as a *Kulturkampf* (cultural war) between them. However, as nationality gradually replaced religion as the dominant ideology of Switzerland's subnations, it so happened that sizable proportions of both Catholics and Protestants were included among the sectors speaking both German and French or Italian. Whatever antipathy arose either between religious or between language groups was mitigated by the fact that adversaries in one context could be allies in the other.[40]

Moreover, the proportions of the several subnations remained more or less the same for over a century. Nothing is so likely to exacerbate interethnic antagonism as what French Canadians call *la revanche des berceaux*—the vengeance of the cradles. With a greater number of births leading to a more rapid growth of one sector, every agreement is tentative, in force only till the day, eagerly awaited or fearfully dreaded, when one minority reaches 51 percent. By happenstance, the greater natural increase of the German Swiss was offset by their higher rate of emigration. Nor did the movement within the country disturb its structural balance: since the language of the schools is set locally, children typically adopt the language of the canton into which their parents had moved.

In more recent times, the balance that was reached by these fortuitous circumstances seems to have been endangered by the very large influx of foreign workers, who were more numerous relative to the native population than anywhere else in Europe. As one horn of the country's dilemma, the rapid postwar development of the economy had been built on a broad base of imported labor, which could not be replaced entirely by natives. In the summer of 1971 the government officially reported a total of only fifty-one unemployed in the whole country. For lack of help, retail shops and other small establishments had to restrict their activities or even close down altogether.

In the 1990s about 45 percent of the population were Protestant, 48 percent Catholic, and the rest of other faiths or irreligious. In contrast to the less than half of native Swiss who are Catholic, more than three-quarters of resident foreigners belong to that church. In a country with a population of only

6.5 million, the presence of 660,000 permanent, mainly Catholic, aliens has resulted in an *"Überfremdung"* (in French, *"hyperxénie"*; in English translation, a surplus of foreigners). Many Swiss have seen the large number of foreigners as a danger to the society mainly because most come from areas quite alien to Swiss culture (southern Italy, Spain, and other Mediterranean countries), also because legal impediments to acquiring citizenship are so great that most are unassimilable by definition. Naturalization is difficult even for a Swiss-born child of alien parents, and one may apply for the right of permanent residence only after ten years of renewed temporary visas.[41]

One reason for the legal barriers to immigration is that xenophobic parties can bring pressure through the use of the initiative. If 100,000 signatures are gathered within eighteen months, the proposal must be submitted to a popular vote. The most memorable instance was the 1989 vote to abolish the Swiss army, which was defeated by two to one, but under the law even so extreme a proposal had to be submitted to the electorate.[42] Though most initiatives fail, the federal government often adopts legislation as a preventive reform. In 1970, for example, an initiative that would have cut the number of aliens by 44 percent was defeated, but over the next several years the federal government stopped immigration altogether. "Switzerland did not have to issue a formal halt in immigration: the quantitative limits on seasonal workers, quotas, institutionalized preferences for native Swiss workers over foreigners, and other policies to reduce the foreign presence had the same outcome."[43]

In this thoroughly middle-class society, where the embourgeoisement of workers and of socialists in particular has been all but total, foreign laborers introduced a new type of proletariat. Thus, the remarkable industrial peace—a full generation without a single strike or lockout—was broken, for example, by Spanish workers constructing a new building of the International Labor Organization in Geneva. The presence of aliens has also affected interethnic relations of the Swiss themselves. Italian, which once had been more or less restricted to the single canton of Ticino, became an important second language, particularly in the cities of German Switzerland, where most of the immigrants work. If they are allowed to stay, they and particularly their children will adopt the language of the area. Thus, the large immigration of Italians, which reduced German speakers to the lowest proportion in Swiss history, may in the long run have the contrary effect, greatly reinforcing the German ascendancy over French.

In sum, Switzerland's famous ethnic harmony is too well established in deeply rooted institutions to be broken entirely, but several trends have been troublesome. The most notable episode, the demand of French-speaking Catholics in the Jura for their own autonomous canton, is less important than the disparity between the economic need for foreign workers and the unwillingness of many Swiss citizens to have them assimilated into the population. In spite of the fact that more foreigners have been permitted to come in than restrictionists would prefer, the lack of low-skill workers has squeezed the economy.

In the 1970s the federal government's power was extended with respect to the protection of the family, the national economy, atomic energy, national roads, the movie industry, oil pipelines, university scholarships, the protection of nature, and regional zoning.[44] This miscellany is made up of matters that clearly transgress cantonal boundaries, but also issues that have become important only recently. If most of the problems associated with modernity are to be assigned to the federal government, the functions of the cantons will shrink proportionally. As another reflection of the same trend, the country has been divided into 106 microregions as a guide to the central government in its efforts to assist those areas most in need of aid.[45] Seemingly, any heightened hostility between language or religious groups could be offset by an augmented central authority.

In 1991, when Switzerland celebrated the three-hundredth anniversary of its founding, some cynics were callous enough to remark that the actual nation had been born much later. Even so, it was an occasion for thinking about the past and about the future.

In an ever more urban country, where there are more city workers than farmers, there remains an agrarian nostalgia expressed in a persistent alpine folklore.... The Swiss person living in today's world is still tied to yesterday, however much his thoughts and dealings are international when they pertain to technical or commercial matters.... Politically the typical Swiss thinks first of all communally, regionally, and cantonally.... This country's history follows from its tensions, with each resolution generating new tensions—tensions by nativity, tradition, and commerce and the economy, but also by a humanitarian-social openness to the world.[46]

Conclusions

It is difficult for anyone living today to imagine a world not organized by the principle of nationality, which is so pervasive that its absence would strike one as unnatural. Yet the nation as we know it is less than two hundred years old. There were antecedents, of course: city-states in which at least the dominant classes were tied to a particular locale, or the more general attachment of virtually everyone to his province and local culture. But these were not sentiments used to legitimize the existence and boundaries of large multiethnic states.

Very few actual nations conform to the abstract definition of a large human aggregate characterized by a common territory, language, religion, genealogy, and way of life, or some partial combination of these. Perhaps much of Japan's exceptional history derives from the fact that among large countries it is all but unique in its ethnic homogeneity. There is a downside to this favorable circumstance: Japan is incapable of assimilating aliens, and such foreigners as the Korean minority have never been fully accepted.

Switzerland started from a great ethnic diversity and succeeded in building a genuine sense of national being. Like that of the United States, Switzerland's democracy permitted a full and legitimate expression of ethnicity through a strongly federal political system supplemented by local or provincial unofficial organizations. In neither Switzerland nor the United States has there been complete justice for all subnations, but in both most of the people of whatever ethnic affinity have felt that on balance the country warrants their loyal support.

What is a people? What determines the dimensions of a nation that demands the right of political selfhood? The contrast between Japan and Switzerland is intriguing. Japan is a nation because of its unique homogeneity; Switzerland is one in spite of its marked heterogeneity.

14

Who is a Jew?

In the analysis of any action that is based on a moral decision, the most relevant ethnic distribution would presumably be a breakdown by religious faiths. To fashion such a classification incurs several special problems. In the United States the only data in this century are one sample survey by the Bureau of the Census and statistics compiled by various private polling firms.[1]

Gathering religious data is especially difficult with respect to Jews, for in their case totally irreligious persons may choose, under some circumstances but not others, to define themselves as part of what they see as an ethnos. And if they decide that they are not Jews, others may nevertheless overrule that choice and apply anti-Semitic measures against them. In short, the recurrent dilemma in gathering ethnic data—the preliminary definition of a person's ethnicity—is particularly perplexing in this case.

Who is a Jew in History?

From the earliest periods of Jewish history the ethnic label has been ambiguous. The word *Jew,* from the Hebrew *Yehudi,* first designated a member of the tribe of Judah. Subsequently, when King David's kingdom was split between Israel in the north and Judea in the south, a resident of the former was known as a Yeduhi irrespective of his tribal identity. Still later the word referred to adherents of a religion; those who called themselves Israelites were designated by outsiders as Yehudim. The dominance of religious identity, however, is largely a consequence of the fact that most writings about Jews' earliest history have been by religious Jews. In the words of J. L. Talmon, an Israeli professor of history, there have been "heterodox and even secular trends in Judaism, but their voices have been suppressed by the priestly scribes and compilers." In the second century, according to Talmon's account, some Jews "gambled on horses, worshiped Aphrodite, prayed to Greek gods, coveted other men's wives, dodged bill collectors, and concocted ways to become invisible."[2]

The word *Judaism* is of relatively recent coinage, not to be found in the Bible, rabbinic literature, or very often in medieval literature. The nucleus of

Judaic identity, the core of the faith, is the Mosaic covenant—the treaty by which God promised to free the Jews from slavery in Egypt and they promised to obey His commandments. According to the American historian Chaim Potok, those who fled Egypt were a motley assemblage of frightened and quarrelsome Asians of various ethnic backgrounds who became Israelites only after they accepted the obligation to adhere to the Ten Commandments.[3] Over the centuries a believer's responsibilities were supplemented by layer after layer of elaboration in the Talmud, next to the Torah (or Bible) the most sacred work. Judaism sets no sharp distinction between secular and religious law; *halakhah* (Hebrew for law) derives from the Talmud and post-talmudic exegesis. As spelled out by Akiva Orr, a modern secular Israeli,

> Judaism...demands that the believer demonstrate acceptance by practicing daily religious rules for the conduct of ordinary life (*mitsvot*).... Matters of washing, food, dress, work, and rest are prescribed in some 613 religious rules which regulate daily life.... The initiation ceremony of the Jewish adolescent is called "Bar-mitsvah," i.e., "capable of performing the mitsvot," indicating that this is the essence of the community which this youth is joining.... The only valid definition of "a Jew" is—one who performs the mitsvot. All other definitions...are mere stopgaps designed to keep in the fold those who are about to stray away.[4]

With so voluminous and continually evolving a dogma, Judaism developed into a faith of considerable complexity.

In the first and second centuries A.D., after being disastrously vanquished in their homeland, Jews dispersed from the Near East throughout the world—to India and China, to Italy and from there to northern Europe and then to the New World. Early in the Middle Ages Christians began to denounce Jews as the murderers of Christ, and eventually this hostility became a routine element of Christianity. In a remarkable table in his book on the Holocaust, the American political scientist Raul Hilberg listed in parallel columns anti-Jewish canon laws of the Roman Catholic Church and strikingly similar measures decreed in Nazi Germany.[5] Martin Luther's book, *About the Jews and Their Lies,* pictured them "like a plague, pestilence, pure misfortune in our country," demons who want to rule the world and in the process stealing and dismembering Christian children and poisoning the water that Christians drink.[6]

Though the basis of anti-Semitism was originally religious, after many Jews converted or became agnostics, antipathy continued with a mercantile or social-class rationale, then under the Nazis a racial one, then in Communist and Islamic countries a nationalist one based on a deliberate confusion of Judaism with Zionism. Antipathy toward Jews spread even to peoples who may never have encountered any, whether in life or in literature. An anonymous work denouncing the Chinese in Southeast Asia, allegedly written by the King of Siam, was titled *The Jews of the East.*[7] The Ijebu, a tribe in the Nigerian territory from which many of the middlemen in the nineteenth-century slave traffic were drawn, were known as "the Jews of Yorubaland."[8]

Apart from the Diaspora itself, several factors encouraged diversity within Judaism. Active proselytizing in the early period brought large numbers of believers into the originally small Jewish population. Most conversions or half-conversions, however, were rather of Jews into the religions of the host populations. In Spain the *conversos,* Jews who had become Christians, were known as *"marranos,"* or swine. They were suspected (in some cases, correctly) of continuing in secret to practice their prior faith, and in spite of their possibly dubious loyalty to Catholicism, many had risen to prominence. In 1478 Ferdinand and Isabella of Castille developed an irregular and spasmodic judicial system into a permanent Inquisition to test the sincerity of their conversions.

A surge of anti-Semitism spread throughout Western Europe. Jews were expelled from England in 1290, then from France, Portugal, and parts of Germany, from Spain in 1492. By 1600 few professing Jews were left in Western Europe. In their migration eastward they divided into two broad denominations—Sephardim, who fled from Spain or Portugal to the eastern Mediterranean basin and spoke Ladino, a mixture of Spanish, Hebrew, Aramaic, and the local languages; and Ashkenazim, who were ousted from Germany and spoke Yiddish, derived from German with Hebrew, Aramaic, and local admixtures. In the segregated small towns of tsarist Russia and in Europe's remaining ghettos, Jews lived for several centuries in relative isolation from their host countries' cultures. Cut off from the modern world, they turned inward, developing ever more intricate exegeses of Judaic orthodoxy in a *pilpul,* or talmudic study, that became hairsplittingly disputatious.

France of the eighteenth century was the center of the Enlightenment, and most of its proponents, the so-called *philosophes* (what we today would call intellectuals), opposed any religious intrusion into secular life. Whether Christians, deists, or atheists, all were anticlerical. For the divine right of kings they substituted the natural rights of all and a social contract underlying government. Reason became more important than faith; nature was redefined as good; and for the decline from God's grace there was substituted a probable or inevitable progress.

Since Christianity was the dominant site of anti-Semitism, most Jews welcomed the challenge to churches' power, and some of their hopes for reform were realized. Throughout Western Europe laws keeping them at an inferior civil status were revoked. The Napoleonic decree, which became the usual formula of this emancipation, was limited: "The Jew as an individual is to be given every right, but Jews as a nation [to be understood in the then usual meaning of community] are to be denied any right."[9] From Eastern Europe, where Jews were being murdered in periodic pogroms, many fled to the small settlements remaining in countries of the West. Responses varied among those who could now choose to convert, to remain a Jew, or to seek some intermediate status.

The French Enlightenment, in Europe the main font of modern secular ideology, also helped develop the nonreligious variant of anti-Semitism. Virtually every *philosophe* followed the lead of Voltaire, who was obsessed with Jewry. During Hitler's domination of Europe, a history teacher named Henry Labrou compiled a 150-page book of Voltaire's anti-Jewish writings. Of the 118 articles in Voltaire's *Dictionnaire Philosophique,* 30 pertain to Jews, whom he described as "the most abominable people in the world," "a totally ignorant nation" whose "priests have always sacrificed human victims with their sacred hands." All men were worthy of freedom except the Jews, because Jews were not of the same species as the rest of mankind.[10]

Socialists on Jews

Of the various new types of denigration of Jews that arose after religious anti-Semitism lost its legal underpinning, perhaps the most influential was that of the socialist movement. Marx described Judaism as "the petty haggling of the hawker"; "money is the universal value of everything." Some years later he characterized the Jews in Prussia's Polish province as "the filthiest of all races." He denounced Ferdinand Lassalle, the leader of a competing German socialist party, as a "Jewish nigger." In Engels's phrase, Lassalle was rather "a greasy Jew disguised under brilliantine and flashy jewels."[11] Socialists have had to grapple with this all too blunt record to maintain the pious fiction that their founding fathers were not anti-Semitic.

The maniacal antipathy was taken over by the French socialists, who saw themselves as the principal heirs of the Enlightenment. In the words of a founder of the movement, Charles Fourier, the emancipation of those "parasites, merchants, usurers" was "the most shameful of all recent vices of society." France's most important socialist theorist, Pierre-Joseph Proudhon, demanded that they be denied any employment and be expelled from France, for "the Jew is the enemy of the human race. One must send this race back to Asia or exterminate it."[12] It was only after the second trial of Charles Dreyfus, a Jewish officer in the French army who was convicted of treason with forged evidence, that Jean Jaurès called on his fellow French socialists to come to his support. Karl Liebknecht and Rosa Luxemburg, who were virtually canonized after soldiers murdered them, denounced Jaurès's stand, for in their view it was impossible for a member of the ruling class to be condemned unjustly.[13]

English socialists, though generally less well-known than their comrades on the Continent, followed along the same path. H. M. Hyndman, founder of the Social Democratic Federation, called the conflict in South Africa "an abominable war on behalf of German-Jew mine owners and other international interlopers." In his book *Anticipations* (1902), H. G. Wells denounced the "swarms of black, and brown, and dirty-white, and yellow people.... The whole tenor and meaning of the world, as I see it, is that they have to go."[14]

From Voltaire and Marx, there was an unbroken line to Stalin and beyond. "Socialist anti-Semitism," in the words of the American social analyst George

Lichtheim, "was in its origins the poisoned root of a tree planted—alongside the more familiar tree of liberty—in the decades following the French revolution. The anticapitalist and anti-Jewish themes were intertwined."

> [There is a] striking contrast between Marx's benevolent desire to liberate the toiling masses from the tyranny of their capitalist exploiters and his ferocious attacks upon those who appeared to stand in the way of his messianic hopes—the "idiotic" peasants and the "rapacious" Jews, for example. Long after Marx's death his followers in Soviet Russia were acting quite in accordance with their master's views when they eliminated the kulaks and persecuted the Jews.[15]

Moreover, aberrant socialists constituted a pathway by which anti-Semitism was transferred from socialism to protofascist or fascist movements.

One day after their coup, the Bolsheviks established a Commissariat for Jewish National Affairs (or *Evkom*). One of Evkom's first acts was to abolish the autonomous institutions of the Jewish community and to transfer their property and funds to itself. The Jewish Sections within the Communist party, now the sole political force of Soviet Jewry, busied themselves assaulting competing political or cultural institutions of Jews, beginning with the "bourgeois-clerical Zionists" and proceeding with Hebrew schools. The campaign culminated in 1922, when some 3,000 Zionists were arrested and sentenced to exile in Siberia, Kazakhstan, or the Solovetski Islands. Dr. Julius Margolin, a Zionist who from 1940 on was himself imprisoned in several camps, wrote later that "an entire generation of Zionists has died in Soviet prisons, camps and in exile." They got no help from the Zionist movement, in good part because Western liberals, including the Jews and the Zionists among them, were generally unwilling to face up to Soviet brutality. "We did not care," Margolin recalled. "I do not remember seeing a single article about [the victims] in the prewar papers. Not the least effort was made to mobilize public opinion and alleviate their fate."[16]

After the Union of Soviet Socialist Republics was formally established at the beginning of 1923, the party vigorously promoted Yiddish newspapers, schools, courts, and soviets. Attempts to metamorphose Jews into agriculturists were intensified, culminating in the establishment of a Jewish Autonomous Oblast in Birobidzhan, about as far from European Russia as one could get within the USSR. The project's principal purpose was not to provide a place where Jews could settle, but to strengthen militarily and politically a region on the border of China. Though a total failure as a Jewish settlement, for years Birobidzhan served as an effective morsel of propaganda among sympathetic Jews in Western countries.[17]

Almost all the Jewish Communist leaders became victims of the 1930s purges. As objects of the party's antipathy, Jews were refashioned from "national bourgeois," "Zionist sympathizers," "Bundists," or whatever to simply Jews as Jews, Jews *tout court*. Defendants in the several show trials were known by their party pseudonyms and so identified in Soviet accounts. When their original names were recognizably Jewish, however, the Soviet press routinely cited them as, for instance, "Kamenev (Rosenfeld)" or "Trotsky (Bronstein)." During a period when millions were being killed off in a man-made famine and a massive purge, it was decidedly useful for the party to label the standard scapegoat.

Even traits once regarded favorably became a basis for hostility and discrimination. Between the mid-1930s and the late 1940s, the meaning of "cosmopolitan" changed from a citizen of the world (in a socialist context a positive designation) to a traitor to one's country. By a gradual process, in an effort to reconstitute Russian patriotism as a weapon against Nazi Germany, cosmopolitanism was defined as "a reactionary theory that preaches indifference to the fatherland, to national traditions, and to national culture." Then, after the war an article in *Pravda* (28 January 1949) carried the new meaning one step farther. Those guilty of cosmopolitanism were identified as persons associated with international Jewry, Zionism, pro-Americanism, and Catholicism; and in the following months the target was more narrowly specified as Soviet Jews.[18]

Anti-Semitism rose to a new climax in 1948 to 1953. The most dramatic event was the so-called doctors' plot: nine Jewish physicians were to be unmasked as agents of an American-Zionist conspiracy, allegedly masterminded by the Joint Distribution Committee (an American relief agency active in Eastern Europe but not in the Soviet Union). If Stalin had not died in 1953, the physicians would certainly have been executed, and it is likely that the carefully structured plot was intended also as a prelude for a much more extensive slaughter of Soviet Jews.

In 1963 an intensified campaign of defamation was launched with the publication by the Ukrainian Republic Academy of Sciences, of *Judaism without Embellishment*. A crudely anti-Semitic tract, it combined absurd fabrications with cartoons hauntingly reminiscent of those that had earlier been printed in Julius Streicher's *Der Stürmer* (The Stormtrooper), the most viciously anti-Jewish Nazi publication. According to an article in the Soviet journal, *Literaturnaia Gazeta* (Chronicle of Literature, 10 February 1953), the author, Trofim Kichko, had been a collaborator during the Nazi occupation of the Ukraine and, after the war, had been expelled from the party. The outcry against his book was so strong in the West, including Western European Communist parties, that the work was withdrawn—to be replaced by others, including one by the same Trofim Kichko, *Judaism and Zionism* (1968).

As before, Jews were sent off to camps in large numbers, no longer as political prisoners, but generally for violation of this or that decree. Soviet anti-Semites were adept at manipulating decrees concerning participation in the ubiquitous black market, bribery, dealing in foreign currency, and so on. In the mid-1960s more than a third of those sentenced to death for breaches of such laws were Jews, and the fact was emphasized in every Soviet newspaper account.

Jews have had to live with an ambivalent status in many countries, but seldom have the contradictions been as sharp as in the Soviet Union. As a mainly urban people with a tradition of learning, Jews could rise within an economy undergoing modernization, and some did so. But the anti-Semitism endemic in both Eastern Europe and socialist doctrine rose periodically to maniacal extremes, leaving no path to security for many Jews.

> On the one hand, the authorities want the Jews to assimilate; on the other hand, they irrationally fear the full penetration of Soviet life which assimilation implies. So the Jews are formally recognized as a nationality, as a religious group, as equal citizens—but are at the same time deprived of their national and religious rights as a group, and of full equality as individuals.[19]

Jews as a Race

Elsewhere the widespread secularization made it imperative to rewrite anti-Jewish laws and even myths, and it was no simple task to devise a suitable revision. For example, in the 1890s sixteen members of the German Reichstag had an unofficial platform on who is a Jew:

Was er glaubt is einerlei; In der Rasse liegt die Schweinerei.

(His faith is a matter of indifference; it is in race that the rottenness lies.) Yet the anti-Jewish legislation they would have liked to sponsor always foundered on the issue of how to identify their intended victims. As another example, Karl Lueger, a leader of Austria's notoriously anti-Semitic Christian Social party and mayor of Vienna from 1897 to his death in 1910, included Jews not only among his "best friends," but as employees of municipal bureaus; he even allowed them to be students of the Gymnasium and the university. In a famous declaration he asserted, *"Wer Jude ist, bestimme ich"* (I decide who is a Jew). Like many other anti-Semites, Lueger assumed he was privileged to single out the wheat from the chaff.

The fateful question of who in Nazi Germany was a Jew took two and half years to work out.[20] As Raul Hilberg traced the route the first formulation, in April 1933, was to divide the population between Aryans and non-Aryans according to whether or not they had at least one Jewish grandparent. But the Japanese protested that, as non-Aryans, they were classified with Jews. According to some party members, moreover, Jews should have been differentiated by the amount of their non-Aryan blood. In September a second attempt was made in a decree setting qualifications for German citizenship, but this also had to be discarded. The final decrees were written under pressure at the highest party level, for in another decree with criminal sanctions "Jew" and

"German" had already been used without precise definitions as approximate equivalents of non-Aryan and Aryan. Yet it took until 14 November 1935 for the citizenship law to reach its final form.

A Jew was defined as:

- A person with three or four Jewish grandparents; or
- A person with two Jewish grandparents who
  — belonged to a Jewish religious community on 15 September 1935 or subsequently joined one; or
  — was married to a Jew on that date or subsequently married one; or
  — was the offspring of a marriage with a three-quarter or full Jew contracted after that date; or
  — was the offspring of an extramarital relationship with a three-quarter or full Jew and was born after 31 July 1936.

Defined as not a Jew but as a *Mischling,* or person of partly Jewish blood, were the following:

- A person with two Jewish grandparents who
  — did not adhere to the Jewish religion on 15 September 1935, and did not join it subsequently; or
  — was not married to a Jew on that date and did not marry one subsequently.
- A person with one Jewish grandparent.

In principle *Mischlinge* were not to be destroyed but were subject to various types of less total discrimination.

A new profession of *Sippenforscher* (or genealogical researchers) came into being, for anyone who sought employment by the Reich or membership in the party had to submit seven documents—the birth or baptismal certificates of four grandparents, two parents, and himself. Doubtful cases were taken to Germany's highest court, which by a racial criterion classified a few persons with four "German" grandparents as Jews because they had adopted the Judaic religion or married a Jew. Court cases concerning *Mischlinge* were especially common and confusing. A *Mischling* of the first degree could be transformed into one of the second degree; and one of the second degree could be transformed into a "German." "Pseudoliberation" resulted from a clarification of the law or correction of prior false evidence, and "true liberation" was awarded for "merit."

As Germany conquered large portions of Europe during the first years of World War II, the allies it acquired also issued new or revised decrees defining the Jews who were to be persecuted. In Croatia, Slovakia, and Bulgaria, volunteers for military service, decorated or incapacitated veterans, and war orphans were not subject to the same degree of discrimination. In Bulgaria a person with three or four Jewish grandparents was not a Jew if he had been baptized and married in a Christian rite. A Croatian decree incorporated a prior decision of a German court defining the spouse of a Jew as also one. In Hungary a person born in 1920 to a Jew converted to Christianity, if his forebears had lived in Hungary for a century or more, was a Jew in 1938, a non-Jew in 1939, and again a Jew in 1941.[21]

Though both Germany and these various partial imitators loudly proclaimed their classifications as racial, in fact they continued the earlier religious categories. No attempt was made to classify the populations by the shape of the nose (in accordance with the universal anti-Semitic stereotype) or, as another criterion, by blood type. Persons were identified as Jews either by their own religion or by that of their parents or grandparents (or, however ridiculous in a racial classification, by that of their spouse). Though ideologues held that pollution persists indefinitely, even the fanatics who established the categories did not consider tracing the "tainted blood" back more than two generations.

Remarkably, one response to this ostensibly racial typology was to accept the propaganda and argue, in opposition to a palpable fabrication, that Jews do not in any sense constitute a race—or even that in the human species there are no subspecies of any sort.[22] Indeed, given the history of Jewry, one would expect a wide range of all genetic characteristics. However, if one understands race to be a human grouping with a relatively high probability of inherited characteristics, and if one applies this definition to particular sectors of the world's Jewish population, one finds discernible racial pockets with a markedly higher incidence, for instance, of certain genetic diseases.[23]

Paradoxically, some Jewish writers have contended that there is a biological basis of Jewish superiority. The theory was spelled out in greatest detail by the American economist Nathaniel Weyl in his book, *The Creative Elite in America* (1966): the smartest young men became rabbis, married the daughters of the wealthiest men in their communities, and thus were able to bring up a large progeny. In short, in Weyl's words, "Jewish intellectual eminence can be regarded as the result of seventeen centuries of selective breeding for scholars." The sociologist-philosopher Lewis Feuer wrote a lively critique that challenges every element of the hypothesis. The smartest Jews, who had the greatest possibilities for advancement in the Christian or Muslim world, were generally the most likely to convert and move out of Jewry. Among the forty-nine Nobel laureates listed in the *Encyclopaedia Judaica,* precisely one was descended from rabbinic forebears; of twenty-eight famed rabbis of modern times, all but six were descended from rabbis. "Possibly selective breeding heightened the acumen of rabbinical intelligence; it may also have extinguished qualities of venturesomeness and originality."[24]

The bigotry endemic in socialism and maniacal in Nazism confirmed beyond contest the fear that secularization would not bring a full or permanent relief to those who had been persecuted as non-Christians. Even those totally alien to both Judaism and Jewishness were denied full entry into some gentile societies.

What's in a Name?

If Judaism is the *sine qua non* of being Jewish, then why should a secular Jew, not to say one who has converted to Christianity or Islam, continue to carry a label that invites harassment and discrimination? One avenue of escape has been to adopt a non-Jewish name, and the Judaic tradition itself provided many precedents. Benzion Kaganoff, who has written a number of articles and two books on the names of Jews, summed up as follows: "Even the most religiously motivated and identity-conscious Jews have become acculturated as far as their names are concerned."[25]

For a period in early modern times, that most intimate of the labels of one's persona, one's name, varied over the years. According to a number of studies cited by the historical demographer Roger S. Schofield, in various English-speaking countries the same persons listed in various records had different spellings of their name in from 4 to as many as 25 percent of the cases. Similar proportions were found in other countries.[26] People who up to that time had lived with only a given personal name were also obliged to adopt a surname. So long as Jews lived isolated in their own communities, one name usually sufficed to distinguish an individual. As a first step in their emancipation in modern Europe, Jews were obliged to cut through the confusion of identities by adopting a family name that would remain constant through succeeding generations.

German files of applications for changes of name still exist in two archives, in Merseburg and Berlin, and a historian has analyzed them for two periods, 1840 to 1867 and 1900 to 1932.[27] One purpose of Prussia's law mandating family names was to give Jews who wanted it a degree of anonymity, but anti-Semites resented a device that permitted their intended targets to become less visible. Over the decades, thus, German Jews were sometimes urged and sometimes forbidden to adopt a gentile name. The surnames were sometimes recognizably Jewish, but especially in Germany many were not. Some bureaucrats welcomed an occasion to supplement their income with a new kind of blackmail. Jews able to pay handsomely could buy surnames containing such attractive labels as *Gold-*, *Fein-* (fine), or *-blum* (flower). Those who could not afford to reward their tormentors were saddled with such identities as *Schmalz* (grease), *Ochsenschwanz* (oxtail), or *Eselkopf* (donkey's head).

As late as the 1920s about 4,000 Germans a year petitioned to adopt a new name, and courts of the Weimar Republic approved virtually all the applications. Responding to the official encouragement of full acculturation, many Jews took on surnames that helped them melt into the general population. In a continual search for the latest fashion, some names chosen as ultragentile became identified as quasi-Jewish. In Germany this happened to Siegfried, in the United States to Milton and Seymour. Such a German name as Morgenstern (morning star), as one example, was both associated with Jews and held by many gentiles; and as the Nazis became more powerful, some 15,000 of the latter organized a National Association of Morgensterns in order to avoid confusion between its members and the targets of anti-Semites.

When the National Socialist government undertook to set Jews apart by their names (as well as a J on their identity cards and a yellow Star of David on their clothing), it took from 1933 to two final decrees in 1938 to complete the task. All Jews were required to change their given names to one of those in a list of 185 for males and 91 for females, prescribed for them and forbidden for all others. Some biblical names that had become popular among gentiles (Joshua and Esther, for instance) were omitted from the list, and many were spelled in "the Yiddish fashion" in order to make them stand out more sharply.

In the United States, Joey Adams, who changed his name from Abramowitz when he started as a stand-up comedian, used to tell his audiences about a club date in Boston. Wendell Adams, one of the New England Adamses, came up after the show and, as a joke, asked whether they might be related. "I don't know," Joey responded; "what was your name before you changed it?" The reason this is funny, of course, is that everyone assumes that all such families as the Adamses have an unblemished genealogy. Contrary to the usual supposition, however, the eventual white Anglo-Saxon Protestants who dominated the upper class some decades ago included a significant minority who, as they moved up, had changed their ethnic identity as well as their social class.[28]

An article in *Aufbau* (6 August 1943), New York's German-language newspaper for refugees from Nazism, advised its readers to make a "sensible choice" in choosing a new name. The piece was titled *"Müssen Sie Washington heissen?"*—Do you have to call yourself Washington? According to a survey among its readers, a few respondents had carefully preserved the Jewish character of the earlier name. Others noted that since they did not speak English well, they avoided too Anglo-Saxon an appellation. Some alterations were total. Many translated the name to the English equivalent, and others translated only part of a compound name. Long names were cut by dropping the end, the beginning, or the middle. The sound of words was approximated, or letters were transposed.

Most interesting were the reasons cited for what all respondents took to be an important decision:

- to shift from a name hard for Americans to spell or pronounce;
- to complete the break with the past; for example, various combinations with *Deutsch* (German) were discarded;
- to avoid anticipated anti-Semitism;

- of soldiers, as officially counseled by the U.S. Army, to avoid special persecution in case they were taken prisoner;
- to adopt names of relatives who had immigrated earlier.

Many expressed satisfaction with their new names, which they said removed the immigrant or Jewish element and helped them assimilate. A minority, who were also more reluctant to discuss their motives, regretted having made the change.

Refugees during and immediately after Hitler's war undoubtedly constituted a special case, and their stated motives differed from those noted in some other studies. For the same period, of 1,107 consecutive petitioners to the Los Angeles Superior Court, 46 percent (as against 6 percent of the Los Angeles population at that time) were Jews. Non-Jewish petitioners wanted, for example, to return to a maiden name after a divorce or to rid themselves of a name difficult to pronounce. Most of the Jews, it was presumed, hoped to avoid being identified as such.[29]

Undoubtedly the adoption of a new name is so charged an issue, often raising pangs of guilt, because many see it as one step toward apostasy. However, when several sociologists compared two samples from the National Jewish Population Study with or without distinctively Jewish names, they found no significant difference in such demographic attributes as age or place of birth or in such religious/ethnic indicators as belonging to a synagogue, attending a seder, or even having friends most of whom were Jews.[30]

American Jews

Jews in America had long been divided by their national origin, which was closely associated with the period of their immigration. Sephardic and German Jews, relatively well established by the 1880s, were overwhelmed during the following decades by far larger numbers from Poland, Lithuania, and the Ukraine. The later immigrants spoke Yiddish, a language that many of the earlier settlers stigmatized. As early as 1888 East Europeans had established 130 Orthodox congregations in New York City, and some struggled to maintain such traditional communities in America's infertile soil. They had to overcome not only a widespread trend toward secularism, but the rise of new denominations within Judaism.

The Reform movement, which started in Germany, flourished especially in the United States. Like Protestantism, Reform Judaism was faced with a persistent dilemma in deciding how to define religious authority. Some of those associated with it eventually became no more than ambiguously Jewish or entirely irreligious, and a portion of those remaining returned part way to traditional orthodox rituals. Conservative Judaism was established as a less than total adaptation to modern life, in accord with the flexibility that its leaders perceived in the *halakhah* itself. Based on both a premodern doctrine and an accommodation to modern values, however, it is in perpetual tension.

Two momentous happenings, the Holocaust and the founding of Israel, broke down many prior divisions, and by the 1950s most American Jews fitted into a middle range. For many observing Jews religion had become a family affair. For them attendance at the synagogue has been restricted to the High Holy Days and Passover, and burdensome restrictions on personal behavior have been cut to comfortable levels. Many analysts of Jewry have watched the accommodation to gentile norms with increasing apprehension. As one small but telling example, consider college fraternities and sororities. Up to World War II most non-Jewish ones excluded Jews; subsequently, in response to increasing pressure, they admitted them on the same basis as gentiles. But one unofficial function of these social groups is to furnish adolescents a choice among suitable marriage partners, and the "specter" of rising intermarriage rates induced Jewish community leaders to reverse the earlier demand and sponsor segregated Jewish fraternities and sororities.[31]

It is a commonplace that American Jews, once concerned about whether they would be accepted, are now anxious about whether they will survive their all but total acceptance. As Prime Minister of Israel, Golda Meir held that Jewish-gentile marriages in the United States were a kind of continuation of the Holocaust in Europe. The same sentiment, though usually lacking the preposterous comparison, has become a routine commentary also among American Jewish spokesmen.

As of the 1990s, more than half of young Jews are marrying outside the faith, and conversions of non-Jewish partners are in a distinct minority. Jewish knowledge and education are, for most Jews, thin at best and becoming thinner.... The Jewish proportion of the population will drop below 2 percent within the next century.... More American Jews today see themselves as members of an "ethnic" group than of a "religious" group, [and there has been a] decline of ethnicity into nostalgia.[32]

How many Jews are there in the American population? There is no simple answer to that question, mainly because there is no simple answer to who is a Jew. In 1970 to 1971 the Council of Jewish Federations undertook a national survey. Three criteria were used to define the ethnos: whether any in a housing unit had been born Jewish, had a parent who had been born Jewish, or regarded themselves as being Jewish. When corrections were made for sampling and other errors, the total was estimated to be between 5.6 and 6.0 million.[33] Only very small proportions of those who had been born Jewish (or gentile) did not report themselves as such. But many non-Jews–that is, gentile spouses of Jews and children not being raised as Jews—lived in the households included in the survey.

In 1990, after several years of preparation, there was another survey. The sample design was intended to ensure the widest possible coverage, ranging from those who strongly identified themselves as Jewish to those on the margins of the community or even outside it. Persons who had been born Jews who no longer considered themselves Jewish, as well as gentile spouses and children of Jewish household members, were to be counted. With this wide a net, an initial screening identified 5,146 households with one or more Jews or quasi-Jews. Detailed interviews on their social and economic characteristics were completed with 6,507 persons in 2,439 of these households.

> One might question whether individuals should be counted as part of the Jewish population if they do not regard themselves as currently Jewish, even though born of one or two Jewish parents or raised as Jews, and particularly if they currently report identification with another religion.... [But] unless it is known how many are in each category, including those on the margins and those who have left, the community cannot design realistic programs to maintain its strength, to retain those in it—especially those on the margins—and to attract back those who have opted out.[34]

According to the 1990 survey, the estimate was 8.1 million Jews or former Jews. But of these, only 4.2 million identified themselves as Jews by a religious criterion and 1.1 million as secular Jews, giving a total of 5.5 million in the "core Jewish population."

> Major challenges face the community as a result of intermarriage, the persistence of low fertility, the greater dispersal of the population, comparatively high rates of marital instability, the evidence of growing secularism, the loss of the more traditional members through aging and death, and growing Americanization. Yet...American Jews continue their efforts to find a meaningful balance between being American and being Jewish.[35]

In a useful summary of analyses of American Jews, the sociologist Nathan Glazer paraphrased the works of what he termed transformationists, mainly the American sociologists Calvin Goldscheider and Steven M. Cohen:

> American Jews remain different in family structure, occupations, education, political values, and social behavior from non-Jewish Americans. These differences have nothing to do with discrimination or the failure of American Jews to integrate. Indeed, some of these differences—as in the greater amount of education and the concentration in the professions—are due to the very openness of American society. The ability to integrate leads, paradoxically, not to American Jews paralleling American educational achievements and occupational structure, but to their diverging on the basis of open opportunity. Furthermore, these differences are sustained by and help to sustain a pattern of social life in which Jews interact for the most part with other Jews.[36]

Jews in Israel

Parallel with the anti-Semitic redefinition of Jews as a race rather than as a religious community, there had been the Zionist redefinition: Jews are a people rather than, or as well as, a religious community. The rise of political (as distinguished from messianic) Zionism followed a reversal of the prior trend in Europe toward greater tolerance and full emancipation. From the first progenitors of the movement through the rancorous Zionist congresses to the politics of Israel after it was founded in 1948, many issues have remained the same—and most of them pertain to the question of Jewish identity.

- Most fundamentally, Zionism was opposed by assimilationists. A French Jew, for example, may regard himself as a Frenchman who happens to be a Jew or a Jew who happens to live in France. If he sees himself as the former, he might well find the latter designation not only wrongheaded but dangerous, for it aggravates anti-Semites' doubts about Jews' loyalty to France.
- Among Zionists, the most important conflict has been between messianic and political advocates. In 1935 the extremist wing of religious Zionists founded a small sect that evolved into the "Guardians of the City," in whose view it was blasphemous to establish a Jewish state before the coming of the messiah. Currently religious Zionists in Israel are divided into two broad groups, each with about a tenth of the Jewish population: the ultra-Orthodox (in Hebrew, *haredim*, or zealots) and the Orthodox (in Hebrew, *dati'im*). The former do not, and the latter do, serve in the armed forces and otherwise support the Israeli state.
- Before the state was founded, a corollary question concerned its site. Various places were suggested: "Neujudäa," the American Midwest purchased from the United States, or Uganda. That the movement settled on "the Land of Israel" was an implicit concession to religious Zionists rather than the result of comparing alternative localities on other grounds.
- Zionist ideology has rejected the culture that Jews had developed in exile. The agricultural commune of the kibbutz was represented as therapy for the alienation allegedly generated in the ghetto or the urban environments that followed it. Reflecting its determination to break with the past, Israel was for many years hostile to both Yiddish and the Yiddishist movement established to honor the culture associated with that language.

Jews of all types, that is to say, resisted the idea of Zionism or some of its manifestations—religious zealots, patriots who opposed a dual nationality, socialists who opposed any form of national identity, aficionados of the culture associated with Yiddish. No one really believed the Zionist slogan, "a land without people for a people without a land." From before the founding of the state, its advocates had to face the problem of an Arab population in the territory they claimed as their own. Socialist Zionists rationalized their program with the vision of an Arab proletariat, downtrodden by their callous ruling class, gaining enormously in a Jewish state. Revisionist Zionists, somewhat more realistically, anticipated that Arabs would defend their homeland militantly, and that in the struggle to establish a new state violence could be mitigated but not evaded. Many Zionists took a middle position and hoped that things could be worked out by some sort of accommodation.[37]

That, in spite of these obstacles, a Jewish state was established in Palestine was a near-miracle, and Israel's survival through almost five decades of persistent hostility from its neighbors and their allies has been a true miracle. In spite of all its achievements, however, Israel has not solved "the Jewish question." The ambivalent identity of the Jew in exile and the psychological alienation supposedly resulting from that status have not ended now that he is a citizen of what Zionists call "his own country," no longer impelled to imitate the culture of a gentile majority.

According to the declaration of independence on 14 May 1948, "We hereby proclaim the establishment of the Jewish State in Palestine, to be called the State of Israel." Shortly thereafter, the Knesset (Parliament) passed unanimously a Law of Return, which announced that "every Jew has the right to immigrate to the country." Two years later it was supplemented by a Nationality Law that stipulated who was or could become an Israeli citizen. Thus, both the founding document and the laws setting Israel's future population pertained to "Jews," who were not defined either there or elsewhere.

With the establishment of the state, all divisions within the Jewish population became more significant and therefore sharper. The number of parties competing for seats in the Knesset was twenty-one in 1949, seventeen in 1951, eighteen in 1955, twenty-five in 1959, and so on. During the first decades the dominant party, Mapai (Labor), never had a majority. Having to form coalition governments with Mapam (Left Labor), General Zionists (moderate Right), or the religious bloc, it typically chose the last, for its members were indifferent to most secular issues. Orthodox rabbis accumulated power over all matters related to Judaic norms.[38]

In the population register and on the identity card that every Israeli is required to carry, his identity is specified according to three categories. The first, Citizenship, is "Israeli," and the few problems pertaining to it have concerned those with dual citizenship. The second item, in Hebrew *le'um,* is often translated nationality; it does not mean a politically defined membership of a state (obviously, since there is a separate entry for citizenship in the same register), but rather ethnic group or people. But the ethnicity of a "Jew," ambiguous from the founding of the state, has remained a contentious issue. The third item, Religion, can also be ambiguous depending on whether one accepts each respondent's declaration or follows the Orthodox definition.

How each Jew is specified can affect significantly not only the automatic right to immigrate but, among other matters, the right to define the identity of oneself and one's children. For a time it was the custom to accept an immigrant's statement that he was a Jew, but when a move was made to change that practice into official policy, a debate broke out that has persisted to this day. Religious parties held that only the Chief Rabbinate could rule who is a Jew; the Left parties demanded that religion and nationality be deleted from Israeli identity cards.[39]

During World War II, Oswald Rufeisen, a Polish Jew and in his youth an ardent Zionist, used forged papers to work as a police interpreter in Nazi-occupied Poland. In that post he helped hundreds of Jewish and gentile anti-Nazis before he was betrayed and arrested. Managing to escape, he took refuge in a convent, where eventually he converted to Catholicism and became Brother Daniel, a Carmelite friar. As an immigrant to Israel he designated himself as of Christian religion and Jewish nationality and requested, and was denied, automatic Israeli citizenship under the Law of Return. On appeal, the Supreme Court ruled in a three-to-two decision that a Jew who had voluntarily converted to Christianity is no longer a Jew under Israeli law. Under Judaic law, on the contrary, a male child of a Jewish mother who had been circumcised and confirmed in a bar mitzvah is defined as a member of *Ahm Yisrael,* which can be construed, with contradictory conclusions for policy, as the Jewish people, Jewish community, or Jewish nation. As Akiva Orr interpreted the ruling,

> [t]he legal wrangle exposed a crisis of identity. The secular majority in the Knesset hesitated to legislate a secular definition of this crucial term [that is, *Jew*], while the secular courts refused to utilize the only existing definition, the religious one...This produced an inherently contradictory situation in which a nonreligious court, for nonreligious considerations, ruled that a person's religious belief is a criterion of his nonreligious nationality.... Zionism succeeded in creating a secular Jewish state only to discover that it was clinging to definition of Jewishness based on religion.[40]

From 1955 to 1972 the country was torn apart by a case involving a brother and sister, Hanoch and Miriam Langer, both of whom were forbidden to marry because they had been conceived in a second marriage before the mother divorced her first husband. Since there is no civil marriage for Jews in Israel, the prohibition of a religious ceremony was decisive. Eventually a commission headed by the Chief Rabbi resolved the case by a finding that the children's father, a convert to Judaism who had immigrated to Israel, was not really a Jew, and therefore the marriage was invalid and the children were not bastards. The names of those who had served on a commission with the Chief Rabbi were kept secret, for feelings ran so high that it was feared they would be attacked.[41]

In 1968, Benjamin Shalit, a native-born Israeli naval officer, married in a civil ceremony a gentile woman whom he had met while studying in Scotland. When he returned home with his wife, she became an Israeli citizen. They registered their first child as Nationality: Jewish; Religion: (left blank). The registration clerk changed this to Nationality: Father Jewish, Mother non-Jewish; Religion: Not registered. Shalit applied to the Supreme Court for relief, in effect asking it to declare that there is a Jewish nationality distinct from Judaism. In 1970, after more than a year in process, the Supreme Court ruled by five to four that "the determination of the affiliation of an individual to a given religion or a given nationality derives principally from the subjective feeling of the person concerned." As they stressed in their ruling, it pertained not to identity in general but only to who is a Jew in the population register. Only one justice of the majority held that the Shalit children were Jewish by nationality; the other four ruled only that the registration clerk must record whatever the parent tells him. But suppose, as might well happen in a mixed marriage, that the father and the mother disagree on how their children should be officially designated. The possible complications, whatever their temporary solution, would not be settled for the children, whose right to marry in Israel could be challenged on the basis of a falsely recorded *le'um*.

Shortly after the Shalit decision, the government proposed an amendment to the registration procedure to prevent the case from setting a legal precedent. Debate in the Knesset was exceptionally sharp, and Golda Meir's highly emotional speech in support of the bill represented a succinct statement of the ethnic dilemma embedded in political Zionism. "Above anything else in the world," she declared, is "the existence of the Jewish people," religious and secular alike. Speaking as an avowed atheist, she defended Judaism as the only force that over the centuries had prevented Jewry from disappearing.

In over twenty cases rabbinical courts have affirmed and specified in detail their own designation: a person is a Jew who was born of a Jewish mother or who converted to Orthodox Judaism and did not profess another religion. Members of the Bene Israel, a Jewish sect in India, were denied full status in Israel until the Rabbinical Council yielded to the Knesset's entreaty to make this one exception. Another sect, the Karaites, were forbidden to intermarry with other Jews. In the case of Mrs. Rina Eitani, born in Germany and after her immigration a political activist who served with distinction in the Israeli army, the Israeli courts used Nazi records on Aryan and non-Aryan forebears to prove she had a Jewish father but a gentile mother.

Several prominent cases involved foreign-born gentiles who had been converted by Reform rabbis and were denied Jewish identity in Israel. According to an Orthodox source quoted in the *Jerusalem Post* (7 February 1987), some 80,000 to 90,000 "non-Jews" had been registered in Israel as "Jews," so no one can any longer tell who is a Jew.

> Given the vagueness of the law and the incompatibility of secularist and Orthodox canon, civil servants tended to meet hard cases...by improvisation. Precision was avoided in order to deter a political showdown.[42]

Of the most prominent court cases—concerning, respectively, an apostate, an irreligious Jew, and converts to non-Orthodox Judaism—the last have been most damaging to the state. They have opened a division between Israel and the non-Orthodox American Jews on whose support the country partly depends. Reform and Conservative spokesmen have found it galling that the small Orthodox minority in Israel has presumed to define other denominations as non-Jews. In 1995 the Israeli Supreme Court ruled that a Brazilian woman born a Christian and converted by a non-Orthodox rabbi had to be recognized as a Jew. But Chief Rabbi Yisrael Lau commented that the court's order was not acceptable and that he and his associates would continue to deny the legitimacy of such conversions.[43]

The dilemmas reflected in the early decisions of Israeli courts have not been resolved. With the passage of time many have become more acute, and each year one or two new cases have involved virtually the same issues. So long as an electoral system persists that gives the ultra-Orthodox disproportionate power, many Jews in Israel will oppose the power of rabbis whose rulings they find objectionable. No compromise can result in more than a temporary respite, for the religious parties see these issues as absolute. Their determination has gained them not only significant victories but also the will to continue the struggle.

Many Jews, both in Israel and elsewhere, opposed the rapprochement between the Israeli government and the Palestine Liberation Organization (PLO). Especially after a Jewish religious fanatic assassinated Prime Minister Yitzhak Rabin, some Leftists demanded that the power of the ultra-Orthodox be curtailed, with a concomitant greater freedom for secular Jewry and a substitution of humanist cosmopolitanism for socialist nationalism. In the opinion of an opponent of this antireligious trend, "They want an Israeli politics without traditional Judaism."[44] In the mid-1990s the debate over how to define a Jew has sharpened.

Conclusions

Jews constitute, in whole or in part, a religious community, a nation, an ethnic group, a cultural group, a race. Not only is there no necessary congruence among these several classifications but each of them represents a continuum from an undeniable core through more or less determinate sectors to a dubious periphery. Specified by religion, Jews range from an ultra-Orthodox rabbi through an occasional Reform practitioner to a confirmed atheist; by nationality or ethnicity, from a Zionist partisan through a supporter of Israel to an anti-Zionist nationalist of some other country; by culture, from an enthusiastic Yiddishist to one indifferent to any element of the Jewish tradition; by race, from one with typical genetic characteristics through one with some of them to one with none. The separate strands, distinguishable in the abstract, intermingle in actual life. As a notable example, many East European immigrants to the United States perceived Jewry as an ethnic community; but since American law had no place for such a unit but did guarantee freedom of religion, they established religious institutions with a strong ethnic orientation.

The ambiguity of Jewishness was forecast by Heinrich Heine, who was not only a great poet but also a perceptive analyst of his status as a Jew in nineteenth-century Germany. He summarized his conclusions in what has become known as "Heine's law": *"Wie es sich Christelt, so Jüdelt es sich"*—roughly, as Christians behave, so also do Jews. And one might add: except that they do the same things with greater intensity and often, therefore, with more success. A great paradox of American society is that certain minorities—many Asians and some Hispanics, as well as Jews—both are set off from the majority and also in important respects are more successful than the majority.

15

Ethnicity in the New Nations of the Post-Colonial World

The right of self-determination, which became a guiding policy in Central and Eastern Europe after World War I, was reaffirmed after World War II, not only in Europe but throughout the world. The push toward national independence, though sometimes hesitant and wavering, came from both sides of the imperial bond: nationalist leaders argued for the right of self-determination with texts they had studied at the London School of Economics, the Sorbonne, or Harvard, and their demands were supported by many of their professors and fellow students. Virtually all the colonies of Western powers were converted into "new nations."

With this transformation of the world's map, the questions of what a nation is, what nationalism signifies, were posed with renewed urgency. Earlier, a few large areas of Asia, for instance, had attained a certain coherence through China's sentiment of imperial greatness and India's Hinduism. Even in those countries, however, primary loyalties were usually as parochial as they had been in Europe before the French Revolution. To foster a sentiment of broad unity that would transcend the natural bonds of clan and locality, the new nationalists undertook to rediscover (or, very often, to invent) a common cultural heritage. Other elements of European history also recurred: "modern India's imagery of the ancient village community resembles the idealization of traditional societies that has accompanied the modernization of Western Europe."[1] However, even the scholarship underlying such a renovation of the past was largely the product of Europeans, available primarily or only in European languages. The shedding of the imperial bond was possible only by emphasizing, however inadvertently, the immeasurable and typically unacknowledged debt owed to the imperialist powers.

The nationalism of less developed countries is concentrated in their cities, many of which are the outright creation of European peoples. Other large urban centers grew from small towns or villages mainly as a consequence of Western influences. Consider the great cities of Southeast Asia as one example:

In 1800, Rangoon, Saigon, and Singapore did not yet exist in city form; Bangkok, the new capital of Thailand, was less than twenty years old; Manila and Batavia

243

(Jakarta), though then about two hundred years old, were merely small coastal towns. They began to grow rapidly after...the consolidation of Western control, direct or indirect, over most of Southeast Asia in the 1890s.[2]

As these Southeast Asian countries attained their independence (or, in the case of Thailand, greatly extended the range of its prior nominal independence), they chose as their capitals cities that almost without exception had been products of Western trade and imperial rule: New Delhi, Karachi, Colombo, Rangoon, Bangkok, Kuala Lumpur, Jakarta, Manila, and Singapore. Because each of these cities was closely associated with the foreign power that had created it, in every country some nationalists called for a shift of the capital to an inland location more in the native tradition and nearer to the country's geographical center. But in practical terms the sites that other nationalists had selected were usually the best choice—typically the largest urban aggregate, in some cases the only real one.[3] In short, even if occasionally with a fresh name to recall the pre-colonial grandeur, the centers of new nationalism were indisputable products of the colonial rule. And in the post-colonial era the same capitals typically became the nucleus of a new elite hardly less distant from the rural mass than the alien rulers had been.

If colonial tradition persisted in the capitals of various new nations, many of those nations were too small to exert much of a counterforce. The proliferation of ministates could have been merely ludicrous except that giving inconsequential areas genuine power has reduced the effectiveness of international bodies, seldom very high, to a new low. Take, for instance, a random sample of some of the tiny member states of the United Nations (see table 15.1). The dates of the population estimates, as listed in a United Nations directory, suggest that these countries are rather casual about the collection of basic data. Representatives of these nations, with fewer inhabitants than a middle-sized American town, sit on United Nations committees that at least ostensibly make decisions affecting world affairs.

A list of the world's countries compiled two decades ago by the U.S. Central Intelligence Agency had forty-one more entities than the United Nations.[4] Some of these had been excluded from the international body for political reasons (North and South Korea, for example); others had an ambiguous status (Namibia, Faroe Islands); some had found it inappropriate to apply for membership in the United Nations (Switzerland, Vatican, and—at that time but not later—Andorra, San Marino).

The most inclusive count of quasicountries is given in a detailed list in the United Nations *Demographic Yearbook*. It provides basic data on the population and area for every country or other unit with "at least 50 inhabitants," a total of 216 in the world.[5] However, since in the work's tables most of the smallest were incorporated into other entities, the problem of whether to grant the wee ones a quasistatehood was bypassed.

TABLE 15.1
Some Tiny Member States of the United Nations

Ministate	Date of Admission	Estimated Population	Date of Estimate
Andorra	1993	5,664	1954
Bahrain	1971	350,798	1981
Brunei Darussalam	1984	192,832	1981
Cape Verde	1975	289,027	1980
Comoros	1975	385,890	1980
Djibouti	1977	81,200	1961
Domenica	1978	74,625	1981
Grenada	1974	89,088	1981
Marshall Islands	1991	43,380	1988
Monaco	1993	27,063	1982
San Marino	1992	19,149	1976
Sao Tomé and Principe	1975	96,611	1981
Seychelles	1976	68,598	1987

Source: *U.N. Statistical Yearbook 1992*, 39th Issue (New York, 1994), table 9.

One might conclude that the principle of the self-determination of nations has been applied rather too openhandedly. In fact, most of the new nations, however tiny, include two or more ethnic subpopulations that compete vigorously and sometimes violently for dominance in the unprecedented setting. As in Central Europe so in the rest of the world, it proved to be impossible to bestow its own nationhood on every ethnic grouping of a jumbled population.

The problems of statehood, critical in almost every one of the so-called new nations, may be most serious in Africa south of the Sahara.[6] As the president of Zambia wrote in his autobiography, "The question being asked all over Black Africa is, 'Who am I?'"[7] Of the three typical responses, based respectively on tribal, national, and racial criteria, only the first derives from a thoroughly embedded group sentiment. Just because tribes are the basic ethnic unit, those who are trying to build nations (as well as their Western sympathizers) routinely denounce "tribalism." As I have noted earlier, in the opinion of some analysts, "the word 'tribe' and its derivatives are best banned from the social science vocabulary."[8] But however one designates them, they and not the nations are Black Africa's most significant cultural units. The point is made dramatically in the subtitle of a book by the British Africanist Basil Davidson: "Africa and the Curse of the Nation-State."[9]

In a study of what the author called "situational ethnicity," he surveyed students in three Ghanaian universities—that is, a sample of the country's elite. When communicating within a linguistic or tribal group, the student generally identified himself as a native of his home town or kin group. When the interaction was in an ethnically heterogeneous grouping, such as a university residence hall, he typically identified himself as a member of a linguistic or tribal group. Only when confronted by foreigners, did the person call himself a Ghanaian.[10]

The continent of Africa is conventionally divided into two quite distinct areas, north and south of the Sahara desert. North Africa is populated by a race once known as Hamitic, but the very name is now dismissed as a remnant from the racist writings of the past century. However one terms it, there is a racial boundary between the area along the Mediterranean and that south of the Sahara. In antiquity three designations, subsequently adopted as the names of countries, marked this border zone: Ethiopia, Sudan, and Guinea, derived respectively from the Greek, Arabic, and Berber for "land of the black men."[11]

Ethnicity in the European Colonies

The Europeans who once governed their empires were distinguished from the general population first of all, of course, by their power; and since in most colonies the subject peoples were not Caucasian, the most visible sign of social status was usually race. Units of India's civil service and army, though staffed in subordinate or provincial positions with Indian personnel, were always headed by Europeans. Quarters assigned to each grade or wage level paralleled the native segregation by caste, with a consequent inordinately complex residential pattern.[12] Stamford Raffles, the British colonial administrator of the early nineteenth century, in most respects tried to substitute universalist principles for autocracy or mercantilism. But he zoned the Singapore he built by race, and the city's Chinatown has long marked the site of the old restricted quarter.[13]

In many colonies, however, races were classified by cultural as well as physical attributes. In most of the towns of colonial Africa that Europeans built, no residential segregation was planned, for apart from domestic servants Africans were originally expected to live in compounds outside the city. The restrictions that developed subsequently differed greatly from one colony to another. Though in British Nigeria, for instance, discrimination by color was based on "the firm conviction that peaceful colonial administration and the perpetuation of imperial rule were directly dependent upon the doctrine of white superiority,"[14] Europeans were merely advised, not compelled, to live in their own quarters. The government abolished even this degree of control some years before independence was granted. In Kenya as of 1950, on the other hand, if the 70,000 Africans in Nairobi had really been confined to their small location, they might well have claimed an attempted genocide. In fact, nearly half were housed by their European or Indian employers. In Southern Rhodesia as of the same date, the segregation was founded on "cultural differences," and mulattos were exempt.[15]

French Africa and particularly Algeria were subject to Paris's *mission civilisatrice,* and a very few assimilated natives ended up in France as civil equals of the French, some even as Senators. Those who remained in the colonies, however, were required to live in their own quarters. Segregation "sometimes result[ed] from deliberate policy, instituted at the [city's] very founding, but fairly frequently it was brought about simply by physical features and maintained and hardened more or less inadvertently."[16]

In Portugal's African colonies also, the population was classified into categories somewhat irrespective of race. For example, in Portuguese Angola around 1950, the "civilized" sector (so designated on the basis of education, occupation, and income) comprised all of the 79,000 whites, 85 percent (or 26,000) of the mulattos, and 0.75 percent (or 30,000) of the Africans. "The authorities, in order to ensure a true assimilation of the Africans, admit[ted] them to the civilized status only parsimoniously, taking care that their number [did] not exceed that of the Europeans," but those that did cross the line allegedly suffered no racial discrimination. "Men of all colors live[d] and work[ed] together on the basis of full equality in commerce, industry, administration, the army, and the church."[17] This partial dissolution of racial barriers was coupled with living conditions that made Angola notorious the world over. Corrupt officials subjected the mass of the African population to forced labor, flogging, and torture, and the victims had no legal redress.

In the Netherlands East Indies, a Eurasian, an Indonesian, or a Chinese who showed himself to be fit for European social life—by criteria that changed over time but included such characteristics as religion, education, occupation, and marriage to a white—could become "European" by decree. About 5 percent of the 245,000 Europeans enumerated in the 1930 census were of this type.[18] Some 60 to 70 percent of the roughly 250,000 Dutch in Indonesia at the outbreak of World War II were of mixed racial ancestry. This subpopulation was heterogeneous also in cultural attributes; their Dutch, often spoken with a Eurasian accent, usually had some admixture of Indonesian words or grammatical forms.[19] There was racial antipathy not only between Dutch and natives but also between "real" Dutch and the so-called Indos.

As the contrast between British and Portuguese areas shows most graphically, some of the colonies that came closest to applying color-blind standards operated least in accord with Western democratic principles, while the colonies that benefited most from the partial democratization of political and economic life maintained the social bar most rigorously. The class/ethnic/racial structure was more tangled than in its usual presentation.

Ethnicity in Africa

Physical anthropologists have classified Black Africans into various group-ings, but there is only one clear division, that between the Khoisan (also called Bushmen or Hottentots) and all the rest. Except for the Khoisan, no people of pre-colonial Africa was set apart by a combination of physical type, language, and other cultural attributes.

If one includes post-colonial times, there is one exception to this state-ment—the Cape Colored of South Africa, a product of both race mixture and the development of what is generally regarded as a separate culture. They have no tribal homelands, they are not tribally organized, they speak mostly Afrikaans (as well as English in many cases) rather than a language of one of the black peoples. For many years they had a separate juridical status, differ-ent from that of both whites and blacks. Their situation was especially am-biguous; the very name Colored was attacked, and some writers punctiliously put it between quotation marks. Though the authors of a book on the inequi-ties of apartheid would have liked to dispense with racial designations alto-gether, they were forced to use them in order to discuss the actualities of South African life:

> In terms of the Population Registration Act of 1950, everybody in South Africa was classified according to their [sic] "race" as defined by the Act; the four major classifications being established as "white," "native" (subsequently Bantu, sub-sequently black), "colored," and "Indian."...In this book the term "black" is used to include all those who are disenfranchised [sic] and are not classified as white; it thus includes all the people who are politically classified as Bantu/black, col-ored, or Indian. However, since the apartheid legislation affects these different sections of the black population differently in certain important respects, it is often necessary to distinguish between people along official lines, and in those instances we have used the terms "African," "Indian," or "colored."[20]

If, as such critics charge, the term *Colored* was imposed on the group by the state, it is no less the case that the critics were trying to impose the term *black* on the same people—who would have preferred a designation with no racial specification. Within the framework of South African society as it was then constituted, they preferred the official label. It was part of the name of a number of organizations (among others, the Federal Colored People's party). Individuals expressed pride in being a member of the Colored group, both in response to survey questions and, with fuller detail, in speeches and articles.[21]

In contrast, a government commission headed by Erika Theron, a former professor of social work at Stellenbosch University, was appointed to review government policies affecting the Colored population. What could be regarded as its key recommendation read as follows:

> There is no culture in the Colored community that is essentially different from [that of] the Afrikaans- or English-speaking Whites.... They have no separate

culture of their own. Differences that do exist in the lowest stratum must be ascribed, as in all population groups, to standards of literacy, education, and living conditions.... The commission therefore recommends that the idea be abandoned that the Colored population is a community which is culturally different and culturally distinguishable from the White population groups; and that the advancement and pursuit of culture be dealt with within the same organizational framework as for Afrikaans-speaking and English-speaking Whites.[22]

Three years were spent in preparing this report, but the government rejected most of its proposals within a week of its submission, including the one that in effect canceled the principle of apartheid for this one minority.

Before the institution of apartheid in 1948, the Colored had been favored over blacks in law, politics, and employment. Then they lost virtually all of their special privileges and were pushed down to the low status of blacks. In the 1980s, in a second reversal, they began to acquire important improvements in several key determinants of their way of life. A 1983 Constitution Act restored to them (and to Indians) the right to a limited participation in government, and two years later laws prohibiting marriage or sexual intercourse across race lines were repealed. These were among the first steps toward the abolition of apartheid soon to take place. After that momentous transformation, the fate of the 35 million colored improved in some respects, but far less than one might suppose. They are not eligible under various affirmative action programs because, for instance, they do not speak Xhosa or another African language. As one colored woman put it, "Before, we were too black to be white. Now we're too white to be black."[23]

In the rest of Black Africa's population, the differentiation by various cultural attributes is very great. The American anthropologist George Murdock's *Ethnographic Atlas* (as corrected and amended) set central and southern Africa as the largest of his major units of the continent. He calculated a total of 410 ethnic units in the area.[24] The enormous complexity of the populations of Black Africa is evident first of all in the range of *languages*. Some authors speak loosely of a "Bantu stock" or a "Bantu civilization," but Bantu (like Aryan) refers properly only to a family of languages, spoken by peoples who differ considerably in their other traits.[25] One cannot state precisely the number of African languages, for not only is our knowledge often partial and of dubious quality, but the crucial distinction between language and dialect is sometimes arbitrary. The French linguist Pierre Alexandre made a conservative estimate of 800, with an average of about 200,000 persons per language. But only those widespread languages with a written form that is taught in schools (e.g., Swahili, Yoruba, Hausa) have a genuine unity, for the spoken dialects are so different that, in Alexandre's words, "one hesitates to consider [the languages] as constituting single entities," thus raising the total by several hundred more. According to another authority, these figures represent a consensus:

Over 2,000 languages are distinguished by individual names, but this number may be reduced by almost half if interintelligible languages are treated together....

Around 50 major languages may be singled out as being each spoken by at least one million people in Africa.... The major boundaries of Africa have little or no relevance to the distribution of African peoples and their languages.[26]

Because of the political, commercial, religious, or cultural dominance of their native speakers, such non-African languages as English, French, Portuguese, and Arabic became not only the main means of communication among small native elites, but sometimes also the foundations of new African languages. These non-African languages, while a useful *lingua franca* among francophone or anglophone elites, also constituted one more barrier separating the countries' rulers. According to President Senghor of Senegal, "the division between anglophones and francophones was the most serious problem that the West African subregion had to face"![27]

Of the new states in Black Africa, only four very small ones are linguistically homogeneous. Sometimes the numerically dominant language is strongly opposed by minorities. In Kenya the Kikuyu and Lwo have rejected Swahili, and in Uganda the smaller tribes are unwilling to accept Ganda. Sometimes one can discern a possible new language of the future: most of the inhabitants of Mali speak some form of Mande, from which a common speech could evolve. In other states the number of dominant languages ranges from two in Togo to roughly a hundred in Cameroon.[28]

If a language has no written form, nationalist sentiments are likely to set decisions about establishing a writing system or converting it to a technically better one. At one time, one could base such guidelines on linguistic efficiency alone. As part of his work with missionaries in the United Bible Society, William A. Smalley established a number of criteria—to maximize the ease of learning the written language, the learner's motivation, the consistent representation of spoken sounds, the transfer to other languages, and the ease of reproduction in print.[29] When ethnic allegiance outweighs such technical factors, the political circumstances can foster diametrically opposed policies. In Cameroon, for instance, some of the tribes opposed writing their languages with symbols borrowed from French, which was associated with the colonial regime.

Nor is Black Africa more unified by criteria other than language. Divisions by *religion* seldom coincide with the borders of the new states. Native faiths are subsumed under the term *animism,* indicating the recurrence of some basic characteristics but no unifying force. The social effects of creed, ritual, and organization have been, on the contrary, to tie each individual more closely to his extended family or local territory. Missionaries encouraged conversions to Islam or Christianity by many nonreligious inducements, ranging from coercion to monetary advantages and often including a significant adaptation to prior religious customs.[30] Of those listed as Muslims or Christians, therefore, some are truly so and some merely carry the label; probably most combine the universalist religion with older beliefs and rituals into a mixture that can be as divisive as traditional animism. One important effect of the conflict among rival faiths may have been to encourage secularism, which in its varying strengths adds yet another dimension to the confusion.[31]

The main reason that African states are so poorly aligned with *national units,* of course, is that typically their boundaries were set by competing imperialist powers with no regard for tribal areas. Often a large people was cut in half. If a mixture of smaller tribes was brought together under an alien rule for no more than several dozen years, its members hardly had time to assimilate the political-cultural norms of the tiny administrative class controlling the colony. In the considerable body of writings on Pan-Arabism, for instance, some fundamental questions remain unresolved: how Arabism relates to Islam and thus to Christian Arabs and to non-Arab Muslims, of whom there are many in Black Africa.

Cutting across Pan-Arabism is another transnational movement, Pan-Africanism. The Organization of African Unity, founded in 1963, adhered for a while to its unwritten law that discussions shall keep clear of all intra-African controversies; but since the late 1970s this rule has been repeatedly ignored. The dominant ideology of the OAU, a kind of black racism, has brought about some strange paradoxes. As Kwame Nkrumah wrote in his autobiography, when he first arrived in London as a young man, he saw a news placard, "Mussolini Invades Ethiopia." "It was almost as if the whole of London had declared war on me personally," he wrote. "My nationalism surged to the fore."[32] It is a new meaning of the word when the nationalism of a future leader is aroused by an attack on a country 3,000 miles from a not-yet-born Ghana and alien in every respect except, in part, race; and when, because of the surge of that strange type of nationalism, democratic Britain is identified as one with Fascist Italy because both are inhabited by white Europeans.

Whatever coherence was achieved in a colony, moreover, was dissipated with the establishment of independence, for the new rulers invariably sought a legitimizing precedent not in the alien intrusions they had opposed but in pre-colonial African states. Little was known about those ancient kingdoms, and the spread of independence was followed immediately by the institution of African history as an academic subject. Scholars organized research institutes in French and Belgian Africa, and three English-language programs were started almost simultaneously at the University of Ibadan, the University of Ghana, and the School of Oriental and African Studies in London.[33]

But what is the *history* of a region with no written languages? In a 1963 television speech, Hugh Trevor-Roper, Regius Professor of Modern History at Oxford, summarily dismissed the proposed extension of his discipline: "Perhaps in the future there will be some African history," he said, "but at present there is none; there is only the history of Europeans in Africa. The rest is darkness, and darkness is not a subject of history."[34] To counter this view, those engaged in developing a history of Africa have defended oral tradition as an appropriate alternative source. The quality of written and oral sources, they argue, differs not in kind, but only in degree. Any historian evaluates the material available to him in order to approximate historical truth, and one who uses an oral tradition does the same. "No doubt he will arrive at a lower degree of probability than would otherwise be attained, but that does not rule out the fact that what he is doing is valid, and that it is history."[35]

In the abstract one might accept the contention that legend, myth, folk tale, and fable are legitimate sources, but in a field already burdened with political bias, extending the range so far has had some unfortunate consequences. For instance, in summing up the record to date in African history, two Marxists denounced "the cult of facts" and "the fallacy of objectivism." Following the counsel of the British Communist E. P. Thompson, they recommended a dialectical interplay between theory and empirical matter.[36] The use of oral tradition, according to one interpretation, results in a composite of which history may be no more than one indecipherable element:

> Africa's colonial rulers and mentors began the process of intellectual colonization by telling Africans what they had to be ashamed of.... Nationalist historians unwittingly perpetuated it by telling them what they had to be proud of.[37]

At the beginning of the colonial period about a quarter of the people in West Africa lived in stateless societies. The first European observers assumed that those who had established states were more advanced, but some subsequent analysts challenged this appraisal as simplistic. The distinction should be based, the latter held, not on whether authority was concentrated or dispersed, but rather on the level of culture. States were formed, one can hypothesize, mainly to wage war, either defensive or offensive, or to conduct large-scale trade more efficiently. The earliest states, which were in existence by the tenth century, were strung along the border between the Sahara and the savanna: Takrur, Ghana, Gao, Kanem.

That the modern state of Ghana took over the ancient name does not mean that there is an actual continuity between the two. Present-day Ghana is hundreds of miles to the southeast of its namesake. The inhabitants of ancient Ghana called it the Kingdom of Wagandu; the name by which it is known today comes from Arabic writers, one of whom noted that in fact the designation was not the name of a country, but only the title of the king.[38]

When one after another the colonies of Black Africa became independent, many of their inhabitants, as well as sympathetic observers in the West, anticipated that from this base of self-government the people would build veritable utopias. "Instead," according to Julius Nyerere, the first president of Tanzania, "injustice, even tyranny, is rampant." The 60,000 troops that Nyerere sent into Uganda to rid the world of Idi Amin, one of Africa's most notorious and bloodthirsty despots, soon began looting and killing on their own. Nyerere's Tanzania permitted no dissent, had no independent press; in 1979 it had more political prisoners than South Africa.[39] During the first two decades of independence, native governments murdered more than a million people. Emperor Bokassa I of the Central African Empire had eighty schoolchildren beaten to death because they had been disrespectful. Life President Francisco Macias Nguema of Equatorial Guinea had his soldiers slaughter an estimated eighth of his country's population.[40] In Burundi, "massacre is established as a routine of political competition, and conflict escalates to the search for an ultimate solution in genocide."[41] Armies of the new states have overthrown governments at least once in most of them, and in several more than once.[42]

That African states are ethnically heterogeneous by almost any measure is, of course, related to the fact that their recent history has not been auspicious. According to one analysis of ethnic data from black African nations,

> [c]ultural pluralism increases the likelihood of conflict between members of communal groups.... Greater degrees of variation in the ethnic background of elites...further increase the likelihood of elite instability. [But] modernization decreases the likelihood of political instability in these nations.[43]

A fissiparous predisposition has so dominated the cultural-social-political structure of most African countries that the wonder is how any have managed to survive as ongoing entities. However autocratic, arbitrary, or cruel it may be, political control does not generate legitimacy, for it has almost never been based on recognized institutional authority. Very often, on the contrary, there has been a competition between chiefs as carriers of native tradition and the new urban-based rulers. State-run economies, generally corrupt and inefficient, have not promoted a greater coherence in the multiethnic populations. In such a setting the one type of coercion relevant to economic development is taxation, but the typical one-party state offers no meaningful return for taxes paid by agriculturists, urban workers, or entrepreneurs; only bureaucrats and the army benefit from the levies that the state imposes. According to United Nations estimates, based on egregiously poor statistics, the economies of thirty of sub-Saharan Africa's forty-six countries retrogressed after they became independent.[44]

Two American political scientists have hypothesized that the improbable survival of African states has been made possible by the international recognition bestowed on the post-colonial status quo.[45] When Western journalists and academics take note of inefficiency, corruption, and mass murder, they often call these blemishes the aftereffects of colonialism or the continuing baneful influence of neocolonialism—though before such excuses were needed, the same journalists and academics quoted African politicians' declamations about the immediate benefits from political independence. This "literature of apologetics" has reminded some critics of the 1930s, when liberal democrats regularly supported the grossly undemocratic Soviet Union.[46]

According to the West Indian economist W. Arthur Lewis, Western democrats who give African democrats no support are thereby expressing their racism:

> Only democracy can solve the problems [of West Africa, he wrote], since that is the only framework which makes it possible for men of different tribes, languages, and religions to live at peace with each other.... [Yet] political scientists...fall over themselves to demonstrate that democracy is suitable only for Europeans and North Americans, and in the sacred name of "charisma," "modernization," and "national unity," call upon us to admire any demagogue who, aided by a loud voice and a bunch of hooligans, captures and suppresses his rivals.[47]

Nigeria as a Prototype

The problems that the new African states face can be seen in focus by concentrating on a particular case. When Nigeria attained independence in 1960, it was the largest and wealthiest country of Black Africa, with a body of civil servants whom their British predecessors had trained. There was a mood of joyful expectancy not only in the country itself, but among many foreign observers—those unable or unwilling to look behind the facade to the patchwork holding the new state together.

The conquest of what became Nigeria had begun in 1852, when Britain implemented its effort to end the slave trade by establishing control over Lagos, one of the main ports through which slaves were exported. A treaty with the local potentate specified that the traffic would be abolished and that legitimate trade and missionaries would be encouraged,[48] and these remained important concerns for half a century.

It was not until 1914 that several British-controlled regions were assembled into "Nigeria." The London *Times* (or, according to other accounts, the woman who later married Nigeria's first governor-general) coined the name for "the agglomeration of pagan and Mohammedan states which have been brought, by the exertion of the Royal Niger Company, within the confines of a British Protectorate, and thus need for the first time in their history to be described as an entity." Within this area an estimated 248 languages were spoken, some by no more than several hundred, others by as many as five million. Since the larger peoples were not wholly within the country's boundaries (Fulani, for instance, were spread over much of northern and western Africa), their cohesion also threatened Nigeria's continued existence.[49]

Fulani, Hausa, and two smaller peoples, Kanuri and Nupe, are mostly Muslims. Together with the Tiv, a highly independent tribe little influenced by either Hausa-Islamic or European-Christian culture, these Muslim peoples make up about two-thirds of the Northern Region's population, with the remainder comprising a large number of so-called pagan tribes. The coastal area is yet more diverse. The dominant ethnos of the Western Region (that is, the hinterland of Lagos) is the Yoruba, made up of many subtribes distinguished in both dialect and politics. In the Eastern Region, much of which is covered by dense forest, the main people is the Ibo, second in size to the Hausa. Before the civil war of 1967–1970, the Ibo were divided into thirty subtribes, sixty-nine clans, and about five hundred more or less autonomous villages or village groups.[50] Though part of British Nigeria, the Ibo had never been subordinate to the Hausa or any other of the region's peoples.

After the British consolidated Nigeria, one important effect of their policies was to reinforce sectional differences. In the North, even before the establishment of the country, Sir Frederick (later Lord) Lugard implemented a policy of indirect rule as a permanent basis of his administration. As he wrote in his first annual report, "The Fulani rule has been maintained as an experiment, for I am anxious to prove to these people that we have no hostility to them and only insist on good government and justice, and I am anxious to utilize, if possible, their wonderful intelligence, for they are born rulers."[51]

The local chieftains continued as before except that, within the broad local authority permitted them, their power was increased by support from the colonial government. Natives collected taxes and remitted a percentage to the British administration. Courts were under native judges, who ran them mainly by Islamic precepts. The local British representative was termed "the Resident" rather than by a more officious title, and "the attitude of the Resident," in Lugard's words, "is that of a watchful adviser, not of an interfering ruler, but he is ever jealous of the rights of the peasantry, and of any injustice to them."[52]

Lugard intended indirect rule to be a process by which the chiefs would themselves become the instruments of modernization, but under his successors the policy gradually lost this perhaps unrealistic purpose, becoming simply an expedient course of minimum interference. "Before the British took over the country...the system was one of autocracy tempered by assassination. The Emirs today are maintained by British bayonets."[53] The colonial administration barred Christian missionaries from the Muslim North, and as a result of this isolation, Nigerian Islam remained more conservative than its Levantine counterpart, as indicated, for instance, by the more rigid observance of the Ramadan fast.[54] When constitutional conventions tried to include human rights provisions in the constitutions of 1979 and 1992, both times the Muslim delegates were able to protect the Sharia, or Islamic law, by exempting Muslims from guarantees in the basic federal law.[55]

The reality is more complex than any classification of Nigeria's population into separate peoples. Take the way that the Hausa identify themselves as one instance. The British political scientist William Miles surveyed two villages, one in Nigeria and the other in contiguous francophone Niger, using eight components of Hausa identity to indicate the differences between them: religion, birthplace, ancestral home, clan/community, country, tribe or language, city, and skin color. He then compared his two samples to see whether they identified themselves as Hausa or as members of one of the nations. He found the interaction between ethnic/tribal and national identities to be complicated; both types of belonging were "fluid, multilayered, and evolutionary."[56]

The persistence of traditional Islamic culture in the North was in sharp contrast to the rapid transformation particularly of the Ibo. They had fought long against the imposition of British rule, and they were the last major tribe to be pacified. But within several decades they began to take full advantage of the new opportunities offered by their contacts with the West. While the solidly built Islamic culture of the North was relatively impermeable to modernization, the more primitive Ibo, paradoxically, proved to be better able to absorb Western civilization. "Their passion for education and their desire to catch up with other groups were insatiable."[57] By 1965 nearly half of the Nigerians being trained at England's Sandhurst Military Academy were Ibo, and they gained a similar degree of dominance also in Nigeria's federal civil service.[58] Before 1938 there had been precisely one Ibo studying in the United States; by 1953–1954 just over half of the 318 Nigerians in American colleges were Ibo. The pioneer, Nnamdi Azikiwe, played an important role in the nationalist movement.

Even during the last two decades of colonial rule, when all the nationalists' efforts were concentrated on the single aim of bringing the British administration to an end, intertribal jealousy was still too great to be altogether subdued. Until 1941, for example, the nationalist leaders of the South cooperated in the Nigerian Youth Movement; then the Ibo and Ijebu withdrew and eventually set up a rival movement.[59] After independence, local patriotisms influenced national politics much more. Officially, membership in political parties was open to any resident of a region; ostensibly, any Nigerian in the South could join the parties of that region, and anyone in the North could join either of the other two. In fact, the distribution of party strength and the composition of local affiliates reflected ethnic or religious solidarity.[60] In such a country as Nigeria one finds, a half-inch under the surface of competition through modern political institutions, a continuation of traditional hostilities.

With tribal leaders exercising the main power in the state, the relative size of the regions' populations was crucial. According to the census the British had administered in 1952–1953, the North had 17.6 million people out of a total of 31.8 million, thus getting an absolute majority in the federal House.[61] When independent Nigeria held its own census in 1962, the North had reportedly increased by 30 percent over the decade, and the East and West by 70 percent. A British administrator rejected the latter figure as "grossly inflated," and eventually the whole set of data was discarded. The following year another census was taken, and the inhabitants of the North were found to have increased from 22.5 million in 1962 to 29.8 million in 1963.[62] This time the governor of the East rejected the results. "I regret that the inflations disclosed are of such astronomical proportions that the figures obtained, taken as a whole, are worse than useless." Together, the two censuses cost a total of £4 million—as well as much hope for a viable democracy.

In 1966, only six years after Nigeria had become independent, the Northern-dominated civilian government in Lagos was overthrown in a military coup headed by an Ibo general. In retaliation, between 5,000 (the army's estimate) and 30,000 (the victims' figure) Ibo and other Southerners living in Northern cities were slaughtered. In May, 1967 the Ibo-dominated East seceded and proclaimed itself the independent state of Biafra.[63] In the view of the Nigerian state, two factors related to the secession were of prime importance: much of the country's oil, it so happened, was located in Biafra; and if any part of Nigeria was permitted to leave, that might well prove to be a disastrous precedent.

According to the all too prophetic words of Biafra's national anthem (written by Azikiwe himself), "If the price is death for all we hold dear, [then] spilling our blood we'll count as privilege." The United States took the position that this was an internal conflict and recognized only the federal government as legitimate. Britain and the Soviet Union sent supplies to the federal government, France to Biafra.[64]

Three years later, a reunited Nigeria was set afloat again on a sea of Ibo corpses. According to various estimates, between 500,000 and 2,000,000 Biafran civilians died, mostly from starvation. An embargo that Nigeria imposed on Biafran ports prevented trade with an area that had imported food in normal times and was heavily populated even before the arrival of large numbers of refugees.[65] Nigerian officials either refused offers of humanitarian assistance or stipulated that food supplies had to be delivered to a federally controlled airport and shipped by road from there. According to a survey by Dr. Karl Western of the U.S. Centers for Disease Control, over 30 percent of the Biafran population was suffering from famine edema, and two-thirds showed a dangerous loss of weight. Almost all of the little assistance the Biafrans received was amassed and flown in by private relief agencies, foremost among them the International Rescue Committee, based in New York.

When the fighting ended in 1970, a news blanket was drawn over Biafra, and official Nigerian agencies' report of an amicable reconciliation between the combatants was confirmed by a pronouncement from U Thant, the secretary general of the United Nations. The subsequent history of Nigeria consists of an alternation between civilian and military governments, neither of which could impede a decline in the economy, politics, and civil life.[66] In 1995 the despotic regime of General Sani Abacha hanged Ken Saro-Wiwa, an internationally famous author, and eight other members of the Movement for the Survival of the Ogoni People. Like that of the Ibo, the home of the Ogoni is the site of Nigeria's oil. Extracting it was destroying the agricultural base of their tribal life, but the vast sums from oil exports were absorbed by the grossly inefficient and corrupt central government.[67]

No single factor has brought about Nigeria's decline, but the sharp and often violent competition among the several peoples making up the country's population certainly was one important cause.

16

The Conglomeration that is India

With 884 million people in 1991 (or with the disputed Jammu and Kashmir, 899 million), India is after China the world's most populous nation. In size and complexity, it is more like Europe than a single European state. It is often said that the bond that holds India together is Hinduism, but the country's principal religious faith is less a unifying force than the contrary. Being a Hindu defines one's place in Indian society far less than being in one or another of the castes into which Hindus are divided. The English word caste is used to translate two Hindi words, *varna* and *jati,* which must be distinguished in order to understand the institution. The literal meaning of varna is color, a significant criterion of differentiation. "A light skin color is valued almost universally.... In many Indian languages [as also in English] the words *fair* and *beautiful* are used synonymously.... Virginity and a light skin are among the most desirable qualities in a bride."[1]

There are four varnas, identified by the occupation with which each was traditionally associated: in hierarchical order, *Brahman,* priest or scholar; *Kshatriya,* warrior or ruler; *Vaishya,* merchant; and *Sudra,* peasant or craftsman. A more important broad classification divides Hindu India into only three parts: the twice-born top three varnas, members of which undergo a rite of passage that brings them fully into the community; the once-born Sudras; and Untouchables, who are below all the varnas.

At the local level Hinduism divides society not into three to five broad orders, but perhaps 3,000 castes and subcastes—some subunits of varnas, some associated with particular territories or traditional occupations, some the consequence of the spread of Hinduism to tribal peoples, and so on. These smaller units are the *jatis,* the breeding units of the population. The essence of caste is endogamy; the rule is that one must marry within one's jati or, by extension, within a comparable jati that the classification of varnas helps one identify.

The distinction between varna and jati, however, merely begins to map the complexity of the caste system. A survey of how the pattern is changing in particular areas of India begins with defining the key terms that the author has used:

Unfortunately, a single term "caste" is employed to connote different structural orders such as the smallest endogamous sub-subcaste for which local words like *jati, quom, dudh* (milk), and *biradari* are used; a higher order consisting of several subcastes and a still higher order of *varna*. The term "caste" is also used to refer to a category of cognate subcastes as a unit of association across different regions of India. It is used to refer to a category of different named subcaste groups at the pan-India level. Finally it is used to refer to ideology as in caste ideology.[2]

Of all the characteristics of the institution, the association of some castes with traditional occupations has been most eroded by urbanization and modernization, but in other respects the caste system has not only survived, but flourished.

The establishment of Pax Britannica set the caste free from the territorial limitations inherent in the pre-British political system.... The building of roads all over India, and the introduction of railways, postage, telegraph, cheap paper, and printing—especially in the regional languages—enabled castes to organize as they had never done before.[3]

The numerous restrictions on social intercourse relate particularly to the transfer of water: one takes water from one's equals or superiors, not from one's inferiors. Since defilement can be by any member of specified groups, efforts to avoid it go beyond regulating relations among individuals. Untouchables still typically live in segregated areas at a village's outskirts, and sometimes various other castes also have had their own segregated quarters or streets.

"The Hindu social order," to sum up in the words of the American demographer Kingsley Davis, "is the most thorough attempt known in history to introduce absolute inequality as the guiding principle in social relations."[4] According to Philip Mason, an English analyst of race relations, the caste system at its height "embodied a differentiation between people more extreme and explicit than is to be found even in the plantation slavery of the Southern United States or in South Africa today [that is, in the mid-1960s]."[5] "In the hierarchical scheme [of Hinduism] a group's acknowledged differentness whereby it is contrasted with other groups becomes the very principle whereby it is integrated into society.... More than an orthodoxy, Hinduism is an 'orthopraxy'"—requiring an acceptance of regulated behavior more than of doctrinal belief.[6]

Enumerations in British India

Under Britain's administration a series of comprehensive enumerations established a record unique for a non-Western country in the nineteenth century. This stocktaking began with so-called gazetteers, which first the East India Company and then its governmental successor developed in order to inform administrators about the alien civilization over which Britain was assuming control. Eventually the gazetteers constituted "a comprehensive description of a district or state of British India...including historical, archaeological, political, economic, sociological, commercial, and statistical data."[7]

This wide range was continued in the decennial national censuses that began in 1871–72. Some of the most renowned Western scholars of Hindu civilization were associated with the subsequent censuses—for example, Sir George Grierson, who compiled a monumental nineteen-volume *Linguistic Survey of India* (1903–1928); Sir Herbert Risley, who wrote *The People of India* (1908); E. A. H. Blunt, author of the classic study *The Caste System of Northern India* (1931); and J. H. Hutton, author of *Caste In India* (1946).

The report of the Census Committee appointed to recommend procedures for the 1881 enumeration recounted the typical dilemmas that had to be faced. "An important question is the definition of the term nationality. As regards foreigners...there is no difficulty; but it is not easy in the case of the various Native races which inhabit the different provinces of India."[8] As a compromise, respondents were asked to give their mother tongue and their place of birth. Christians were classified into eight denominations plus Others; but the parallel division of Hindu castes was rather more cursory. The Committee found it "not possible" to distinguish among castes or subcastes.

As it developed, the census markedly affected the structure of the caste system, especially by facilitating upward mobility.[9] In the very first enumeration, in 1871–72, two Tamil peasant jatis wanted to be recorded as belonging to a higher varna than that generally conceded to them, and others followed this precedent. Risley, the census commissioner in 1901, tried to have the jatis in each local hierarchy ranked in order as well as identified with the varna associated with each of them. As might have been anticipated, this innovation stimulated antagonisms, and many more caste leaders tried to upgrade their groups. In the struggle to get the best rank possible in the official hierarchy, after the 1901 count more jatis than ever before united into broader caste associations, and local breeding groups were thus transformed into politically conscious organizations over larger territories. Before the 1911 count, as a census volume reported, hundreds of petitions were received requesting a new caste name, a higher place in the list, an assignment to a higher varna, and so on. "There is a general idea in Bengal that the object of the census is not to show the number of persons belonging to each caste, but to fix the relative position of different castes and to deal with questions of social superiority."[10]

In 1941, partly because of this experience and partly presumably because of the exigencies of a country at war, except for Untouchables caste was reportedly removed from the census schedule. A subsequent review of census operations, however, specifically noted that "a record was made of the race, tribe, or caste of every person enumerated.... In the case of a person belonging to a Scheduled Caste [that is, an Untouchable], his definite caste was recorded."[11] Whatever the new procedure was, it was followed also in 1951.

Though the categories used to classify India's population were often imprecise and fluid, every count had to be preceded by a definition. Instructions to enumerators had to specify what it meant not only to be in this or that caste, but to be a Hindu, to speak a particular language, and so forth. Should the rubric Hindus include Untouchables, who one might say had been cast out of that religious community? Should it include such marginal groups as Sikhs, who founded their religion in the fifteenth century to reconcile Hinduism with Islam, but who in modern times were often a partner with Hindus against Muslims and, still more recently, a sometimes violent proponent of secession? Or, as another instance, in 1890 a sect rejected the name Hindu as derogatory and insisted on being called Aryas; they pressured the census officials to add their designation to the list and thus to recognize them as a new religion.

Each such decision, even if made on narrowly technical grounds, became a political act. By being enumerated and included in an official document, members of a loose community acquired an enhanced being as well as a set of characteristics based on quantified data. "Religions became communities mapped, counted, and above all compared with other religious communities."[12]

Christian and Muslim missionaries have long been converting Hindus; and the Hindus, reading the comparative figures on adherents, have responded with propaganda for reconversion. Using census data from 1872 through 1901, one U. N. Mukerji extrapolated the decline of Hindus to their ultimate extinction. They were "A Dying Race"! Such works, the focus of much discussion, became the nucleus of an organization to promote Hindu rights. Caste Hindus even made some efforts to ameliorate the condition of Untouchables, who were the most likely to convert to other religions.

At the beginning of this century, when the government of British India was considering granting Indians some electoral rights, a group of distinguished Muslims called on the viceroy and asked him to resolve the contradiction between their importance in Indian society and their position (as shown in the 1901 census) as a minority that would be defeated in every election. In accordance with Britain's parliamentary principle that significant interest groups should be recognized in the political system, the Muslims got what they asked for: separate electorates with a guaranteed number of seats in future legislative assemblies. Hostility between Hindus and Muslims, endemic in the subcontinent's history, was of course exacerbated by this reform. The precedent of a special electorate for Muslims, moreover, was followed with preferments for various other groupings. When a reform of 1919 extended the franchise and introduced the direct election of representatives, it also set up special constituencies for such diverse interest groups as universities, landlords, and industry and commerce, as well as special seats for Muslims, Sikhs, and two racial categories of Indian Christians. The more democratic the country became, the more census-based communal representation was used to define the political balance.

Ethnic Divisions in Independent India

In the census process Untouchables were originally defined in a religious context—that is, if such a person touched a high-caste Hindu, a purification ritual would be imperative. India's Constitution of 1950 outlawed the status of Untouchability, and some would regard that designation as therefore obsolete. Yet in postcolonial India Untouchables have been the ethnic unit that received the most benefits in "protective discrimination."[13]

In British India a Schedule had been maintained in order to identify groups of Untouchables entitled to compensatory assistance. Under the Constitution of independent India, in each state the list of Scheduled castes and tribes was initially specified by the President, and any change in it could be made only with the approval of Parliament. It proved to be impossible, however, to draw up a Schedule that was even approximately accurate. For example, the Rajbanshis, a very large caste of Bengal, were not listed because they claimed that inclusion would degrade them, but five years later they appeared on the official Schedule and remained there; they had opted for money rather than status.[14] Similar confusions in the specification of Scheduled or Untouchable groups were to be found throughout the country.

In some parts of [the state of] Gujarat, Bhil and Garasia are considered by some to be synonymous, but others would consider it derogatory for a Garasia to be equated with a Bhil. A few decades ago, in Uttar Pradesh the Jatav would furiously refute any connection with the Chamar; but now they do not. In the early 1960s, the Hmar in the Manipur would not identify themselves with the Mizo, but in Mizoram they merged their separate identities into a larger Mizo tribal entity. In Manipur the Kipgen would sometimes identify themselves with the Thadou and would sometimes swing back to a distinct identity.[15]

This continuous flux in names and identities was made more complex by the inconsistent decisions of India's courts, which have ruled that under equivalent circumstances persons were both entitled and not entitled to benefits.

The list of acts outlawed in the Untouchability (Offences) Act of 1955 suggests the range of discrimination against Untouchables. It abrogated the prior prohibition of access to temples, shops, restaurants, water sources, and other public accommodations and conveyances, particular occupations and trades, hospitals and schools, and so on. Since the defendant, the prosecutor, and the judge in cases tried under this law have always been caste Hindus, the Untouchables gained little by it. Fewer than one in a hundred of the population was ever charged for widely prevailing illegal practices, and the infrequent convictions resulted in very small fines.[16]

According to a 1968 report of a government Commission on Untouchability, three ex-Untouchables had been shot dead in Madhya Pradesh for daring to curl their mustaches upward in the style of the Kshatriyas. Philip Mason remarked, "As the report rightly states, the fact that incidents occur and are reported is a step forward; it is not long since...none would have dared to curl his mustache."[17]

Particular sectors of the population have received special benefits related not only to education, but to working conditions, housing, agriculture, cottage industries, cooperatives, animal husbandry, medical care and public health, rehabilitation, community centers, and aid to voluntary agencies. Such so-called positive or reverse discrimination, instituted in order to blur caste divisions, has sharpened them. Quotas of government jobs and places in colleges are set nationally, but it is the states that specify allotments for castes designated as "backward."

In the south most jobs and college places are reserved—in Tamil Nadu, for instance, 50 percent for castes designated as "backward," plus 18 percent for Scheduled castes and tribes. If annual quotas are not filled, the assigned places are accumulated, so that some institutions in the state of Gujarat have quotas as high as 80 percent.

> Guess what? People are now struggling to be *admitted* to the lower castes. Such as India's Christians. Most of their ancestors converted to escape the caste system. But now they want to get back in. And while their bishops closed some 20,000 schools in protest, the parishioners have been staging faux-crucifixions to draw attention to their demand for formal entry into the pantheon of outcasts.[18]

As one might suppose, such reverse discrimination has been much resented by the new victims. In 1985 and 1986, riots related to caste politics resulted in some four hundred deaths. In the northern states of Bihar and Uttar Pradesh, land-owning castes organized private armies to protect their property against caste-related land reforms, and these illegal but well armed mercenaries have killed Untouchables.[19]

At the periphery of the Hindu population there are the so-called tribals, members of primitive tribes, some of which are in the process of adapting to the norms of the majority. Counts of tribes, it is generally agreed, have been the least dependable of India's ethnic statistics. With or without good reason enumerators have often listed an indeterminate "Tribal" as Hindu,[20] but there have been few guides to indicate when such a people undergoing acculturation should be reclassified, or whether the criterion should be ascription by the enumerator, self-identification, or public reputation. No tribals were listed in the state of Uttar Pradesh in 1961, but a decade later the number was 198,565; in other instances large populations have disappeared. "The census engaged simultaneously in genocide and resuscitation of tribal groups by statistical manipulation."[21]

Divisions within Hindu India were overlaid by the still sharper conflicts between Hindus and those of other religions. In 1947 such antagonisms led to the partition between Muslim Pakistan and Hindu India. Mass disorders on both sides of the border resulted in an estimated half million violent deaths, and hostilities flared up in renewed Indian-Pakistani wars in 1965 and 1971. The partition, however, did not really separate adherents of the two religions. Compared with the 64 million Muslims who ended up in the new state of Pakistan, there were 36 million who remained in India. Since most of their political leaders had gone to Pakistan, the Muslims in post-1947 India have been at a distinct disadvantage. The All-India Muslim League, the remnant of the Muslim party before the partition, was able to garner only three seats in the Lower Chamber in 1980, two in 1984, and none at all in 1989 and 1991. Similarly, neither of two competing political parties of Untouchables, the Republican Party of India and the Party of the Majority, has been able up to the mid-1990s to elect a single representative to the Lower Chamber.

The divisive effects of religion and caste have been aggravated also by India's multiplicity of *languages*. In the *Linguistic Survey of India* already mentioned, George Grierson listed 179 languages and 544 dialects in British India. After the separation of Pakistan, the Indian census of 1951 raised this to 1,652. Many of these are of minor importance, but Indians do use fourteen or fifteen major languages in addition to English.

Since members of local castes have typically spoken the same language, many disputes about language policy have been half-hidden manifestations of the perennial caste conflict.[22] The Government of India Act of 1935 extended local self-government by giving provincial and municipal bodies the authority to choose their official language, and this reform aggravated existent disputes. With the rising antagonism between the two principal religious blocs, differences have increased between Urdu and Hindi, related languages spoken respectively by Muslims and Hindus. The effort to promote Hindustani as a compromise between the two failed.[23] Hindu-Sikh rivalry has resulted, similarly, in a growing divergence between the closely related Hindi and Punjabi. Opposition to Hindi as a national language is especially strong in South India, where the native speech is one or another of the unrelated Dravidian languages.

During the decades that newly independent India was working out what its official language should be, English was by far the commonest second language, but nationalist opposition to its formal acceptance was reinforced by class conflict. Members of the old elite had gone to English-language schools and colleges, but most in the lower classes know little or nothing of the colonial rulers' speech. In the Constitution the official status of English was limited to a transitional period lasting till 1965, but a law passed before the expiration of its supposed term made its use, in addition to Hindi, optional for official state purposes and in Parliament.[24] In effect, the nation has two official national languages, Hindi and English, plus the language that in each state is spoken by the majority of its inhabitants.

In short, language policy is about not only an issue very important in itself, but also one that embodies disputes by caste and social class, by religion and region, and by a nationalist versus a Western orientation. Each of the more important disputants has its language association, which in the heated arguments for its point of view frequently uses census statistics to demonstrate a controversial thesis. Yet an Official Language Commission (like Alajos Kovács in another context[25]) viewed the determination of linguistic policy as essentially a technical assignment.

Members of the Commission were certain that they represented the interests of the nation. Behind this certainty one could detect a clear assumption that language planning is like any other rational administration. Once priorities have been set, efficient execution puts the plan into practice. In this process political conflicts are irrelevant, if not outright reactionary. Official policymakers have viewed the politics of language communities as a menace that needs to be eradicated rather than a political issue which demands a political solution.[26]

In this as in other ethnic controversies, in other countries as in India, every party to a dispute tries to be accepted as the neutral arbiter, the proponent of science and rationality. Sometimes the planners believe in their role, but undoubtedly many consciously use the pose to gain a polemical advantage. One need not ascribe any but the highest professional motives to census officials to conclude that, nevertheless, the work they compiled was very often a part of the political process. And the larger the electorate, the more pertinent the data became in the struggle for relatively greater power among an increased number of interest groups.

As an official document of the British raj, the census was authoritative. One group could cite it in competing with another one for this or that advantage. After the establishment of independent India, representation (including quotas) in the Lower Chamber of Parliament and in the state assemblies was adjusted every decade on the basis of census returns. This provision reinforced the earlier link between enumeration and politics. What was conceived as a neutral instrument became a catalyst. The census described and by its description stimulated change among the nation's ethnic groups in their response to the census's data. Ten years later the next census described the altered world created in part by the previous census, thus establishing a cycle of description, action, change, followed by another description.[27]

The widespread effort to reduce fertility in independent India has added another factor to interethnic hostility. According to Hindu extremists, the gradual increase in the proportion of Muslims from each census to the next has been building up to a time when Hindus will be a minority at the mercy of non-Hindus. For example, the newspaper *Organiser* printed stories under such provocative headlines as: "Polygamy for Muslims and Birth Control for Hindus Would Be National Suicide"; "Family Planning or Death Wish?"; "How Family Planning Lost Us Our Lahore"; "When Will We Need to Import Our Soldiers?"[28] Politicians of the Bharatiya Janata party, the major voice of Hindu nationalism, have accused Muslims of not practicing family planning in order to overtake the Hindu majority. Over the period 1951 to 1991, the proportion of Muslims in the Indian population did indeed rise—from 9.9 to 12.1 percent.[29]

At the 1975 U.N. World Population Congress in Bucharest, Karan Singh, India's newly appointed Minister for Health and Family Planning, had asserted that if India was to realize its goal of lowering the birth rate to 25 per thousand by 1983–84, the country might have to "think the unthinkable"—a legal limitation on family size. A month later he wrote to Prime Minister Indira Gandhi that he saw "no alternative but to think in terms of introduction of some element of compulsion in the larger national interest."[30] After trying several means of contraception without much success, India's officials decided to concentrate on sterilization, for with only one contact with a person, he or she became permanently incapable of adding to the country's population.

There was considerable opposition to the sterilization program, and it was greatly exacerbated by charges that the Hindu majority was using it to reduce the proportions of Untouchables and particularly of Muslims. A Muslim slum was cleared of its inhabitants at gun point and then razed; when the people were allowed back to where their homes had been, their ration cards would be renewed, they were told, only if the men underwent an operation forbidden by their religion. Police and family planners were killed; in one ugly incident, according to seven opposition members of Parliament, several dozen protesters were shot down and 150 were wounded in antisterilization riots. The opposition was a significant reason for the fall of the Gandhi government in 1977. Under the Janata government in office from 1977 to 1980, not only was such compulsion strongly condemned, but any type of family planning was given far less attention than in earlier decades.[31]

Anglo-Indians

One group in the Indian population has not yet been mentioned, the offspring in India of mixed white-Asian marriages. Many of the general works on marginality cite Anglo-Indians as a prime example of an ethnic group in constant tension between two cultures, supposedly "lacking in self-confidence, devoid of ambition, and wanting in thrift and independence.... A sense of inferiority accompanies their constant struggle for European recognition."[32]

It has not been easy for them to provide a satisfactory answer to the question, Who am I? Because of their alienation from both the British and the Indians, they were almost literally forced to think of themselves as a people apart, and this self-image has persisted to this day.[33]

Such descriptions are closer to stereotypes than to the products of research, of which there has been little of significance. In a 1964 survey of college students, most of whom were Bengali Hindus, Anglo-Indians were characterized *not* as unstable, oversensitive, restless, and depressed, but as "energetic," "good-natured," "friendly," "persevering," and "able to work hard." These judgments were made in spite of the respondents' criticism of Anglo-Indians' "imitation of the British" and their "anti-Indian attitude." Nor did a 1967 survey of Anglo-Indian students in Bangalore elicit the replies that one would anticipate from a prototypical marginal group. Asked to make a choice concerning their future, nine out of ten opted for either maintenance of a separate community in India or emigration, only 8 percent for full acculturation into Hindu society. Two-thirds said that they were "well treated" by other Indians, and four-fifths reported a "good friend" outside their community. In their self-appraisals, the respondents most often cited "hard-working," followed by "efficient," "courageous," "dependable," and "helpful," as well as "extravagant" and "unambitious."[34]

How did this group come into being? From the sixteenth century a population of mixed European-Indian parentage evolved in several of the country's cities. Apart from the fact that most were Christian and spoke a European language, they were culturally and socially quite heterogeneous. With the gradual consolidation of their dominion over the subcontinent, the British felt threatened by these Eurasians, who around 1800 outnumbered the whites. In a series of legal acts, the British barred Eurasians from the army, many civil-service posts, and the schools and clubs that they had established for themselves. It was from being classed together as an intermediate sector of British India that a sense of group identity began to develop.[35] Though many were not of English descent, they came to prefer the designation "Anglo-Indian" to any of the several alternatives, and this was officially adopted in the 1911 census.[36]

In a reversal of government policy beginning in the mid-nineteenth century, Anglo-Indians were given preference for certain posts in transportation and communications, then a route to clerical or technical positions that required proficiency in English but no more than elementary or occasionally secondary schooling. Comfortable with this patronage, most Anglo-Indians were reportedly "literate but uneducated, proficient only in a few skilled trades but by and large innocent of commercial or professional skills, and with few exceptions landless."[37] They formed a distinctive and relatively cohesive community, with English as its first language, a specific cuisine and way of life.

This cohesion was shattered by developments following the Montagu-Chelmsford Report of 1919, which recommended the Indianization of the railways and other public services in which Anglo-Indians had had a near monopoly. The consequence was widespread unemployment among a population that had few resources, insufficient training for other middle-level jobs, and too much pride to compete with other Indians for unskilled labor. Anglo-

Indian slum areas appeared in Calcutta, Madras, Bangalore, and Delhi. "The tragedy of the community was that they always relied on the British to look after them. They were willing to accept an inferior position in return for job reservations."[38] Following the establishment of India's independence in 1948, the new government continued what was left of their preferential status for another ten years and then discontinued it altogether.

Fairer women in the group often married European or American men and raised their children as members of their husbands' nationalities. On the other hand, when native Christian women married Anglo-Indian men, their children acquired Anglo-Indian identities. Because of this differential selection of marriage partners, Anglo-Indians are becoming physically indistinguishable from the rest of the population.[39]

Today an Anglo-Indian can be defined informally as a native-born Indian Christian who speaks English as his first language, typically wears Western clothes and follows a European diet, and is employed in one of a relatively few occupations. The official definition is also vague enough to allow for considerable movement in and out. According to India's 1950 Constitution, an Anglo-Indian is one "whose father or any of whose other male progenitors in the male line is or was of European descent but who is domiciled within the territory of India, and is or was born within such territory of parents habitually resident therein and not established for temporary purposes only." The ambiguity of the identity is reflected in population estimates, which range widely. In spite of the imprecise boundaries, those who identify themselves as members of the community often have a strong group consciousness.

In what has become a subcultural rather than a racial grouping, ties to the English language and British ways are crucial. In the words of Frank Anthony, one of the Anglo-Indian leaders, "Without our schools and without our language, English, we cannot be an Anglo-Indian community."[40] But the offspring of those who before independence studied only English now have to learn also Hindi and sometimes also a regional language, as well as Indian history and culture.

One can hardly sum up this account of Anglo-Indians with any such single concept as marginality. Components of the community, originally discrete and heterogeneous, fused in response to discrimination during the spread of British rule. For a period Anglo-Indians had preferential access to certain jobs controlled by the state, and then they lost this special entry to the work force. Many have emigrated, and others have found a way to integrate into the general Indian society.

Conclusions

Not only did the censuses of British and independent India attempt to depict the country's ethnic complexity, but there has been a persistent interaction between record keeping and the heterogeneity that the censuses measured. Perhaps more than anywhere else, the recognition of an aspirant caste or subcaste in an official count helped bring that new ethnic group into being. It is symptomatic that the word sanskritization, which I have used to indicate an upward mobility by means of the manipulation of symbols,[41] originated with an Indian scholar writing about his native country.

The caste system has been remarkably persistent. The colonial rulers abolished such abominable features as, for instance, *suttee,* the rule that the widow of a high-caste Hindu must be burnt on the same pyre as her deceased husband. In the nineteenth century a number of prominent Indians began to fight against child marriage. But the efforts of independent India to raise the level of the Untouchables have not only failed; the principal effect has been to aggravate the distinctions between them and the rest of the population.

17

Conclusions

Epistemology—the study of knowledge, its basis, and its reliability—has been a major branch of philosophy since the early Greeks posed some new questions.[1] Essentially the various positions they took can be compressed into two, which in current jargon are labeled *realism* and *nominalism*. Realists hold that universals exist independently and can be perceived only imperfectly in their empirical counterparts. Nominalists hold that abstract concepts, general terms, or universals exist only in the names that we give to mind-made categories.

A number of the recurrent themes in this epistemological controversy are relevant to any analysis of ethnicity. The belief that universals have an independent existence defines the doctrine of racism: there is an archetype of the white race (or the black, or any other race) derived from a particular path of evolution, and differences between actual white and black persons partly reflect these "real" distinctions. The concept is similar to deduction in logic, the process by which a conclusion follows necessarily from an accepted premise by an inference from the general to the specific.

Nominalism is similar to induction in logic, the process by which particular facts or instances are built into general principles. Universals are concepts to which we give names, but they do not exist in any other sense. There are white and black persons, and from these individuals we order the world into contrasting categories, which we term *races*. For a realist the nature of a white or a black is given, and if anyone deviates from the prototype this merely personal aberration does not invalidate the pattern. A nominalist, on the contrary, is always willing to adapt his representation of universals to new empirical evidence.

Some analysts have been so intent on combating racism that they have gone beyond nominalism to assert that "there are no races," or "there is only one race, the human race." Daily experience tells us differently. Ashley Montagu's work, *Man's Most Dangerous Myth,* is not subtitled the delusion of racism, but *The Fallacy of Race.* Yet he begins by admitting the inescapable:

An African Negro and a white Englishman must have had a somewhat different biological history, and their obvious physical differences would justify the biologist in classifying them as belonging to two different races.... Four distinctive major groups of mankind are the Negroid or black, the Archaic white or Australoid, the Caucasoid or white, and the Mongoloid.... [However,] it is preferable to speak of these four large groups of mankind as *major groups* rather than as races, and to speak of the varieties of men which enter into the formation of these major groups as *ethnic groups*.[2]

Though many others in the social disciplines also abjure the word *race,* few have accepted *major group* as an alternative term. Manifestly the individuals in any one of the categories Montagu lists do not constitute a *group* as this word is generally understood. Nor does his definition of *ethnic group*— "part of a species population in process of undergoing genetic differentiation"[3]—conform to the usual sense of a population sector distinguished by either its physical or its cultural characteristics. This kind of dispute over terms is common in writings about ethnicity, but I do not find it useful. Races exist, and calling them that does not contribute to racism.

Ethnic Identity

Before one counts members of an ethnic unit one must identify them. "Various suggestions have been offered," according to the *Oxford English Dictionary,* concerning the origin of the word *identity*. Presumably it derived from *idem,* same, and eventually it came to mean "the condition or fact that a person or thing is itself and not something else; continuity of personality." When Philip Gleason traced the concept through the works of such sociologists as Erving Goffman and other members of the symbolic-interaction school, he ended up quoting Arthur Lovejoy's remark about the word *romantic,* which had "come to mean so many things that, by itself, it means nothing. It has ceased to perform the function of a verbal sign." In Gleason's opinion, identity has also been worn down to an almost meaningless remnant.[4] I would not go quite so far, but it is true that the collection of ethnic data, a formidable task in itself, begins with a yet more difficult one, specifying the precise boundaries of the units to be assembled.

Everyone defines himself in relation to the groups with which he is associated, as William James pointed out with characteristic charm:

> I, who for the time being have staked all on being a psychologist, am mortified if others know much more psychology than I. But I am content to wallow in the grossest ignorance of Greek.... Had I "pretensions" to be a linguist, it would have been just the reverse.[5]

James, however, was not only a psychologist, but also an aspirant professional painter, a physician, a physiologist, and a philosopher; and his service as president of the Society for Psychical Research marked him as an aberrant among conventional psychologists. Like almost everyone else, he was a member of several families—the son of Henry James, a prolific author of works on religion; the brother of Henry and Alice, both writers of fiction; and the husband of Alice Howe Gibbens. As a professor at Harvard, he influenced many students and younger colleagues. An American who helped found the typically American school of pragmatism, he studied in Germany and had close ties there and also with prominent English and French contemporaries. In short, James was a member not only of the community of psychologists, but also of many others. He sometimes was only partly in any group and thus not wholly of most of them.

To one degree or another, everyone has many identities; all persons are peripheral to several cultures and subcultures; in some respects, each of us is a marginal man. Persons with a particular attribute that marks them as units in a statistical aggregate have more than one identity, so that the presumed unity is only partial. Yet the process of defining an ethnos is often ignored by those who collect or use ethnic data.

One of the more interesting attempts to write of identity as a jointly personal/communal concept is Harold Isaacs's "basic group identity":

> The baby acquires a *name*, an individual name, a family name, a *group* name. He acquires the *history* and *origins* of the group into which he is born. The group culture-past automatically endows him, among other things, with his *nationality* or other condition of national, regional, or tribal affiliation, his *language, religion,* and *value system*…all shaping the outlook and way of life upon which the new individual enters from his first day.[6]

In fact, many babies do not acquire a group name quite so automatically. As I have noted in several contexts, usually a group-in-formation has to deal with a recurrent dilemma in deciding what to call itself, whether colored or Negro or black or African American, whether Mexican American or Chicano, whether Flemish or Southern Dutch. And a baby whom his parents define as a Catholic may become, as an adult, a Protestant or an agnostic; a German may emigrate and become an American; and so on through the whole ever-changing ethnic mosaic.

The school of what have been termed primordialists, with Isaacs as a significant spokesman, hold that the collective identity that we call ethnicity is a given in human relations. So-called instrumentalists maintain, on the contrary, that ethnicity is a highly adaptive and malleable phenomenon, with the boundaries of an ethnic group expanding or contracting in response to new conditions, different leaders, or changed stimuli. Both points of view are partly valid. Ethnic collectivities have a base in reality as solid as that of any other type of social grouping, but from that base many variations can evolve.[7]

Richard Alba has offered a useful classification of theories about ethnic identity:[8]

- Ethnicity is a working- or lower-class style, as in Herbert Gans's *The Urban Villagers.*

- Ethnicity is a means of organizing politics, as in Nathan Glazer and Daniel Patrick Moynihan's *Beyond the Melting Pot*.
- Ethnicity is a revival of immigrant sentiments, as in Marcus Lee Hansen's "What the son wishes to forget, the grandson wishes to remember."
- Ethnicity is merely symbolic, signifying little more than a step in the complete withering away of differences, as in Stephen Steinberg's *The Ethnic Myth: Race, Ethnicity, and Class in America*.

The point is not that one or another of these alternatives is correct, but that they all are, of different subgroups, to different degrees, at different times, in different contexts.

How problematic ethnic identity is can be illustrated by reviewing, as I have done in chapter 14, the many answers to the perennial question, Who is a Jew? For an Orthodox rabbi, a Jew is a person born of a Jewish mother who has been brought into the community by specified rituals and currently follows the very many rules governing everyday life. By that criterion, most Jews in the United States or in Israel are not really Jews. Is an irreligious person who defines himself as Jewish on national or cultural grounds misusing the label? And what of those who declare themselves to be non-Jewish by any index and yet are seen as appropriate targets by anti-Semites? Or, to take another example, consider the religious identities recorded in the past several censuses of the Netherlands. The Roman Catholics constituted a sizable plurality but, in fact, in the several titanic social-political upheavals since the 1940s, Dutch Catholics were on both sides of every issue. Statistics on religion, however accurate in form, were meaningless in substance.

Aggregating to What?

Ethnic data are collected from individuals, and they are published as characteristics of groups. How do the "groups" get defined, and how much difference does it make where the boundaries are drawn? Apart from the general complications in the process of aggregation, the most persistent problem in moving from personal identity to ethnic group is whether one has chosen the appropriate category.

How many ethnic groups are there, say, in the United States? Since many Americans respond to a question on their ethnicity by declaring themselves to be simply "American," a possible answer is that the whole population constitutes a single ethnic group. Such an uncomplicated rejoinder might serve in Luxembourg, for instance, but hardly in any country larger that such a ministate. Manifestly Americans are of many ethnic heritages, and someone in the statistical bureau has to decide how many are to be distinguished and how each is to be differentiated from the others.

This choice of groups included in an enumeration is always more or less arbitrary. The people being counted affect the result first of all by each person's often flexible self-identification (if this is the criterion the statistical agency uses) and then by the lobbying of ethnic spokesmen. No result is determined, and no consistency should be expected.

One way of fixing the number has been to take those coming to the United States from each European country as a nationality, which either persists for two generations (as in the "foreign stock" as defined by the Bureau of the Census) or goes on forever (as in the base by which the immigration quotas were set in the 1920s). In any case, the assumption that those coming from multiethnic empires were ethnically unitary was not well based: as the data were collected, immigrants were identified with nations to which they were indifferent or, probably more often, hostile. Filipinos, Asian Indians, Chinese, and Japanese each comprise several quite disparate subgroups, which are not distinguished in the statistics. On the other hand, though the tribal identity of many American Indians is often of little relevance even to the persons themselves, the Bureau asked every one of them to list his tribe, collated the responses, and printed them in detailed tables.

A fundamental principle of classification used to be that insiders are distinguished from outsiders. But in today's climate of opinion, that differentiation has become blurred. Even citizenship has been redefined, so that in a number of Western countries aliens are now permitted to vote. One aim of the U.S. Bureau of the Census was once to measure how well immigrants were assimilating to American culture; now it is more often to calculate how many persons of minority status are to receive various kinds of special aid.

A generation ago some anthropologists formed a school of "culture and personality," which elevated stereotypes to pretentious scholarly appraisals of what they labeled national character. Not only are there cultural configurations that can be uncovered and precisely described, members of the school believed, but each society includes a corresponding modal personality structure. From such premises it was deemed possible to extract the essence of a culture without laborious field work (Margaret Mead and Rhoda Métraux edited a book on "the study of culture at a distance"[9]); but some who had analyzed those cultures on the spot found the facile generalizations to be false. The national character of Russians, as an egregious instance, was ascribed to the practice of swaddling infants,[10] a conjecture that passed over the fact that the custom had long since disappeared among the members of the ruling classes who were used to exemplify the supposed relation.

It is a widely held view that a well-adjusted personality includes not only self-respect, but pride in one's heritage. Such pride usually implies a comparison by which every other heritage is depreciated. The American social psychologist A. A. Roback compiled a dictionary of ethnophaulisms, as he called them, such as the more than a hundred nicknames and phrases used in

American slang to denigrate a score or more of immigrant peoples.[11] There are similar epithets in every language to belittle every people with which those speaking it have any dealings.

Now that political correctness has been applied to ethnic relations, Roback's compilation must be expanded with words that anyone may find offensive. A good illustration of the standards now recommended in formal speech is a volume issued by a Task Force on Bias-Free Language of the Association of American University Presses.[12] One caustic reviewer cited some examples:

> We are warned off "the many common English expressions that originate in a disparaging characterization of a particular group or people." "Siamese twins," "get one's Irish up," and even "to shanghai" are cited.... Objection is made to the designation Latin American "because not all persons referred to as Latin American speak a Latin-based language."..."Gratuitous characterizations of individuals, such as well-dressed, intelligent, articulate, and qualified...may be unacceptably patronizing in some contexts, as are positive stereotypes—the polite, hard-working Japanese person or the silver-tongued Irish person."[13]

Some of those who have written about Black Africa want everyone to abandon the concept "tribe" and look on all who reside in Nigeria, for example, as one people. That members of other tribes killed huge proportions of the Ibo, such analysts do not regard as pertinent. In Central Europe the boundaries of each ethnos of every country have been routinely set in order to shape the nation's ethnic contours in the manner the political elites desired. In India, on the contrary, official efforts to classify the inordinately complex population have often reflected the revised self-definitions by members of various castes and subcastes.

Toward the End of Ethnicity?

That query, the title of chapter 2, is still with us. Two books published in 1995 were titled *The End of the Nation State* and *The End of the Nation-State*.[14] The first, without a hyphen, is by Kenichi Ohmae, a management consultant; the second, with a hyphen, is by Jean-Marie Guéhenno, France's envoy to the European Union. Both authors stress the globalization of economics and business, leading to an eventual borderless world. In its original French version, Guéhenno's work was titled *La fin de la démocratie*—the end of democracy, for he believes that the social values associated with capitalist democratic states are also endangered.

Prophecies that the nation state is moribund have been with us for a long while. Campaigns for an international language, for universal disarmament, for the goals of ecumenicism, and so on rose to a climax following the end of World War I, when the Allies established the League of Nations. Following the end of World War II, the victors founded the United Nations as a successor to the League. To put it no stronger, this second international body has

also failed to live up to its founders' lofty expectations. Among all the attempts to transgress nations' prerogatives, the most successful have been agree-
ments to reduce impediments to free trade. In the negotiations leading to
these pacts, however, no country gave up its sovereignty; rather, in razor-
sharp deals each derived some benefit from its improved position in international commerce.

Paradoxically, one important reason that some nation states have become
weaker is that their ethnic components are stronger. For much of the twentieth century statesmen have used population transfers in an attempt to create
ethnically homogeneous nations. But the implementation of Woodrow Wilson's
"right of self-determination" has brought about not the desired goal, but two
unanticipated consequences. The world now contains many ministates too
small to carry the burdens of independence. And the stress on the "right" of
every ethnic unit to its very own state has everywhere exacerbated discord.

Even if we are in the final stage of nationalism—a proposition I find dubious—ethnicity is still with us, and becoming sturdier, more pervasive, sometimes more radical. The title of this book is a play on words. Ethnicity
counts—that is to say, it is important. But the counts of ethnic groups are
fundamentally flawed. For a statistical bureau the classification of ethnic/
racial groups is both important and, given the conditions set by laws and
circumstances, impossible.

If these data are irremediably flawed, as is the case, why should they be
collected, compiled, and published? Not to have official racial and ethnic
statistics would mean both in the United States and in many other countries
that several dozen laws that have set various policies based on the supposed
distribution of such groups would have to be repealed. Further, in most instances it would mean that in a society far from indifferent to ethnic/racial
distinctions we would be substituting ignorance for knowledge, even if partial and defective.

For several decades in the recent past, it is true, many persons in Western
countries believed that no data should be collected on the races, nationalities,
and religious communities that make up their populations. But when, for
example, various American agencies tried to assist blacks in getting jobs or to
improve the academic achievement of Hispanics, without data on ethnicity it
was impossible to check on which programs had succeeded and which had
not. An interesting article from the mid-1960s highlighted the dilemma:

> In the past, the removal of racial designation from forms has been a prime objec-
> tive of the civil rights movement. With the passage of recent legislation to assure
> these rights, the absence of an item on race from statistical and administrative
> forms may, in fact, contribute to frustrating enforcement of the legislation.[15]

Whenever there is an information vacuum, it is likely to be filled with a
makeshift substitute. At the time of the war in Vietnam, since the American

armed forces kept no records by race, it was impossible to check on the accuracy of a widely reported contention that blacks were bearing the brunt of the fighting. John van Allen, a correspondent in Vietnam at the time, reported that for five hours he was once at Danang air terminal, the point of exit and entry for most of the troops. By his count blacks invariably came out at 10 to 14 percent of a unit, or about the same proportion as in the general population of the United States.[16] Of course, those batches of soldiers may have been atypical, or the reporter may have miscounted, whether inadvertently or in order to make his point. Yet, inadequate at it was, this compilation was better than no evidence at all concerning a recurrent theme of political propaganda.

In an imperfect world, we must make do with less than the ideal. On the mass scale of a national census, it will never be possible to classify a population accurately into real ethnic groups. In some instances improvements on the past record may be possible, but only up to a point.

Of all the caveats to users of ethnic statistics, the most important is the generalization that a statistical bureau's task is not simply to count what exists in the real world. Statisticians play a part in fashioning the data they produce, and many sectors of a society influence their decisions.

Notes

Introduction

1. Thomas Sowell, *Race and Culture: A World View* (New York: Basic Books, 1994). Donald L. Horowitz, *Ethnic Groups in Conflict* (Berkeley: University of California Press, 1985).
2. Theresa F. Rogers, "Interviews by Telephone and in Person: Quality of Responses and Field Performance," *Public Opinion Quarterly* 40 (1976): 51–65.
3. Philip E. Converse, "Attitudes and Non-attitudes: Continuation of a Dialogue," in Edward R. Tufte, ed., *The Quantitative Analysis of Social Problems* (Reading, Mass.: Addison-Wesley, 1970).
4. Alan Ryan, "Our Dishevelled World," *Times Literary Supplement* (23 June 1995).
5. Richard D. Alba, *Ethnic Identity: The Transformation of White America* (New Haven: Yale University Press, 1990): 311–12.
6. Joshua A. Fishman, *Language in Sociocultural Change: Essays* (Stanford, Calif.: Stanford University Press, 1972), chap. 5.
7. E. H. Simpson, "The Interpretation of Interaction in Contingency Tables," *Journal of the Royal Statistical Society*, Ser. B, 13 (1951): 238–41.
8. Nathan Keyfitz, "Heterogeneity and Selection in Population Analysis," Statistics Canada, *Research Paper*, no. 10 (Ottawa, 1984).
9. Stanley Lieberson and Lawrence Santi, "The Use of Nativity Data to Estimate Ethnic Characteristics and Patterns," *Social Science Research* 14 (1985): 31–56.
10. Cf. Robert A. Nisbet, *The Sociological Tradition* (New York: Basic Books, 1966), chap. 5.
11. Oskar Morgenstern, *On the Accuracy of Economic Observations*, 2nd ed. (Princeton, N.J.: Princeton University Press, 1963), 40.
12. Ibid., 40n.
13. Ansley J. Coale and Frederick F. Stephan, "The Case of the Indians and Teen-Age Widows," *Journal of the American Statistical Association* 57 (1962): 338–47.
14. Judith Banister, "Use and Abuse of Census Editing and Imputation," *Asian and Pacific Census Forum* 6 (February 1980): 1–2, 16–20.
15. Charles E. Johnson, Jr., "Consistency of Reporting Ethnic Origins in the Current Population Survey," U.S. Bureau of the Census, *Technical Papers*, no. 31 (Washington, D.C., 1974).
16. M. N. Srinivas, *Caste in Modern India and Other Essays* (Bombay: Asia Publishing House, 1962).

1. Toward the End of Ethnicity?

1. John Stone, *Racial Conflict in Contemporary Society* (Cambridge, Mass.: Harvard University Press, 1985).

2. John Rex, *Race Relations in Sociological Theory* (London: Weidenfeld and Nicolson, 1970).
3. Many of the recent books on ethnicity begin with a long list of ethnic conflicts the world over. As a typical example, see Anthony D. Smith, *The Ethnic Revival* (Cambridge: Cambridge University Press, 1981), chap. 1.
4. William Godwin, *Enquiry concerning Political Justice and Its Influence on Morals and Happiness* (1793; Toronto: University of Toronto Press, 1946), vol. 2, 528.
5. Karl Marx and Friedrich Engels, *The Communist Manifesto* (1848), in Saul K. Padover, ed., *Karl Marx on Revolution* (New York: McGraw-Hill, 1971), 95–96.
6. See 15–19.
7. Nathan Glazer and Daniel P. Moynihan, eds., *Ethnicity: Theory and Experience* (Cambridge, Mass.: Harvard University Press, 1975), 4.
8. Gunnar Myrdal, *An American Dilemma: The Negro Problem and Modern Democracy* (New York: Harper, 1944), 1024.
9. William Petersen, "Prejudice in American Society: A Critique of Some Recent Formulations," *Commentary* (October 1958): 342–48.
10. Israel Zangwill, *The Melting Pot,* rev. ed. (New York: Macmillan, 1921). Israel Zangwill (1864–1926) was a prominent member of Britain's Jewish literary circle. In 1905 Theodor Herzl, the founder of modern Zionism, went to England specifically to meet him and then returned to Vienna to work up his notes into his manifesto, *Der Judenstaat* (1896). Zangwill himself later became involved in Zionist affairs. That this one man should have become prominently associated both with the total assimilation of immigrants in the United States and also with renascent Jewish nationalism is something of a historical curiosity.
11. Robert E. Park, *Race and Culture* (Glencoe, Ill.: Free Press, 1950), chap. 26.
12. Maurice B. Davie, *World Immigration, with Special Reference to the United States* (New York: Macmillan, 1949), 498–99.
13. Theodore M. Newcomb, Ralph H. Turner, and Philip E. Converse, *Social Psychology: The Study of Human Interaction* (New York: Holt, Rinehart and Winston, 1965), 430.
14. T. Lynn Smith, *Social Problems* (New York: Crowell, 1955), 423–24.
15. John Harding, Bernard Kutner, Harold Proshansky, and Isidor Chein, "Prejudice and Ethnic Relations," in Gardner Lindzey, ed., *Handbook of Social Psychology* (New York: Random House, 1954), vol. 2, 1021–61.
16. Paul Johnson, *Modern Times: The World from the Twenties to the Eighties* (New York: Harper and Row, 1983), chap. 3.
17. Gertrude Himmelfarb, *The De-Moralization of Society: From Victorian Virtues to Modern Values* (New York: Knopf, 1995), 11–12.
18. Ruth Benedict, *Patterns of Culture* (Boston: Houghton Mifflin, 1934). On several occasions I assigned *Patterns of Culture* as one of the readings in an introductory sociology class, and most students were able to detect that Benedict's pretense not to judge among the three primitive peoples she described *was* a pretense. Some understood as well that the description of three Indian cultures was in part a commentary on American politics: the contrast between the warlike Dobu or the highly competitive Kwakiutl on the one side and the quiet, peaceable Zuñi on the other was one anthropologist's restatement of the reactionary-progressive, aggressive-peaceloving dichotomy of that day's liberal stand on international relations.
19. Clyde Kluckhohn, Melville J. Herskovits, Charles F. Voegelin, Cora DuBois, William W. Howells, Ralph L. Beals, and W. W. Hill, "Statement on Human Rights," *American Anthropologist* 49 (1947): 539–43.
20. A. L. Kroeber, "Anthropology," *Scientific American* 183 (September 1950): 87–94.

21. Bronislaw Malinowski, *A Diary in the Strict Sense of the Term* (New York: Harcourt Brace, 1967).
22. Hans Vaihinger, *The Philosophy of "As If": A System of the Theoretical, Practical, and Religious Fictions of Mankind,* 2nd ed. (London: Routledge & Kegan Paul, 1935).
23. David Bidney, "Cultural Relativism," *International Encyclopedia of the Social Sciences* (New York: Macmillan/Free Press, 1968), vol. 3, 543–47.
24. Cf. William Petersen, "Forbidden Knowledge," in Saad Z. Nagi and Ronald G. Corwin, eds., *The Social Contexts of Research* (New York: John Wiley, 1972).
25. William Graham Sumner, *Folkways: A Study of the Sociological Importance of Usages, Manners, Customs, Mores, and Morals* (Boston: Ginn, 1907), 87.
26. Milton J. Esman, *Ethnic Politics* (Ithaca, N.Y.: Cornell University Press, 1994), 11–12.
27. P. P. V. D. Balsdon, *Romans and Aliens* (London: Duckworth, 1979).
28. Paul White, "Ethnic Minority Communities in Europe," in Daniel Noin and Robert Woods, eds., *The Changing Population of Europe* (Oxford: Blackwell, 1993).
29. John S. Lindberg, *The Background of Swedish Emigration to the United States: An Economic and Sociological Study of the Dynamics of Migration* (Minneapolis: University of Minnesota Press, 1930).
30. Thomas Sowell, *Race and Culture: A World View* (New York: Basic Books, 1994), 4.
31. Gino Germani, "Mass Immigration and Modernization in Argentina," in William Petersen, ed., *Readings in Population* (New York: Macmillan, 1972).
32. Donald L. Horowitz, *Ethnic Groups in Conflict* (Berkeley: University of California Press, 1985), 29.
33. K. M. Panikkar, *Asia and Western Dominance* (New York: Day, n.d.), 150. See also below: 15–4.
34. Jack E. Weller, *Yesterday's People: Life in Contemporary Appalachia* (Lexington: University of Kentucky Press, 1966), 30.
35. Horace Kephart, *Our Southern Highlanders* (New York: Macmillan, 1941).
36. Representative works include *Southern Regions of the United States* (1936), by Odum and *Human Geography of the South,* 2nd ed. (1968), Vance.
37. Richard Drake, "Appalachian America: The Emergence of a Concept, 1895-1964," *Mountain Life and Work* 41, 1 (1965), 6–9.
38. *Wall Street Journal* (1 April 1996).
39. David M. Heer, "Intermarriage," *Harvard Encyclopedia of American Ethnic Groups* (Cambridge, Mass.: Harvard University Press, 1980).
40. Marcus Lee Hansen, *The Problem of the Third Generation Immigrant* (Rock Island, Ill.: Augustana Historical Society, 1938); reprinted in *Commentary* (November 1952): 492–500.
41. Martin Kilson, "Blacks and Neo-Ethnicity in American Political Life," in Glazer and Moynihan, *Ethnicity: Theory and Experience.*
42. See, for example, Horace M. Kallen, et al., *Cultural Pluralism and the American Idea: An Essay in Social Philosophy* (Philadelphia: University of Pennsylvania Press, 1956), covering a symposium in which Kallen defended his fully elaborated thesis against several critics. See also Philip Gleason, "American Identity and Americanization," *Harvard Encyclopedia of American Ethnic Groups* (Cambridge, Mass.: Harvard University Press, 1980).
43. Samuel Lubell, *The Future of American Politics,* 2nd ed. (Garden City, N.Y.: Doubleday-Anchor, 1956).
44. V. O. Key, Jr., *The Responsible Electorate: Rationality in Presidential Voting, 1936–1960* (Cambridge, Mass.: Belknap Press, 1960), 50.

45. John Higham, "Current Trends in the Study of Ethnicity in the United States," *Journal of American Ethnic History* 2 (1982): 5–15. See also Herbert Gutman, *Work, Culture and Society in Industrializing America: Essays in American Working Class and Social History* (New York: Random House, 1976), 3–78; Philip Gleason, "Pluralism and Assimilation: A Conceptual History," in John Edwards, ed., *Linguistic Minorities: Policies and Pluralism* (New York: Academic Press, 1984).
46. Milton M. Gordon, *Assimilation in American Life* (New York: Oxford University Press, 1964), chap. 4.
47. John Courtney Murray, *We Hold These Truths: Catholic Reflections on the American Proposition*, 2 vols. (New York: Harper, 1944).
48. Michael Novak, *The Rise of the Unmeltable Ethnics: Politics and Culture in the Seventies* (New York: Macmillan, 1972), 20, 47.
49. Herbert J. Gans, "Symbolic Ethnicity: The Future of Ethnic Groups and Cultures in America," *Ethnic and Racial Studies* 2 (1979): 1–20.
50. *Wall Street Journal* (6 June 1985).
51. Cf. William Petersen, "Spanish As She Is Spoke in California," *Alta Vista* (Monterey, Calif.), 28 April 1991.
52. Aimé Césaire, *Cahier d'un retour au pays natal*, with "Un grand poète noir," by André Breton (New York: Brentano's, 1947). See also Anon., "Twilight of a Dark Myth," *Times Literary Supplement* (16 September 1965).
53. Gary B. Mills and Elizabeth Shown Mills, "Roots and the News 'Faction': A Legitimate Tool for Clio?" *Virginia Magazine of History and Biography* 89 (1981): 3–25.
54. Richard Bernstein, *Dictatorship of Virtue: Multiculturalism and the Battle for America's Future* (New York: Knopf, 1994), Prologue. See also Lewis S. Feuer, "From Pluralism to Multiculturalism," *Society* 29 (1991): 19–22.

2. Concepts of Ethnicity

1. Stephan Thernstrom, ed., *Harvard Encyclopedia of American Ethnic Groups* (Cambridge, Mass.: Harvard University Press, 1980), Introduction.
2. See 4–7.
3. Louis Wirth, "The Problem of Minority Groups," in Ralph Linton, ed., *The Science of Man in the World Crisis* (New York: Columbia University Press, 1945).
4. Alexis de Tocqueville, *Democracy in America* (1835; New York: Vintage, 1959).
5. Louis Dumont, *Homo Hierarchicus: An Essay on the Caste System* (Chicago: University of Chicago Press, 1970).
6. Walker Connor, *Ethnonationalism: The Quest for Understanding* (Princeton, N.J.: Princeton University Press, 1994), xi.
7. E. K. Francis, "The Nature of the Ethnic Group," *American Sociological Review* 52 (1947): 393–400. Cf. Tomas Hammar, "Citizenship: Membership of a Nation and of a State," *International Migration* 24 (1986): 735–48.
8. Elie Kedourie, *Nationalism*, 4th ed. (Cambridge, Mass.: Blackwell, 1993), chap. 5.
9. John Lukacs, "American History: The Terminological Problem," *American Scholar* (Winter 1992): 17–32.
10. Guy Héraud, *L'Europe des ethnies* (Paris: Presses d'Europe, 1963).
11. A few English-language works on ethnicity have done so; see, for example, Anthony D. Smith, *Theories of Nationalism*, 2nd ed. (London: Duckworth, 1983), 189 and passim; John Hutchinson, *Modern Nationalism* (London: Fontana Press, 1994), chap. 1.

12. John C. Loehlin, Gardner Lindzey, and J. N. Spuhler, *Race Differences in Intelligence* (San Francisco: W. H. Freeman, 1975).

13. Stephen Molner, *Human Variation: Races, Types and Ethnic Groups*, 3rd ed. (Englewood Cliffs, N.J.: Prentice-Hall, 1992).

14. A. James Gregor, "Notes on a 'Scientific' Controversy," *Mankind Quarterly* 2 (January–March 1962): 14–23.

15. A. Littlefield, L. Lieberman, and L. Reynolds, "Redefining Race: The Potential Demise of a Concept in Physical Anthropology," *Current Anthropology* 23 (1982): 641–55. See also Eugenia Shanklin, *Anthropology & Race* (Belmont, Calif.: Wadsworth Publishing Co., 1994), chap. 5.

16. José Pérez de Barradas, *Los mestizos de América* (Madrid: Cultura Clásica y Moderna, 1948), 184–85. See also Magnus Mörner, "The History of Race Relations in Latin America: Some Comments on the State of Research," *Latin American Research Review* 1 (1966): 17–44.

17. William Stanton, *The Leopard's Spots: Scientific Attitudes toward Race in America, 1815–59* (Chicago: University of Chicago Press, 1960), 58–67.

18. Ibid., 196.

19. Gilberto Freyre, *The Masters and the Slaves, Black into White: Race and Nationality in Brazilian Thought*, 4th ed. (New York: Knopf, 1947), 91.

20. Joseph A. Page, *The Brazilians* (Reading, Mass.: Addison-Wesley, 1995), chap. 2.

21. Ronald Segal, *The Black Diaspora* (London: Faber, 1995), quoted in a review by Roland Oliver, *Times Literary Supplement* (2 June 1995).

22. Pierre L. van den Berghe, *Race and Racism: A Comparative Analysis* (New York: Wiley, 1967), 9; "Class, Race, and Ethnicity in Africa," *Ethnic and Racial Studies* 6 (1983): 221–36.

23. Francis, "The Nature of the Ethnic Group." See also Francis, "Minority Groups— A Revision of Concepts," *British Journal of Sociology* 2 (1951): 219–29, 254.

24. John A. Armstrong, *Nations before Nationalism* (Chapel Hill: University of North Carolina Press, 1982), 228–32.

25. Ibid., 139.

26. See 271–72.

27. Ravi Pendakur, "Visible Minority as a Redefinition of Race," International Union for the Scientific Study of Population, *International Population Conference, Montreal, 1993* (Liège, Belgium, 1993), vol. 3, 469–82.

28. Franz Boas, "Changes in Bodily Form of Descendants of Immigrants," in U.S. Senate Immigration Commission, *Report* 38 (Washington, D.C., 1911).

29. Joseph B. Birdsell, "The Problem of the Evolution of Human Races: Classification or Clines?" *Social Biology* 19 (1972): 136–62.

30. A. G. Erskine and Wladyslaw W. Socha, *Principles and Practice of Blood Groupings*, 2nd ed. (St. Louis: Mosby, 1978). R. R. Race and Ruth Sanger, *Blood Groups in Man*, 5th ed. (Philadelphia: F. A. Davis, 1968).

31. Abraham Kaplan, *The Conduct of Inquiry: Methodology for Behavioral Science* (San Francisco: Chandler, 1964), 71. See also Timothy Williamson, *Vagueness* (London: Routledge, 1995).

32. Edward Sapir, *Language: An Introduction to the Study of Speech* (New York: Harcourt, Brace, 1921).

33. See 176–77.

34. Einar Haugen, *Language Conflict and Language Planning: The Case of Modern Norwegian* (Cambridge, Mass.: Harvard University Press, 1966).

35. Isabelle Kreindler, "The Changing Status of Russian in the Soviet Union," *International Journal of the Sociology of Language*, no. 33 (1982): 7–39.

36. John DeFrancis, "Language and Script Reform in China," in Joshua A. Fishman, ed., *Advances in the Creation and Revision of Writing Systems* (The Hague: Mouton, 1977).

37. Fulmer Mood, "The Origin, Evolution, and Application of the Sectional Concept, 1750–1900," in Merrill Jensen, ed., *Regionalism in America* (Madison: University of Wisconsin Press, 1965).

38. See chap. 13.

39. Connor, *Ethnonationalism*, 29–30.

40. Ira S. Lowry, *Science and Politics of Ethnic Enumeration*, Rand Paper no. P-6435-1 (Santa Monica, Rand Corporation, 1980).

41. See 164–66.

42. United Nations, *Demographic Yearbook, 1956* (New York, 1957), 32–33.

43. Crawford Young, *Ethnic Diversity and Public Policy* (Geneva: U.N. Research Institute for Social Development, 1994).

44. See 66–68.

45. For example, Juanita Tamayo Lott, "Do United States Racial/Ethnic Categories Still Fit?" *Population Today* (January 1993): 6–9.

46. E. M. Schreiber, "Dirty Data in Britain and the USA: The Reliability of 'Invariant' Characteristics Reported in Surveys," *Public Opinion Quarterly* 39 (1975–76): 493–506.

47. United Nations, *Demographic Yearbook, 1977* (New York, 1978).

48. Thomas Sowell, *Race and Culture: A World View* (New York: Basic Books, 1994), 255–56.

49. William Alonso and Paul Starr, eds., *The Politics of Numbers* (New York: Russell Sage Foundation, 1987).

50. Nicholas Eberstadt, *The Tyranny of Numbers: Mismeasurement and Misrule* (Washington, D.C.: AEI Press, 1995), Introduction.

51. David A. Swanson, "An Evaluation of 'Ratio' and 'Difference' Regression Methods for Estimating Small, Highly Concentrated Populations: The Case of Ethnic Groups," *Public Data Use* 6 (July 1978): 18–27.

3. American Politics and the Measurement of Ethnicity

1. John P. Roche, "Immigration and Nationality: A Historical Overview of United States Policy," in Uri Ra'anan and Roche, eds., *Ethnic Resurgence in Modern Democratic States: A Multidisciplinary Approach to Human Resources and Conflict* (New York: Pergamon Press, 1980).

2. J. Hector St. John de Crèvecoeur, *Letters from an American Farmer* (London, 1782; reprinted, New York: Albert and Charles Boni, 1925), 54–55.

3. J. van Hinte, *Nederlanders in Amerika: Een studie over landverhuizers en volkplanters in de 19e en 20e eeuw in de Vereenigde Staten van Amerika*, 2 vols. (Groningen: Noordhoff, 1928).

4. Henry A. Pochmann, *German Culture in America: Philosophical and Literary Influences, 1600–1900* (Madison: University of Wisconsin Press, 1961), 3.

5. Marcus Lee Hansen, *The Immigrant in American History* (Cambridge, Mass.: Harvard University Press, 1948), 24–25.

6. Hans Kohn, *American Nationalism: An Interpretative Essay* (New York: Macmillan, 1957).

7. Alexander Hamilton, James Madison, and John Jay, *The Federalist Papers* (New York: New American Library, 1961), 341.

8. Edmund S. Morgan, *The Birth of the Republic, 1763–89* (Chicago: University of Chicago Press, 1977). Forrest McDonald, *Novus Ordo Seculorum: The In-*

tellectual Origins of the Constitution (Lawrence: University Press of Kansas, 1985).

9. Robert A. Goldwin, "Why Blacks, Women & Jews Are Not Mentioned in the Constitution," *Commentary* (May 1987): 28–33.

10. *Dred Scott* v. *Sandford,* 19 Howard 393, 1857. For an enlightening analysis, see Roche, "Immigration and Nationality."

11. Quoted in Kohn, *American Nationalism,* 58.

12. Walker Connor, *Ethnonationalism: The Quest for Understanding* (Princeton, N.J.: Princeton University Press, 1994), 69.

13. Kathleen Neils Conzen, "Germans," in *Harvard Encyclopedia of American Ethnic Groups* (Cambridge, Mass.: Harvard University Press, 1980).

14. Andrew M. Greeley, *That Most Distressful Nation: The Taming of the American Irish* (Chicago: Quadrangle Books, 1972), chap. 6.

15. Philip Gleason, "American Identity and Americanization," *Harvard Encyclopedia of American Ethnic Groups*. See also above, 67–68.

16. See 25.

17. Robert A. Nisbet, *The Quest for Community: A Study in the Ethics of Order and Freedom* (New York: Oxford University Press, 1953), 280.

18. See 25.

19. John Hope Franklin, *The Emancipation Proclamation* (New York: Doubleday, 1963), chap. 5.

20. Ralph A. Rossum, "Justice Harlan's Constitution," *Weekly Standard* (13 May 1996): 31–33.

21. William Bradford Reynolds, "Legitimizing Race as a Decision-Making Criterion: Where Are We Going?" Forum on Law and Social Justice, Amherst College, Amherst, Mass., 1983 (unpublished manuscript).

22. Nathan Glazer, *Affirmative Discrimination: Ethnic Inequality and Public Policy* (New York: Basic Books, 1975). On so contentious an issue as affirmative action, no single work suffices to represent the range of opinion. Glazer is recommended for his detailed contrast between the original law and the subsequent interpretation; see also his later discussion, "Black and White after Thirty Years," *Public Interest,* no. 121 (1995): 61–79. A sharper critique is given in Paul Craig Roberts and Lawrence M. Stratton, *The New Color Line: How Quotas and Privilege Destroy Democracy* (Washington: Regnery, 1995). A longer perspective is given in Terry Eastland and William J. Bennett, *Counting by Race: Equality from the Founding Fathers to* Bakke *and* Weber (New York: Basic Books, 1979). R. A. Rossum is a good analysis of its topic, *Reverse Discrimination: The Constitutional Debate* (New York: Marcel Dekker, 1980). C. J. Livingston gives a spirited defense of "affirmative action" against "equality of opportunity" in his *Fair Game: Inequality and Affirmative Action* (San Francisco: W. H. Freeman, 1979). This sample of works grew over the decades to a small library, particularly when a movement arose to abolish affirmative action.

23. Lawrence J. Siskind, "Rule of Law," *Wall Street Journal* (12 July 1995).

24. Ira S. Lowry, *Counting Ethnic Minorities in the 1990 Census* (privately published, 1989), 2.

25. Thomas Sowell, *Preferential Policies: An International Perspective* (New York: Morrow, 1990), chap. 7 and passim.

26. Seymour Martin Lipset and William Schneider, "The Bakke Case," *Public Opinion* (March–April 1978): 38–44.

27. Quoted in Terry Eastland, *Ending Affirmative Action: The Case for Colorblind Justice* (New York: Basic Books, 1996), 166–67.

28. Abraham D. Lavender, and John M. Forsyth, "The Sociological Study of Minority Groups as Reflected by Leading Sociological Journals: Who Gets Studied and Who Gets Neglected?" *Ethnicity* 3 (1976): 388–98. One might object that the result of this survey may have been the factitious consequence of the choice of journals; many papers on Jews, for instance, appear in specialized journals, but there are also such serials as *Phylon,* devoted almost entirely to blacks. Lavender and Forsyth cited a number of other studies that came to the same conclusion that they did. Subsequently, with the rapid rise of a new feminism in all its various guises, much of the stress shifted from ethnic/racial relations to gender.

29. Thomas Sowell, *Ethnic America: A History* (New York: Basic Books, 1981), chap. 2 and passim. See also Stanley Lieberson, *A Piece of the Pie: Blacks and White Immigrants since 1880* (Berkeley: University of California Press, 1981); Nathan Glazer, *Ethnic Dilemmas* (Cambridge. Mass.: Harvard University Press, 1983), chap. 5.

30. Andrew M. Greeley, *Ethnicity in the United States: A Preliminary Reconnaissance* (New York: Wiley, 1974); Greeley, "Political Participation among Ethnic Groups," *American Journal of Sociology* 80 (1974): 170–204.

31. Nathan Glazer and Daniel Patrick Moynihan, *Beyond the Melting Pot: The Negroes, Puerto Ricans, Jews, and Irish of New York City,* 2nd ed. (Cambridge, Mass.: M.I.T. Press, 1970). See also Glazer, *"Beyond the Melting Pot* Twenty Years After," *Journal of American Ethnic History* 1 (1981): 43–55.

32. Illinois Department of Human Rights, "Report of Public Hearings on the Department's Proposed Rules Governing Equal Employment Opportunity and Affirmative Action by State Executive Agencies" (Chicago: mimeographed, 1982).

33. Philip Gleason, "Pluralism and Assimilation: A Conceptual History," in John Edwards, ed., *Linguistic Minorities: Policies and Pluralism* (New York: Academic Press, 1984).

34. Margo J. Anderson, *The American Census: A Social History* (New Haven: Yale University Press, 1988). Carroll D. Wright and William C. Hunt, *The History and Growth of the United States Census* (56th Cong., 1st sess., Senate Document no. 194, 1900; reprinted, New York: Johnson Reprint Corp., 1966).

35. Oskar Morgenstern, *On the Accuracy of Economic Observations,* 2nd ed. (Princeton, N.J.: Princeton University Press, 1963), chap. 3.

36. U.S. Office of Federal Statistical Policy and Standards, "Race and Ethnic Standards for Federal Statistics and Administrative Reporting," Directive no. 15 (Washington, D.C., May 1978). See also Katherine K. Wallman and John Hodgdon, "Race and Ethnic Standards for Federal Statistics and Administrative Reporting," *Statistical Reporter,* no. 77-10 (July 1977): 450–54.

37. Ira S. Lowry, *The Science and Politics of Ethnic Enumeration,* Rand Papers Series, no. P-6435-1 (Santa Monica, Calif., 1980), 19. See also Stanley Lieberson and Mary Waters, "Ethnic Mixtures in the United States," *Sociology and Social Research* 70 (1985): 43–51.

38. For an excellent analysis of the issues, see Daniel Melnick, "The 1980 Census: Recalculating the Federal Equation," *Publius: The Journal of Federalism* 11 (1981): 39–65.

39. See Ian I. Mitroff, Richard O. Mason, and Vincent P. Barabba, *The 1980 Census: Policymaking and Turbulence* (Lexington, Mass.: Lexington Books, 1983).

40. U.S. Bureau of the Census, *Census of Population and Housing, 1990,* Content Determination Report no. 1990 CDR-6, "Race and Ethnic Origin" (Washington, D.C., 1991).

41. U.S. Bureau of the Census, *1990 Census of Population, Population Characteristics, United States* (Washington, D.C., 1992), B-13.

42. Sam Roberts, *Who We Are: A Portrait of America Based on the Latest U.S. Census* (New York: Times Books, 1993), 15–16.
43. U.S. Bureau of the Census, *1990 Census of Population and Housing, Summary Population and Housing Characteristics, United States* (Washington, D.C., 1992), B-13.
44. *Wall Street Journal* (13 September 1995).
45. See William Stanton, *The Leopard's Spots: Scientific Attitudes toward Race in America, 1815–59* (Chicago: University of Chicago Press, 1960), 58–67.
46. See 106.
47. Charles A. Price, "Methods of Estimating the Size of Groups," *Harvard Encyclopedia of American Ethnic Groups*.
48. Lowry, *Science and Politics of Ethnic Enumeration*.
49. Mitroff, Mason, and Barabba, *The 1980 Census*.

4. Identification of Americans of European Descent

1. Christopher A. Ford, "Administering Identity: The Determination of 'Race' in Race-conscious Law," *California Law Review* 82 (1994): 1231–85.
2. Ibid.
3. Cited in Albert Bernhardt Faust, *The German Element in the United States, with Special Reference to Its Political, Moral, Social, and Educational Influence* (New York: Steuben Society of America, 1927), vol. 2, chap. 1. See also Erich Rosenthal, "The Equivalence of United States Census Data for Persons of Russian Stock or Descent with American Jews: An Evaluation," *Demography* 12 (1975): 275–90.
4. See 51.
5. W. S. Rossiter, *A Century of Population Growth, from the First Census of the United States to the Twelfth, 1790—1900* (Washington, D.C.: Government Printing Office, 1909), chaps. 10 and 11.
6. Faust, *German Element in the United States*, vol. 2, chap. 1.
7. Donald H. Akenson, "Why the Accepted Estimates of the Ethnicity of the American People, 1790, Are Unacceptable," *William and Mary Quarterly* 41 (1984): 102–19. See also Forrest McDonald and Ellen Shapiro McDonald, "Ethnic Origins of the American People," *William and Mary Quarterly* 37 (1980): 179–99.
8. U.S. Senate, "Immigration Quotas on the Basis of National Origin," *Miscellaneous Documents*, no. 65, 70th Cong., 1st sess. (Washington, D.C., 1928).
9. Kristin A. Hansen and Amara Bachu, "The Foreign-born Population: 1994," U.S. Bureau of the Census, *Current Population Reports, Population Characteristics*, P20-486 (Washington, D.C., August 1995).
10. Frederick Rose, "Muddled Masses: The Growing Backlash against Immigration Includes Many Myths," *Wall Street Journal* (26 April 1995).
11. A. E. C. W. Spencer, "Catholics in Britain and Ireland: Regional Contrasts," in D. A. Coleman, ed., *Demography of Immigrants and Minority Groups in the United Kingdom* (London: Academic Press, 1982).
12. James Barr, *Fundamentalism* (London: SCM Press, 1977), 1.
13. Shailer Mathews, *The Faith of Modernism* (New York: Macmillan, 1924), 22–36.
14. *Washington Times* (22 July 1985). On conflict in the Methodist church, see *Insight* (16 February 1987).
15. Merton P. Strommen, et al., *A Study of Generations* (Minneapolis: Augsburg Publishing House, 1972).
16. Associated Press dispatch, 30 August 1986.
17. See, for example, Harold J. Abramson, *Ethnic Diversity in Catholic America* (New York: Wiley, 1973).

18. U.S. Bureau of the Census, "Religion Reported by the Civilian Population of the United States, March 1957," *Current Population Reports,* Ser. P-20, no. 79 (1958). See also Dorothy Good, "Questions on Religion in the United States Census," *Population Index* 25 (1959): 3–16; Charles R. Foster, *A Question of Religion* (New York: Inter-University Case Program, no. 66; Indianapolis: Bobbs-Merrill, 1961); William Petersen, "Religious Statistics in the United States," *Journal for the Scientific Study of Religion* 1 (1962): 165–78.

19. Sidney Goldstein, "Socioeconomic Differentials among Religious Groups in the United States," *American Journal of Sociology* 74 (1969): 612–31.

20. Conrad Taeuber, "Census," *International Encyclopedia of the Social Sciences* 2: 360–65.

21. Data from the Princeton Religious Research Center. See also Martha Farnsworth Riche, "The Fall and Rise of Religion," *American Demographics* 4 (May 1982): 14–19, 47.

22. David E. Weissbrodt, *Immigration Law and Procedure in a Nutshell* (St. Paul, Minn.: West Publishing Co., 1984). Charles Gordon and Ellen Gittel Gordon, *Immigration and Nationality Law,* Desk Edition (New York: Matthew Bender, 1986).

23. Wolf Blitzer, "The State Department Has No Record of Golda Meir's Renouncing Her American Citizenship," *Present Tense* (Spring 1986): 51–53.

24. *Insight* (8 December 1986). Cf. Mona Harrington, "Loyalties: Dual and Divided," *Harvard Encyclopedia of American Ethnic Groups.*

25. See 171.

26. *Wall Street Journal* (10 March 1987).

27. Cf. George M. Scott, Jr., "To Catch or Not to Catch a Thief: A Case of Bride Theft among the Lao Hmong Refugees in Southern California," *Ethnic Groups* 7 (1988): 137–51.

28. Stanley Lieberson and Mary C. Waters, "The Ethnic Responses of Whites: What Causes Their Instability, Simplification, and Inconsistency?" *Social Forces* 72 (1993): 421–50.

29. For example, Michael J. Levin and Reynolds Farley, "Historical Comparability of Ethnic Designations in the United States," American Statistical Association, Social Statistics Section, *Proceedings of the Annual Meeting, 1982* (Washington, D.C., 1982).

30. Deborah Pomerance and Diane Ellis, *Ethnic Statistics: A Compendium of Reference Sources* (Arlington, Va.: Data Use and Access Laboratories, 1954).

31. Ansley J. Coale, "The Population of the United States in 1950 Classified by Age, Sex, and Color—A Revision of Census Figures," *Journal of the American Statistical Association* 50 (1955): 16–54.

32. Richard F. Tomasson, "Bias in Estimates of the U.S. Nonwhite Population as Indicated by Trends in Death Rates," *Journal of the American Statistical Association* 56 (1961): 44–51.

33. V. R. Andress, "Ethnic/Racial Misidentification in Death: A Problem Which May Distort Suicide Statistics," *Forensic Science* (Lausanne) 9 (1977): 179–83.

34. See chap. 6.

35. Tom W. Smith, "Ethnic Measurement and Identification," *Ethnicity* 7 (1980): 78–95. See also Smith, "Problems in Ethnic Measurement: Over-, Under-, and Misidentification," General Social Survey Project, *Technical Report* no. 29, 1982.

36. National Research Council, *Counting the People in 1980: An Appraisal of Census Plans* (Washington, D.C.: National Academy of Sciences, 1978).

37. Barbara A. Bailar, Roger A. Herriot, and Jeffrey S. Passel, "The Quality of Federal Censuses and Survey Data," *Public Data Use* 10 (1982): 203–18. See also Stanley Lieberson and Lawrence Santi, "The Use of Nativity Data to Es-

timate Ethnic Characteristics and Patterns," *Social Science Research* 14 (1985): 31–56.

38. U.S. Bureau of the Census, *Census of Population and Housing, 1990*, Content Determination Report no. 1990 CDR-6, "Race and Ethnic Origin" (Washington, D.C., 1991).

5. Differentiation among Blacks

1. See 14–15, 267–69.
2. Abraham Kaplan, *The Conduct of Inquiry: Methodology for Behavioral Science* (San Francisco: Chandler, 1964), chap. 9.
3. Thomas Sowell, "Three Black Histories," in Sowell, ed., *Essays and Data on American Ethnic Groups* (Washington, D.C.: Urban Institute, 1978).
4. Quoted in Reynolds Farley, *Growth of the Black Population: A Study in Demographic Trends* (Chicago: Markham Publication Co., 1970), 27.
5. John Cummings, *Negro Population, 1790–1915* (Washington, D.C.: U.S. Bureau of the Census, 1918; reprinted, New York: Arno Press, 1968), chap. 11.
6. Thomas Sowell, *Ethnic America: A History* (New York: Basic Books, 1981), 219.
7. See 68–69.
8. "The Jeweler's Dilemma," *New Republic* (10 November 1986). One of the more interesting comments on this query was from Walter E. Williams, a distinguished economist who is himself black. One day, when he was picking up litter about his house, a white man stopped to ask whether when he finished he would come over to his home to work there. Williams's comment was, "Mistaken identity is always at least a bit unpleasant, but it is not the same as racism" (ibid.).
9. Dinesh D'Souza, *The End of Racism: Principles for a Multiracial Society* (New York: Free Press, 1995), 245–87.
10. See, for example, Reynolds Farley and Suzanne M. Bianchi, "The Growing Gap between Blacks," *American Demographics* 5 (July 1983): 15–18.
11. William Julius Wilson, *The Declining Significance of Race: Blacks and Changing American Institutions* (Chicago: University of Chicago Press, 1978). Like any other attempt to show that discrimination against Negroes is no longer all-pervasive, Wilson's book was not well received by many other blacks. An "Association of Black Sociologists" declared itself to be "outraged over the misrepresentations of the black experience" and "extremely disturbed over the policy implications that may derive from this work." The book was important enough to stimulate a full volume of commentary and response: Charles Vert Willie, ed., *The Caste and Class Controversy* (Bayside, N.Y.: General Hall, 1979).
12. Claudette E. Bennett, "The Black Population in the United States: March 1994 and 1993," U.S. Bureau of the Census, *Current Population Report, Population Characteristics*, P20-480, January 1995.
13. *Economist* (8 July 1995).
14. Nathan Glazer, "Black and White after Thirty Years," *Public Interest*, no. 121 (Fall 1995): 61–79.
15. Arch Puddington, "The Disappearance of the 'Vital Center,'" *Weekly Standard* (15 January 1996): 31–35.
16. Belgian Flemings represent a parallel case in a totally different setting; see chap. 11.
17. William E. Cross, Jr., *Shades of Black: Diversity in African-American Identity* (Philadelphia: Temple University Press, 1991), 135.
18. Ibid., 157.
19. Janet E. Helms, ed., *Black and White Racial Identity: Theory, Research, and Practice* (Westport, Conn.: Greenwood Press, 1990), chap. 2.

20. W. Augustus Low and Virgil A. Clift, *Encyclopedia of Black America* (New York: McGraw-Hill, 1981), 656–57. See also Halford H. Fairchild, "Black, Negro, or Afro-American? The Differences Are Crucial!" *Journal of Black Studies* 16 (1985): 47–55.

21. Cf. Arna Bontemps and Jack Conroy, *Anyplace But Here* (New York: Hill & Wang, 1966). In the 1950s such popular magazines as *Ebony* and *Negro Digest* carried series of articles depicting the psychic cost to a person leading a double life, or describing the exceptional white who passed as a Negro, arguing in sum that the phenomenon of "passing" (then generally written between quotation marks) was itself a passing fad.

22. From one such calculation it was estimated that each year between 1900 and 1910, 25,000 blacks passed into the white community; see Hornell Hart, *Selective Migration as a Factor in Child Welfare in the United States* (Iowa City: University of Iowa, 1921).

23. Brewton Berry, *Almost White* (New York: Macmillan, 1965).

24. Calvin L. Beale, "Census Problems of Racial Enumeration," in Edgar T. Thompson and Everett C. Hughes, eds., *Race: Individual and Collective Behavior* (Glencoe, Ill.: Free Press, 1958).

25. James H. Dormon, "Louisiana Cajuns: A Case Study in Ethnic Group Revitalization," *Social Science Quarterly* 65 (1984): 1043–57.

26. George E. Kent, "Struggle for the Image: Selected Books by or about Blacks during 1971," *Phylon* 33 (1972): 304–23.

27. See 28–29.

28. Gunnar Myrdal, *An American Dilemma: The Negro Problem and Modern Democracy* (New York: Harper, 1944), 965–66.

29. J. L. Dillard, *Black English, Its History and Usage in the United States* (New York: Random House, 1972). P. Grade, in Dillard, ed., *Perspectives on Black English* (The Hague: Mouton, 1975).

30. Joan G. Fickett, in Dillard, *Perspectives on Black English*.

31. Joan C. Baratz, in Robert H. Bentley and Samuel D. Crawford, eds., *Black English Reader* (Glenview, Ill.: Scott, Foresman, 1973); italics in the original.

32. Henry H. Mitchell, in Arthur L. Smith, ed., *Language, Communication, and Rhetoric in Black America* (New York: Harper, 1972).

33. William Labov, "Objectivity and Commitment in Linguistic Science: The Case of the Black English Trial in Ann Arbor," *Language in Society* 11 (1982): 165–201.

34. Cf. "Booker T. Washington, Pro and Con," in Herbert Aptheker, ed., *A Documentary History of the Negro People in the United States* (Secaucus, N.J.: Citadel Press, 1974), vol. 1, 876–86; vol. 2, 1–15.

35. Quoted in Samuel R. Spencer, Jr., *Booker T. Washington and the Negro's Place in American Society* (Boston: Little, Brown, 1955), 101.

36. Cf. Harold R. Isaacs, *The New World of Negro Americans* (New York: John Day, 1963), 195–230. Eric J. Sundquist, "W. E. B. DuBois: Up to Slavery," *Commentary* (December 1986): 62–67.

37. Glenn C. Loury, *One by One from the Inside Out: Essays and Reviews on Race and Responsibility in America* (New York: Free Press, 1995), 65–66.

38. Edmund David Cronen, *Black Moses: The Story of Marcus Garvey and the Universal Negro Improvement Association* (Madison: University of Wisconsin Press, 1968). See also Isaacs, *The New World*, 136–46.

39. Cronen, *Black Moses*, chaps. 4–6.

40. R. L. Watson, "American Scholars and the Continuity of African Culture in the United States," *Journal of Negro History* 63 (1978): 375–86.

41. Melville J. Herskovits, *The Myth of the Negro Past* (1941; reprinted, Boston: Beacon Press, 1958).
42. Ibid., 111, 263, 171–72.
43. E. Franklin Frazier, *The Negro Family in the United States*, rev. ed. (Chicago: University of Chicago Press, 1966).
44. The opposed points of view were expressed first in two books, Frazier's *The Negro Family in the United States* (1939) and Herskovits's *The Myth of the Negro Past* (1940), reviewed by Frazier in *The Nation* (14 February 1942). The most direct confrontation was in three articles on the Negro family in Bahia, Brazil, reprinted in Pierre van den Berghe, ed., *Intergroup Relations: Sociological Perspectives* (New York: Basic Books, 1972).
45. Lee Rainwater and William L. Yancey, *The Moynihan Report and the Politics of Controversy* (Cambridge, Mass.: M.I.T. Press, 1967). This reprints the report by Moynihan and some of the most prominent criticisms of it.
46. Bennett, "The Black Population in the United States."
47. Larry Freshnock and Phillips Cutright, "Models of Illegitimacy: United States, 1969," *Demography* 16 (1979): 37–47.
48. U.S. Bureau of the Census, *Census of Population and Housing, 1990*, Content Determination Reports, no. 1990 CDR-6, "Race and Ethnic Origin" (Washington, D.C., 1991).

6. Who is an American Indian?

1. Barry T. Klein, *Reference Encyclopedia of the American Indian*, 6th ed. (West Nyack, N.Y.: Todd Publications, 1993).
2. Charles F. Voegelin, and Florence M. Voegelin, *Map of North American Indian Languages*, American Ethnological Society, Publication no. 20, rev. (New York, 1966).
3. Quoted in D. F. Johnston, *An Analysis of Sources of Information on the Population of the Navaho*, Bureau of Ethnology, Smithsonian Institution, Bulletin 197 (Washington, D.C., 1966): 66ff.
4. Harold E. Driver, *Indians of North America*, 2nd ed. (Chicago: University of Chicago Press, 1969), chap. 17.
5. *New York Times* (5 and 7 January 1978).
6. Driver, *Indians of North America*, 309, 320, 324.
7. Everts Boutell Greene and Virginia D. Harrington, *American Population before the Federal Census of 1790* (New York: Columbia University Press, 1932). See also Patricia Cline Cohen, *A Calculating People: The Spread of Numeracy in Early America* (Chicago: University of Chicago Press, 1982), chap. 2.
8. Quoted in Daniel Boorstin, *The Americans: The Colonial Experience* (New York: Random House, 1958), 348.
9. James H. Cassedy, *Demography in Early America: Beginnings of the Statistical Mind, 1600–1800* (Cambridge, Mass.: Harvard University Press, 1969), chap. 4.
10. Quoted in ibid., 103n.
11. Woodrow Wilson Borah, "The Historical Demography of Latin America: Sources, Techniques, Controversies, Yields," in Paul Deprez, ed., *Population and Economics* (Winnipeg: University of Manitoba Press, 1970).
12. James Mooney, "Population," in Frederick Webb Hodge, ed., *Handbook of the American Indians North of Mexico*, Bureau of American Ethnology, Smithsonian Institution, Bulletin 30 (Washington, D.C., 1910); *The Aboriginal Population of*

America North of Mexico, Smithsonian Institution, Miscellaneous Collection 80, no. 7 (Washington, D.C., 1928).

13. Henry F. Dobyns, "Estimating Aboriginal American Population: An Appraisal of Techniques with a New Hemispheric Estimate," *Current Anthropology* 7 (1966): 395–416. Dobyns also set a very high figure for the pre-Columbian population of North and South America. Among the estimates often cited are those of the well-known American anthropologist A. L. Kroeber (8.4 million) and the Argentine ethnologist Ángel Rosenblat (13.4 million). Dobyns's estimate was 90–112 million.

14. William M. Denevan, ed., *The Native Population of the Americas in 1492* (Madison: University of Wisconsin Press, 1976), 7–12. Douglas H. Ubelaker, "Prehistoric New World Population Size: Historical Review and Current Appraisal of North American Estimates," *American Journal of Physical Anthropology* 45 (1976): 661–66.

15. Russell Thornton and Joan Marsh-Thornton, "Estimating Prehistoric American Indian Population Size for the United States Area: Implications of the Nineteenth-Century Population Decline and Nadir," *American Journal of Physical Anthropology* 55 (1981): 47–53. See also Russell Thornton, "Recent Estimates of the Prehistoric California Indian Population," *Current Anthropology* 21 (1980): 702–04.

16. The phrase was coined by D. Ian Pool in *The Maori Population of New Zealand, 1769-1971* (Auckland, N.Z.: Auckland University Press, 1977), 13.

17. Wilbert E. Moore, *Industrialization and Labor: Social Aspects of Economic Development* (Ithaca, N.Y.: Cornell University Press, 1951), 216. See also Julian Pitt-Rivers, "Mestizo or Ladino?" *Race* 10 (1969): 463–77; "Race in Latin America: The Concept of 'Raza,'" *European Journal of Sociology* 14 (1973): 3–27.

18. John D. Early, "Revision of Ladino and Maya Census Populations of Guatemala, 1950 and 1964," *Demography* 11 (1974): 105–17.

19. The reports of Morse and Schoolcraft were summarized in the 1890 census report; see U.S. Census Office, "Report on Indians Taxed and Not Taxed in the United States (except Alaska)," in *Eleventh Census of the United States, 1890* (Washington, D.C., 1894).

20. Johnston, *The Population of the Navaho,* 101–04.

21. Ibid., 81.

22. S. Lyman Tyler, *A History of Indian Policy* (Washington, D.C.: U.S. Bureau of Indian Affairs, 1973).

23. U.S. Bureau of Indian Affairs, *Information about the Indian People* (Washington, D.C., 1981).

24. Alan L. Sorkin has written several informative works on this topic. His book on federal programs devoted to Indians in and around reservations has chapters on schools, health services, agricultural development, industrial development, manpower development, property and income management, and welfare services: *American Indians and Federal Aid* (Washington, D.C.: Brookings Institution, 1971). One notable program that subsidized migration from reservations to urban areas was an implicit admission that the many efforts to improve conditions in the context of reservation life were not succeeding: "Some Aspects of American Indian Migration," *Social Forces* 48 (1969): 243–50. Roughly half of the Indians in the United States now live in cities, where their level of living is also deplorable. Indians contribute to the slums' social ills, particularly through high rates of alcoholism. Their health is poor, and the dropout rate from schools is very high. For a view two decades ago, see Sorkin, *The Urban American Indian* (Lexington, Mass.: Lexington Books, 1978), chap. 9 and passim.

25. U.S. Commissioner of Indian Affairs, "Report," in *Report of the Secretary of the Interior*, House of Representatives, 52nd Cong., 2nd sess., Executive Documents 1, part 5, vol. II (Washington, D.C., 1982): 31–37.

26. See Alison R. Bernstein, *American Indians and World War II: Toward a New Era in Indian Affairs* (Norman: University of Oklahoma Press, 1991).

27. Cf. Nancy Oestreich Lurie, "The Indian Claims Commission," *Annals of the American Academy of Political and Social Science* 436 (1978): 97–110.

28. James A. Clifton, ed., *The Invented Indian: Cultural Fictions and Government Policies* (New Brunswick, N.J.: Transaction Publishers, 1990), chap. 1.

29. Ronald L. Trosper, "Native American Boundary Maintenance: The Flathead Indian Reservation, Montana, 1860–1970," *Ethnicity* 3 (1976): 275–303.

30. Cf. *Felix S. Cohen's Handbook of Federal Indian Law* (republished in a facsimile printing: Albuquerque: University of New Mexico Press, 1942).

31. U.S. Census Office, "Report on Indians Taxed and Not Taxed."

32. Russell Thornton, "Demographic Antecedents of a Revitalization Movement: Population Change, Population Size and the 1890 Ghost Dance," *American Sociological Review* 46 (1981): 88–96.

33. S. Ryan Johansson and Samuel H. Preston, "Tribal Demography: The Hopi and Navaho Populations as Seen through Manuscripts from the 1900 U.S. Census," *Social Science History* 3 (1978): 1–33.

34. Brian W. Dippie, *The Vanishing American: White Attitudes and U.S. Indian Policy* (Middletown, Conn.: Wesleyan University Press, 1982).

35. U.S. Bureau of the Census, *Historical Statistics of the United States: Colonial Times to 1957* (Washington, D.C., 1960), 3.

36. J. Nixon Hadley, "The Demography of the American Indians," *Annals of the American Academy of Political and Social Science* 311 (1957): 23–30.

37. Jeffrey S. Passel, "Provisional Evaluation of the 1970 Census Count of American Indians," *Demography* 13 (1976): 397–409.

38. For example, Milton M. Goldberg, "A Qualification of the Marginal Man Theory," *American Sociological Review* 6 (1941): 52–58; David Riesman, "Marginality, Conformity, and Insight," in *Individualism Reconsidered* (Glencoe, Ill.: Free Press, 1954).

39. Sol Tax, "The Impact of Urbanization on American Indians," *Annals of the American Academy of Political and Social Science* 436 (1978): 121–36.

40. U.S. Bureau of the Census, *Census of Population and Housing, 1990*, Content Determination Report, no. 1990 CDR-6, "Race and Ethnic Origin" (Washington, D.C., 1991), III-1.

41. Ibid.

42. U.S. Bureau of the Census, *1990 Census of Population and Housing, Summary Population and Housing Characteristics, United States* (Washington, D.C., 1992), III-1.

43. Ibid., B-11.

7. The Creation of Hispanics

1. Claudio Lomnitz-Adler, *Exits from the Labyrinth: Culture and Ideology in the Mexican National Space* (Berkeley: University of California Press, 1992), chap. 15. See also Alberto Ruy-Sánchez, "Approaches to the Problem of Mexican Identity," in Robert L. Earle and John D. Wirth, eds., *Identities in North America: The Search for Community* (Stanford, Calif.: Stanford University Press, 1995).

2. Ralph C. Guzmán, *The Political Socialization of the Mexican American People* (New York: Arno Press, 1970), 187.

3. Fernando Peñalosa, "Toward an Operational Definition of the Mexican American," *Aztlán* 1 (1970): 1–11.
4. Quoted in John H. Burma, *Spanish-Speaking Groups in the United States* (Durham, N.C.: Duke University Press, 1954; reprinted, Detroit: Blaine Ethridge, 1974).
5. Peter Skerry, *Mexican Americans: The Ambivalent Minority* (Cambridge, Mass.: Harvard University Press, 1995).
6. Guzmán, *The Political Socialization of the Mexican American People*, 86ff.
7. John Skirius, "Vasconcelos and *México de Afuera* (1928)," *Aztlán* 7 (1976): 479–97.
8. Tino Villanueva, "Sobre el termino 'Chicano,'" *Cuadernos Hispanoamericanos*, no. 336 (1978): 387–410.
9. Gaynor Cohen, "Alliance and Conflict among Mexican Americans," *Ethnic and Racial Studies* 5 (1982): 175–95.
10. Rodolfo de la Garza, "Demythologizing Chicano-Mexican Relations," in Susan Kaufman Purcell, ed., "Mexico-United States Relations," *Proceedings of the Academy of Political Science* 34 (1981): 88–96.
11. Cf. Doris L. Meyer, "The Language Issue in New Mexico, 1880-1900: Mexican-American Resistance against Cultural Erosion," *Bilingual Review* 4 (1977): 99–106.
12. A. J. Jaffe, Ruth M. Cullen, and Thomas D. Boswell, *The Changing Demography of Spanish Americans* (New York: Academic Press, 1980), chap. 5. Cf. Leo Grebler, Joan W. Moore, and Ralph Guzmán, *The Mexican-American People: The Nation's Second Largest Minority* (New York: Free Press, 1970).
13. Dorothy Waggoner, "Statistics on Language Use," in Charles A. Ferguson and Shirley Brice Heath, eds., *Language in the USA* (New York: Cambridge University Press, 1981). Cf. U.S. Bureau of the Census, "Mother Tongue of the Foreign Born: Selected Characteristics of Foreign Born by Language Spoken before Coming to the U.S.," *U.S. Census of Population, 1960*, Final Report PC(2)-1E (Washington, D.C., 1966).
14. David E. Lopez, "Chicano Language Loyalty in an Urban Setting," *Sociology and Social Research* 62 (1978): 267–78. See also Calvin J. Veltman, "Melting Pot USA: L'anglicisation des Hispano-américains," *Cahiers Québécois de Démographie* 10 (1981): 31–48.
15. David H. Hunter, "The 1975 Voting Rights Act and Language Minorities," *Catholic University Law Review* 25 (1976): 250–70. See also Edith McArthur, "How Wide Is the Language Gap?" *American Demographics* 3 (May 1981): 28–33.
16. William E. Morton, "Demographic Redefinition of Hispanos," *Public Health Reports* 85 (1970): 617–23.
17. Robert Schoen, Verne E. Nelson, and Marion Collins, "Intermarriage among Spanish-Surnamed Californians, 1962-1974," *International Migration Review* 12 (1978): 359–69. See also Gillian Stevens and Robert Schoen, "Linguistic Intermarriage in the United States," *Working Papers in Population Studies* (Urbana-Champaign: University of Illinois, 1986).
18. See also 75–77.
19. Edward W. Fernandez, "Comparison of Persons of Spanish Surname and Persons of Spanish Origin in the United States," U.S. Bureau of the Census, *Technical Report*, no. 38 (Washington, D.C., 1975).
20. Charlotte A. Redden, "Identification of Spanish Heritage Persons in Public Data," *Public Data Use* 4 (1976): 3–11.
21. Mexican-American Population Commission of California, *Mexican-American Population in California as of April, 1973, with Projections to 1980* (San Francisco, 1973), Appendix B.

22. The large number of studies on this issue show little or no agreement on any of the debatable points. For a comparison of several estimates, with an excellent discussion of the issues involved in arriving at plausible figures, see Jacob S. Siegel, Jeffrey S. Passel, and J. Gregory Robinson, "Preliminary Review of Existing Studies of the Number of Illegal Residents in the United States," in *U.S. Immigration Policy and the National Interest: The Staff Report of the Select Commission on Immigration and Refugee Policy* (Washington, D.C., 1980), Appendix E.

23. Mark Reisler, *By the Sweat of Their Brow: Mexican Immigrant Labor in the United States, 1900–1940* (Westport, Conn.: Greenwood Press, 1976). V. M. Briggs, Jr., "Mexican Workers in the United States Labour Market: A Contemporary Dilemma," *International Labour Review* 12 (1975): 351–68.

24. *New York Times* (28 and 29 March 1980).

25. Constanza Montana, "Latino Schism: Hispanic Communities in the U.S. Are Divided by Influx of Mexicans," *Wall Street Journal* (21 October 1986).

26. José Hernández, Leo Estrada, and David Alvírez, "Census Data and the Problem of Conceptually Defining the Mexican American Population," *Social Science Quarterly* 53 (1973): 671–87.

27. Suzanne Oboler, *Ethnic Labels, Latino Lives: Identity and the Politics of (Re)Presentation in the United States* (Minneapolis: University of Minnesota Press, 1995), chap 2.

28. Jack D. Forbes, "The Hispanic Spin: Party Politics and Governmental Manipulation of Ethnic Identity," *Latin American Perspectives* 19 (1992): 59–78.

29. Ernest Garcia, "Chicano Spanish Dialects and Education," *Aztlán* 2 (1971): 67–77. E. Hernández-Chávez, A. D. Cohen, and A. F. Beltramo, eds. *El lenguaje de los chicanos* (Arlington, Va.: Center for Applied Linguistics, 1975).

30. Thomas G. Exter, "Focus on Hispanics," *American Demographics* 7 (August 1985): 29–33.

31. See, for example, Frank D. Bean, Jorge Chapa, Ruth R. Berg, and Kathryn A. Sowards, "Educational and Sociodemographic Incorporation among Hispanic Immigrants to the United States," in Barry Edmonston and Jeffrey S. Passel, eds., *Immigration and Ethnicity: The Integration of America's Newest Arrivals* (Washington, D.C.: Urban Institute, 1983).

32. Ilan Stavans, *The Hispanic Condition: Reflections on Culture and Identity in America* (New York: HarperCollins, 1995), 131.

33. José Hernández Alvarez, *Return Migration to Puerto Rico* (Berkeley: Institute of International Studies, University of California, 1967; reprinted, Westport, Conn.: Greenwood Press, 1976).

34. Nathan Glazer and Daniel P. Moynihan, *Beyond the Melting Pot,* 2nd ed. (Cambridge, Mass.: M.I.T. Press, 1970), xii.

35. Jaffe et al., *The Changing Demography of Spanish Americans,* chap. 7. See, as one example, an account of Puerto Rican settlements in three small cities of Massachusetts: Ramón Borges-Mendez, "Migration, Social Networks, Poverty and the Regionalization of Puerto Rican Settlements: Barrio Formation in Lowell, Lawrence and Holyoke, Massachusetts," *Latino Studies Journal* 4 (1993): 3–21.

36. See, for example, Clara E. Rodriguez, "Puerto Rican Circular Migration: Revisited," *Latino Studies Journal* 4 (1993): 93–113.

37. Linda Chavez, *Out of the Barrio: Toward a New Politics of Hispanic Assimilation* (New York: Basic Books, 1991), 152.

38. Language Policy Task Force, "Language Policy and the Puerto Rican Community," *Bilingual Review* 5 (1978): 1–39.

39. Américo Paredos, "On Ethnographic Work among Minority Groups: A Folklorist's Perspective," in Ricardo Romo and Raymund Paredos, eds., *New Directions in*

Chicano Scholarship (La Jolla, Calif.: Chicano Studies Program, University of California, 1979).

40. Rosalie Pedalino Porter, *Forked Tongue: The Politics of Bilingual Education* (New York: Basic Books, 1990).

41. Benigno E. Aguirre, "Differential Migration of Cuban Social Races: A Review and Interpretation of the Problem," *Latin American Research Review* 11 (1976): 103–24. See also Richard R. Fagen, Richard A. Brody, and Thomas J. O'Leary, *Cubans in Exile: Disaffection and the Revolution* (Stanford, Calif.: Stanford University Press, 1968).

42. Joseph P. Fitzpatrick and Lourdes Travieso Parker, "Hispanic-Americans in the Eastern United States," *Annals of the American Academy of Social and Political Science* 454 (1981): 98–110. See also Alejandro Portes and Robert L. Bach, *Latin Journey: Cuban and Mexican Immigrants in the United States* (Berkeley: University of California Press, 1985).

43. Quoted in *American Demographics* 2 (June 1980): 7.

44. Rodolfo O. de la Garza, Louis DeSipio, F. Chris Garcia, John Garcia, and Angelo Falcon, *Latino Voices: Mexican, Puerto Rican, and Cuban Perspectives on American Politics* (Boulder, Colo.: Westview Press, 1992), 7.

45. Ibid., 13–14, 62–64, 84, 96, 121.

46. Patricia A. Montgomery, "The Hispanic Population in the United States, March 1993," U.S. Bureau of the Census, *Current Population Report, Population Characteristics*, Series P20-475 (Washington, D.C., May 1994).

47. U.S. Bureau of the Census, *Census of Population and Housing, 1990,* Content Determination Report, no. 1990 CDR-6, "Race and Ethnic Origin" (Washington, D.C., 1991).

48. Alfred N. Garwood, ed., *Hispanic Americans: A Statistical Sourcebook* (Boulder, Colo.: Numbers & Concepts, 1992), table 8.19.

49. Morris Janowitz, *The Reconstruction of Patriotism: Education for Civic Consciousness* (Chicago: University of Chicago Press, 1983), 129, 137.

8. Americans of Asian Stocks

1. Cf. Naosaku Uchida, *The Overseas Chinese: A Bibliographical Essay Based on the Resources of the Hoover Institution* (Stanford, Calif.: Stanford University, 1959).

2. Maurice Freedman, *The Study of Chinese Society,* G. William Skinner, ed. (Stanford, Calif.: Stanford University Press, 1979).

3. Persia C. Campbell, *Chinese Coolie Emigration to Countries within the British Empire* (London: P. S. King, 1923), 135ff.

4. Gladys C. Hansen, *The Chinese in California: A Brief Bibliographic History* (San Francisco Public Library, 1970).

5. Stuart C. Miller, *The Unwelcome Immigrant: The American Image of the Chinese, 1785–1882* (Berkeley: University of California Press, 1969), 153.

6. Thomas Sowell, *Ethnic America: A History* (New York: Basic Books, 1981), chap 6.

7. S. W. Kung, *Chinese in American Life: Some Aspects of Their History, Status, Problems, and Contributions* (Seattle: University of Washington Press, 1962), 91–92.

8. Rodman W. Paul, "The Origin of the Chinese Issue in California," in Leonard Dinnerstein and Frederic C. Jaher, eds., *The Aliens: A History of Ethnic Minorities in America* (New York: Appleton-Century-Crofts, 1970).

9. Dudley O. McGovney, "The Anti-Japanese Laws of California and Ten Other States," *California Law Review* 35 (1947): 7–60.

10. See 143, 149.
11. Romanzo C. Adams, "Japanese Migration Statistics," *Sociology and Social Research* 13 (1929): 436–45.
12. Allan R. Bosworth, *America's Concentration Camps* (New York: W. W. Norton, 1967). William Petersen, *Japanese Americans: Oppression and Success* (New York: Random House, 1971), chaps. 3–4. Michi Weglyn, *Years of Infamy: The Untold Story of America's Concentration Camps* (New York: Morrow, 1976).
13. Cf. Walter F. Banse, ed., *Adjudications of the Attorney General of the United States*, 1: *Precedent Decisions under the Japanese-American Evacuation Claims Act, 1950–1956* (Washington, D.C., 1956).
14. Sowell, *Ethnic America*, 148–52.
15. William Wei, *The Asian American Movement* (Philadelphia: Temple University Press, 1993), 45.
16. Ibid., 144.
17. Dudley O. McGovney, "Race Discrimination in Naturalization," *Iowa Law Bulletin* 8 (1922–23): 211–44.
18. Charles B. Keeley, "Philippine Migration: Internal Movements and Emigration to the United States," *International Migration Review* 7 (1973): 177–87. H. Brett Melendy, *Asians in America: Filipinos, Koreans, and East Indians* (Boston: Twayne Publishers, 1977).
19. H. Brett Melendy, "Filipinos," in *Harvard Encyclopedia of American Ethnic Groups* (Cambridge, Mass.: Harvard University Press, 1980). See also above, 315–17, on the use of Spanish surnames to identify Hispanics.
20. See 210–11.
21. Ivan Light, "Immigrant Entrepreneurs in America: Koreans in Los Angeles," in Nathan Glazer, ed., *Clamor at the Gates: The New American Immigration* (San Francisco: ICS Press, 1985).
22. Won Moo Hurh and Kwang Chung Kim, *Korean Immigrants in America: A Structural Analysis of Ethnic Confinement and Adhesive Adaptation* (Rutherford, N.J.: Fairleigh Dickinson University, 1984).
23. Hyung-chan Kim, "Koreans," in *Harvard Encyclopedia of American Ethnic Groups.*
24. Melendy, *Asians in America*, chap. 19. Sripati Chandrasekhar, "A History of United States Legislation with Respect to Immigration from India," in Chandrasekhar, ed., *From India to America* (La Jolla, Calif.: Population Review, 1982).
25. Maxine P. Fisher, "Indian Ethnic Identity: The Role of Associations in the New York Indian Population," in Paramatma Saran and Edwin Eames, eds., *The New Ethnics: Asian Indians in the United States* (New York: Praeger, 1980). See also chap. 16.
26. Anand Mohan, "Acculturation, Assimilation, and Political Adaptation," in Saran and Eames, *The New Ethnics.*
27. Ranjan Borra in a letter to the *New York Times* (29 August 1976).
28. Arif Ghayur, "Pakistanis," in *Harvard Encyclopedia of American Ethnic Groups.*
29. John Barton and Anthony Paul, *Murder of a Gentle Land: The Untold Story of Communist Genocide in Cambodia* (New York: Crowell, 1977).
30. Barry Wain, *The Refused: The Agony of the Indochinese Refugees* (New York: Simon and Schuster, 1981).
31. *New York Times* (20 February 1989).
32. U.S. Bureau for Refugee Programs, *World Refugee Report* (Washington, D.C.: Department of State, 1985).
33. Paul James Rutledge, *The Vietnamese Experience in America* (Bloomington: Indiana University Press, 1992).

34. Elizabeth Aoki, "Which Party Will Harvest the New Asian Votes?" *California Journal* (November 1986): 545–46.
35. U.S. Bureau of the Census, *Census of Population and Housing, 1990,* Content Determination Report no. 1990 CDR-6, "Race and Ethnic Origin" (Washington, D.C., 1991).
36. Tom Waldman, "Monterey Park: The Rise and Fall of an All-American City," *California Journal* (May 1989): 203–08.
37. U.S. Bureau of the Census, *1990 Census of Population.* "Asian and Pacific Islanders in the United States." 1990 CP-3-5. (Washington, D.C., 1993).
38. Ibid., B-25.

9. Hawaii

1. Isabella L. Bird, *Six Months in the Sandwich Islands* (1873; Honolulu: University of Hawaii Press, 1964), 133–34.
2. Norma McArthur, "Essays in Multiplication: European Sea-farers in Polynesia," *Journal of Pacific History* 1 (1966): 91–105.
3. The classic study is Romanzo Adams, *Interracial Marriage in Hawaii* (New York: Macmillan, 1937). It has been supplemented by a large literature: for example, Robert C. Schmitt, "Demographic Correlates of Interracial Marriage," *Demography* 2 (1965): 463–73; Margaret A. Parkman and Jack Sawyer, "Dimensions of Ethnic Intermarriage in Hawaii," *American Sociological Review* 32 (1967): 593–607.
4. U.S. Bureau of Labor Statistics, *Report of the Commissioner of Labor on Hawaii, 1902* (Washington, D.C., 1903), 22.
5. Newton E. Morton, Chin S. Chung, and Ming-pi Mi, *Genetics of Interracial Crosses in Hawaii* (New York: S. Karger, 1967).
6. Robert C. Schmitt, "1970 Treatment of Ethnic Stock," Memorandum of the State Department of Planning and Economic Development, no. 6204 (Honolulu: 1968).
7. Lawrence H. Fuchs, *Hawaii Pono: A Social History* (New York: Harcourt, Brace, 1961). The book offered so unfavorable a view of upper-class whites that in their circle it became something of a literary scandal. Yet the author, in spite of his academic liberal stance, found much to praise in the rule of these same upper-class whites.
8. Robert C. Schmitt, *Demographic Statistics of Hawaii: 1778–1965* (Honolulu: University of Hawaii Press, 1968), chap. 3.
9. Cf. chap. 8.
10. Bernhard L. Hormann, "'Racial' Statistics in Hawaii," *Social Process in Hawaii* 12 (1948): 27–35.
11. Cited in Ralph S. Kuykendall, *The Hawaiian Kingdom:* vol. III, *1874–1893: The Kalakaua Dynasty* (Honolulu: University of Hawaii Press, 1967), 174.
12. Fuchs, *Hawaii Pono,* 76.
13. Robert C. Schmitt, "How Many Hawaiians?" *Journal of the Polynesian Society* 76 (1967): 467–75.
14. Romanzo Adams, "Census Notes on the Negroes in Hawaii Prior to the War," *Social Process in Hawaii* 9–10 (1945): 25–27.
15. U.S. Bureau of the Census, *Census of Population, 1900,* II, part II (Washington, D.C., 1902), ccxvi–ccxix.
16. Adams, "Census Notes on Negroes."
17. Cf. 20–21.
18. Adams, *Interracial Marriage,* 113.
19. Elizabeth Wittermans, *Interethnic Relations in a Plural Society* (Groningen: Wolters, 1964).

20. U.S. Bureau of the Census, *Census of Population, 1960,* I, part 13 (Washington, D.C., 1963), table 15.
21. Schmitt, *Demographic Statistics of Hawaii,* 105.
22. Cf. 20.
23. Robert C. Schmitt, "Migration Statistics in an Island State: The Hawaii Experience," *American Statistician* 22 (1968): 20–23.
24. Schmitt, *Demographic Statistic of Hawaii,* 82.
25. Romanzo Adams, *The Peoples of Hawaii* (Honolulu: University of Hawaii Press, 1933), 9; *Interracial Marriage in Hawaii,* 8.
26. Adams, *Interracial Marriage in Hawaii,* 87.
27. Carol Esaki-Brunson, "Japanese Education on Kauai: Surveying Community Needs," M.A. Thesis, Monterey Institute of International Studies, 1991.

10. Some European Nations and Subnations

1. For example, Lewis M. Killian, "The Collection of Official Data on Ethnicity and Religion: The US Experience," *New Community* 5 (Autumn–Winter 1985): 74–82.
2. Julian Huxley and A. C. Haddon, *We Europeans: A Survey of "Racial" Problems 1935,* quoted in Pat Shipman, *The Evolution of Racism: Human Differences and the Use and Abuse of Science* (New York: Simon & Schuster, 1994), 148.
3. Max Weber, *Economy and Society: An Outline of Interpretive Sociology* (1956; New York: Bedminster Press, 1968), vol. 1, 385ff.
4. Alexis de Tocqueville, *Democracy in America* (1835; New York: Vintage, 1959), vol. 1, 176.
5. Elie Kedourie, *Nationalism,* 4th ed. (Cambridge, Mass.: Blackwell, 1993), 67.
6. Anthony D. Smith, *Theories of Nationalism,* 2nd ed. (London: Duckworth, 1983), 168.
7. Carl J. Friedrich, *Europe: An Emergent Nation?* (New York: Harper & Row, 1969).
8. John Hutchinson, *Modern Nationalism* (London: Fontana Press, 1994), 162.
9. Jacques Attali, *Europe(s)* (Paris: Fayard, 1994), 9.
10. Keith Webb, *The Growth of Nationalism in Scotland* (Glasgow: Molendinar Press, 1977), 29.
11. Ibid., 45–46.
12. H. J. Hanham, *Scottish Nationalism* (Cambridge, Mass.: Harvard University Press, 1969), 24.
13. Guy Héraud, *L'Europe des ethnies* (Paris: Presses d'Europe, 1963), 19.
14. See, for example, John Geipel, *The Europeans: The People—Today and Yesterday—Their Origins and Interrelations* (New York: Pegasus, 1970).
15. Erich Gruner and Beat Junker, *Bürger, Staat und Politik in der Schweiz* (Basel: Lehrmittelverlag, 1968), 9–10.
16. Franck Jotterand, "La politique culturelle," in Erich Gruner, ed., *Die Schweiz seit 1945: Beiträge zur Zeitgeschichte* (Bern: Francke, 1971), 281–82.
17. L. Pietersen, *Die Friesen en hun taal* (Drachten, Netherlands: Lavermen N.V., 1969).
18. Mancur Olson, *The Logic of Collective Action* (New York: Schocken, 1971), 2; italics in the original.
19. W. J. Argyle, "Size and Scale as Factors in the Development of Nationalist Movements," in Anthony D. Smith, ed., *Nationalist Movements* (London: Macmillan Press, 1976).
20. Cf. Alfred Cobban, *The Nation State and National Self-Determination* (New York: Crowell, 1969), 296.

21. Ibid., 41.
22. Robert A. Kann, *A History of the Habsburg Empire, 1526–1918* (Berkeley: University of California Press, 1974), 256ff. Cf. Stephen M. Horak et al., *Eastern European National Minorities, 1919-1980: A Handbook* (Littleton, Colo.: Libraries Unlimited, 1985).
23. Kann, *A History of the Habsburg Empire,* 72–74.
24. Ibid., 298.
25. Victor L. Tapié, *The Rise and Fall of the Habsburg Monarchy* (New York: Praeger, 1971), 296, 299.
26. Eugene M. Kulischer, *Europe on the Move: War and Population Changes, 1917–47* (New York: Columbia University Press, 1948).
27. Stephen P. Ladas, *The Exchange of Minorities: Bulgaria, Greece and Turkey* (New York: Macmillan, 1932). Carlile Aylmer Macartney, *Hungary and Her Successors: The Treaty of Trianon and Its Consequences, 1919–1937* (London: Oxford University Press, 1937), 430–49.
28. Stanley B. Kimball, "The Austro-Slav Revival: A Study of Nineteenth-Century Literary Foundations," *Transactions of the American Philosophical Society,* N.S., vol. 63 (1973), part 4, chap 3.
29. Ibid.
30. Quoted in Victor S. Mamatey, "The Establishment of the Republic," in Mamatey and Radomír Luža, eds., *A History of the Czechoslovak Republic, 1918–1948* (Princeton, N.J.: Princeton University Press, 1973).
31. Cf. Tom B. Bottomore and Patrick Goode, *Austro-Marxism: Texts Translated and Edited* (Oxford: Clarendon Press, 1978). Otto Bauer, *Die Nationalitätenfrage und die Sozialdemokratie* (Vienna: Volksbuchhandlung, 1907).
32. Thomas Masaryk, *The Making of a State: Memories and Observations, 1914–1918* (New York: Frederick A. Stokes, 1927), 78–80. Mamatey, "The Establishment of the Republic."
33. Quoted in Cobban, *The Nation State and National Self-Determination,* 69.
34. Joseph A. Mikus, *Slovakia: A Political History, 1918–1950* (Milwaukee, Wisc.: Marquette University Press, 1963), 6. See also Robert B. Pynsent, *Questions of Identity: Czech and Slovak Ideas of Nationality and Personality* (Budapest: Central European University Press, 1994).
35. Václav L. Beneš, "Czechoslovak Democracy and Its Problems, 1918–1920," in Mamatey and Luža, *A History of the Czechoslovak Republic.*
36. Radomír Luža, *The Transfer of the Sudeten Germans: A Study of Czech-German Relations, 1933–1962* (New York: New York University Press, 1964), 26, 42–43.
37. Kedourie, *Nationalism,* 124.
38. D. Perman, *The Shaping of the Czechoslovak State: Diplomatic History of the Boundaries of Czechoslovakia, 1914–1920* (Leiden: Brill, 1962), chaps. 5, 10.
39. George F. Kennan, *From Prague after Munich: Diplomatic Papers, 1938–1940* (Princeton, N.J.: Princeton University Press, 1968), 14.
40. Inis L. Claude, Jr., *National Minorities: An International Problem* (Cambridge, Mass.: Harvard University Press, 1955), chaps. 2–3. Cobban, *The Nation State,* chap. 5.
41. Alajos Kovács, "La connaissance des langues comme contrôle de la statistique des nationalités," *Bulletin de l'Institut International de Statistique* 23 (1928), part 2: 246–346.
42. Mario Strassoldo, *Lingue e nazionalità nelle rilevazioni demografiche,* Contributi e Ricerche Scienze Politiche Trieste, no. 8 (Trieste: CLUET, 1977).
43. Ibid., 48–51.
44. Ibid., 13–16.

45. Dudley Kirk, *Europe's Population in the Interwar Years* (League of Nations; Princeton, N.J.: Princeton University Press, 1946), 224–26.
46. *Economist* (14 December 1985; 25 January 1986).
47. Ali Eminov, "The Education of Turkish Speakers in Bulgaria," *Ethnic Groups* 5 (1983): 129–50.
48. Gwynne Dyer, "Bizarre Vanishing Act in Bulgaria," *Washington Times* (18 March 1985). *Wall Street Journal* (4 March 1985; 28 November 1985). *Insight* (14 September 1987).
49. U.S. Helsinki Watch Committee, *Destroying Ethnic Identity: The Expulsion of the Bulgarian Turks* (New York, 1989).
50. Chauncy D. Harris, "New European Countries and Their Minorities," *Geographical Review* 83 (1993): 301–20.
51. Ibid.
52. Georgios Tsiakalos, *Ausländer Feindlichkeit* (Munich: C. H. Beck, 1983).
53. Michel Wieviorka, "Tendencies to Racism in Europe: Does France Represent a Unique Case, or Is It Representative of a Trend?" in John Wrench and John Solomos, eds., *Racism and Migration in Western Europe* (Oxford: Berg, 1993); *Economist* (27 April 1996): 53.
54. Aleksandra Ålund and Carl-Ulrik Schierup, "The Thorny Road to Europe: Swedish Immigrant Policy in Transition," in Wrench and Solomos, *Racism and Migration in Western Europe.*
55. Tomas Hammar, "Swedish Immigration Policy: A Country Report," in *European Immigration Policy* (Cambridge, England: University Press, 1985).
56. Martin O. Heisler, "Transnational Migration as a Small Window on the Diminished Autonomy of the Modern Democratic State," *Annals of the American Academy of Political and Social Science* 485 (1986): 153–66.
57. Heléne Lööw, "The Cult of Violence: The Swedish Racist Counterculture," in Tore Björgo and Rob White, eds., *Racist Violence in Europe* (New York: St. Martin's Press, 1993).
58. Donald L. Horowitz, *Ethnic Groups in Conflict* (Berkeley: University of California Press, 1985), 195.
59. Dirk J. van de Kaa, "The Netherlands: No More Censuses?" *Population Today* (March 1986): 5, 10.
60. Tomas Hammar, "Political Participation and Civil Rights in Scandinavia," in Wrench and Solomos, *Racism and Migration in Western Europe.*
61. Tomas Hammar, "The Political Rights of Foreign Nationals—Immigrant Participation in Swedish Politics," *Current Sweden,* no. 305 (Stockholm: Svenska Institutet, 1983).
62. Heisler, "Transnational Migration."

11. A Comparison of American Blacks and Belgian Flemings

1. According to a Flemish source, however, the francophone administrators of the former Belgian Congo (present-day Zaire) used "Flamand" as their harshest epithet against an African native.
2. Gunnar Myrdal, *An American Dilemma: The Negro Problem and Modern Democracy* (New York: Harper, 1944), 208.
3. Ibid., 305.
4. E. Franklin Frazier, *Black Bourgeoisie: The Rise of a New Middle Class in the United States* (Glencoe, Ill.: Free Press, 1957).
5. Frank E. Huggett, *Modern Belgium* (London: Pall Mall, 1969).

6. U.S. Bureau of the Census, "Differences between Income of White and Negro Families by Work Experience of Wife and Region, 1970, 1969, and 1959," *Current Population Reports,* Ser. P-23, no. 39 (1971). See also Daniel Patrick Moynihan, "The Schism in Black America," *Public Interest,* no. 27 (1972): 3–24.
7. Myrdal, *An American Dilemma,* 1065–70.
8. N. Vanhove, *De ontwikkeling van de Vlaamse economie in internationaal perspectief* (Brussels: Gewestelijke Economische Raad voor Vlaanderen, 1973).
9. Max Lamberty, *De Vlaamse opstanding,* vol. 1 (Louvain: Davidsfonds, 1971). H. J. Elias and A. W. Willemsen, "Beknopte geschiedenis van de Vlaamse beweging," in J. Deleu et al., eds., *Encyclopedie van de Vlaamse beweging* (Tielt, Belgium: Lannoo, 1973), vol. 1, 17–47. M. Ruys, *The Flemings: A People on the Move, A Nation in Being* (Tielt, Belgium: Lannoo, 1973).
10. P. Kluft and F. van der Vorst, "Enquête à Bruxelles: Le problème linguistique et politique (Brussels: Institut de Sociologie, Université de Bruxelles, 1970; mimeographed).
11. P. M. G. Lévy, *La querelle du recensement* (Brussels: Institut Belge de Science Politique, 1960); "La mort du recensement linguistique," *Revue Nouvelle* 18 (1962): 145–54.
12. Nathan Glazer, *Affirmative Discrimination: Ethnic Inequality and Public Policy* (New York: Basic Books, 1975).
13. Daniel Seligman, "How 'Equal Opportunities' Turned into Employment Quotas," *Fortune* (March 1973): 160ff.
14. Quoted in Diane Ravitch. "Multiculturism: E Pluribus Unum," *American Scholar* (Summer 1990): 337–54.
15. *Kultuurraad voor Vlaanderen, Tweede Jaarboek* (Antwerp, 1961).
16. This may not be as anomalous as it seems, given the vagaries of nationalist movements. An array of Irish writers, from George Bernard Shaw to James Joyce and beyond, could not bear living in Ireland, but after their deaths reside there in honor.
17. Melville J. Herskovits, *The Myth of the Negro Past* (Boston: Beacon Press, 1958), 190–93.
18. See Harold R. Isaacs, *The New World of Negro Americans* (New York: Viking, 1963), 62–71.
19. J. L. Pauwels, "Moeilijkheden met de benaming van onze taal," in G. Geerts, ed., *Taal of taaltje? Een bloemlezing taalpolitieke beschouwing over het Nederlands* (Louvain: Acco, 1972).
20. Ibid.
21. Umberto Eco, *The Search for the Perfect Language* (Oxford: Blackwell, 1995), 96–97.
22. Myrdal, *An American Dilemma,* 928.
23. See 98.
24. A. W. Southall, "Population Movements in East Africa," in K. M. Barbour and A. W. Southall, eds., *Essays on African Population* (London: Routledge & Kegan Paul, 1961).
25. Harold R. Isaacs, "Back to Africa," *New Yorker* (13 May 1961).
26. *New York Times* (5 September 1971).
27. Pieter Geyl, *Eenheid en tweeheid in de Nederlanden* (Lochem: De Tijdstroom, 1946); *History of the Low Countries: Encounters and Problems* (New York: St. Martin's Press, 1964).
28. Henri Pirenne, *Histoire de Belgique,* 7 vols. (Brussels: H. and M. Lamertin, 1900–48).

29. S. S. H. M. Boelen, "De Nederlandse taal in Vlaanderen," in Geerts, *Taal of taaltje*; italics in the original.

30. There has been a beginning response from the Walloon side, of which the most prominent item was a history of Wallonia: L. Genicot, ed., *Histoire de la Wallonie* (Toulouse: Edouard Privat, [1973]). It was not only published in France but was one of a series on "the history of the provinces"!

31. English-speaking persons are more likely to use the French version, but sometimes there is a third variation. The English Brussels, thus, seems to have been a compromise between the French Bruxelles and the Dutch Brussel. Even when the local name is carried over into English, the often bizarre pronunciation (as of Waterloo, for instance) makes it unrecognizable to either Fleming or Walloon.

32. Einar Haugen, *The Ecology of Language* (Stanford, Calif.: Stanford University Press, 1972), 341.

12. Ethnic Relations in the Netherlands

1. For example, Paul Scholten, *Het geloof in het nederlandse volksleven* (Amsterdam: Ploegsma, 1941).

2. L. J. Rogier, *Katholieke herleving: Geschiedenis von katholiek Nederland sinds 1853* (The Hague: Pax, 1956), chap. 1.

3. J. A. Loeff et al., eds., *Het katholiek Nederland, 1813–1913: Ter blijde herinnering aan het eerste eeuwfest onzer nationale onafhangelijkheid*, 2 vols. (Nijmegen: L. C. G. Malmberg [1913]).

4. See 152–53.

5. W. G. Versluis, *Geschiedenis van de emancipatie der katholieken in Nederland van 1795–heden* (Utrecht: Dekker & Van de Vegt, 1948), 74.

6. Jos. van Wely, *Schaepman: Levensverhaal* (Bussum: Brand, 1952).

7. One consequence of the schism was a migration to Canada and the United States, where the settlers tried to establish a Christian society in microcosm. Just before World War I, a Christian party was organized in the United States; and in 1921 the *Christian Standard* was founded, supplementing several Dutch-language newspapers. A Christian Labor Association, or trade union based on Calvinist principles, followed. Christian schools were founded to teach children Old Testament ethics. Calvin College in Grand Rapids, begun on a small scale in 1876, offered bachelors' degrees by 1920. All these were faithful reflections of comparable institutions that had prospered in the Netherlands, but in the quite different social climate of the United States all but the church and the schools failed within a few years.

8. It was restored in 1954, but only for primary grades.

9. P. Kasteel, *Abraham Kuyper* (Kampen: Kok, 1938), 229.

10. Herman Bakvis, *Catholic Power in the Netherlands* (Kingston: McGill-Queen's University Press, 1981), chap. 1.

11. Carleton J. H. Hayes, *A Generation of Materialism, 1871–1900* (New York: Harper, 1941), 199.

12. J. P. Kruijt, *Verzuiling* (Zaandijk: Heijnis, 1959), 14.

13. L. J. van Apeldoorn, *Inleiding tot de studie van het nederlandse recht*, 12th ed. (Zwolle: Tjeenk Willink, 1954), 288–92.

14. Dudley Kirk, *Europe's Population in the Interwar Years* (League of Nations; Princeton, N.J.: Princeton University Press, 1946), 180–82.

15. *Van Alphen's nieuw kerkelijk handboek tevens complete predikantenboek omvattende alle protestantse kerken en gemeenten in Nederland, Nederland Overzee en de hollandse gemeenten in het buitenland* (Gouda: Koch en Knuttel,

1958), Bijlage F, "Tractementen, emolumenten en pensioenen voor predikanten, predikantsweduwen en wezen."

16. Kruijt, *Verzuiling*, 12–13.
17. J. P. Kruijt and Walter Goddijn, "Verzuiling en ontzuiling als sociologisch proces," in A. N. J. den Hollander et al., eds., *Drift en koers: Een halve eeuw sociale verandering in Nederland* (Assen: Van Gorcum, Prakke & Prakke, 1961).
18. *De Volkskrant* (25 October 1951).
19. H. Ernst, "Overbevolking en geboorteregeling," in Werkgenootschap van Katholieke Theologen in Nederland, *Jaarboek 1953* (Hilversum: Gooi, 1953).
20. Katholieke Volkspartij, "Documentatie gezinspolitiek," The Hague, mimeographed, 1957.
21. Frederik van Heek, *Het geboorte-niveau der nederlandse Rooms-Katholieken: Een demografisch-sociologische studie van een geëmancipeerde minderheidsgroep* (Leiden: Stenfert Kroese, 1954). For an English-language summary, see van Heek, "Roman-Catholicism and Fertility in the Netherlands: Demographic Aspects of Minority Status," *Population Studies* 10 (1956): 125–38.
22. A. J. van 't Veer, "Het geboorteniveau van de Rooms-Katholieken in het drostambt Tudderen," *Mens en Maatschappij* 37 (1962): 24–28. I translated the article for William Petersen, ed., *Readings in Population* (New York: Macmillan, 1972), 342–46.
23. John A. Coleman, *The Evolution of Dutch Catholicism, 1958–1974* (Berkeley: University of California Press, 1978), 1–2.
24. Jan Blokker, "Omdat wij er tegen zijn," in Blokker et al., eds., *Verzuiling: Een nederlands probleem al of niet voorzichtig benaderd* (Zaandijk: Heijnis, 1959).
25. Douglas Nobbs, *Theocracy and Toleration: A Study of Disputes in Dutch Calvinism from 1600–1650* (Cambridge, England: University Press, 1938).
26. Bisschoppen van de Rooms Katholieke Kerk, *De katholiek in het openbare leven van deze tijd: Bisschoppelijk Mandement, 1954* (Utrecht, 1954).
27. B. M. I. Delfgaauw, "Persoonlijke waarheid en georganiseerde macht," *Te Elfder Ure* 1 (1954): 279–85.
28. J. M. G. Thurlings, "The Case of Dutch Catholicism: A Contribution to the Theory of Pluralistic Society," *Sociologia Neerlandica* 7 (1971): 118–36. See also Thurlings, *De wankele zuil: Nederlandse katholieken tussen assimilatie en pluralisme* (Nijmegen: Dekker & Van de Vegt; Amersfoort: De Horstink, 1971); "Pluralism and Assimilation in the Netherlands, with Special Reference to Dutch Catholicism," in William Petersen, ed., *The Background to Ethnic Conflict* (Leiden: Brill, 1979).
29. Bakvis, *Catholic Power*, chaps. 5–6.
30. Coleman, *The Evolution of Dutch Catholicism*, chap. 6.
31. Gordon F. Sander, "Innocence Lost," *New York Times Magazine* (22 August 1976). See also J. E. Ellemers, "The Netherlands in the Sixties and Seventies," *Netherlands Journal of Sociology* 17 (1981): 113–35.
32. Samuel J. Eldersveld, Jan Kooiman, and Theo van der Tak, *Elite Images of Dutch Politics: Accommodation and Conflict* (Ann Arbor: University of Michigan Press, 1981).
33. Henry L. Mason, "Reflections on the Politicized University: II. Triparity and Tripolarity in the Netherlands," *AAUP Bulletin* 60 (1974): 383–400.
34. Hans Daalder, "The Dutch Universities between the 'New Democracy' and the 'New Management,'" *Minerva* 12 (1974): 228–31.
35. Ivan Gadourek and J. L. Jessen, "Proscription and Acceptance of Drug-taking in the Netherlands," *Sociologia Neerlandica* 8 (1972): 14–40.
36. *Wall Street Journal* (23 April 1996).

37. *New York Times* (16 November 1975; 8 December 1984).
38. *Wall Street Journal* (23 April 1996).
39. Organization for Economic Development, *Netherlands: OECD Economic Surveys* (Paris, 1986).
40. *Insight* (6 June 1986).
41. See 170–71.

13. Two Case Studies: Japan and Switzerland

1. M. Inez Hilger, *Together with the Ainu, A Vanishing People* (Norman: University of Oklahoma Press, 1971).
2. George Sansom, *A History of Japan to 1334* (Stanford, Calif.: Stanford University Press, 1958), 9.
3. Ibid., 16–17, 64–65.
4. John Whitney Hall and Richard K. Beardsley, *Twelve Doors to Japan* (New York: McGraw-Hill, 1965), 16.
5. George Sansom, *A History of Japan, 1334–1615* (Stanford, Calif.: Stanford University Press, 1961), vi.
6. Sansom, *A History of Japan to 1334,* 17–18, 129–31.
7. Basil Hall Chamberlain, *Japanese Things* (Rutland, Vt.: Tuttle, 1971), 17–19.
8. Herbert Passin, "Japanese Society," *International Encyclopedia of the Social Sciences,* vol. 8, 236–49.
9. Sumikazu Taguchi, "A Note on Current Research on Immigrant Groups in Japan," *International Migration Review* 17 (1983): 699–714.
10. Elizabeth Stevenson, *Lafcadio Hearn* (New York: Macmillan, 1961).
11. R. F. Dore, "Japan as a Model of Economic Development," *European Journal of Sociology* 5 (1964): 138–54.
12. William Petersen, "Thoughts on Writing a Dictionary of Demography," *Population and Development Review* 9 (1983): 677–87.
13. Richard K. Beardsley, in Hall and Beardsley, *Twelve Doors to Japan,* 312–17.
14. Donald Keene, *Living Japan* (Garden City, N.Y.: Doubleday, 1959), 108.
15. Korean Overseas Information Service, *A Handbook of Korea* (Seoul: Seoul International Publishing House, 1987), 47–54.
16. Ibid., 84–110.
17. Richard H. Mitchell, *The Korean Minority in Japan* (Berkeley: University of California Press, 1967), chaps. 1–4, 6–9. See also Changsoo Lee and George DeVos, *Koreans in Japan: Ethnic Conflict and Accommodation* (Berkeley: University of California Press, 1981).
18. George A. DeVos, William O. Wetherall, and Kaye Stearman, *Japan's Minorities: Burakumin, Koreans, Ainu and Okinawans* (London: Minority Rights Group, 1983).
19. Hiroshi Wagatsuma, "The Social Perception of Skin Color in Japan," *Daedalus* 96 (1967): 407–43.
20. George Fields, "Racism Is Accepted Practice in Japan," *Wall Street Journal* (10 November 1986).
21. John Price, in George A. DeVos and Hiroshi Wagatsuma, *Japan's Invisible Race: Caste in Culture and Personality* (Berkeley: University of California Press, 1966), chap. 1.
22. DeVos, Wetherall, and Stearman, *Japan's Minorities.*
23. Milton Ezrati, "Losing the Thread in Japan," *American Scholar* (Spring 1996): 177–92.
24. Wolf Linder, *Swiss Democracy: Possible Solutions to Conflict in Multicultural Societies* (London: St. Martin's Press, 1994), 5–6.

25. Hans Kohn, *Nationalism and Liberty: The Swiss Example* (London: Allen and Unwin, 1956), 111.
26. Hermann Weilenmann, *Pax Helvetica, oder die Demokratie der kleinen Gruppen* (Zurich: Eugen Rentsch, 1951), 268.
27. Blaise Lempen, *Un modèle en crise: La Suisse* (Lausanne: Editions Payot, 1985), 154.
28. See 152.
29. Denis de Rougemont, "Swiss Federalism," in Théo Chopard, ed., *Switzerland, Present and Future: A Small Country Re-examines Itself* (Bern: New Helvetic Society, 1963).
30. Kohn, *Nationalism and Liberty,* 89, 94.
31. Ibid., 127.
32. Rougemont, "Swiss Federalism." It is indicative of Rougemont's ambivalence that at the age of thirty he moved to Paris and became known to the literary world as a Frenchman.
33. Georg Kreis, "Die besseren Patrioten: National Idee und regionale Identität in der französischen Schweiz vor 1914," in Schweizerische Akademie der Geistes-wissenschaften, *Auf dem Weg zu einer schweizerischen Identität, 1848–1914* (Freiburg: Universitätsverlag Freiburg, 1987).
34. *Economist* (23 March 1996): 54.
35. Rebecca Posner, "Thirty Years On," supplement to Iorgu Iordan and John Orr, *An Introduction to Romance Linguistics: Its Schools and Scholars* (Berkeley: University of California Press, 1970), 419.
36. Joseph Hanse et al., *Chasse aux Belgicismes* (Brussels: Fondation Charles Plisnier, 1971).
37. Max Petitpierre et al., *Premier rapport de la Commission confédérée de bons offices pour le Jura du 13 Mai 1969* (Bern, 1969).
38. Kurt B. Mayer, "The Jura Problem: Ethnic Conflict in Switzerland," *Social Research* 35 (1968): 707–41.
39. John R. G. Jenkins, *Jura Separatism in Switzerland* (Oxford: Clarendon Press, 1986), chap. 7.
40. Kurt B. Mayer, *The Population of Switzerland* (New York: Columbia University Press, 1952), chap. 8; Linder, *Swiss Democracy,* 18–25.
41. Kurt B. Mayer, "Postwar Immigration and Switzerland's Demographic and Social Structure," in William Petersen, ed., *Readings in Population* (New York: Macmillan, 1972), 241–55.
42. Linder, *Swiss Democracy,* 84.
43. Patrick R. Ireland, *The Policy Challenge of Ethnic Diversity: Immigrant Politics in France and Switzerland* (Cambridge, Mass.: Harvard University Press, 1994), chaps. 4–5.
44. Jean-François Aubert, "Histoire constitutionelle," in Erich Gruner, ed., *Die Schweiz seit 1945* (Bern: Francke, [1971]).
45. Organization for Economic Cooperation and Development, *Regional Problems and Policies in Switzerland* (Paris, 1991).
46. Ulrich Im Hof, *Geschichte der Schweiz,* 5th ed., (Stuttgart: Verlag W. Kohlhammer, 1991), 150–51.

14. Who is a Jew?

1. See 78–81.
2. J. L. Talmon, "Who Is a Jew?" *Encounter* (May 1965): 28–36.
3. Chaim Potok, *Wanderings: Chaim Potok's History of the Jews* (New York: Knopf, 1978), 69.

4. Akiva Orr, *The unJewish State: The Politics of Jewish Identity in Israel* (London: Ithaca Press, 1981), 3–5.

5. Raul Hilberg, *The Destruction of the European Jews* (Chicago: Quadrangle Books, 1967), 5–6. One should note that the Catholic Church has tried to undo the centuries of anti-Semitism. The Holy Week prayers used to refer to the "perfidious Jews" who had killed Jesus, and these passages were removed by the Second Vatican Council. John Paul II went farther and recognized Jews as the "elder brothers" of Catholics [*New York Times* (3 April 1994)].

6. Hilberg, *The Destruction of the European Jews,* 8–10, 689–90.

7. G. William Skinner, *Chinese Society in Thailand: An Analytical History* (Ithaca, N.Y.: Cornell University Press, 1957), 164–65.

8. James S. Coleman, *Nigeria: Background to Nationalism* (Berkeley: University of California Press, 1960), 228.

9. H. I. Bach, *The German Jew: A Synthesis of Judaism and Western Civilization, 1730–1930* (New York: Oxford University Press, 1984), 75.

10. Potok, *Wanderings,* 366.

11. W. H. Chaloner and W. O. Henderson, "Marx/Engels and Racism," *Encounter* (July 1975): 18–23.

12. George Lichtheim, "Socialism and the Jews," *Dissent* 15 (1968): 314–34.

13. Alain Finkielkraut, *Le Juif imaginaire* (Paris: Editions du Seuil, 1980), 99–100.

14. Quoted in George Watson, "Race & the Socialists: On the Progressive Principle of Revolutionary Extermination," *Encounter* (November 1976): 15–23.

15. Lichtheim, "Socialism and the Jews."

16. Quoted in Robert Conquest, *The Great Terror: Stalin's Purge of the Thirties* (Harmondsworth, England: Penguin Books, 1971), 683.

17. C. Abramsky, "The Biro-Bidzhan Project, 1927–1959," in Lionel Kochan, ed., *The Jews in Soviet Russia since 1917,* 3rd ed. (New York: Oxford University Press, 1978).

18. R. N. Carew Hunt, *A Guide to Communist Jargon* (New York: Macmillan, 1957), 36–40.

19. Moshe Decter, "The Status of Jews in the Soviet Union," *Foreign Affairs* (January 1963): 420–30.

20. Hilberg, *The Destruction of European Jews,* chap 4. See also Yitzhak Arad, Yisrael Gutman, and Abraham Margaliot, eds., *Documents on the Holocaust: Selected Sources on the Destruction of the Jews of Germany and Austria, Poland, and the Soviet Union* (Jerusalem: Yad Vashem, 1981).

21. Hilberg, *The Destruction of European Jews,* 453ff.

22. See 40, 86.

23. William Petersen, "Jews as a Race," *Midstream* (February–March 1988): 35–37.

24. Lewis S. Feuer, "The Sociobiological Theory of Jewish Intellectual Achievement: A Sociological Critique," in Joseph B. Maier and Chaim I. Waxman, eds., *Ethnicity, Identity, and History* (New Brunswick, N.J.: Transaction Books, 1983).

25. Benzion C. Kaganoff, *A Dictionary of Jewish Names and Their History* (New York: Schocken Books, 1977), xii.

26. See the symposium in *Annales de Démographie Historique* (1972). See also E. A. Wrigley, ed., *Identifying People in the Past* (London: Edward Arnold, 1973).

27. Dietz Bering, *Der Name als Stigma: Antisemitismus im deutschen Alltag* (Stuttgart: Klett-Cotta, 1989).

28. Robert C. Christopher, *Crashing the Gates: The De-Wasping of America's Power Elite* (New York: Simon & Schuster, 1989). As has been noted in another context (see 199–202), a commission that had been assigned to set immigration restrictions according to the national origins of the population of the United States used a monograph by W. S. Rossiter as their starting point. He had classi-

fied by presumed nationalities the names listed in the 1790 census, but even at the founding of the Republic the names of its citizens were not an accurate index of their ethnic origins. The association between surname and origin became ever more dubious with the larger number of immigrants from various countries.

In 1939, when the Social Security Board issued an analysis of the 43,900,000 names then on its roll, one person in ten carried one of the fifty commonest surnames, beginning with the 471,190 Smiths down to the 26,000 named Nichols. Of these fifty family names, only one—Cohen—was not of British origin. Schmidts had become Smiths and Müllers Millers; Scots or Irish had dropped the Mac or Mc from their names; such a Dutch name as Kouwenhaven ended up as Cowan or Conover. See H. L. Mencken, *The American Language: An Inquiry into the Development of English in the United States,* Supplement II (New York: Knopf, 1975), 396–98.

A generous sample of a New York City file of petitions to municipal courts from 1848 to 1924 gives an impression of who wanted to change his name and why. A hope of wider business contacts, accommodation to new friends or acquaintances, a desire to escape the stigma they perceived to be attached to their ethnic identity—the motives as spelled out in the applications generally were variations on a very few themes. From 1895 on, East European petitions outnumbered those of other nationalities, but mostly because those who had arrived earlier had already gone through the process. See Arthur Scherr, "Change-of-Name Petitions of New York Courts," *Names* 34 (1986): 284–302.

29. Leonard Broom, Helen P. Beem, and Virginia Harris, "Characteristics of 1,107 Petitioners for Change of Name," *American Sociological Review* 20 (1935): 33–39. The assumption that Jews were motivated by a desire to avoid being identified, which is repeated in many studies of the matter, is contradicted by the behavior of the senior author, Leonard Broom, who made no secret of his change of name from Bloom. Another prominent sociologist, Robert Merton, not only did not hide his Jewish origin but used to joke in his classes about having selected a new name generally known as that of a Catholic philosopher.

30. Harold S. Himmelfarb, R. Michael Loar, and Susan H. Mott, "Sampling by Ethnic Surname: The Case of American Jews," *Public Opinion Quarterly* 47 (1983): 247–60. See also Werner Cohn, "What's in a Name: A Comment on Himmelfarb, Loar, and Mott," with a "Comment by Himmelfarb et al.," *Public Opinion Quarterly* 48 (1984): 660–65.

31. In contrast to a series of apocalyptic accounts, a book on "reinventing Jewish culture, 1880–1950," gives a detailed history of the myriad ways that American Jews have adapted to the general culture of their country. One chapter is titled "Kitchen Judaism," about the various ways that one compromised with *kashruth,* the demanding Judaic dietary laws. One of the first escapes was to eat out, with "out" meaning away from both the home and the restrictions set there. Eschewing pork and other patently *treif* foods in their own kitchens, Jews indulged their appetite for chop suey and ballpark hot dogs, not to say "kosher-style" delicacies of all sorts. Two schools of experts arose, one trying to show that modern science supports the rules of *kashruth* on how to keep healthy, the other criticizing the poor nutrition of the traditional Jewish cuisine. See Jenna Weissman Joselit, *The Wonders of America: Reinventing Jewish Culture, 1880–1950* (New York: Hill and Wang, 1994), chap. 5.

32. Seymour Martin Lipset and Earl Raab, *Jews and the New American Scene* (Cambridge, Mass.: Harvard University Press, 1995), chap. 3.

33. Bernard Lazerwitz, "An Estimate of a Rare Population Group: The U.S. Jewish Population," *Demography* 15 (1978): 389–94.

34. Sidney Goldstein, *Profile of American Jewry: Insights from the 1990 National Jewish Population Survey,* Occasional Paper no. 6 (New York: Council of Jewish Federations, 1993), 77.
35. Ibid., 141.
36. Nathan Glazer, "New Perspectives in American Jewish Sociology," *American Jewish Yearbook, 1987* (New York: American Jewish Committee, 1987).
37. Milton J. Esman, *Ethnic Politics* (Ithaca, N.Y.: Cornell University Press, 1994), chap. 5.
38. Howard M. Sachar, *A History of Israel: From the Rise of Zionism to Our Time* (New York: Knopf, 1976), 368.
39. Yossi Beilin, *Israel: A Concise Political History* (New York: St. Martin's Press, 1992), 79.
40. Orr, *The unJewish State,* 96.
41. Beilin, *Israel,* 81–82.
42. Noah Lucas, *The Modern History of Israel* (New York: Praeger, 1975), 419.
43. AP dispatch (13 November 1995).
44. Yoram Hazony, "The Zionist Idea and Its Enemies," *Commentary* (May 1996): 30–38.

15. Ethnicity in the New Nations of the Post-Colonial World

1. Reinhard Bendix, *Nation-Building and Citizenship: Studies of Our Changing Social Order,* rev. ed. (Berkeley: University of California Press, 1977), 266.
2. Norton S. Ginsburg, "The Great City in Southeast Asia," *American Journal of Sociology* 60 (1955): 455–62.
3. Rhoads Murphey, "New Capitals of Asia," *Economic Development and Cultural Change* 5 (1957): 216–43.
4. U.S. Central Intelligence Agency, *National Basic Intelligence Factbook* (Washington, D.C., 1979).
5. United Nations, *Demographic Yearbook,* 44th Issue (New York, 1994), Introduction.
6. Cf. Anthony D. Smith, *State and Nation in the Third World: The Western State and African Nationalism* (Brighton, Sussex: Wheatsheaf Books, 1983).
7. Kenneth Kaunda, *A Humanist in Africa: Letters to Colin Morris* (London: Longmans, 1966), 57.
8. Pierre L. van den Berghe, "Class, Race, and Ethnicity in Africa," *Ethnic and Racial Studies* 6 (1983): 221–36.
9. Basil Davidson, *The Black Man's Burden: Africa and the Curse of the Nation-State* (New York: Times Books, 1992).
10. Joseph M. Kaufert, "Situational Ethnic Identity in Ghana: A Survey of University Students," in John N. Paden, ed., *Values, Identities, and National Integration: Empirical Research in Africa* (Evanston: Northwestern University Press, 1980), chap. 4.
11. J. D. Fage, *A History of Africa* (London: Hutchinson, 1978), 13–14n.
12. K. M. Panikkar, *Asia and Western Dominance* (New York: Day, n.d.), 150.
13. D. W. Fryer, "The 'Million City' in Southeast Asia," *Geographical Review* 43 (1953): 474–94.
14. James S. Coleman, *Nigeria: Background to Nationalism* (Berkeley: University of California Press, 1960), 152.
15. J. L. L. Comhaire, "Urban Segregation and Racial Legislation in Africa," *American Sociological Review* 15 (1950): 392–97.

16. Jacques Denis, *Le phénomène urbain en Afrique Centrale*, Bibliothèque de la Faculté de Philosophie et Lettres de Namur, Belgium, 22 (1958): 110–11.
17. Ibid., 123–24.
18. A. van Marle, "De groep der Europeanen in Nederlands Indië: Iets over onstaan en groei," *Indonesië* 5 (1951–1952).
19. J. H. Kraak, "The Repatriation of the Dutch from Indonesia," *REMP Bulletin* 6 (1958): 27–40.
20. Laurine Platzky and Cherryl Walker, *The Surplus People: Forced Removals in South Africa* (Johannesburg: Raven Press, 1985), xiii.
21. H. F. Dickie-Clark, *The Marginal Situation: A Sociological Study of a Coloured Group* (London: Routledge and Kegan Paul, 1966), 161–62.
22. Quoted in Platzky and Walker, *The Surplus People,* 99.
23. *Economist* (13–19 April 1996): 36.
24. George P. Murdock, *Ethnographic Atlas* (Pittsburgh: University of Pittsburgh Press, 1967); "Addenda and Corrigenda to the Ethnographic Atlas," *Ethnology,* vols. 6–9 (1967–71).
25. Pierre Alexandre, *An Introduction to Languages and Language in Africa* (London: Heinemann, 1972), 75. Cf. Maxwell Owusu, "Ethnography of Africa: The Usefulness of the Useless," *American Anthropologist* 80 (1978): 310–34.
26. David Dalby, "African Languages," in *Africa South of the Sahara, 1992,* 21st ed. (London: Europa Publications, 1992), 95–97. Cf. David Lamb, *The Africans* (New York: Random House, 1982), 14–16.
27. Quoted in Kay Whiteman, "Mutual Perceptions in Africa," in Anthony Kirk-Greene and Daniel Bach, eds., *State and Society in Francophone Africa since Independence* (Oxford: St. Martin's Press, 1995), chap. 18.
28. Alexandre, *An Introduction to Languages,* 88–91.
29. Jack Berry, "'The Making of Alphabets' Revisited," in Joshua A. Fishman, ed., *Advances in the Creation and Revision of Writing Systems* (The Hague: Mouton, 1977).
30. J. Spencer Trimingham, *Islam in West Africa* (Oxford: Clarendon Press, 1959), chap. 5.
31. Monica Wilson, *Religion and the Transformation of Society: A Study in Social Change in Africa* (Cambridge, England: University Press, 1971), chap. 1. See also Geoffrey Parrinder, "The Religions of Africa," in *Africa South of the Sahara, 1992,* 90–94.
32. Quoted in Margery Perham, *The Colonial Reckoning: The End of Imperial Rule in Africa in the Light of the British Experience* (New York: Knopf, 1962), 52.
33. Philip D. Curtin, *Precolonial African History* (Washington, D.C.: American Historical Association, 1974), 9–10.
34. Quoted in Ali A. Mazrui, "Introduction," UNESCO, *The Methodology of Contemporary African History* (Paris, 1984), 16.
35. Jan Vansina, *Oral Tradition: A Study in Historical Methodology* (London: Routledge and Kegan Paul, 1965), 186.
36. Arnold Tema and Bonaventure Swai, *Historians and Africanist History: A Critique* (London: Zed Press, 1981), chap. 4.
37. Caroline Neale, *Writing "Independent" History: African Historiography, 1960–1980* (Westport, Conn.: Greenwood Press, 1985), 186.
38. Fage, *A History of Africa,* 58n.
39. Lamb, *The Africans,* 43, 67.
40. Ibid., 104.
41. Leo Kuper, *The Pity of It All: Polarization of Racial and Ethnic Relations* (Minneapolis: University of Minnesota Press, 1977), chap. 5.

42. Robert H. Jackson and Carl G. Rosberg, "Why Africa's Weak States Persist: The Empirical and Juridical in Statehood," *World Politics* 35 (1982): 1–24.
43. Donald G. Morrison and H. Michael Stevenson, "Cultural Pluralism, Modernization, and Conflict: An Empirical Analysis of Sources of Political Instability in African Nations," in Paden, *Values, Identities and National Integration*, chap. 1.
44. Lamb, *The Africans*, 20.
45. Jackson and Rosberg, "Why Africa's Weak States Persist."
46. Susan Ritner and Peter Ritner, "Africanism's Constitutional Malarkey," with comments by Immanuel Wallerstein and Herbert J. Spiro and a reply by the Ritners, *New Leader* (10 and 22 June 1963).
47. W. Arthur Lewis, *Politics in West Africa* (New York: Oxford University Press, 1965), 89–90.
48. Alan Burns, *History of Nigeria* (London: George Allen and Unwin, 1969), chaps. 10–11.
49. Cf. A. H. M. Kirk-Greene, "The Linguistic Statistics of Northern Nigeria: A Tentative Presentation," *African Language Review* 6 (1967): 75–101.
50. Coleman, *Nigeria*, chap. 1.
51. Quoted in Michael Crowder, *The Story of Nigeria* (London: Faber and Faber, 1973), 220.
52. Ibid., 245.
53. Ibid., 258.
54. Peter P. Ekeh, in Joseph Okpaku, ed., *Nigeria: Dilemma of Nationhood: An African Analysis of the Biafran Conflict* (New York: The Third Press, 1972).
55. Barbara Callaway and Lucy Creevey, *The Heritage of Islam: Women, Religion, and Politics in West Africa* (Boulder, Colo.: Lynne Rienner Publishers, 1994), 193.
56. William F. S. Miles, *Hausaland Divided: Colonialism and Independence in Nigeria and Niger* (Ithaca, N.Y.: Cornell University Press, 1994), chap. 3.
57. Richard L. Sklar, *Nigerian Political Parties: Power in an Emergent African Nation* (Princeton, N.J.: Princeton University Press, 1963), chaps. 10–11. See also Larry Diamond, "Class, Ethnicity, and the Democratic State: Nigeria, 1950–1966," *Comparative Studies in Society and History* 25 (1983): 457–89.
58. T. C. McCaskie, "Recent History," in *Africa South of the Sahara, 1992*, 761–73.
59. Coleman, *Nigeria*, 224.
60. Moyibi Amoda, in Okpaku, *Nigeria*.
61. S. A. Aluko, "How Many Nigerians? An Analysis of Nigeria's Census Problems, 1901–63," *Journal of Modern African Studies* 3 (1965): 371–92. Kurt Krieger, "Die Bedeutung statistischer Erhebungen für die Völkerkunde am Beispiel der Stadt Anka in Nord-Nigeria," *Sociologus* 4 (1954): 67–81. R. Mansell Prothero, "The Population Census of Northern Nigeria, 1952: Problems and Results," *Population Studies* 10 (1956): 166–83.
62. Thomas H. Eighmy, "Problems of Census Interpretation in Developing Countries: The Western Nigerian Case," *Svensk Geografisk* 44 (1968): 151–72. T. O. Ogunlesi, "Before and After a Population Census Operation in Nigeria—A Physician's Experience," T. M. Yesufu, "The Politics and Economics of Nigeria's Population Census," and Reuben K. Udo, "Population and Politics in Nigeria (Problems of Census-taking in the Nigerian Federation)," in John C. Caldwell and Chukuka Okonjo, eds., *The Population of Tropical Africa* (New York: Columbia University Press, 1968). "Census Migration in Nigeria," *Nigerian Geographical Journal* 13 (1970): 3–7. Ian Campbell, "The Nigerian Census: An Essay in Civil-Military Relations," *Journal of Commonwealth and Comparative Politics* 14 (1976): 242–54.

63. *New York Times* (28 May 1967).
64. *New York Times* (6 February 1968).
65. E. Wayne Nafziger, *The Economics of Political Instability: The Nigerian-Biafran War* (Boulder, Colo.: Westview Press, 1983), 166.
66. Peter H. Koehn, *Public Policy and Administration in Africa: Lessons from Nigeria* (Boulder, Colo.: Westview Press, 1990), chap. 8.
67. *Wall Street Journal* (13 November 1995).

16. The Conglomeration that is India

1. André Béteille, "Race and Descent as Social Categories in India," *Daedalus* 96 (1967): 444–63.
2. M. S. A. Rao, "Some Conceptual Issues in the Study of Caste, Class, Ethnicity, and Dominance," in Francine R. Frankel and Rao, eds., *Dominance and State Power in Modern India: Decline of a Social Order,* vol. 1 (Delhi: Oxford University Press, 1989), 22.
3. M. N. Srinivas, *Caste in Modern India and Other Essays* (Bombay: Asia Publishing House, 1962), 16. See also Pauline Kolenda, *Caste in Contemporary India: Beyond Organic Solidarity* (Menlo Park, Calif.: Benjamin/Cummings Publishing Co., 1978).
4. Kingsley Davis, *The Population of India and Pakistan* (Princeton, N.J.: Princeton University Press, 1951), 170.
5. Philip Mason, *Race Relations: A Field of Study Comes of Age* (London: University of London, 1968), 137.
6. Louis Dumont, *Homo Hierarchicus: An Essay on the Caste System* (Chicago: University of Chicago Press, 1970), 191–92.
7. Henry Scholberg, *The District Gazetteers of British India: A Bibliography* (Zug, Switzerland: Inter-Documentation Company, 1970).
8. Quoted in D. Natarajan, "Indian Census through a Hundred Years," *Census of India, 1971*; Census Centenary Monograph, no. 2, part 1, chaps. I and II (New Delhi: Office of the Registrar General, 1972).
9. See 9, 270.
10. Quoted in M. N. Srinivas, *Social Change in Modern India* (Berkeley: University of California Press, 1969), 95.
11. S. G. Srivastava, "Indian Census in Perspective," *Census of India, 1971,* Census Monograph no. 1 (New Delhi: Office of the Registrar General, 1971).
12. Kenneth W. Jones, "Religious Identity and the Indian Census," unpublished paper, n.d.
13. Lelah Dushkin, "Scheduled Caste Politics," in J. Michael Mahar, ed., *The Untouchables in Contemporary India* (Tucson: University of Arizona Press, 1972).
14. Harold R. I. Isaacs, *India's Ex-Untouchables* (New York: John Day, 1964), chap. 2.
15. B. K. Roy Burman, "Census of India—Scheduled Castes and Scheduled Tribes," in Ashish Bose et al., eds., *Population Statistics in India* (New Delhi: Vikas Publishing House, 1977).
16. Dilip Hiro, *The Untouchables of India* (London: Minority Rights Group, 1975). See also Marc Galanter, "The Abolition of Disabilities—Untouchability and the Law," in Mahar, *The Untouchables in Contemporary India*.
17. Mason, *Race Relations,* 185.
18. *Wall Street Journal* (26 December 1995; emphasis in the original).
19. "India's Castes," *Economist* (6 September 1986).

20. For example, Davis, *The Population of India,* 188–91.
21. R. A. Schermerhorn, "Minorities in the Census of India, 1971," *Demography India* 3 (1974): 315–27.
22. Selig S. Harrison, *India: The Most Dangerous Decades* (Princeton, N.J.: Princeton University Press, 1960), 105–14.
23. Jyotirindra Das Gupta, *Language Conflict and National Development: Group Politics and National Language Policy in India* (Berkeley: University of California Press, 1970), chap. 4.
24. Ibid., 236.
25. See 164–65.
26. Das Gupta, *Language Conflict and National Development,* 225–26.
27. Jones, "Religious Identity."
28. Theodore P. Wright, Jr., "The Ethnic Numbers Game in India: Hindu-Muslim Conflicts over Conversion, Family Planning, Migration, and the Census," in William C. McCready, ed., *Culture, Ethnicity and Identity: Current Issues in Research* (New York: Academic Press, 1983).
29. *Economist* (19 August 1995).
30. Quoted in Pravin M. Visaria, and Leela Visaria, "India's Population: Second and Growing," *Population Bulletin* 36 (October 1981): 1–54.
31. Ved Mehta, *The New India* (New York: Penguin Books, 1978), chap. 5.
32. Paul F. Cressey, "The Anglo-Indians: A Disorganized Marginal Group," *Social Forces* 14 (1935): 263–68. Cf. Robert E. Park, "Human Migration and the Marginal Man," *American Journal of Sociology* 33 (1928): 881–93; reprinted in Park, *Race and Culture* (Glencoe, Ill.: Free Press, 1950), chap. 26. Everett V. Stonequist, *The Marginal Man: A Study in Personality and Culture Conflict* (New York: Scribner, 1937), 12–18.
33. Noel P. Gist, "The Anglo-Indians of India," in Gist and Anthony Gary Dworkin, eds., *The Blending of Races: Marginality and Identity in World Perspective* (New York: Wiley, 1972).
34. Noel P. Gist and Roy Dean Wright, *Marginality and Identity: Anglo-Indians as a Racial Minority in India* (Leiden: E. J. Brill, 1973).
35. Dorris W. Goodrich, "The Making of an Ethnic Group: The Eurasian Community in India." Doctoral dissertation, University of California, Berkeley, 1952.
36. H. W. B. Moreno, "Some Anglo-Indian Terms and Origins," *Proceedings of the Indian Historical Records Commission* 5 (1923): 76–82.
37. W. T. Roy, "Hostages to Fortune: A Socio-political Study of the Anglo-Indian Remnant in India," *Plural Societies* 7 (1976): 55–63.
38. Coralie Younger, *Anglo-Indians: Neglected Children of the Raj* (Delhi: B.R. Publishing Co., 1987), 74.
39. Elmer L. Hedin, "The Anglo-Indian Community," *American Journal of Sociology* 40 (1934): 165–79. D. K. Bhattacharya, "The Anglo-Indians in Bombay," *Race* 10 (1968): 163–72.
40. V. R. Gaikwad, *The Anglo-Indians* (Bombay: Asia Publishing House, 1967), 174.
41. See 9, 270.

17. Conclusions

1. Alfred J. Ayer, *The Problem of Knowledge* (Harmondsworth, England: Penguin Books, 1957).
2. Ashley Montagu, *Man's Most Dangerous Myth: The Fallacy of Race,* 4th ed. (Cleveland: World Publishing Co., 1964), 25, 28; emphasis in the original.

3. Ibid., 80, Appendix B.
4. Philip Gleason, "Identifying Identity: A Semantic History," *Journal of American History* 69 (1983): 910–31. See also Arthur O. Lovejoy, *Essays in the History of Ideas* (1948), 232, quoted in ibid.; Gleason, "American Identity and Americanization," *Harvard Encyclopedia of American Ethnic Groups* (Cambridge, Mass.: Harvard University Press, 1980); Orrin E. Klapp, *Collective Search for Identity* (New York: Holt, Rinehart, and Winston, 1969).
5. William James, *The Principles of Psychology* (1890; reprint, Cambridge, Mass.: Harvard University Press, 1981), vol. 1, 310.
6. Harold R. Isaacs, "Basic Group Identity: The Idols of the Tribe," in Nathan Glazer and Daniel P. Moynihan, eds., *Ethnicity: Theory and Experience* (Cambridge: Mass.: Harvard University Press, 1975); italics in the original. See also Isaacs, *Idols of the Tribe: Group Identity and Political Change* (New York: Harper & Row, 1975).
7. See Milton J. Esman, *Ethnic Politics* (Ithaca, N.Y.: Cornell University Press, 1994), chap. 9 and passim.
8. Richard D. Alba, *Ethnic Identity: The Transformation of White America* (New Haven: Yale University Press, 1990), 27–30.
9. Margaret Mead and Rhoda Métraux, eds., *The Study of Culture at a Distance* (Chicago: University of Chicago Press, 1953).
10. Geoffrey Gorer and John Rickman, *The People of Great Russia* (1950; reprint, New York: Norton, 1960).
11. A. A. Roback, *A Dictionary of International Slurs (Ethnophaulisms)* (1944; reprint, Cambridge, Mass.: Sci-Art Publishers, 1979).
12. Marilyn Schwartz and the Task Force on Bias-Free Language of the Association of American University Presses, *Guidelines for Bias-Free Writing* (Bloomington: Indiana University Press, 1995).
13. P. J. O'Rourke, Review of Schwarz, *Guidelines for Bias-Free Writing, American Spectator* (August 1995): 62–64.
14. Kenichi Ohmae, *The End of the Nation State* (New York: HarperCollins, 1995). Jean-Marie Guéhenno, *The End of the Nation-State* (Minneapolis: University of Minnesota Press, 1995).
15. Albert Mindlin, "The Designation of Race or Color on Forms," *Public Administration Review* 26 (1966): 110–18.
16. *Encounter* (March 1989): 78.

Bibliography

The volume of writings on ethnicity grows more massive year by year. There would be little point in supplementing the endnotes with general works, and this list is therefore limited to recommended readings on the narrow subject of the book, namely, how an ethnos is identified and measured.

To read numerical data with understanding one should be minimally acquainted with statistical jargon and techniques. Of the dozen or so elementary texts on *statistics* in print, those I have seen differ only in details. The most concise, more useful perhaps for those who need not instruction but a jogging of memory, is any edition of *An Outline of Statistical Methods*, which Barnes & Noble publishes in its College Outline Series. An especially pertinent background is available in Margo J. Anderson, *The American Census: A Social History* (New Haven: Yale University Press, 1988).

In line with the spirit of this book are two books warning the reader against the careless acceptance or interpretation of alleged facts presented in numbers: Darrell Huff, *How to Lie with Statistics* (New York: Norton, 1954), and Richard P. Runyan, *How Numbers Lie: A Consumer's Guide to the Fine Art of Numerical Deception* (Lexington, Mass.: Lewis Publishing Co., 1981).

A work to be recommended as a catchall of *statistical flaws* can be used as a test of how wary the reader has become: Bernard Siskin, Jerome Staller, and David Rorvik, *What Are the Chances? Risks, Odds, and Likelihood in Everyday Life* (New York: Crown Publishers, 1989). It consists of a list of questions and—often—silly answers. For example (page 4):

> Given the prevalence of terrorism around the world, just how risky is overseas travel?
>
> Overseas travel is very safe. Your chances of being killed by terrorists overseas is 1 in 650,000. Better you should worry about being struck by lightning or by being killed by Americans in Baltimore. (The chances of the latter happening are greater than 1 in 4,000!)

An example of what one might term *Superabundant Aggregation*: terrorist Libya is one with democratic Switzerland, unruly Northern Ireland with peaceful Canada. The conclusion is as well based as, say, whatever the Bureau of the Census publishes about Hispanics or Asians and Pacific Islanders.

Another example (pages 64–65):

> What are the chances I will die while giving birth?

315

The death rate for white females is currently 5 per 100,000 live births—10 times less than it was in 1950.

For black females, however, the current death rate is nearly 21 per 100,000—more than 4 times that of the white rate.

The issue here is the one-to-one comparison of whites' and blacks' rates—a contrast that is routine in works on ethnicity. To make a genuine contrast, at least two additional breakdowns are needed—between working- or middle-class Negroes and underclass blacks and, second, between women of both races in the prime reproductive ages and those either younger or older.

Two of the most general works on *ethnic identity* are Philip Gleason, "Identifying Identity: A Semantic History," *Journal of American History* 69 (1983): 910–31, a detailed investigation of the meanings given to the concept, and Orrin E. Klapp, *Collective Search for Identity* (New York: Holt, Rinehart, and Winston, 1969). Gleason has also analyzed the development of ethnic identities in American history: "American Identity and Americanization," *Harvard Encyclopedia of American Ethnic Groups* (Cambridge, Mass.: Harvard University Press, 1980). This is brought up to date in Richard D. Alba, *Ethnic Identity: The Transformation of White America* (New Haven: Yale University Press, 1990).

The legal scholar Dudley O. McGovney wrote two interesting papers on how American courts attempted to deal with ethnicity: "Race Discrimination in Naturalization," *Iowa Law Bulletin* 8 (1922–23): 211–44; "The Anti-Japanese Laws of California and Ten Other States," *California Law Review* 35 (1947): 7–60. See also Sripati Chandrasekhar, "A History of United States Legislation with Respect to Immigration from India," in Chandrasekhar, ed., *From India to America* (La Jolla, Calif.: Population Review, 1982). That the various juridical dilemmas have, if anything, become sharper is spelled out in Christopher A. Ford, "Administering Identity: The Determination of 'Race' in Race-conscious Law," *California Law Review* 82 (1994): 1231–85.

Many works concentrate on ambiguities in determining the identity of particular minorities. On changes in *blacks'* self-identification, much background material is concisely presented in W. Augustus Low and Virginia A. Clift, *Encyclopedia of Black America* (New York: McGraw-Hill, 1981). The differences between slaves, free colored, and West Indian immigrants—as well as their progeny over several generations—are presented in Thomas Sowell, "Three Black Histories," in Sowell, ed., *Essays and Data on American Ethnic Groups* (Washington, D.C.: Urban Institute, 1978). Of the rather few works on passing, one is recommended: Arna Bontemps and Jack Conroy, *Anyplace But Here* (New York: Hill & Wang, 1966). Most attention has been given to the latest shift, symbolized by the displacement of "Negro" by "black" or "Black." Characteristic works include William E. Cross, Jr., *Shades of Black: Diversity in African-American Identity* (Philadelphia: Temple University Press, 1991); Janet E. Helms, ed., *Black and White Racial Identity: Theory, Re-*

search, and Practice (Westport, Conn.: Greenwood Press, 1990); George E. Kent, "Struggle for the Image: Selected Books by or about Blacks during 1971," *Phylon* 33 (1972): 304–23; Halford H. Fairchild, "Black, Negro, or Afro-American? The Differences Are Crucial!," *Journal of Black Studies* 16 (1985): 47–55.

Census enumerators, while they were still required to identify ethnicity, were often baffled by *multiracial* groups. See, for example, Brewton Berry, *Almost White* (New York: Macmillan, 1965); Calvin L. Beale, "Census Problems of Racial Enumeration," in Edgar T. Thompson and Everett C. Hughes, eds., *Race: Individual and Collective Behavior* (Glencoe, Ill.: Free Press, 1958); James H. Dormon, "Louisiana Cajuns: A Case Study in Ethnic Group Revitalization," *Social Science Quarterly* 65 (1984): 1043–57.

American *Indians,* both in the United States and in Latin America, have probably been the category with the least determinate boundaries. The most general work, a delight to read, is James A. Clifton, ed., *The Invented Indian: Cultural Fiction and Government Policies* (New Brunswick, N.J.: Transaction Publishers, 1990). A detailed analysis of the largest tribe in the United States gives many details on enumerators' general frustrations: D. F. Johnston, *An Analysis of Sources of Information on the Population of the Navaho,* Bureau of Ethnology, Smithsonian Institution, Bulletin 197 (Washington, D.C., 1966). This can be usefully supplemented by journal papers on similar themes—for example: S. Ryan Johansson and Samuel H. Preston, "Tribal Demography: The Hopi and Navaho Populations as Seen through Manuscripts from the 1900 U.S. Census," *Social Science History* 3 (1978): 1–33; J. Nixon Hadley, "The Demography of the American Indians," *Annals of the American Academy of Political and Social Science* 311 (1957): 23–30; Jeffrey S. Passel, "Provisional Evaluation of the 1970 Census Count of American Indians," *Demography* 13 (1976): 397–409.

The definitions of the *Hispanic* population, made up of several disparate units each with its own articulate spokesmen, have generated a sizable body of critical writings. See, for example, a number of early papers: William E. Morton, "Demographic Redefinition of Hispanos," *Public Health Reports* 85 (1970): 617–23; José Hernández, Leo Estrada, and David Alvírez, "Census Data and the Problem of Conceptually Defining the Mexican American Population," *Social Science Quarterly* 53 (1973): 671–87; Edward W. Fernandez, "Comparison of Persons of Spanish Surname and Persons of Spanish Origin in the United States," U.S. Bureau of the Census, *Technical Report,* no. 38 (Washington, D.C., 1975); Charlotte A. Redden, "Identification of Spanish Heritage Persons in Public Data," *Public Data Use* 4 (1976): 3–11. The controversy continues in more recent publications: Jack D. Forbes, "The Hispanic Spin: Party Politics and Governmental Manipulation of Ethnic Identity," *Latin American Perspectives* 19 (1992): 59–78; Suzanne Oboler, *Ethnic Labels, Latino Lives: Identity and the Politics of (Re)Presentation in the United States* (Minneapolis: University of Minnesota Press, 1995); Ilan Stavans, *The*

Hispanic Condition: Reflections on Culture and Identity in America (New York: HarperCollins, 1995).

On the ambiguity of race in Latin America, two papers by the anthropologist Julian Pitt-Rivers are informative: "Mestizo or Ladino?" *Race* 10 (1969): 463–77; "Race in Latin America: The Concept of 'Raza'" *European Journal of Sociology* 14 (1973): 3–27.

Ethnic statistics falter not only because of ambiguous identities of individuals, but also because of sometimes indefensible types of aggregation. Two of the sharpest commentaries on American official data are by Ira S. Lowry, formerly with the Rand Corporation and now an independent consultant: *The Science and Politics of Ethnic Enumeration*, Rand Papers Series, no. P-6435-1 (Santa Monica, Calif., 1980); *Counting Ethnic Minorities in the 1990 Census* (privately published, 1989). Less acerbic but just as critical are a number of papers by Tom Smith, whose long experience with private polling by the Center for the Study of American Pluralism of the University of Chicago has given him a broad base for detailed commentary. See, for example, "Ethnic Measurement and Identification," *Ethnicity* 7 (1980): 79–95; "Problems in Ethnic Measurement: Over-, Under-, and Misidentification," General Social Survey Project, *Technical Report* 29 (1982). Among other noteworthy general appraisals are: Charles A. Price, "Methods of Estimating the Size of Groups," *Harvard Encyclopedia of American Ethnic Groups*; Michael J. Levin and Reynolds Farley, "Historical Comparability of Ethnic Designations in the United States," American Statistical Association, Social Statistics Section, *Proceedings of the Annual Meeting, 1982* (Washington, D.C., 1982); Barbara A. Bailar, Roger A. Herriot, and Jeffrey S. Passel, "The Quality of Federal Censuses and Survey Data," *Public Data Use* 10 (1982): 203–18; Stanley Lieberson and Lawrence Santi, "The Use of Nativity Data to Estimate Ethnic Characteristics and Patterns," *Social Science Research* 14 (1985): 31–56; Lewis M. Killian, "The Collection of Official Data on Ethnicity and Religion: The US Experience," *New Community* 5 (Autumn–Winter 1985): 74–82; Stanley Lieberson and Mary C. Waters, "The Ethnic Responses of Whites: What Causes Their Instability, Simplification, and Inconsistency," *Social Forces* 72 (1993): 421–50.

Similar lists of critical essays could be presented concerning the official statistics of other major countries, but to include them would extend this bibliography beyond reasonable limits. Two discussions, however, are of especial interest, for they point to the shift over the past several decades in how statistical fallacies are often perceived, from remediable errors to bureaucratic manipulation of data: Alajos Kovács, "La connaissance des langues comme contrôle de la statistique des nationalités," *Bulletin de l'Institut International de Statistique* 23 (1928): part 2, 246–346; Mario Strassoldo, *Lingue e nazionalità nelle rilevazioni demografiche,* Contributi e Ricerche Scienze Politiche Trieste, no. 8 (Trieste: CLUET, 1977). Additional instances of how ethnic data of diverse countries interact with their ethnic politics are given in Dudley Kirk, *Europe's Population in the Interwar Years* (League of Nations; Princeton, N.J.: Princeton University Press, 1946); Robert C. Schmitt, *Demographic Statistics of Hawaii: 1778–1965* (Honolulu: University of Hawaii Press, 1968); P. M. G. Lévy, *La querelle du recensement* (Brussels: Institut Belge de Science Politique, 1960) and "La mort du recensement linguistique," *Revue Nouvelle* 18 (1962): 145–54; several of the papers in John C. Caldwell and Chukuka Okonjo, eds., *The Population of Tropical Africa* (New York: Columbia University Press, 1968); Raul Hilberg, *The Destruction of the European Jews* (Chicago: Quadrangle Books, 1967); Akiva Orr, *The unJewish State: The Politics of Jewish Identity in Israel* (London: Ithaca Press, 1981).

The *interpretation* of statistical data can be tricky. A very useful guide to the logic underlying correct procedures is given in Abraham Kaplan, *The Conduct of Inquiry: Methodology for Behavioral Science* (San Francisco: Chandler, 1964). Perhaps the most common fault in works on ethnicity/race is a simple comparison of the characteristics of various groups. Unlike most other general works on ethnic groups in the United States, Thomas Sowell, *Ethnic America: A History* (New York: Basic Books, 1981) routinely considers, for example, differences in age structure. Delinquency is high among blacks partly because of their higher proportion of teenagers. Fertility is higher among recent immigrants partly because most of them are young adults. The income of Jews is above that of other minorities partly because a higher proportion are in the age group that has risen to the maximum earnings over a lifetime. To contrast the characteristics or behavior patterns of various minorities without controlling for age structure is to invite a gross misinterpretation. In the old but still very useful book, *Say It with Figures* (New York: Harper, 1947), Hans Zeisel cited a finding that single people eat more candy than married people. One might suppose that the relative lack of sex is compensated by the consumption of more sweets. But when one controls for age, the true explanation is evident: children eat more candy and are generally not married.

This book is based essentially on several decades of research on its subject matter, a period during which I have written a number of books and papers on ethnicity and related matters. Some of this *earlier analysis* has been reworked and updated to fit into the book's overall structure. The most important books and monographs are: *Planned Migration: The Social Determinants of the Dutch-Canadian Movement* (Berkeley: University of California Press, 1955); *Japanese Americans: Oppression and Success* (New York: Random House, 1971); *Population,* 3rd ed. (New York: Macmillan, 1975); with Renee Petersen, *Dictionary of Demography: Terms, Concepts, and Institutions*; *Biographies*; *Multilingual Dictionary,* 5 vols. (1985–86). Editor: *The Background to Ethnic Conflict* (Leiden: E. J. Brill, 1979). Papers on ethnicity include: "Prejudice in American Society: A Critique of Some Recent Formulations," *Commentary*

(October 1958): 441–45; "Religious Statistics in the United States," *Journal for the Scientific Study of Religion* 1 (Spring 1962): 165–78; "The Classification of Subnations in Hawaii: An Essay in the Sociology of Knowledge," *American Sociological Review* 24 (1969): 863–77; "On the Subnations of Western Europe," in Nathan Glazer and Daniel P. Moynihan, eds., *Ethnicity: Theory and Experience* (Cambridge, Mass.: Harvard University Press, 1975); "Ethnic Structure in Western Europe," *Population Review* 20 (January–February 1976): 41–44; "A Comparison of a Racial and a Language Subnation: American Negroes and Flemish," *Ethnicity* 3 (1976): 145–76; "Chinese Americans and Japanese Americans," in Thomas Sowell, ed., *American Ethnic Groups* (New York: Urban Institute, 1978); "Concepts of Ethnicity," *Harvard Encyclopedia of American Ethnic Groups* (1980), reprinted in William Petersen et al., *Concepts of Ethnicity* (Cambridge, Mass.: Harvard University Press, 1982); "Politics and the Measurement of Ethnicity," in William Alonso and Paul Starr, eds., *The Politics of Numbers* (New York: Russell Sage Foundation, 1987).

Index

321